DISABILITY AND DEMOCRACY

Reconstructing (Special) Education for Postmodernity

Edited by
THOMAS M. SKRTIC

Foreword by
JONAS F. SOLTIS

TEACHERS COLLEGE PRESS

Teachers College, Columbia University
New York and London

Published by Teachers College Press, 1234 Amsterdam Avenue, New York, NY 10027

Library of Congress Cataloging-in-Publication Data

Disability and democracy : reconstructing (special) education for
  postmodernity / edited by Thomas M. Skrtic.
    p. cm. – (Special education series)
  Includes bibliographical references and index.
  ISBN 0-8077-3411-X. – ISBN 0-8077-3410-1 (pbk.)
  1. Special education. 2. Handicapped students. 3. Postmodernism–
Social aspects.   I. Skrtic, Thomas M. II. Series: Special
education series (New York, N.Y.)
  LC3969.D57   1995
  371.9–dc20   95-7268

ISBN 0-8077-3410-1 (paper)
ISBN 0-8077-3411-X (cloth)

Printed on acid-free paper

Manufactured in the United States of America

02 01 00 99 98 97 96 95 8 7 6 5 4 3 2 1

Achieving the Complete School:
Strategies for Effective Mainstreaming
> Douglas Biklen with Robert Bogdan,
> Dianne L. Ferguson, Stanford J. Searl,
> Jr., and Steven J. Taylor

Stress in Childhood:
An Intervention Model for
Teachers and Other Professionals
> Gaston E. Blom, Bruce D. Cheney,
> and James E. Snoddy

Curriculum Decision Making for
Students with Severe Handicaps:
Policy and Practice

Interpreting Disability:
A Qualitative Reader
> Philip M. Ferguson, Dianne L. Ferguson,
> and Steven J. Taylor, Editors

On Being L.D.: Perspectives
and Strategies of Young Adults
> Stephen T. Murphy

Toward Effective Public School
Programs for Deaf Students:
Context, Process, and Outcomes
> Thomas N. Kluwin, Donald F. Moores,
> and Martha Gonter Gaustad, Editors

ound:
nunication Is
al Views of
sability

ation Training

Mental
Stories
Steven J. Taylor

ols?
n Dyson, and
rs

racy:
al) Education for

ditor

For my mother, Caroline Skrtic,
whose inward beauty and generosity
are admired by all who know her,
especially me.

Contents

Foreword

This is a book nominally about special education. It is, in fact, a special book about education, democracy, neopragmatism, postmodernism, philosophy of social science, and progressive social reconstruction. Skrtic has an amazing grasp of a vast literature that gives framework and substance to his far-ranging analysis of what has gone right and wrong with education, educational research, educational administration, and special education, which he treats as a representative case of optional paradigms at work, explaining and critiquing social, political, and educational appearances and realities.

Whether focusing on the mainstreaming and inclusion debates in special education or on the reform and restructuring debates in general education, Skrtic brings multiple perspectives to bear on their analysis (deconstruction) and clarification (reconstruction) with masterful skill and range. Anyone who has lived through the multifaceted contemporary revolution in thought in this last part of the twentieth century will appreciate Skrtic's ability to pull much of it together and use it effectively in this ambitious book. *Disability and Democracy* should be required reading for graduate students in foundations, philosophy, curriculum theory, administration, sociology, policy, educational research, and of course, special education. It is a very special book.

Jonas F. Soltis
November 1994
William Heard Kilpatrick Professor
of Philosophy of Education, Emeritus

Preface and Acknowledgments

To find out what our society means by sanity, perhaps we should investigate what is happening in the field of insanity.

Michel Foucault

The idea for this book began to take shape in 1982 when, upon completing the fieldwork for an implementation study of the Education for All Handicapped Children Act of 1975 (EHA), I began searching for a way to explain what my colleagues and I had found in our case studies. After reading broadly in the areas of policy implementation and educational change, I realized that I needed to know more about schools as organizations. With this in mind, I turned to the interdisciplinary field of organization analysis, which eventually led me to the social disciplines themselves, and finally to philosophy. The first thing I found was that, in a sense, there were too many explanations for our findings. Understanding things as social as public policy and organizational change depends on the frame of reference one brings to bear on the subject. More important, I began to see that the act of choosing a frame of reference has profound moral and political implications for individuals and society, which of course got me thinking about the way special education and disability have been framed historically.

The second thing I found was that the social disciplines and philosophy were in the midst of an intellectual crisis over the very question of frames of reference, or paradigms. Of course, some intellectual infighting in these fields is to be expected. As a discourse on the transition from traditional to modern society, much of social science is a debate over the best paradigm for theorizing the nature and effects of modernity, with philosophy serving as the arbiter. But this crisis was different, more fundamental and of far greater consequence. Beginning in the 1960s, a series of socioeconomic and cultural transformations had changed modernity itself, thus calling the very object of modern social theorizing into question. For many, these changes signify the opening of a new period in human history–a postmodern era that raises serious questions about the epistemological and moral groundings of our modern institutions, the resolution of which requires new postmodern forms of theorizing. These questions and the discourse on postmodernism itself got

me thinking about the grounds of the modern institution of public education, particularly how it and its institutional practice of special education
might be more productively theorized.

The advantage of postmodernism is that it provides a number of fundamentally different ways to theorize the social, and thus a multiplicity of
ways to interpret social phenomena like education, special education, and
disability. An apparent problem with postmodernism, however, is its relativistic outlook, the idea that there is no cognitively certain way to choose
among interpretations as a guide to action. As such, the concern in the early
1980s was that postmodernism's cognitive relativism necessarily implies a
form of moral relativism that undermines all modern ideas and institutions,
including those of liberty, equality, justice, and democracy itself. But this
fear of relativism, what Richard Bernstein called the "Cartesian anxiety," is a
hold-over from modernism's foundational or monological epistemology—the
belief that the only way to justify a social practice or institution is to show
that it is based on the truth about the world. As both a tonic for Cartesian
anxiety and a means to capitalize on the positive possibilities of postmodern
theorizing, Bernstein and other contemporary philosophers such as Richard
Rorty proposed the antifoundational or dialogical method of pragmatism, the
turn-of-the-century philosophy which, in the United States, is associated
most often with John Dewey.

Pragmatism is a method for social theorizing under conditions of uncertainty, conditions in which it is accepted that there are no independent,
cognitive criteria for choosing among interpretations of the social world.
Whereas the aim of modern social inquiry is to justify social practices and
institutions by showing that they are based on a true representation of the
world, the goal of pragmatism is to change social practices and institutions
by reconciling them with useful and thus desirable moral ideals. As such,
pragmatism avoids modernism's problem of theoretical representation and
postmodernism's alleged moral relativism by focusing on the consequences of
social theorizing, on the question of whether acting upon a particular social
theory contributes to the practical realization of desirable social values, particularly those associated with democracy.

By now it was 1985, and after submitting the final report on the EHA
implementation study I began to write about the crisis in modern knowledge
and the implications of postmodernism for the field of special education. My
first paper on the topic was published in 1986, a particularly opportune time
because a crisis of sorts had developed in the field of special education itself.
Under the rubric of the "regular education initiative," leading special educators and key government officials were criticizing the EHA and the associated
practice of mainstreaming and calling for a new, more integrated or inclusive
approach to special education. Of course, the field of special education was

no stranger to criticism or change; the EHA and mainstreaming themselves resulted from criticism of segregated special classrooms in the 1960s. But this round of criticism was more contentious and divisive, largely because there was far more to lose in the 1980s in terms of hard-won rights and resources for students with special educational needs.

For me, the most interesting aspect of the regular education initiative debate was that the current system of special education was being criticized for creating virtually the same problems as the former special classroom approach. Rather than resolving the problems of the 1960s, the EHA and mainstreaming had merely reproduced them in the 1980s – precisely what my colleagues and I had found in our implementation study. What was so troubling, however, was that the debate focused exclusively on special education models and practices rather than the assumptions and theories in which they are grounded. As I argued in the 1986 paper, and in a subsequent one published in 1987, the danger was that, like the round of criticism that resulted in the EHA and mainstreaming, the current debate would merely reproduce the problems of special education practice rather than resolve them. What the field of special education needed, I proposed, was a critical discourse that, although ultimately concerned with the nature and effects of its models and practices, must be carried out at the level of grounding theories and paradigms.

Had these papers appeared in the mid-1970s, or even in the early 1980s, I doubt they would have received much notice in the special education community. By the mid-1980s, however, apparently there was enough confusion and uncertainty in the field for them to attract the attention of several people in leadership positions at the Council for Exceptional Children (CEC), the main professional association of the field of special education. As a result, I was asked to discuss my ideas at two special education conferences in 1986 and 1987, which eventually led to an invitation from the CEC to organize the preconvention program at its annual meeting in 1989. I accepted the invitation with the proviso that, although the program would address the question of the ethics and efficacy of special education models and practices, it would do so from the perspective of the field's largely unquestioned theoretical and paradigmatic grounding.

Like most applied fields, special education is largely atheoretical, and thus historically it had neither developed a theoretical discourse of its own nor paid much attention to the small body of critical work on special education carried out in the social sciences. This began to change in the 1980s, however, when several people in or associated with the field began to publish theoretical work on the nature and implications of special education and its practices. And it was to this group that I turned for help in organizing and carrying out the preconvention program. Drawing on those whose work I felt represented the most accessible theoretical criticism of special education, I assembled a small international working group which, over the course of several months in 1988, produced a preconvention program entitled, "Exploring the Theory/Practice Link in Special Education." As things began to take shape, however, some of the staff at the CEC became increasingly concerned that the program's theoretical bent would dissuade participation, and thus fail to attract the customary 100 or so preconvention participants. Nevertheless, the working group pressed on and subsequently delivered the program to an audience of over 700 special educators in San Francisco on April 21–22, 1989.

Originally, the preconvention papers were to be published by the CEC as a book or monograph. However, as the regular education initiative evolved into the more radical "inclusive education" movement, the leadership at the CEC changed and, for reasons about which I can only speculate, in the end the plan to publish the papers was dropped. At that point my colleagues and I expanded our papers somewhat and submitted the revised manuscript to Teachers College Press, which accepted it for publication and, on the recommendation of two anonymous reviewers and the editor who had been assigned to the project, asked that we expand it by further highlighting the political implications of special education and by linking the crisis in the field to the broader question of educational reform and democratic renewal. The result, then, is *Disability and Democracy: Reconstructing (Special) Education for Postmodernity.*

The word "special" is bracketed in the subtitle for three reasons that are central to the arguments put forth in the book. As we will see, reconstructing special education for postmodernity necessarily requires eliminating it as an institutional practice of public education. At the same time, however, one cannot ethically eliminate special education without first making the institution of public education a more special or humane place for every student. In this sense, bracketing "special" before the word "education" signifies the need to erase it as a reference to a separate system of education, but only under conditions in which it remains there as a trace, as a broader reference to the nature of public education itself.

Bracketing "special" in the subtitle is also a political tactic, a way of reminding educators that they are perhaps the most powerful group in contemporary society. From a postmodern perspective, knowledge is power when its accumulation by certain groups gives them the authority to define reality for others, and particularly when it gives them the authority to define others as abnormal and to treat their bodies. Given the pervasiveness and centrality of education in industrialized societies, the power of educators is particularly evident and alarming when we consider that, acting through special educators, they continue to classify more and more students as abnormal at younger and younger ages.

The third reason for bracketing "special" in the subtitle can be understood by referring back to Michel Foucault's opening comment on sanity/insanity. One of the central methodological themes running through all of Foucault's work is that the most insightful way to understand a social institution is to consider it from its dark side, from the perspective of the professions and institutional practices that emerge to contain its failures. In this sense, special education is the dark side of public education – the institutional practice that emerged in twentieth-century industrialized democracies to conceal its failure to educate all citizens for full political, economic, and cultural participation in democracy. Here, bracketing "special" signifies a methodological approach, a way of finding out what industrialized societies mean by education by investigating what is happening in the field of special education. Ultimately, then, bracketing "special" before "education" in the subtitle – as a trace, a political tactic, and a methodological approach – signifies that *Disability and Democracy* has as much, and perhaps more, to say about public education as it does about special education.

The book is divided into three sections. Part 1 includes two chapters which delegitimize or deconstruct modern (special) education theory and practice and recommend the epistemological and moral framework of pragmatism as a way to reconstruct it for the emerging postmodern era. Part 2 contains four chapters, each of which presents an alternative paradigm for theorizing special education and disability, and notes its practical and political consequences as a frame of reference for grounding the field and its practices. Finally, Part 3 includes four chapters, the first three of which illustrate the implications of choosing among paradigms by providing different theoretical interpretations of special education and disability grounded in one or more of the Part 2 paradigms. The last chapter of Part 3 ties together the major themes of the book by showing how deconstructing special education necessarily deconstructs public education, proposing an alternative structure and mode of professional discourse for public education, and justifying these alternatives on moral, political, and economic grounds.

I begin the process of deconstruction in Chapter 1 by presenting the modern or objectivist view of the professions and showing how it is undermined by the subjectivist philosophy of science vindicated in the work of Kuhn and others. Here, I am concerned ultimately with the rise of subjectivism in the modern social sciences and its implications for education and special education, which, like all applied fields, are premised on the objectivist view of the professions. By exposing the contradictions in the objectivist view, my aim in Chapter 1 is to raise doubts about the legitimacy of modern professional knowledge and the process of professionalization itself.

I continue the process of deconstruction in Chapter 2 by showing how postmodernism calls all forms of modern social knowledge–objectivist and subjectivist–into question, thus raising even greater concerns about the legitimacy of professional knowledge and, moreover, about the possibility of choosing an alternative form of social knowledge as a grounding for it. I begin the chapter by developing an intellectual map of modern social knowledge, a conceptual framework that exposes the metatheoretical presuppositions behind each of four modes of modern social theorizing: the functionalist, interpretivist, radical structuralist, and radical humanist paradigms. I use the map to highlight the epistemological and moral dilemma that postmodernism poses, first for the social disciplines and then for social professions like education and special education which draw their knowledge claims from them. Following this, I consider the epistemological and moral framework of pragmatism and, after noting its positive possibilities as an approach to postmodern theorizing, recommend it as a method of social analysis for deconstructing and reconstructing special education theory and practice. Finally, I explicate my approach to pragmatism by describing four analytic techniques–immanent critique, ideal types, deconstruction, and genealogy–and alert readers to the ways in which they are being used in the book.

Each of the Part 2 chapters presents an optional metatheoretical description of special education, disability, and progress from the perspective of one of the four modern paradigms. This format is meant to show that, when viewed from different paradigms, special education, disability, and progress have fundamentally different meanings and thus profoundly different implications for ethical practice and for a just society. I present the first paradigmatic perspective–the functionalist view of special education and disability–in Chapter 3. As the dominant mode of social theorizing in the modern era, functionalism is the traditional frame of reference of the social sciences and social professions, and thus the metatheoretical grounding of conventional theory and practice in education and special education. I begin with a discussion of the way the functionalist theories of organizational rationality and human pathology shaped schooling in the twentieth century; then, drawing on this discussion, I show how functionalist schooling creates the institutional practice of special education and the very idea of student disability as artifacts of the system. Next, I characterize special education as an extreme form of functionalist education and discuss the social and political implications of such a metatheoretical grounding for students, for the field of special education, and for the institution of education. I conclude the chapter by considering the field's response to criticism and by once again recommending pragmatism, this time as a mode of professional discourse in which, as a matter of course, special educators continuously construct, deconstruct, and reconstruct their professional knowledge and practices.

In Chapter 4, Philip Ferguson and Dianne Ferguson characterize the interpretivist paradigm—a frame of reference that emphasizes the importance of perspective—as a metatheoretical grounding for special education theory and practice. Throughout the chapter they elaborate on the concept of perspective with the literary metaphor of telling stories, arguing that, if the special educators were to assume an interpretivist stance, they would listen to the personal stories of individuals with disabilities and reorient their practices on the basis of an insider's understanding of what it is like to be viewed as disabled in our society. In presenting the metatheoretical presuppositions of the interpretivist paradigm, the Fergusons contrast them with those of functionalism, specifying the arguments that interpretivists make in favor of their outlook as a guide to action. They discuss interpretivism's philosophical heritage and, drawing upon its key theoretical tenets, show how such an approach to inquiry would change the nature of special education theory and practice. They conclude the chapter with a discussion of interpretivism's implications for progress and social justice, noting that from this perspective both require that special educators listen to the voices of those they claim to serve.

Sally Tomlinson presents the radical structuralist view of special education and disability in Chapter 5. She identifies the paradigm's intellectual forbearers and key theoretical approaches and, after a brief critique of the functionalist and interpretivist paradigms, turns to a radical structuralist interpretation of the development and expansion of special education in the industrialized nations, using Britain as a case in point. The radical structuralist perspective draws heavily on conceptualizations of social and cultural reproduction and interest group conflicts. According to Tomlinson, if the field of special education were to ground itself in this paradigm, it would question the expansion of special education and the identification of ever-larger numbers of students as disabled, two developments which are occurring in most industrialized societies. Considering these developments from the radical structuralist perspective, she argues that the expansion is driven by attempts to restructure education to fit the needs of technologically-based societies in which academic and technical elites are required, but in which more citizens will be partially or permanently unemployed. Tomlinson questions the politics and morality of a special education system that legitimizes an inferior economic and social position for increasing numbers of citizens, and concludes the chapter with an examination of the reforms that radical structuralists would require before conceding progress toward a just system of education.

In Chapter 6, Dwight Kiel presents the radical humanist view of special education and disability. He begins by characterizing the paradigm in terms of its intellectual forbearers and metatheoretical presuppositions, noting that, despite some important differences, humanists share the belief that the dominance of functionalism in the modern era has retarded the capacity of humans for development, fulfillment, and self-reflection. After comparing the radical humanist outlook to those of the other modern paradigms, Kiel turns to a discussion of the humanist view of education and special education. If special educators were to ground their theory and practice in radical humanism, he contends, ultimately they would be concerned with the question of whether education and special education contribute to or detract from the development of self-reflective, autonomous citizens. Next, Kiel considers the moral and political significance that humanists attach to this and related questions, and characterizes the reforms that humanists would propose to achieve social justice in public education. Finally, he concludes the chapter and Part 2 of the book with a discussion of postmodernism in which he reviews postmodern theorists' criticisms of the radical humanist paradigm.

Part 3 includes four chapters, each of which provides a theoretical critique of special education and the notion of student disability by drawing theory from one or more of the four paradigmatic perspectives presented in Part 2. In Chapter 7, Christine Sleeter draws theory from the radical structuralist paradigm and uses it to reinterpret the emergence and expansion of the disability category and the field of learning disabilities. She argues that, given a radical structuralist reading, the category was created to explain away the academic failures of primarily white middle- and upper-class students in the wake of post-Sputnik school reforms. Sleeter discusses the basic tenets of conflict theory, a principal school of thought within the radical structuralist paradigm, as well as the sorts of questions they suggest for examining a field such as learning disabilities. After recommending several additional areas of special education practice that beg for a radical structuralist analysis, she concludes the chapter by noting that such analyses are important because they reaffirm the need to confront racism and classism in schools and society, to support practices that treat all students fairly, and to celebrate diversity.

In Chapter 8, Lous Heshusius argues against the mechanistic (functionalist) principles that have shaped education and special education historically, and makes a case for grounding them in what she calls the "emergent holistic paradigm." In terms of the conceptual framework of the book, holism draws insights from two of the four modern paradigms—interpretivism and radical humanism. However, true to the holistic principle that the whole is greater than the sum of its parts, Heshusius argues that, although holism incorporates insights from these paradigms, it cannot be reduced to them. After noting the dissatisfaction with the mechanistic view in a number of fields, Heshusius discusses the negative implications of special education's mechanistic outlook and explains the field's reluctance to abandon this way of thinking. Finally, after explicating several holistic principles and applying them to education and special education, she concludes the chapter by noting that, although holism tends to be resisted or co-opted by mechanistically oriented educators, it is nonetheless increasingly found in a variety of avant-garde educational settings.

In Chapter 9, I draw organization theory from each of the four modern paradigms and, using the pragmatist approach to postmodern theorizing, combine them dialogically to form a metatheory of school organization and change. I use the metatheory to reinterpret special education and student disability from an organizational perspective, characterizing them as organizational pathologies – unintended negative consequences arising from the contradiction between the democratic ideal of universal public education and the bureaucratic structure of schooling in twentieth-century industrialized societies. To support this claim, I use the metatheory to redescribe the emergence and expansion of special education in this century, including the rise and fall of the special classroom approach and the failure of the EHA and mainstreaming to resolve the field's problems of professional practice. Finally, by relating this analysis of the field's models and practices to its guiding theories and metatheoretical paradigm, I deconstruct special education as an institutional practice of public education.

In Chapter 10, I bring the book full-cirle by considering the relationship between disability, democracy, and the necessary reconstruction of (special) education in light of the historical contingencies of an emerging postindustrial political economy. I begin by using the metatheory of school organization and change developed in Chapter 9 to analyze the inclusive education reform movement in special education and the school restructuring movement in education. By treating the former as a discourse on equity and the latter as a discourse on excellence, I show that, given a critical reading, the two discourses converge to deconstruct the institution of public education itself. I begin the process of reconstructing (special) education by showing that, given a nascent postindustrial political economy, the social goals of educational excellence and educational equity require the same things of public education: a nonbureaucratic or "adhocratic" organizational structure and a pragmatic mode of professional discourse. The combination of pragmatism and adhocracy, I contend, not only holds the promise of making schools more excellent and equitable for all students, but at the same time raises the possibility of making industrialized democracies like the United States more democratic. In this latter regard, I argue that pragmatism and adhocracy provide the methods and conditions of discourse necessary to revive the idea of progressive education in these nations, which in turn holds out the possibility of reviving the critical project of democratic renewal through cultural transformation and a social reconstruction of society.

Disability and Democracy was written to justify and promote the deconstruction of special education and the twentieth-century notion of student disability, as well as to provide some substantive and methodological resources for reconstructing (special) education in terms of the historical contingencies of an emerging postmodern culture and postindustrial political economy. Its aim is to tempt the rising generation of educators to construct new educational knowledge, practices, discourses, and organizations—ones that are more consistent with the ideal of serving the best educational and political interests of all students, and thus ultimately the democratic needs of contemporary society.

I am indebted to several individuals and institutions for their support and encouragement. First, I want to thank the chapter authors for helping me pull off the CEC preconvention program in 1989, and particularly for sticking with me over the several years it took to turn the program into this book. I also would like to thank the University of Kansas which, through one of its Intra-University Visiting Professorships, provided me with free time in the mid-1980s to pursue my research interests in organization theory and social and political philosophy. In this regard, I owe a tremendous intellectual debt to Bob Antonio, Dwight Kiel, and Gary Shapiro who, as my mentors during and after the professorship, guided me through the discourses on postmodernism and led me to pragmatism, as well as to Egon Guba and Yvonna Lincoln whose intellectual companionship and generosity in the early 1980s led me to see that I needed something like the professorship.

I also am indebted to the Danforth Foundation and the University of Kansas Hall Center for the Humanities, which provided me with fellowships in 1978–84 and 1986–87, respectively, and thus with invaluable opportunities to expand my ideas about special education, disability, and democracy, and to test them on an interdisciplinary audience. I also would like to thank the faculty members and students of the Department of Educational Administration at Syracuse University, the Cambridge Institute of Education at the University of Cambridge, and the Institutes for Special Education and Educational Research and the Faculty of Social Science at the University of Oslo. The opportunity to teach courses and participate in colloquia at these institutions in the early 1990s gave me access to an important, largely international testing ground for my work as it was taking shape. In this regard, I also must thank the Russian participants in the Russian–American Seminar on Legislative Issues in the Education of Students with Disabilities. Over the course of a cold and dreary week in Moscow in 1994, these individuals helped me appreciate more fully the extremely dire power/knowledge implications of special education in an industrialized society without democracy.

I will always be indebted to Brian Ellerbeck at Teachers College Press for his intellectual and moral support during the book production process, as well as to Harry Dahl, former President of the CEC (1989–1990), and to Ed Gickling, former Assistant Executive Director for Professional Development at the CEC (1987–1990). Without the personal and political support of Harry and Ed while they were at the CEC, the preconvention program would never have taken place and perhaps *Disability and Democracy* would never have been written.

Finally, in addition to the individuals I encountered at Syracuse, Cambridge, Oslo, and Moscow, I am indebted to a number of students and former students at the University of Kansas, especially Gwen Beegle, Mary Brownell, Jane Dickinson, David Egnor, Rocky Hill, Marilyn Kaff, Jim Knight, Chris Nelson, Brenda Oas, Stephen Smith, Chriss Walther-Thomas, Linda Ware, and Ron Wolf, each of whom in her or his own way advanced my thinking on a number of fronts. Beyond this, and except for the constant support and encouragement of my loving parents and sister, these individuals did more than they will ever know to comfort me as I struggled through the work that led to this book.

In earlier forms, Chapters 1–9 appeared as invited addresses given at the preconvention program of the 1989 annual meeting of the Council for Exceptional Children.

Portions of Chapter 1 appeared in "School Psychology and the Revolution in Modern Knowledge," an invited address given at the 1990 annual meeting of the American Psychological Association, and in "The Crisis in Professional Knowledge: Implications for School Psychology and Educational Reform," a keynote address given at the 1991 annual meeting of the National Association of School Psychology.

Portions of Chapter 2 appeared in "Collaboration and Possibility," a keynote address given at the preconvention program of the 1990 annual meeting of the Council for Exceptional Children, and in "Disciplinary Power as Vulgar Pragmatism: The Case of Special Education in Industrialized Democracies," a paper presented at the 1993 Congress of the International Institute of Sociology.

In a different form, portions of Chapter 4 appeared in *Interpreting Disability: A Qualitative Reader*, Philip M. Ferguson, Dianne L. Ferguson, and Steven J. Taylor, Eds. (New York: Teachers College Press, 1992).

In a different form, portions of Chapter 7 appeared in *Exceptional Children, 53* (1986), pp. 46–54.

Portions of Chapter 8 appeared in *A Cognitive Approach to Learning Disabilities*, D. Kim Reid and Wayne P. Hresko, Eds. (Houston: Pro-Ed Publications, 1991, 2nd ed.).

Portions of Chapter 9 appeared in "Students with Special Educational

Needs: Artifacts of the Traditional Curriculum," a keynote address given at the 1990 International Special Education Congress, which was subsequently published in *Effective Schools for All*, Mel Ainscow, Ed. (London: David Fulton, 1991), pp. 20–42.

Portions of Chapter 10 appeared in "Inclusion: A Real Possibility in the Post-Industrial Era," an invited address given at the 1993 annual meeting of the Council for Exceptional Children, and in "Inclusive Education and the Postindustrial Political Economy," the 1993 Samuel Laycock Memorial Lecture, University of Saskatchewan.

PART 1

Deconstructing/ Reconstructing the Professions

CHAPTER 1

Theory/Practice and Objectivism:
The Modern View of the Professions

Thomas M. Skrtic

The professions rose to a position of prominence and authority in society on the basis of two claims, one practical and one political. The practical claim was that the professions have exclusive access to knowledge that society needs to solve its problems. The political claim was that professionals will apply this knowledge to society's problems in a disinterested way, in the interest of their clients and the common good rather than for personal gain (Haskell, 1984b). The argument for professionalization was framed as the victory of science over traditional authority and the institutionalization of the ethic of service. Advocates of professionalization argued that joining scientific authority and moral obligation in a culture of professionalism would release a new class of citizens in society: individuals who, because they were mentally disciplined, fiercely autonomous, and socially committed, would act as a liberating force in society–a restraint on capitalistic self-interest and thus a model of democratic leadership (Bledstein, 1976).

Over the past 30 years, however, the legitimacy of these claims has been called into question by three waves of criticism: a sociological critique of professional practice, a philosophical critique of professional knowledge, and a political critique of professional power. The sociological critique questions the practical argument by pointing to the contradiction between the convergent, bureaucratic nature of the professions and the divergent, democratic character of society (Collins, 1979). As society has become more dynamic, its problems have become so complex that they require professionals to think divergently and to work across disciplinary lines. But the professions have become increasingly convergent and specialized, thus limiting the type of interdisciplinary effort that is needed (Gilb, 1966). Moreover, because virtually all professionals work in bureaucracies, the application of professional knowledge to social problems is largely determined by the nature and needs of the organizations themselves (Scott, 1981; Chapter 9), which creates serious ethical problems, particularly when the needs of the organization are in conflict with those of its clients or of society (Schein, 1972). Indeed, given the contradictions of specialization and bureaucratization, many of society's most pressing problems are the result of professional activity itself (Freidson, 1988; Schein, 1972).

Perhaps the most troubling aspect of the sociological critique is that it questions the ideal of service to society. Whereas turn-of-the-century intellectuals characterized professionalization as "a grand cultural reform, capable of restoring sanity to a capitalist civilization intoxicated with self-aggrandizement" (Haskell, 1984b, p. 177), today it is seen as merely another form of self-aggrandizement, "a capitalist remedy for the defects of capitalism" (Haskell, 1984a, p. 219; Collins, 1979). Moreover, critics argue, the radical idea of professional as autonomous democrat has had only conservative consequences. The professionalization of social problems such as ignorance, poverty, crime, and disease has meant that "every sphere of American life now [falls] within the power of the . . . professional to set apart, regulate, and contain" (Bledstein, 1976, p. 92).

Although the sociological critique raises serious doubts about the legitimacy of professional practice, the philosophical and political critiques are based on a far greater uncertainty that is spreading throughout intellectual and cultural life. Behind this uncertainty is the fact that Western civilization is undergoing a change in worldview. A worldview, or paradigm, is a shared pattern of basic beliefs and assumptions about the nature of the world and how it works. These assumptions tell us what is real and what is not; they shape our cultural identity and guide and justify our institutional practices. In this sense, paradigms are enabling; they unrandomize reality so we can act in the world. But paradigms are also normative because they conceal the very reasons for our actions in their unquestioned assumptions (Patton, 1975). We are rarely conscious of our paradigms because they tend to surface mainly when they are changing. The uncertainty that we feel today stems from the fact that we are undergoing a fundamental change in worldview, one that questions the very ideas upon which our modern institutions are premised, including the institution of the professions.

The change in worldview is occurring on two levels, the first of which is located within the modern outlook itself. This change represents a shift from objectivism, the dominant philosophy of science in the modern era, to subjectivism, another modern philosophy of science that, until recently, had been largely overshadowed by the apparent success of objectivism, particularly in the English-speaking world (see Burrell & Morgan, 1979).[1] Although subjectivism is not a new philosophy of science, over the past 30 years it increasingly has become the preferred view of science and scientific knowledge (Bernstein, 1976; Rorty, 1979; below). The implications of the rise of subjectivism for the professions is the topic of this chapter. The second level of change, which is taken up in Chapter 2, involves the far more revolutionary emergence of *post*modernism, which, among other things, rejects the objectivism–subjectivism dichotomy and thus raises serious questions about the validity and utility of modern knowledge itself.

The professions are implicated in these changes because the legitimacy of a profession's practices (what its members do) and discourses (what they think, say, read, and write about what they do) rests on the adequacy of its grounding knowledge. The very meaning of knowledge has changed in the late twentieth century, which raises fundamental questions about the legitimacy of professional knowledge, including that of the professions of education and special education. Although the redefinition of knowledge creates a crisis in the professions, it also represents a positive opportunity for progress because, as we will see, a crisis in knowledge is a precondition for growth of knowledge in the sciences and the professions.

THE OBJECTIVIST VIEW OF THE PROFESSIONS

The shift from objectivism to subjectivism has profound implications for the professions because modern professionalism is premised on the objectivist view of science and scientific knowledge. Indeed, as we will see below, the essence of professionalism is the assumption that the scientific knowledge that underwrites professional practices and discourses is objective knowledge of reality. In subsequent sections I consider the subjectivist view of science and its implications for the professions. In preparation for that discussion, this section addresses the conventional view of the professions and the objectivist conceptualization of science upon which it is premised.

Professional Work

The most straightforward way to begin a discussion of the professions and professional knowledge is to consider the nature of professional work, which we can do by comparing it with other types of work. Simple work is work that can be rationalized into a series of routine subtasks, each of which can be completely prespecified and then performed by a separate worker (Mintzberg, 1979). By design, this type of work does not require extensive knowledge or complex skills; it is done by "unskilled" workers who can be trained in a matter of days or even hours (Braverman, 1974). Conversely, complex work is too uncertain or variable to be rationalized. It requires judgment on the part of the worker, who, to make the necessary judgments, must have a relatively extensive knowledge base and an associated set of complex skills that take an extended period of time to learn (Schein, 1972).

There are two types of complex work—craft and professional. Although both require extensive knowledge and complex skills, the difference is whether the necessary expertise is grounded in practical or formal knowledge.

The craft worker's expertise is grounded in practical knowledge, in the customs and conventions of a craft culture, which are conveyed from person to person as a tradition of experienced practice (Braverman, 1974). The expertise of the professional, however, is presumed to be grounded in the formal knowledge of science, that is, in the relatively abstract, technical knowledge produced through the scientific method (see below). As such, professionals address the uncertainty of variable client needs by applying "general principles, theories, or propositions" to particular cases (Schein, 1972, p. 8). A related difference is whether the required knowledge and skills have been codified or systematically identified and recorded. The knowledge and skills necessary of a craft are not codified; one learns them as an apprentice under the guidance of a master who learned them from a previous master in the same way (Mintzberg, 1979). The knowledge and skills necessary to do a profession's work, however, are codified as a curriculum of formal study in a professional school (Schein, 1972).

Although considering the nature of professional work provides some insight into the professions, there is a great deal of confusion as to which occupations actually qualify as professions. This is so because the nature of work has not remained constant. Earlier in the century the distinctions were relatively clear, but as new knowledge and technologies have been developed, much of what was craft work has been transformed into simple work through rationalization, or into professional work through codification (Braverman, 1974). In a knowledge-based and increasingly technological society such as ours, understanding the professions and professional knowledge requires consideration of the broader concept of professionalism.

Professionalism

Professionalism is an important concept in the social sciences and humanities (hereafter, social sciences or disciplines) because the professions have a special relationship with society (see Haskell, 1984b; Hughes, 1963; Parsons, 1968; Wilensky, 1964). On the basis of the claim to scientific authority, society allows the professions greater autonomy than it does other social groups. Professions set their own standards, regulate entry into their ranks, discipline their members, and in general operate with fewer restraints than the arts, trades, or business. In return, professionals are expected to serve the public good and to set and enforce higher standards of conduct for themselves than society requires for its citizens, workers, and businesspeople (Bledstein, 1976; De George, 1982). Professionalism is premised on a "logic of confidence" (Meyer & Rowan, 1978). Society gives professionals greater autonomy than it does other social groups on the assumption that their knowledge is valid and useful, and that they will use it on behalf of their clients and the public good.

Because the growth of specialization in this century has increased the prestige, wealth, and autonomy of professionals, many occupational groups claim to be professions. Thus, it has become necessary to specify additional criteria for identifying the professions (see Hughes, 1963; Parsons, 1968; Wilensky, 1964). Synthesizing the work of others, Schein (1972) developed the following criteria, which he noted fit best the traditional or so-called learned professions of law, medicine, and divinity, and fit to varying degrees other professions like social work and education.

1. The professional, as distinct from the amateur, is engaged in a *full-time occupation* that comprises his principal source of income.
2. The professional is assumed to have a *strong motivation* or calling as a basis for his choice of a professional career and is assumed to have a stable lifetime commitment to that career.
3. The professional possesses a *specialized body of knowledge and skills* that are acquired during a *prolonged period of education and training*.
4. The professional makes his decisions on behalf of a client in terms of *general principles, theories, or propositions*, which he applies to the particular case under consideration. . . .
5. At the same time, the professional is assumed to have a *service orientation*, which means that he uses his expertise on behalf of the particular needs of his client. . . .
6. The professional's service to the client is assumed to be based on the *objective needs of the client* and independent of the particular sentiments that the professional may have about the client. . . . The professional relationship rests on a kind of *mutual trust between the professional and client.*
7. The professional is assumed to know better what is good for the client than the client himself. . . . The professional demands *autonomy of judgment of his own performance.* Even if the client is not satisfied, the professional will, in principle, permit only his colleagues to judge his performance. Because of this demand for professional autonomy, the client is in a potentially vulnerable position. . . . The profession deals with this potential vulnerability by developing strong ethical and professional standards [of conduct] for its members . . . usually enforced by colleagues through professional associations. . . .
8. Professionals form *professional associations which define criteria of admission, educational standards, licensing or other formal entry examinations, career lines within the profession, and areas of jurisdiction* for the profession. Ultimately, the professional association's function is to protect the autonomy of the profession. . . .

9. Professionals have great power and status in the area of their expertise, but their *knowledge is assumed to be specific*. A professional does not have a license to be a "wise man" outside the area defined by his training.
10. Professionals make their service available but ordinarily are *not allowed to advertise or to seek out clients*. Clients are expected to initiate the contact and then accept the advice and service recommended, without appeal to outside authority. (pp. 8–9)

As in the relationship between the professions and society, confidence also plays a key role in the relationship between the professional and the client. On the basis of access to professional knowledge, the professional is assumed to know best what is good for the client, who accepts the services on trust, without appeal to an outside authority. Although client vulnerability is recognized and addressed through professional codes of ethics, the standards are developed and enforced by the professionals themselves, through the collective action of their professional associations. The circularity of this proposition stems from the argument that only the professions can judge the adequacy of their performance because they alone have access to the specialized knowledge and skills upon which it is based. Thus, in considering the nature of the professions, two central elements emerge – professional autonomy and professional knowledge.

Professional autonomy is the *sine qua non* of professionalism (Abbott, 1988; Parsons, 1968; Wilensky, 1964). It implies that professionals know best what is good for their clients because of access to the specialized knowledge and skills of their profession. It also implies that all decisions as to the adequacy of this knowledge and skill are made by the professionals themselves. As such, the professions can be understood as exclusive occupational groups whose members are bound by "a common sense of identity, self-regulation, lifetime membership, shared values, a common language, clear social boundaries, and strong socialization of new members" (Schein, 1972, p. 10). A key point to grasp about professional autonomy is its relationship to professional knowledge. Society allows the professions greater autonomy than it does other groups because they control a body of specialized knowledge that society needs, and virtually all decisions about the adequacy of this knowledge are left to the professionals themselves. Thus, a profession is an insulated, self-regulating community whose members share an image of the world that is based on strong socialization and common exposure to the profession's communally accepted definition of valid knowledge. The special relationship between the professions and society yields professional autonomy; the circular relationship between professional autonomy and professional knowledge means that a profession is the sole judge of the adequacy of its knowledge and skills.

Professional Knowledge

The legitimacy of the professions' claims about the validity of their knowledge is premised on the positivist epistemology of knowledge. In its most extreme form, positivism asserts that sense perception is the basis of all human knowledge and that, through objective observation, we can escape the bias of our historical and cultural context and thus discern facts that correspond to reality itself.[2] Interpretation and judgment have no validity for the positivist; anything that cannot be observed objectively is dismissed as meaningless (Harré, 1981). Value neutrality is the hallmark of positivism because it is assumed that only neutral observation will allow "the facts to speak for themselves," unaffected by the distorting effects of history and context. Science is central to positivism because the scientific method is thought to be the only way to achieve the objectivity necessary to see the world as it really is (Bernstein, 1976; Hesse, 1980; Wolf, 1981). As such, the growth of knowledge is assumed to be "a cumulative process in which new insights are added to the existing stock of knowledge and false hypotheses eliminated" (Burrell & Morgan, 1979, p. 5), a process that, over time, ultimately converges upon the truth about the world. Positivism is the conviction that scientific knowledge is cumulative, convergent, and objective – the only source of correct knowledge about reality.

Although positivism is a particular theory of knowledge, it has been so pervasive that, until recently, it has been viewed as the only theory of knowledge. The problem is that, although positivism has been discredited (see Bernstein, 1976; Harré, 1981; Hesse, 1980; Rorty, 1979), it is the theory of knowledge upon which the modern university and its associated professional schools are premised (Glazer, 1974; Schön, 1983; Shils, 1978). As such, positivism is the theory of knowledge that underwrites modern professionalism and thus the professions' claim to scientific authority and autonomy in society. Positivism yields a threefold model of professional knowledge, which Schein (1972) described as

1. An *underlying discipline* or *basic science* component upon which the [profession's] practice rests or from which it is developed.
2. An *applied science* or *"engineering"* component from which many of the [profession's] day-to-day diagnostic procedures and problem-solutions are derived.
3. A *skills and attitudinal* component that concerns the actual performance of services to the client, using the underlying basic and applied knowledge. (p. 43)

According to the model, professional knowledge can be understood as the interdependent, hierarchical relationship among three types of knowledge:

disciplinary, basic, or *theoretical knowledge*; engineering or *applied knowledge*; and knowledge based on skills and attitudes, or *practical knowledge*.

The positivist model of professional knowledge legitimizes professional practice as the product of a formal, rational-technical process of knowledge production (Schön, 1983). The actual performance of professional services to clients rests on applied knowledge, which itself rests on a foundation of basic or theoretical knowledge. Basic or disciplinary science yields theoretical knowledge, which is assumed to be cumulative, convergent, and objective, according to the positivist theory of knowledge. Applied scientists in professional schools receive theoretical knowledge from the disciplinary sciences and engineer it into the models, practices, and tools to be used in professional practice. The professional practitioner receives applied knowledge from applied scientists and uses it in the performance of services to clients. Thus, rigorous professional practice depends on applied scientists developing models, practices, and tools that, given their grounding in the theoretical knowledge of the disciplinary sciences, are themselves assumed to be cumulative, convergent, and objective (Glazer, 1974; Greenwood, 1981).

The distinction between "received" knowledge and "objective" knowledge is important. Both the applied researcher and the professional practitioner are assumed to operate on the basis of the knowledge each receives on faith from the next higher level in the hierarchy of professional knowledge (Greenwood, 1981; Schein, 1972). According to the model, however, the basic or disciplinary scientist does not receive knowledge; he or she "discovers" it through the scientific method, which makes it cumulative, convergent, and objective, according to the positivist theory of knowledge (Glazer, 1974; Schön, 1983). I will return to the distinction between received and objective knowledge below. At this point, I want to consider professional induction, the process by which individuals gain access to professional knowledge and skills.

Professional Induction

Persons are inducted into a profession through a formal program of professional education in which the inductee is given access to the profession's specialized knowledge and skills. The curriculum of professional education follows the hierarchy of knowledge contained in the positivist model of professional knowledge. First, students are given some exposure to the theoretical knowledge of the relevant disciplinary science in colleges of liberal arts and sciences, then more extensive exposure to the applied knowledge of the profession in the relevant professional school, and finally an internship in which, under the guidance of an experienced practitioner, the inductee learns to apply the profession's theoretically grounded applied knowledge to the actual problems of professional practice (Greenwood, 1981; Schön, 1983). Students arc on thcir way to becoming full-fledged professionals when they can demonstrate that they have internalized the knowledge and skills of the profession. But there is more to becoming a professional than internalizing knowledge and skills – the would-be professional also must be socialized.

Socialization is the process by which a new member internalizes the value system, norms, and established behavior patterns of the group he or she is entering (Etzioni, 1961). Professional socialization inculcates inductees with the standards for how members of the profession ought to behave (Schein, 1968). It is a vital part of professional induction because it is the mechanism by which the professions regulate and discipline the professional behavior of their members, according to the special relationship between the professions and society (De George, 1982; Mintzberg, 1979). When students can demonstrate that they have internalized the profession's knowledge, skills, norms, and values – how to think and act as professionals – they are duly certified as professionally competent by the professional school, admitted to the professional community by the relevant professional association, and licensed by the state to practice the profession.

Given the discussion to this point, we can understand a profession as an autonomous community of members who, through strong socialization and common exposure to a body of specialized knowledge and skills, share a perspective on the world, their work and their clients, and themselves. Professional practices and discourses are shaped by this communally shared outlook. Professionalization produces individuals who are certain that they both know and do what is best for their clients because, given the positivist model of professional knowledge, they assume that the knowledge behind their practices and discourses is cumulative, convergent, and, above all, objective.

THE CRISIS IN SCIENTIFIC KNOWLEDGE

Although the positivist theory of knowledge has been under attack for more than a century (Phillips, 1987), perhaps the most influential critique has been that of Thomas Kuhn (1962, 1970b), who used the notions of paradigms and paradigm shifts to discredit the objectivist understanding of science and scientific knowledge. Although Kuhn limited his analysis to the natural sciences, his work has had its most profound effect on the social sciences and, by implication, on what I will call the *social professions* – that is, professions such as education and special education that draw their theoretical knowledge, in whole or in part, from one or more of the social disciplines (see Chapter 2).

Paradigms

Although the concept of a paradigm was the central element in Kuhn's analysis, he was neither clear nor consistent about what he meant by it (see Kuhn, 1970a, 1970b). Masterman (1970) noted more than 20 different uses of the term in Kuhn's original work, which she reduced to a hierarchy of three basic types of paradigms, ranging from most to least abstract. She called Kuhn's most abstract use of the term the *metaphysical paradigm*, the broadest unit of consensus within a given science, a total worldview or gestalt that subsumes and defines the other two types of paradigms. Kuhn used paradigm in this sense to refer to a way of seeing, a perceptual organizer or mental map that yields a corresponding set of theories and guiding assumptions that define for scientists which entities exist (and which do not) and how they behave.

At the next level of abstraction Masterman placed the *sociological paradigm*, which is what Kuhn referred to as a concrete set of habits or practices (1962) based on universally accepted models or exemplars (1970b). The sociological paradigm is a set of habitual practices that are based on exemplary models, which are themselves grounded in the theories and guiding assumptions derived from the metaphysical paradigm. Finally, Masterman called Kuhn's most concrete use of the term paradigm the *construct paradigm*. Kuhn used paradigm in this sense to refer to the specific research tools and instruments that scientists use to produce and collect data, given the logic of their sociological paradigm's models and practices and, ultimately, their metaphysical paradigm's theories and guiding assumptions.

A metaphysical paradigm is a set of implicit basic beliefs or presuppositions that unrandomize complexity and provide scientists with a general picture of the world and how it works. In turn, these presuppositions yield a corresponding set of theories that scientists use to explain and act upon actual phenomena. The presuppositions can be thought of as *meta*theories because, although theories are grounded in scientific observations, the observations themselves are shaped by the scientists' prior conceptual system of meta-theoretical presuppositions (see Mulkay, 1979; Ritzer, 1980; Shimony, 1977). Below metatheories and theories in the hierarchy are implicit guiding assumptions, which are derived from the logic of the theories and, in turn, yield a corresponding set of models that define and subsume an associated set of research practices and tools. Thus, a scientific community can be understood as operating on the basis of the hierarchy of presuppositions depicted in Figure 1.1. Each level of the hierarchy is defined and subsumed by the higher levels, and all levels are ultimately defined and subsumed by the meta-theoretical presuppositions of the metaphysical paradigm.

FIGURE 1.1. Scientific Community's Hierarchy of Presuppositions

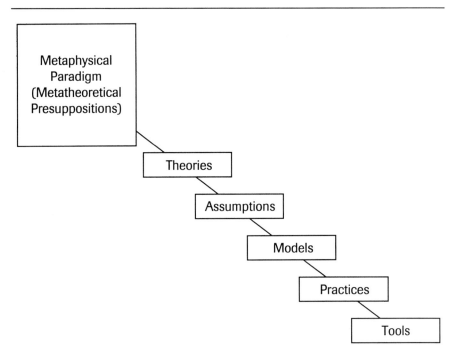

Source: Adapted from G. Burrell and G. Morgan, 1979, *Sociological Paradigms and Organizational Analysis*, p. 29, London: Heinemann Educational Books; G. Ritzer, 1980, *Sociology: A Multiple Paradigm Science*, p. 239, Boston: Allyn & Bacon; and T. M. Skrtic, 1991, *Behind Special Education: A Critical Analysis of Professional Culture and School Organization*, p. 14, Denver: Love Publishing.

Paradigm Shifts

Given this paradigm-based characterization of scientific knowledge and practice, Kuhn used the notion of paradigm shift to reconceptualize the growth of knowledge or progress in the natural sciences. His key insight in this regard was to distinguish between continuous and discontinuous scientific progress. Continuous scientific progress, or what Kuhn called "normal science," progresses by gradual additions to a knowledge base, a highly cumulative and convergent enterprise that articulates a paradigm that already exists. An accepted metatheoretical paradigm is essential for normal science because it unrandomizes the inherent complexity of nature and gives scientists the theories, assumptions, models, practices, and research tools that are necessary to recognize, retrieve, and interpret data (Kuhn, 1970b). Although this is the traditional image of science, Kuhn argued that normal science is merely a necessary prelude to "revolutionary science," which he described as a discontinuous and divergent breakthrough that demands an entirely new paradigm for recognizing and interpreting data.

According to Kuhn (1962, 1970b), revolutionary science uncovers new and previously unsuspected phenomena and invents radical new theories, assumptions, practices, and research tools to describe, collect, and explain data. It begins with the recognition and extended exploration of an anomaly, a violation of the paradigm-induced expectations of normal science. When the anomaly comes to be seen as more than just another normal science puzzle to be solved, the scientific community enters a state of paradigm crisis in which the rules of normal science are blurred. The blurring of the paradigm's rules gives rise to extraordinary research and theoretical speculation, which further loosen the paradigm's stereotypes and begin to expose the parameters of a new metatheoretical paradigm. Although in some cases this foreshadows the shape of the new paradigm, more often the new paradigm emerges all at once, "sometimes in the middle of the night, in the mind of a [scientist] deeply immersed in crisis" (Kuhn, 1970b, p. 90).

In any event, the shift to a new paradigm is revolutionary science. Whereas normal science requires the mutual acceptance of a given metatheoretical paradigm among a community of scientists, revolutionary science requires a paradigm shift, a shift in allegiance to a new paradigm by (more or less) the entire scientific community. After the paradigm shift, normal science begins anew under the guiding framework of the new paradigm. This sets the stage for new anomalies, another paradigm crisis, and eventually the emergence of a new metatheoretical paradigm and its associated theories, assumptions, models, practices, and tools. Kuhn characterized normal science as "a mopping-up operation" (1977b, p. 188), the exploration and further articulation of a paradigm that already exists. Although within-paradigm articulation is the objectivist view of progress, for Kuhn growth of knowledge and progress in the natural sciences is revolutionary; it occurs from consensus to consensus, from paradigm to paradigm.

The Subjectivist View of Science

A key element in Kuhn's reconceptualization of science and scientific progress is the idea that, rather than an objective, rational-technical process, paradigm replacement is a social-political phenomenon, a nonrational-cultural process of persuasion and conversion in which the victorious paradigm is the one that wins the most converts (Barnes, 1985; Ritzer, 1980). Nonrational-cultural factors affect and largely determine the emergence of a new paradigm. Indeed, as ethnographic and historical research on scientific activity shows, paradigms in the natural sciences rise and fall as a result of subjective rather than objective factors (see Bloor, 1976; Knorr, Krohn, & Whitley, 1981; Law, 1975; Phillips, 1973). Natural scientists are "literally constructing their world rather than merely describing it" (Krohn, 1981, p. xi).

Kuhn's work is important for what it had to say about the role of culture and convention in the production of knowledge. His analysis of the conventional nature of knowledge, and the nature of convention itself, contradicted the common perception that science and knowledge are objective, and advanced the idea that both depend on their cultural context for meaning and interpretation. Commenting on the implications of Kuhn's work, Barnes (1982) noted the significance of culture in science by saying that "culture is far more than the setting for scientific research; it is the research itself" (p. 10). The image of scientist as impersonal observer who discovers objective knowledge that is free from time and context has been replaced by the image of scientist as craftsperson who, bound by the culture of a particular place and time, constructs historically situated knowledge that is of temporary validity and utility (Law, 1975; Ravetz, 1971). The revised image of science and scientific progress necessarily undercuts the positivist theory of knowledge. Scientific knowledge, once conceived as the product of "a separate verbal and symbolic high culture [with] the power to reveal, order and enlighten . . . is being brought down to earth, demystified as a human construction" (Krohn, 1981, p. xii).

The subjectivist view of science rejects the objectivist image of science as a neutral, rational-technical undertaking that discovers objective knowledge. It recognizes science as an inherently nonrational-cultural endeavor, a paradigm-bound, communal act of knowledge construction that yields subjective knowledge. From this perspective, science is a form of cultural engagement between an object of study and a community of observers who are conditioned by their paradigm to see the object in a particular way. As Morgan (1983) noted in this regard:

> Scientists engage a subject of study by interacting with it through means of a particular frame of reference. . . . Moreover, since it is possible to engage an object of study in different ways—just as we might engage an apple by looking at it, feeling it, or eating it—we can see that the same object is capable of yielding many different kinds of knowledge. This leads us to see knowledge as a potential-

ity resting in an object of investigation and to see science as being concerned with the realization of potentialities–of possible knowledges. (p. 13)

It is important to note that Kuhn's subjectivist reconceptualization of science is not a critique of science; it is a critique of the objectivist *view* of science (Barnes, 1985). The Kuhnian view leaves the legitimacy of the natural sciences intact; it merely provides a different way of understanding the scientific method and thus the nature of scientific knowledge, practice, and progress. Kuhn and those who have extended his work called into question the objectivist philosophy of science and thus the positivist notion that scientific knowledge is cumulative, convergent, and objective. By showing that science, scientific knowledge, and scientific progress are discontinuous, divergent, and inherently subjective, they vindicated the subjectivist philosophy of science.

THE SUBJECTIVIST VIEW OF THE PROFESSIONS

Given the special relationship between society and the professions and the circular relationship between professional autonomy and professional knowledge, the idea that science produces subjective knowledge rather than objective knowledge has profound implications for the professions. The most obvious implication, of course, is the question of the validity of professional knowledge and, in turn, the claim that the professions know and do what is best for their clients and society. I address these questions with respect to the professions of education and special education in a subsequent section, and more fully in Chapter 2. In this section I want to set the stage for those discussions by reconsidering professional knowledge and professional induction from the subjectivist perspective.

The Subjectivist View of Professional Knowledge

According to the positivist model of professional knowledge, the knowledge of applied scientists and professional practitioners is merely received knowledge, accepted on faith from the basic or disciplinary science level of the hierarchy of professional knowledge. The legitimacy of a profession's claim to know and do what is best for its clients and society ultimately rests on the assumption that basic scientists discover objective knowledge about reality. Given the subjectivist view of science, however, we can see that, like applied scientists and professional practitioners, basic scientists also operate on the basis of received knowledge. The theoretical knowledge of the basic sciences is not objective knowledge about reality; it is knowledge received by looking at the world through a particular metatheoretical paradigm, a process that produces subjective knowledge that is of temporary validity and utility. Like the objectivist image of science and the positivist theory of knowledge, the work of the basic scientist has been demystified and brought down to earth as an act of knowledge construction.

The Subjectivist View of Professional Induction

Although the advantage of standardizing the thought and behavior of scientists and professionals through education and socialization is generally understood (Kuhn, 1970b, 1977a; Mintzberg, 1979; below), the actual process of professional induction has received little critical attention. This is true in all professions (Barnes, 1982; Schön, 1983), including education (Champion, 1984; Haberman, 1983; Koehler, 1985; Popkewitz, 1991; Zeichner & Tabachnick, 1981) and special education (Skrtic, 1986, 1988), because the objectivist view of the professions largely takes induction for granted. The assumption is that the two components of professional induction—education and socialization—are merely different means for accomplishing different ends. Professional education is assumed to be a rational-technical process for conveying an objective body of knowledge and skills, according to the positivist model of professional knowledge (Schön, 1983). Professional socialization is assumed to be a nonrational-cultural process for inculcating a subjective value system and its associated behavior norms, according to the self-regulatory responsibility of the professions (De George, 1982; Greenwood, 1981).

Beyond these assumptions about the nature and aims of professional education and socialization, little is known about the actual process through which professionals are inducted into professional communities. Nevertheless, we can shed some light on this process by turning once again to Kuhn (1970b, 1977a). Kuhn's work is important in this regard because a central feature in his reconceptualization of science is an analysis of scientific education, which for him is a matter of inducting would-be scientists into a scientific community's established knowledge tradition, the accepted metatheoretical paradigm and corresponding theories, assumptions, models, practices, and research tools of a scientific culture (Barnes, 1982). According to Kuhn, scientific education is a process whereby a student is inducted into a culture of customs and conventions, much like the induction of an apprentice into a craft culture. From this perspective, a scientific community's knowledge tradition is the time-honored, mutually agreed-upon conventions and customs of its members. Kuhn's analysis is relevant to the induction process in the professions because, in all its essential elements, professional induction is virtually identical to that of scientific induction (see Cherryholmes, 1988; Skrtic, 1986, 1988).

Of the two objectivist assumptions about professional induction – internalization of objective knowledge through education, and inculcation of subjective norms through socialization – there is no argument about the subjectivity of values and norms, or of socialization itself. But Kuhn's view is that the internalization of knowledge and skills is a subjective process of socialization as well (Barnes, 1982; Popper, 1970). According to this interpretation, professional education, like scientific education, is a process whereby a student is inducted into a culture of customs and conventions; again, like the induction of an apprentice into a craft culture. Professional knowledge is not objective in the sense that it represents an objective reality that exists apart from and prior to its definition by the profession. A profession's knowledge tradition and associated skills are the time-honored, mutually agreed-upon customs and conventions of its members.

Using the Kuhnian view of scientific induction as a frame of reference, professional induction requires the inductee to submit to the institutional legitimacy of the profession and the authority of the teacher, who ordinarily is also an applied scientist. The information conveyed by the teacher is taken on trust by the student because of the context in which it appears. As such, professional education tends to be dogmatic and authoritarian, given its institutional context and the fact that the inductee initially lacks enough of the profession's specialized knowledge to be able to evaluate it on its own terms (Barnes, 1982). And this applies to the professional education of both the applied scientist and the practitioner of the profession. Although the applied scientist learns to engineer theories into models, practices, and tools, and the practitioner learns to apply models, practices, and tools to the problems of professional practice, both are taught in a dogmatic spirit. Each receives knowledge from a higher authority in the hierarchy of professional knowledge, and each accepts it on faith. The would-be professional is regarded as a novice whose very perception must be guided and shaped to conform to the profession's knowledge tradition, to its conventional way of structuring the world and seeing itself and its clients (Barnes, 1982; Greenwood, 1981). The process corresponds to Kuhn's (1970b) characterization of the induction of natural scientists.

> Looking at a contour map, the student sees lines on paper, the cartographer a picture of a terrain. Looking at a bubble-chamber photograph, the student sees confused and broken lines, the physicist a record of familiar subnuclear events. Only after a number of such transformations of vision does the student become an inhabitant of the scientist's world, seeing what the scientist sees and responding as the scientist does. (p. 111)

As in the induction of scientists into scientific cultures, teaching textbooks play a key role in the "transformations of vision" necessary for an inductee to become an inhabitant of the world of a professional culture. The textbook conveys the profession's knowledge tradition to the inductee. In the hands of the teacher, who personifies the authority and legitimacy of the profession, the teaching textbook becomes the principal vehicle for maximizing the authority and credibility of the profession's knowledge tradition (see Barnes, 1982; Kuhn, 1977a). The authority implied by the teaching textbook is essential because professional induction demands complete acceptance of the profession's received knowledge on faith. Anything that questions or offers an alternative to the profession's established knowledge tradition is avoided. Unorthodox perspectives tend to be overlooked in training and rarely find their way into teaching textbooks (Kuhn, 1970b). This sort of education demands complete concentration on one knowledge tradition to the exclusion of all others. The goal is to inculcate in the would-be professional a deep commitment to a particular way of viewing the world and operating in it.

As in the case of Kuhn's reconceptualization of science, his description of scientific induction is not a critique of scientific education; it is a critique of the traditional objectivist *view* of the induction process. Indeed, Kuhn offered his interpretation of the process as an account of an extremely effective system of education (Kuhn, 1970b, 1977a). If we can conceive of a field of endeavor, whether a natural science or a profession, as a collective enterprise grounded in conventionally based, communal judgment, then an authoritarian education is a productive preparation for it. As Barnes (1982) noted with regard to the induction of natural scientists into scientific communities:

> Standardization of perception and cognition facilitates communication, organization, interdependence and division of labor: the more dogmatic their training, the more scientists are bound together into a communal enterprise with all the familiar gains in efficiency which that entails. . . . The consequence of the commitment encouraged by dogmatic training is that investigation is narrowed and focused, and is thus made more productive. (p. 19)

Like scientific work, professional work is too complex to be approached in a random, unsystematic manner. As in the case of scientific knowledge, professional knowledge is premised on a commitment to view the world in a particular way. The advantage of a dogmatic commitment to a particular way of seeing is that it unrandomizes complexity and thus narrows and focuses activity, making it more productive. In this sense, one would expect the same benefits that Kuhn and Barnes noted for the natural sciences to accrue for the professions. However, we will see in Chapter 2 that, although an authoritarian education and a dogmatic commitment to a particular knowledge tradition are advantages for a natural science, they can become a severe disadvantage for a profession, particularly for social professions like education and special education that ground their practices and discourses in the theoretical knowledge of the social sciences.

IMPLICATIONS FOR SPECIAL EDUCATION

The philosophical and political critiques of the professions are based on the implications of subjectivism and the more revolutionary implications of postmodernism, matters that are considered in depth in Chapter 2. I want to conclude this chapter by commenting briefly on the most obvious philosophical implications of the rise of subjectivism for the field of special education.

Inherent in the subjectivist philosophy of science, of course, is a critique of positivism and the objectivist view of scientific knowledge. Special education is implicated in this critique because, like all professions, its legitimacy rests on the positivist epistemology of knowledge, on the assumption that science produces objective knowledge. But subjectivism rejects the objectivist image of science as a purely technical undertaking that yields objective knowledge. As we have seen, the subjectivist view of science is that rather than being a neutral, rational-technical activity, it is a nonrational undertaking, a form of cultural engagement that yields different kinds of socially constructed possible knowledges, depending on the paradigm that serves as the observers' metatheoretical frame of reference. This means that the theoretical knowledge that grounds special education practices and discourses is not objective knowledge about reality; it is subjective knowledge, a social construction based on a particular, historically situated frame of reference. Given the implications of subjectivism, the field of special education must confront the fact that there is nothing inherently true or correct about its professional knowledge, practices, and discourses.

Until now the determination of a valid grounding for professional practice has been left to the discretion of the professions themselves. On the basis of the objectivist view of science and the positivist model of professional knowledge, it was assumed that the validity of professional knowledge is unproblematic and that, with the growth of scientific knowledge generally, incremental refinements are sufficient to revise and extend what is at bottom a solid foundation of objective knowledge about reality. But subjectivism undermines this view, creating a crisis in the profession of special education, an epistemological crisis that turns on the contradiction between the objectivist view of the professions and the subjectivist view of science.

To fully appreciate the significance of the crisis in special education knowledge, however, we must consider the implications of the subjectivist view of science for the social sciences and the knowledge they produce. As we have seen, Kuhn's work is not a critique of science; it is a devastating critique of the objectivist view of science. We will see in Chapter 2 that this has profound implications for the social sciences because, historically, they have modeled themselves after the very objectivist image of science that has been called into question. Moreover, the implications of subjectivism apply with even greater force to the field of special education, given that its legitimacy is premised on the presumed objectivity of its grounding social scientific knowledge.

NOTES

1. The modern era or "modernity" refers to the epoch that follows the Middle Ages or feudalism, the period from about the seventeenth century onward in which a variety of economic, political, social, and cultural transformations emerged in Europe and subsequently became more or less worldwide in their influence (Giddens, 1990; Chapter 2). A key component and, for many, the driving force of modernity is the emergence of science, first the natural sciences in the seventeenth century (Whitehead, 1967), and then the social sciences (largely) in the nineteenth century (Outhwaite, 1987). In this chapter I use "objectivism" and "subjectivism" to refer to the two opposing modern philosophies of *natural* science, and I am concerned with the implications of a shift from an objectivist to a subjectivist philosophy of natural science for the professions, particularly those of education and special education. In Chapter 2 I use "objectivism" and "subjectivism" to refer to the two opposing modern philosophies of *social* science, and I am concerned with the implications of the shift from objectivism to subjectivism in the social sciences for the professions of education and special education. Although objectivism and subjectivism will be addressed more completely in this and the following chapter (see also Chapters 4, 6, and 9), at no point is subjectivism used in the common or mundane sense of mere personal opinion, taste, bias, or idiosyncrasy.

2. This is the classical or nineteenth-century version of positivism. What has come to be seen by many as orthodox positivism in this century is the version offered by Popper (1959). Noting that humans make sense of the world through theories, and that these theories affect the phenomena we are trying to observe, Popper argued that, rather than build theories inductively from observations, we should use empirical observation to attempt to falsify them. According to Popper, no theory can be absolutely true but all can be absolutely falsified, and thus the method of falsification allows us to eliminate inadequate theories, which, over time, gives us an increasingly better grasp of reality, or objective truth. A key difference between classical and Popperian positivism is that, unlike the classical version, Popper recognized the limits of human cognition. Nevertheless, as Hawkesworth (1988) noted, "both [classical] positivist and Popperian conceptions of science are committed to the correspondence theory of truth [i.e., that true statements are those that correspond to reality as it actually is] and its corollary assumption that the objectivity of science ultimately rests upon an appeal to the facts [i.e., upon empirical observation]" (p. 47). For Popper, objective truth exists but merely lies beyond the limits of cognition. By using the

falsification method to progressively eliminate error, however, we can come close to attaining objective truth.

REFERENCES

Abbott, A. (1988). *The system of professions*. Chicago: University of Chicago Press.

Barnes, B. (1982). *T. S. Kuhn and social science*. New York: Columbia University Press.

Barnes, B. (1985). Thomas Kuhn. In Q. Skinner (Ed.), *The return of grand theory in the human sciences* (pp. 83–100). Cambridge: Cambridge University Press.

Bernstein, R. J. (1976). *The restructuring of social and political theory*. Philadelphia: University of Pennsylvania Press.

Bledstein, B. J. (1976). *The culture of professionalism: The middle class and the development of higher education in America*. New York: Norton.

Bloor, D. C. (1976). *Knowledge and social imagery*. London: Routledge & Kegan Paul.

Braverman, H. (1974). *Labor and monopoly capital: The degradation of work in the twentieth century*. New York: Monthly Review.

Burrell, G., & Morgan, G. (1979). *Sociological paradigms and organizational analysis*. London: Heinemann.

Champion, R. H. (1984). Faculty reported use of research in teacher preparation courses: Six instructional scenarios. *Journal of Teacher Education, 35*(5), 9–12.

Cherryholmes, C. H. (1988). *Power and criticism: Poststructuralist investigations in education*. New York: Teachers College Press.

Collins, R. (1979). *The credential society*. New York: Academic Press.

De George, R. T. (1982). *Business ethics*. New York: Macmillan.

Etzioni, A. (1961). *A comparative analysis of complex organizations*. New York: Free Press.

Freidson, E. (1988). *Professional powers: A study of the institutionalization of formal knowledge*. Chicago: University of Chicago Press.

Giddens, A. (1990). *The consequences of modernity*. Cambridge: Polity Press.

Gilb, C. L. (1966). *Hidden hierarchies: The professions and government*. New York: Harper & Row.

Glazer, N. (1974). The schools of the minor professions. *Minerva, 12*(3), 346–364.

Greenwood, E. (1981). Attributes of a profession. In N. Gilbert & H. Specht (Eds.), *The emergence of social work and social welfare* (pp. 241–255). Itasca, IL: F. E. Peacock.

Haberman, M. (1983). Research on preservice laboratory and clinical experiences: Implications for teacher education. In K. R. Howey & W. Gardner (Eds.), *The education of teachers: A look ahead* (pp. 98–117). New York: Longman.

Harré, R. (1981). The positivist-empiricist approach and its alternative. In P. Reason & J. Rowan (Eds.), *Human inquiry: A sourcebook of new paradigm research* (pp. 3–17). New York: John Wiley.

Haskell, T. L. (1984a). Professionalism versus capitalism: R. H. Tawney, Emile Durkheim, and C. S. Peirce on the disinterestedness of professional communities. In T. L. Haskell, *The authority of experts: Studies in history and theory* (pp. 180–225). Bloomington: Indiana University Press.

Haskell, T. L. (1984b). *The authority of experts: Studies in history and theory*. Bloomington: Indiana University Press.

Hawkesworth, M. E. (1988). *Theoretical issues in policy analysis*. Albany: State University of New York Press.

Hesse, M. (1980). *Revolutions and reconstructions in the philosophy of science*. Bloomington: Indiana University Press.

Hughes, E. C. (1963). Professions. *Daedalus, 92*, 655–668.

Knorr, K. D., Krohn, R., & Whitley, R. (Eds.). (1981). *The social process of scientific investigation*. Dordrecht, Holland: D. Reidel.

Koehler, V. (1985). Research on preservice teacher education. *Journal of Teacher Education, 36*(1), 23–30.

Krohn, R. (1981). Introduction: Toward the empirical study of scientific practice. In K. D. Knorr, R. Krohn, & R. Whitley (Eds.), *The social process of scientific investigation* (pp. vii–xxv). Dordrecht, Holland: D. Reidel Publishing.

Kuhn, T. S. (1962). *The structure of scientific revolutions* (1st ed.). Chicago: University of Chicago Press.

Kuhn, T. S. (1970a). Reflections on my critics. In I. Lakatos & A. Musgrave (Eds.), *Criticism and the growth of knowledge* (pp. 231–278). Cambridge: Cambridge University Press.

Kuhn, T. S. (1970b). *The structure of scientific revolutions* (2nd ed.). Chicago: University of Chicago Press.

Kuhn, T. S. (1977a). The essential tension: Tradition and innovation in scientific research. In T. S. Kuhn (Ed.), *The essential tension: Selected studies in scientific tradition and change* (pp. 225–239). Chicago: University of Chicago Press.

Kuhn, T. S. (1977b). The function of measurement in modern physical science. In T. S. Kuhn (Ed.), *The essential tension: Selected studies in scientific tradition and change* (pp. 178–224). Chicago: University of Chicago Press.

Law, J. (1975). Is epistemology redundant? *Philosophy of the Social Sciences, 5*, 317–337.

Masterman, M. (1970). The nature of a paradigm. In I. Lakatos & A. Musgrave (Eds.), *Criticism and the growth of knowledge* (pp. 59–89). Cambridge: Cambridge University Press.

Meyer, J. W., & Rowan, B. (1978). The structure of educational organizations. In M. W. Meyer (Ed.), *Environments and organizations* (pp. 78–109). San Francisco: Jossey-Bass.

Mintzberg, H. (1979). *The structuring of organizations*. Englewood Cliffs, NJ: Prentice-Hall.

Morgan, G. (1983). *Beyond method*. Beverly Hills, CA: Sage.

Mulkay, M. J. (1979). *Science and the sociology of knowledge*. London: Allen & Unwin.

Outhwaite, W. (1987). *New philosophies of social science: Realism, hermeneutics and critical theory*. London: Macmillan.

Parsons, T. (1968). Professions. *The international encyclopedia of the social sciences*. New York: Macmillan.

Patton, M. Q. (1975). *Alternative evaluation research paradigm*. Grand Forks: University of North Dakota Press.

Phillips, D. C. (1973). Paradigms, falsifications and sociology. *Acta Sociologica, 16*, 13–31.

Phillips, D. C. (1987). *Philosophy, science, and social inquiry: Contemporary methodological controversies in social science and related applied fields of research*. Oxford: Pergamon Press.

Popkewitz, T. S. (1991). *A political sociology of educational reform: Power/Knowledge in teaching, teacher education, and research*. New York: Teachers College Press.

Popper, K. R. (1959). *The logic of scientific discovery*. New York: Harper & Row.

Popper, K. R. (1970). Normal science and its dangers. In I. Lakatos & A. Musgrave (Eds.), *Criticism and the growth of knowledge* (pp. 51–58). Cambridge: Cambridge University Press.

Ravetz, J. R. (1971). *Scientific knowledge and its social problems*. Oxford: Clarendon Press.

Ritzer, G. (1980). *Sociology: A multiple paradigm science*. Boston: Allyn & Bacon.

Rorty, R. (1979). *Philosophy and the mirror of nature*. Princeton, NJ: Princeton University Press.

Schein, E. H. (1968). Organizational socialization and the profession of management. *Industrial Management Review, 9*(2), 1–16.

Schein, E. H. (1972). *Professional education*. New York: McGraw-Hill.

Schön, D. A. (1983). *The reflective practitioner: How professionals think in action*. New York: Basic Books.

Scott, R. W. (1981). *Organizations: Rational, natural, and open systems*. Englewood Cliffs, NJ: Prentice-Hall.

Shils, E. (1978). The order of learning in the United States from 1865 to 1920: The ascendancy of the universities. *Minerva, 16*(2), 159–195.

Shimony, A. (1977). Is observation theory-laden? A problem in naturalistic epistemology. In R. G. Colodny (Ed.), *Logic, laws and life* (pp. 185–208). Pittsburgh: University of Pittsburgh Press.

Skrtic, T. M. (1986). The crisis in special education knowledge: A perspective on perspective. *Focus on Exceptional Children, 18*(7), 1–16.

Skrtic, T. M. (1988). The crisis in special education knowledge. In E. L. Meyen & T. M. Skrtic (Eds.), *Exceptional children and youth: An introduction* (pp. 415–447). Denver: Love Publishing.

Skrtic, T. M. (1991). *Behind special education: A critical analysis of professional culture and school organization*. Denver: Love Publishing.

Whitehead, A. N. (1967). *Science and the modern world*. New York: Free Press.

Wilensky, H. L. (1964). The professionalization of everyone? *American Journal of Sociology, 70*, 137–158.

Wolf, F. A. (1981). *Taking the quantum leap*. San Francisco: Harper & Row.

Zeichner, K. M., & Tabachnick, B. R. (1981). Are the effects of university teacher education washed out by school experience? *Journal of Teacher Education, 32*, 7–11.

CHAPTER 2

Power/Knowledge and Pragmatism:
A Postmodern View of the Professions

Thomas M. Skrtic

The knowledge that grounds and legitimizes a profession's practices and discourses is premised on a network of anonymous, historically situated assumptions that organize and give meaning to its practitioners' thought and action (Cherryholmes, 1988; Kuhn, 1970). The assumptions are anonymous because they are grounded in largely unquestioned theories and metatheories; they are historically situated, rather than universal or context free, because they are human constructions, the social products of a particular time and place (Chapter 1). There is an epistemological crisis in the professions because fundamental questions have been raised about the legitimacy of the knowledge that underwrites and justifies their practices and discourses.

In Chapter 1 we saw that one source of uncertainty is the rise of subjectivism, which undermines objectivism, the dominant philosophy of science upon which modern professionalism is premised. In this chapter I want to address the second source of uncertainty, postmodernism, a far more revolutionary development, which, among other things, questions the very objective–subjective dichotomy that defines the parameters of modern knowledge itself. As we will see, postmodernism changes the very meaning of knowledge, which creates a crisis *and* an opportunity for professions like education and special education. The crisis stems from the fact that, even more than subjectivism, postmodernism calls the legitimacy of professional knowledge, practices, and discourses into question. The opportunity arises from two sources. On one hand, a crisis in knowledge is necessary for growth of knowledge, as noted in Chapter 1. On the other hand, postmodernism provides a variety of substantive and methodological insights for reconceptualizing professional knowledge traditions.

The focus of this chapter is modern social knowledge, that is, knowledge of the social world produced since the Enlightenment by what we now think of as the social sciences and humanities (hereafter, social sciences or disciplines). What is so ironic about this knowledge is that over the course of this century, a period in which the objectivist understanding of science was losing its relevance, the social disciplines fought for recognition as genuine sciences by adopting the very objectivist image that was falling out of favor (Bergner, 1981; Bernstein, 1983; Foucault, 1966/1973). As we know, the subjectivist view of science is not a critique of science; it is a devastating critique of the objectivist philosophy of science. And because the social sciences are modeled on the objectivist view, the rise of subjectivism undermines the very claim to legitimacy upon which they are premised. The problem for fields like education and special education is that, by delegitimizing the social sciences' claim to objectivity, subjectivism necessarily calls into question the knowledge, practices, and discourses of the social professions, that is, professions such as education and special education that draw their knowledge claims from the social disciplines.[1]

PARADIGMATIC STATUS OF THE SOCIAL SCIENCES

Although Kuhn (1962, 1970) reserved his conception of paradigms and paradigm shifts exclusively for the natural sciences, his work has been instrumental in advancing our understanding of the social sciences (see Barnes, 1982, 1985; Bernstein, 1976, 1983; Rorty, 1979, 1982). Masterman (1970) made an important contribution in this regard by using Kuhn's paradigm concept to distinguish between natural and social sciences on the basis of their paradigmatic status. According to Masterman, a "paradigmatic" science is one in which there is broad consensus on a single paradigm within the scientific community (e.g., physics after Newton), whereas a "nonparadigmatic" science is one in which consensus is lacking (e.g., natural history or "physics" before Newton). A "dual paradigmatic" state exists immediately before a Kuhnian scientific revolution, when an older, crisis-ridden paradigm and a new one are vying for the dominance that only one of them will achieve. The Newtonian paradigm dominated physics until irreconcilable anomolies set it up for defeat by the Einsteinian paradigm (Clark, 1971). During the period when both paradigms were competing for dominance, physics was a dual paradigm science.

Finally, Masterman characterized the social disciplines as "multiple paradigm" sciences, that is, fields of inquiry in which several viable paradigms compete unsuccessfully for dominance within the scientific community. Unlike the natural sciences, where one paradigm dominates until crisis and revolution replace it with another one, multiple paradigms coexist in the social sciences, which creates two fundamental problems. First, it makes normal science more difficult because social scientists are forced to spend much of their energy winning converts and defending themselves against attacks from rival paradigms (Ritzer, 1980). More important, however, their multiple paradigm status means that Kuhnian scientific revolutions are far more difficult to achieve in the social disciplines, in part because there is simply no single, mutually agreed-upon paradigm to be overthrown (see below). This has slowed the development of the social sciences (relative to the natural sciences) because, as Kuhn (1977) noted, although "one can practice science . . . without a firm consensus, this more flexible practice will not produce the pattern of rapid consequential scientific advance [of the natural sciences, in which] . . . development occurs from one consensus to another" (p. 232). Although it is possible for members of a social scientific community to change paradigms, we will see below that paradigm shifts in multiple paradigm sciences take a different form than those in single paradigm sciences.

FOUR PARADIGMS OF MODERN SOCIAL SCIENTIFIC KNOWLEDGE

Burrell and Morgan (1979) conceptualized the multiple paradigms of the social sciences in terms of the relationship between two dimensions of metatheoretical presuppositions about the nature of social science: one about the nature of science, and one about the nature of society. Using the four strands of debate that have shaped philosophical discourse on the nature of social science in the modern era, Burrell and Morgan formulated their nature of science or "subjective–objective" dimension in terms of the extreme positions on ontology, epistemology, human nature, and methodology (Table 2.1).

According to Burrell and Morgan (1979; see also Morgan & Smircich,

TABLE 2.1. The Subjective–Objective Dimension of Modern Social Theorizing

Subjectivist		**Objectivist**
Nominalism	ontology	Realism
Antipositivism	epistemology	Positivism
Voluntarism	human nature	Determinism
Idiographic	methodology	Nomothetic

Source: Adapted from G. Burrell and G. Morgan, 1979, *Sociological Paradigms and Organizational Analysis*, p. 3, London: Heinemann Educational Books.

1980), realists assume that the social world exists "out there," independent of human awareness, and that it is virtually as hard and concrete as the natural world. Conversely, nominalists assume that the social world is made up of names, concepts, and labels that serve as tools for interpreting and negotiating social reality. Positivists seek to explain and predict social events by searching for regularities and determinate causal relationships through empirical observation (see Chapter 1). Growth of knowledge is seen as a cumulative process in which new information is added to an existing knowledge base and false hypotheses are eliminated. Antipositivists, however, see the social world as essentially relativistic—understandable, but only from the point of view of the individuals directly involved in the activities to be investigated. They reject the notion of objective observer as a valid vantage point for understanding social life (see also Bernstein, 1976).

Burrell and Morgan (1979) characterized determinists as social scientists who assume that humans respond mechanistically or even deterministically to the situations they encounter in the external world. Voluntarists, on the other hand, assume a much more creative role for humans, one in which they construct their social environments rather than being controlled by them. Social scientists who see the social world as an objective, external reality favor the nomothetic methods of the natural sciences—systematic protocols, standardized instruments, and quantitative analysis—which they use to search for universal laws that explain and govern the objective social reality that is presumed to exist. Conversely, idiographic methods of inquiry (emergent protocols, nonstandardized instruments, qualitative analysis) are adopted by social scientists who assume the importance of the subjective experience of humans engaged in the social construction of reality (see also Bernstein, 1976; Dallmayr & McCarthy, 1977).

Taken together, the extreme positions on ontology, epistemology, human nature, and methodology constitute objectivism and subjectivism, the polar opposite philosophies of social science of the modern era. Objectivism, which has been the dominant view, is

> the attempt to apply the models and methods of the natural sciences to the study of human affairs. It treats the social world as if it were the natural world, adopting a "realist" approach to ontology . . . backed up by a "positivist" epistemology, relatively "deterministic" views of human nature and the use of "nomothetic" methodologies. (Burrell & Morgan, 1979, p. 7)

Although subjectivism has been the favored philosophy of social science in some parts of Europe, until recently it had been virtually ignored in other parts of the West, particularly in the United States (see below). Subjectivism stands in complete opposition to objectivism in that, rather than treating the social world as if it were the natural world, it presupposes that

> the ultimate reality of the [social world] lies in "spirit" or "idea" rather than in the data of sense perception. It is essentially "nominalist" in its approach to social reality . . . "antipositivist" in epistemology, "voluntarist" with regard to human nature and it favours idiographic methods as a foundation for social analysis. (Burrell & Morgan, 1979, p. 7)

The nature of society dimension of modern social knowledge can be considered sociologically or analytically. Burrell and Morgan (1979) approached the problem sociologically, using "sociology of regulation" and "sociology of radical change" to describe the extreme positions on their nature of society or "order–conflict" dimension. Table 2.2 differentiates between the two positions in terms of their presuppositions about social life.

Sociology of regulation has been the dominant position in the West. It reflects the value position of theorists who are concerned about explaining society's underlying unity, order, and cohesion. Conversely, theorists of the sociology of radical change characterize modern society in terms of inherent contradictions, conflict, and modes of domination. They are concerned with emancipating people from existing social arrangements.

In his conceptualization of the multiple paradigms of the social sciences, Ritzer (1980, 1983) used the same subjective–objective distinction relative to

TABLE 2.2. The Order–Conflict Dimension of Modern Social Theorizing

Sociology of regulation (order) is concerned with:	Sociology of radical change (conflict) is concerned with:
the status quo	radical change
social order	structural conflict
consensus	modes of domination
social integration	contradiction
solidarity	emancipation
need satisfaction	deprivation
actuality	potentiality

Source: Adapted from G. Burrell and G. Morgan, 1979, *Sociological Paradigms and Organizational Analysis*, p. 18, London: Heinemann Educational Books.

the nature of social inquiry, but approached the nature of society dimension analytically by using a "levels of social analysis" or "microscopic–macroscopic" distinction, which reflects differences among social scientists in terms of presuppositions about the appropriate target of social analysis. Ranging from the microscopic to the macroscopic level, Ritzer's levels of social analysis include individual thought and action, human interaction, groups, organizations, whole societies, and total world systems.

As used here, Ritzer's microscopic and macroscopic levels correspond to the order and conflict positions, respectively, of the Burrell and Morgan scheme, with the microscopic perspective being the dominant level of analysis in the West. In either case, when the nature of science and the nature of society dimensions are related as in Figure 2.1, they produce four paradigms of modern social scientific thought – the *functionalist* (micro-objective), *interpretivist* (micro-subjective), *radical humanist* (macro-subjective), and *radical structuralist* (macro-objective) paradigms.[2]

Each paradigm of modern social scientific thought represents a mutually exclusive view of the social world and how it might be investigated because each one rests on an incommensurable set of metatheoretical presuppositions about the nature of social science itself. As such, each paradigm produces a particular type of modern knowledge because it is a unique, historically situated way of seeing that defines the metatheoretical frame of reference of the social scientists who work within it (Bernstein, 1976, 1983; Burrell & Morgan, 1979; Ritzer, 1980, 1990; Rorty, 1979, 1991). In turn, each metatheoretical paradigm defines and subsumes a corresponding set of social scientific theories, assumptions, models, practices, and research tools, as noted in Chapter 1 relative to the natural sciences.

Ultimately, the type of theoretical knowledge produced by a community of social scientists depends on whether functionalism, interpretivism, radical structuralism, or radical humanism serves as its metatheoretical frame of reference. This has profound philosophical and political implications for the social professions because the nature and effects of their applied and practical knowledge depend on the paradigmatic grounding of the social discipline or disciplines from which they draw their theoretical knowledge. I will return to these implications below, and Chapters 3 through 6 explore each of the paradigms in depth relative to their implications for special education practices and discourses. At this point I want to review the four modern paradigms briefly as a prelude to a discussion of several recent paradigm shifts and the emergence of postmodernism.

Given the dominance of the objectivist image of science and the microscopic/order view of society, the functionalist paradigm has been the dominant framework for social science in the modern era, particularly in the En-

FIGURE 2.1. Four Paradigms of Modern Social Scientific
Thought

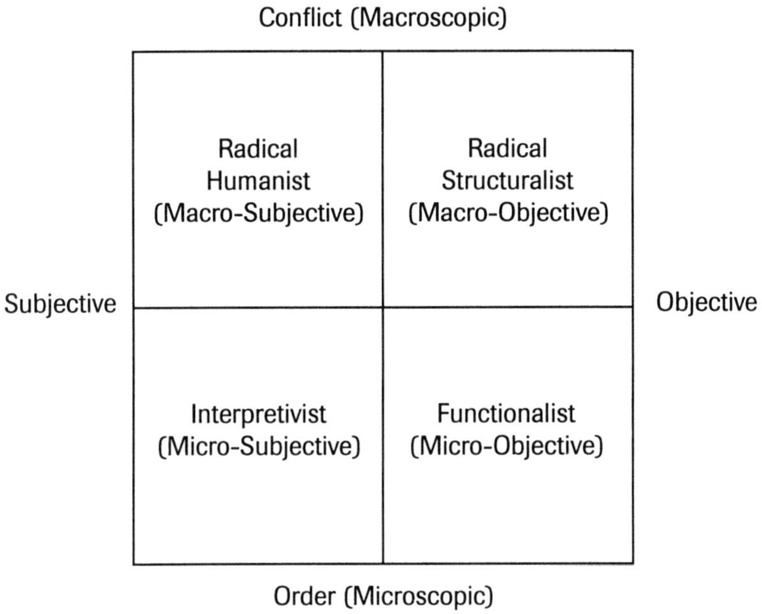

Conflict (Macroscopic)

Radical Humanist (Macro-Subjective)	Radical Structuralist (Macro-Objective)
Interpretivist (Micro-Subjective)	Functionalist (Micro-Objective)

Subjective — Objective

Order (Microscopic)

Source: Adapted from G. Burrell and G. Morgan, 1979, *Sociological Paradigms and Organizational Analysis*, p. 29, London: Heinemann Educational Books; and G. Ritzer, 1980, *Sociology: A Multiple Paradigm Science*, p. 239, Boston: Allyn & Bacon.

glish-speaking world (Bernstein, 1976; Burrell & Morgan, 1979; Foucault, 1966/1973; Ritzer, 1980). Functionalist social science is firmly grounded in the sociology of regulation, takes a more or less microscopic view of social reality, and studies its subject matter from an objectivist point of view. Using an approach to science premised in the tradition of positivism, it seeks to provide rational explanations of social action for the purpose of prediction and control. As such, functionalism represents

the attempt, *par excellence*, to apply the models and methods of the natural sciences to the study of human affairs. . . . The functionalist approach to social science tends to assume that the social world is composed of relatively concrete empirical artifacts and relationships which can be identified, studied and measured through approaches derived from the natural sciences. (Burrell & Morgan, 1979, p. 26)

The functionalist paradigm is equivalent to Ritzer's micro-objective approach to social science. Social scientists operating from this vantage point use positivist methodologies to study microscopic social phenomena–patterns of individual and group behavior and interaction–in an attempt to predict and control various aspects of social life. As Ritzer (1980, 1983) noted, the functionalist views society as a social system composed of interrelated parts, each of which contributes to the maintenance of the others. The parts of society are

> believed to be in a kind of balance with a change in one part necessitating changes in the other parts. The equilibrium of the social system is not static, but a moving equilibrium. Parts of society are always changing, and these changes lead to sympathetic changes in other parts of the system. Thus, change is basically orderly, rather than cataclysmic. (Ritzer, 1980, p. 48)

In the extreme, functionalists argue that all events and structures in society are functional because, if they were not, they would not exist. This leads to the conservative bias that all current aspects of society are indispensable to the system and that, as such, "all structures that exist should continue to exist . . . [which] holds out little possibility of meaningful change within a social system" (Ritzer, 1980, p. 49; Chapter 3).

Burrell and Morgan (1979) characterized interpretivist social scientists as being only implicitly committed to regulation and order. Although they assume that the social world is cohesive, orderly, and integrated, interpretivists (unlike functionalists) are oriented toward understanding the processes through which humans construct their social worlds (see Berger & Luckmann, 1967). Interpretivists address many of the same social issues as functionalists, but they are concerned with understanding the essence of the everyday world as an emergent social phenomenon. When a social world outside the consciousness of humans is recognized, it is regarded as a network of assumptions and intersubjectively shared meanings. Burrell and Morgan's interpretivist paradigm corresponds to Ritzer's micro-subjective perspective. Social scientists of this persuasion are concerned primarily with understanding the social construction of reality (see Dallmayr & McCarthy, 1977; Lincoln & Guba, 1985; Chapter 4).

Radical structuralists share a view of social science with the functionalist paradigm, but their frame of reference is the sociology of radical change. Although they approach social science as objectivists, they use this perspective to mount a critique of the status quo and to advocate change. Working from

Ritzer's macro-objective frame of reference, radical structuralists characterize contemporary society in terms of domination and exploitation, fundamental conflicts that generate change through political and economic crises. Radical structuralists focus their critiques on the material structures of society, on things such as language, economy, technology, bureaucracy, and law (see Giddens, 1981; Chapter 5).

Like radical structuralists, radical humanists' frame of reference is the sociology of radical change. However, in mounting their critique of the status quo they share a view of social science with the interpretivist paradigm. According to Burrell and Morgan, the radical humanist view of society emphasizes the importance of transcending the limitations of existing ideological structures, which they view as distorting true human consciousness. Radical humanists theorize from Ritzer's macro-subjective paradigm and tend to view society as being antihuman, as inhibiting human development, fulfillment, and freedom. Whereas radical structuralists focus their critiques on material structures, radical humanists emphasize ideational structures such as culture, norms, and ideology, and are concerned with the role these structures play in shaping human thought and action (see Bernstein, 1983; Habermas, 1968/ 1971; Chapter 6).

PARADIGM SHIFTS AND THE METALEAP IN THE SOCIAL SCIENCES

Although in principle the multiple paradigm status of the social sciences precludes the kind of paradigm shifts that Kuhn described for the natural sciences (see Kuhn, 1970; Masterman, 1970), paradigm shifts do occur in the social disciplines. One difference is that, whereas a paradigm shift in a natural science is the abandonment of an older crisis-ridden paradigm and the adoption of a new one by (more or less) the entire scientific community (Chapter 1), a paradigm shift in a social science is merely a change in paradigmatic commitment for some members of the scientific community. It affects only those who have changed their paradigmatic allegiance; it does not overthrow the other paradigms or change the outlook of those who remain loyal to them. Although allegiances to particular paradigmatic perspectives have shifted throughout the modern era, and particularly since the 1960s (see below), all four paradigms of modern social scientific thought continue to exist. Paradigm shifts notwithstanding, each one serves as the guiding framework for that portion of the social scientific community that continues to subscribe to it (Bernstein, 1976, 1991; Burrell & Morgan, 1979; Ritzer, 1990).

Because functionalism has been the dominant framework for social science, most modern social theorizing has been premised on the metatheoretical presuppositions of the functionalist paradigm. Over the past 30 years, however, there have been several significant shifts away from the functionalist outlook (Bernstein, 1976, 1983; Burrell & Morgan, 1979; Rorty, 1979).[3] One shift occurred in the 1960s from the functionalist paradigm to the radical structuralist and radical humanist paradigms. It was associated with the emergence of various forms of structuralist social analysis (e.g., Chomsky, 1959; Lévi-Strauss, 1963; Saussure, 1966), as well as increased interest in the social and political philosophy of both the young (radical humanist) and mature (radical structuralist) Marx (see, e.g., Althusser, 1969; Giddens, 1981; Habermas, 1968/1970, 1968/1971; Marcuse, 1964).

Two parallel shifts occurred during the 1970s and 1980s, both of which were associated with the critique of positivism and, following Kuhn, what became a general shift away from the objectivist philosophy of social science (Outhwaite, 1987). One shift occurred at the microscopic (order) level of social analysis, from the functionalist to the interpretivist paradigm, and was associated with renewed interest in various forms of interpretivist social analysis, such as phenomenology, ethnography, and certain forms of hermeneutics (see Bernstein, 1976; Geertz, 1983). The other shift occurred at the macroscopic level, from radical structuralism to radical humanism, which was associated with an expansion of interest in the social and political philosophy of Hegel and the young Marx (see Held, 1980; Jay, 1973), as well as the emergence of new forms of radical humanist inquiry, such as radical ethnography (e.g., B. Bernstein, 1971; Bourdieu, 1977) and radical hermeneutics (see Bernstein, 1976; Caputo, 1987).

Implications for the Social Sciences and Social Professions

There are two key sets of implications associated with the paradigm shifts in the social sciences.[4] The first is related to the general shift in commitment among social scientists from objectivist to subjectivist forms of social theorizing. The second and more important set of implications is related to the emergence (or re-emergence) of antifoundationalism, a perspective on social theorizing that calls the entire four-paradigm matrix of modern social knowledge into question.

The Rise of Subjectivism. The general trend away from functionalist social science over the past 30 years is important because, given functionalism's dominance in the modern era, it has undermined the legitimacy of most modern social theorizing (see Bernstein, 1991; Giddens, 1977; Ritzer, 1990). This is critically important for present purposes because it necessarily calls into question the substantive and methodological legitimacy of the social professions, virtually all of which—including education and special education—have relied explicitly or implicitly on functionalist theory to ground their knowledge, practices, and discourses (see Chapter 3; below). Another important consequence of the paradigm shifts in the social sciences has been the substantive and methodological development of the previously underdeveloped interpretivist, radical structuralist, and radical humanist paradigms (Bernstein, 1976; Burrell & Morgan, 1979). This is an important development in the social sciences because it has produced new forms of social knowledge (Bernstein, 1976, 1983; Rorty, 1979; Ritzer, 1990). It is important for the social professions because the recognition of new modes of theorizing and the availability of new forms of social knowledge have raised the possibility of alternative paradigmatic groundings for fields like education (see, e.g., Apple, 1979, 1985; Cherryholmes, 1988; Giroux, 1983; Soltis, 1984) and special education (see, e.g., Ferguson, 1987; Heshusius, 1982; Iano, 1986; Skrtic, 1986, 1990a, 1991a).

Finally, the paradigm shifts of the 1970s and 1980s have elevated subjectivism to a position of increasing prominence in the social sciences and social professions, which has had both positive and negative effects. As noted above, the advantage is the production and broader utilization of subjectivist forms of knowledge in the social disciplines and social professions. On the negative side, however, the rise of subjectivism has led some long-standing and newly converted interpretivists and radical humanists to see their particular paradigm as the only correct one. This has been true in the social sciences (Bernstein, 1983; Ritzer, 1990; Rorty, 1991) and in education (see Barone, 1992) and special education (see Skrtic, 1990c, 1991a; Chapter 3) because the implications of the rise of subjectivism have been interpreted too narrowly as simply a vindication of subjectivist over objectivist modes of social theorizing, which has tended merely to intensify the historical pattern of political competition among paradigms. Fortunately, however, infighting over paradigms began to subside somewhat in the social sciences by the end of the 1980s, giving rise to what appears to be a new sense of paradigmatic and theoretical diversity, if not pluralism (Bernstein, 1991; Ritzer, 1990). Unfortunately, the same cannot be said about the fields of education and special education where the "paradigm wars" (Gage, 1989) are just beginning. Nevertheless, educators and special educators at least have begun to talk about paradigms, and there even have been some attempts to establish rules of engagement, both in education (Guba, 1990) and special education (Iano, 1987; Skrtic, 1986, 1991a; Chapter 3).

The Emergence of Antifoundationalism. Whereas the paradigm shifts in the social disciplines represent realignments of commitment to various forms of modern social knowledge, a more revolutionary development has been the (re)emergence of the antifoundational view of social knowledge. During the modern period, the conceptualization of knowledge was foundational—the idea that there is a fixed set of foundational criteria against which all knowledge claims can be judged. The modern perspective is monological; it regards knowledge or truth as a monologue spoken in the voice of a single paradigm or theoretical frame of reference, whether an objectivist or a subjectivist one. But antifoundationalism is based on the dialogical idea that there are no independent foundational criteria for judging knowledge claims, and thus that there is no cognitively certain way to establish a particular paradigm or theory as the ultimate frame of reference for interpreting the social world. For the antifoundationalist, the "truth" about the social world is better understood as an ongoing conversation, an open dialogue among many paradigmatic voices and theoretical perspectives (Bernstein, 1983, 1991; Rorty, 1979). Moreover, antifoundationalism blurs the traditional distinctions among the social sciences themselves because, in this view, there is no meaningful way to establish the cognitive authority of one social discipline over another (Geertz, 1983).

Foundational social inquiry is a monological quest for the single best method, theory, paradigm, or discipline for social analysis. But antifoundationalists call for a relativistic form of social analysis, a dialogical discourse in which no modern methodological, theoretical, disciplinary, or paradigmatic perspectives can claim cognitive superiority (Bernstein, 1983, 1991; Ricoeur, 1981; Rorty, 1979, 1991). Generally speaking, postmodernism is a response to antifoundationalism, a frame of reference for social analysis that falls outside the four-paradigm matrix of modern social knowledge itself.[5] Although at present postmodernism is a relatively vague and controversial conception in the social sciences, two predominant forms can be identified (see Antonio, 1989). First, there is radical or Continental postmodernism (e.g., Baudrillard, 1983; Derrida, 1972/1982b; Foucault, 1966/1973; Lyotard, 1979/1984), which rejects all forms of modern social knowledge outright. The Continental postmoderns are incredulous toward paradigms *per se*, regarding them simply as historically situated constructions of the social world, outdated and oppressive metanarratives written in the genre of philosophy (Lyotard, 1979/1984). The second form of postmodernism is the progressive liberal version (e.g., Bernstein, 1983, 1991; Rorty, 1979, 1982, 1991), which is a reappropriation of American pragmatism, the antifoundational philosophy of John Dewey (1920/1982, 1929/1988), William James (1907/1975), George Herbert Mead (1934), and Charles Sanders Peirce (1931–35).[6]

The key difference between the radical and progressive postmoderns is the value they place on modern social knowledge and, more important, modern democratic values such as liberty, equality, community, and social justice. The radical postmoderns reject modern knowledge as oppressive and attempt to free us from its hold by delegitimizing or "deconstructing" it, that is, by exposing its inherent inconsistencies, contradictions, and silences (see below). The problem with this position, however, is the alleged tendency within radical postmodernism to reject modern values as well (see Antonio, 1989; Best & Kellner, 1991; Burbules & Rice, 1991; Stanley, 1992). The progressive postmoderns also want to deconstruct modern knowledge, but they accept it conditionally, as a starting point for "reconstructing" new forms of emancipatory social knowledge through a critical and democratized form of dialogical social inquiry (see Antonio, 1989; Kloppenberg, 1986). Moreover, above all they remain committed to modern democratic values and, recognizing that the expression of these values in modern societies is often more rhetorical than real, seek to "reappropriate, refine, and reground them" (Burbules & Rice, 1991, p. 397; Cherryholmes, 1988; Stanley, 1992). Like the original pragmatist philosophers, the progressive postmoderns or neopragmatists propose that we use modern knowledge pragmatically by ignoring its subjective–objective, micro–macro, and order–conflict dualisms (Kloppenberg, 1986; Rorty, 1979, 1991). They propose a radically open and participatory form of social discourse in which all forms of modern (and postmodern) knowledge are accepted or rejected, in whole or in part, on the basis of their contribution to the realization of democratic social ideals, rather than whether they are true in a foundational sense (Bernstein, 1991; Davidson, 1986; Rorty, 1989, 1991).

THE CRISIS IN SPECIAL EDUCATION

I expand upon pragmatism and, among other things, the notions of deconstruction and reconstruction below. In this section, however, I want to consider the implications of antifoundationalism for the field of special education. As we know, the legitimacy of special education's knowledge tradition rests on the legitimacy of the social knowledge in which it is grounded. As such, antifoundationalism creates a crisis and an opportunity in the field of special education. The crisis stems from the fact that, by delegitimizing modern social knowledge, antifoundationalism calls the legitmacy of special education's knowledge, practices, and discourses into question. As noted above, the opportunity arises from two sources. On one hand, a crisis in knowledge is a precondition for the growth of knowledge; as we have seen, this is the deconstruction side of the progress equation. On the other side of the equation, however, is reconstruction. If the field of special education is to resolve the crisis that antifoundationalism creates, it must have a method for reconstructing its knowledge, practices, and discourses. The opportunity is that antifoundationalism, and particularly the reappropriation of philosophical pragmatism, provides a way for the field of special education to reconcile its practices and discourses with the ideal of serving the best interests of its clients and society. Before commenting further on the opportunity, however, I want to consider the crisis in special education by expanding upon the philosophical implications of antifoundationalism and introducing its political implications.

Philosophical Critique of Special Education Knowledge

As we know from Chapter 1, subjectivism undermines the objectivist philosophy of science and the positivist model of professional knowledge. Special education is implicated in this development because, like all social professions, it is premised on the assumption that its practices and discourses are grounded in objective scientific knowledge. But the subjectivist view is that science is a form of cultural engagement, a social process that yields different kinds of possible knowledges, depending on the observers' paradigmatic frame of reference. This means that the knowledge that grounds special education's practices and discourses is not objective knowledge about reality; it is subjective knowledge based on a particular, historically situated frame of reference.

Given their grounding in the multiple paradigm sciences, social professions such as special education can be thought of as "multiple paradigm professions." As such, antifoundationalism means that these professions have no independent, foundational criteria for determining which of the paradigms of any given social discipline is the correct one for grounding their professional knowledge, practices, and discourses. Moreover, because antifoundationalism blurs the distinctions among the social disciplines themselves, there is no meaningful way to establish the cognitive authority of any particular social science discipline over another. The rise of subjectivism means that special educators must face the fact that there is nothing inherently true or correct about their knowledge, practices, and discourses. The emergence of antifoundationalism means that they must confront the more disturbing realization that there is no cognitively certain way to choose an alternative theoretical grounding from among the various modern (or postmodern) paradigmatic perspectives or disciplinary orientations.

What makes the situation worse for the field of special education is the nature of professional induction. As we saw in Chapter 1, professional induction entails two processes: socialization, an admittedly nonrational-cultural process for inculcating subjective values and norms; and education, a presumedly rational-technical process for conveying objective knowledge and skills.

However, the subjectivist view challenges this characterization on the grounds that neither the knowledge conveyed through professional education nor the process itself is objective. Like professional socialization, professional education is a nonrational-cultural process, a mechanism for inculcating professionals with a deep commitment to a particular way of seeing.

As a means of inducting students into an established knowledge tradition, the induction process is necessarily dogmatic and authoritarian. It requires the inductee to submit to the institutional legitimacy and authority of the profession, to accept the profession's established knowledge tradition on faith as the only correct way of unrandomizing the world and acting upon it. In itself, however, this is not a criticism of the induction process, for as Kuhn (1970, 1977) and Barnes (1982) noted relative to scientific induction, such a transformation of vision is essential if the inductee is to become an inhabitant of the world of a professional culture. In principle, preparation for any collective enterprise that relies on conventional knowledge and communal judgment requires a dogmatic, authoritarian education because, by encouraging commitment to a particular way of unrandomizing complexity, it narrows and focuses activity, making it more productive (Barnes, 1982).

Although we would expect the same benefits that Kuhn and Barnes noted for the natural sciences to apply to the social sciences and social professions, what begins as an advantage for all three groups and remains so for the natural sciences has been a disadvantage for the social sciences and social professions. The degree to which a dogmatic focus remains an advantage depends on the paradigmatic status of the communal enterprise and the conditions under which its work is performed. Paradigmatic status is a key factor because it influences to the degree to which members of a communal enterprise are prepared to recognize anomalies. As Barnes (1985) noted in regard to the natural or single paradigm sciences:

> a group of scientists engaged in normal science is a very sensitive detector of anomaly. Precisely because the group is so committed to its paradigm and so convinced of its correctness, any . . . residue of recalcitrant anomalies . . . may eventually prompt the suspicion that something is amiss with the currently accepted paradigm, and set the stage for its demise. (pp. 90–91)

Given their multiple paradigm status, however, the inherent dogmatism associated with the induction process has been a disadvantage for the social sciences. As we have seen, normal science has been more difficult in the social sciences because of political infighting over the correct paradigm (Ritzer, 1980). More important, however, the multiple paradigm status of the social sciences has slowed their advance relative to the natural sciences because lack of commitment to a particular paradigm renders anomalies more difficult to detect, and thus revolutionary science more difficult to achieve (Kuhn, 1977). Indeed, this is what makes postmodernism so significant. If we think of the four-paradigm matrix of modern social knowledge as a single paradigm composed of different types of foundational knowledge, the emergence of antifoundationalism in the social sciences is equivalent in magnitude, if not in form, to an episode of Kuhnian revolutionary science. As such, postmodernism can be seen as the beginning of normal science in what will become, after the scientific revolution is completed, the postrevolutionary multiple paradigm sciences.

The dogmatic nature of the induction process has been particularly disadvantageous for social professions such as education and special education. First of all, because they are grounded in the multiple paradigm sciences, they suffer the same disadvantages as the social sciences relative to the detection of anomalies. Moreover, the bureaucratic organizations in which educators practice their profession tend to distort anomalies, which further reduces their effect as a source of uncertainty and thus as a mechanism of change (Skrtic, 1991a; Chapter 9). Without the uncertainty caused by anomalies there is nothing to prompt suspicion in the professional culture that something is amiss with the currently accepted paradigm. Lack of suspicion in a professional community reinforces conventional thinking, which ultimately inhibits growth of knowledge and progress.

The professions' special relationship with society yields professional autonomy, which leaves the definition of professional knowledge, practices, and discourses to the professions themselves. As we know from the philosophical critique of the professions, however, there is no cognitively certain way to establish the legitimacy of a professional knowledge tradition because there is no way to establish the cognitive authority of the theoretical knowledge in which it is or could be grounded. Moreover, professional induction is designed to produce professionals with a deep commitment to a particular knowledge tradition. The problem is that, whereas the focused vision of natural scientists uncovers anomalies that force them to question and periodically replace their knowledge tradition, a professional culture such as special education is far less sensitive to anomalies because of the multiple paradigm status of its grounding discipline and the organizational conditions under which it works. The result is that the effectiveness of professional induction in special education produces professionals who rarely question the adequacy of their knowledge tradition. They tend to remain committed to their practices and discourses because, lacking a residue of recalcitrant anomalies, they assume that they are valid and objective, and thus that they serve the best interests of their students and of society.

Political Critique of Special Education Power

The political critique of the social professions is based on the moral and political implications of antifoundationalism. Given a conceptualization of knowledge in which no single interpretation has cognitive authority over another, the act of choosing a grounding for special education practices and discourses is not a neutral, rational-technical undertaking. Ultimately, it is a political and moral act with profound implications for ethical practice and a just society.

An important result of the emergence of antifoundationalism in the social sciences has been a series of revisions in the metaphor for social life – first from an organism to a game, then from a game to a drama, and finally from a drama to a text (Geertz, 1983). The text metaphor implies a mode of social analysis that views human and institutional practices as texts or discursive formations that can be read or interpreted in many ways, none of which is correct in a foundational sense, but each of which carries with it a particular set of moral and political implications. Social analysis under the text metaphor is the study of that which conditions, limits, and institutionalizes social knowledge, practices, and discourses. Ultimately, it asks how power comes to be concentrated in the hands of those in society who have the authority to interpret reality for others (Dreyfus & Rabinow, 1983).

No aspect of social life has received more critical attention under the text analogy than the social professions, for it is this group in modern societies that has the authority to interpret normality, and thus the power to define and classify others as abnormal and to treat their bodies and minds. The principal figure behind this line of criticism is Michel Foucault, the French moral and political philosopher whose work emphasizes the political implications of the knowledge, practices, and discourses of the "human sciences," an inclusive term for the social sciences and social professions (see Foucault, 1980a). Foucault's work focuses on the various modes by which modern societies turn human beings into subjects for investigation, surveillance, and treatment, practices that regularly involve various forms of medicalization, objectification, confinement, and exclusion. His critiques of the power/knowledge relations of the social sciences (1966/1973) and various social professions (1961/1973, 1963/1975, 1975/1979) are concerned with the nature and effects of the power of the human sciences to interpret normality.

Although Foucault (1980a, 1983) was concerned with power, he was not interested in the traditional notion of power, that is, in the centralized and juridical power of the State. Because, for him, knowledge *is* power in the modern world, Foucault was concerned with "the way modern societies control and discipline their populations by sanctioning the knowledge-claims and practices of the human sciences" (Philp, 1985, p. 67). In this regard, he argued that the classical notion of political rule based on sovereignty and rights has been subverted by the human sciences. Foucault referred to this nonsovereign form of power as "disciplinary power" (1980b, p. 105), a type of power that is exercised through the knowledge, practices, and discourses of the human sciences, which together establish and enforce the norms for human behavior in modern societies. "In the end," he argued, "we are judged, condemned, classified, determined in our undertakings, destined to a certain mode of living or dying, as a function of the [knowledge traditions of the human sciences] which are the bearers of the specific effects of power" (1980b, p. 94).

Although Foucault understood disciplinary power as a form of "subjugation," he did not use it in the sense of an intentional desire of certain people to dominate others. Instead, he used disciplinary power in the unconscious or unintentional sense in which professionals, operating under the taken-for-granted conventions and customs of their knowledge tradition, have the effect of turning others into subjects for investigation, surveillance, treatment, confinement, and exclusion. Although Foucault was concerned with the ways in which "subjects are gradually, progressively, really and materially constituted" (Foucault, 1980b, p. 97) by the human sciences, he did not see disciplinary power merely as something that professionals possess and use on their clients. Rather, disciplinary power circulates in a net-like fashion, subjugating professionals as well as their clients (Foucault, 1980b; below).

The significance of disciplinary power for the field of special education is apparent in Philp's (1985) summary of the implications of Foucault's work.

> In workplaces, schoolrooms, hospitals and welfare offices; in the family and the community; and in prisons, mental institutions, courtrooms and tribunals, the human sciences have established their standards of "normality." The normal child, the healthy body, the stable mind . . . such concepts haunt our ideas about ourselves, and are reproduced and legitimated through the practices of teachers, social workers, doctors, judges, policemen and administrators. The human sciences attempt to define normality; and by establishing this normality as a rule of life for us all, they simultaneously manufacture—for investigation, surveillance and treatment—the vast area of our deviation from this standard. (p. 67)

The notion of disciplinary power raises serious moral and political questions about the practices and discourses of the field of special education, given that it is the principal human science that modern industrialized societies use to define normality in schools and, after establishing this standard, to constitute as subjects those students who deviate from it (see Skrtic, 1990b, 1991a, 1991b, 1995a). From a political perspective, these questions concern the nature and effects of the various models, practices, and tools of investigation, surveillance, medicalization, objectification, treatment, confinement, and exclusion that special education has developed and refined over the course of the twentieth century. What makes these questions even more troubling, of course, is the philosophical implications of antifoundationalism. Not only must the field of special education respond to these unsettling political questions, it must do so knowing that there is no way to justify its professional knowledge, practices, and discourses by an appeal to scientific authority. This, then, is the epistemological and moral crisis that special education faces at the end of the modern era.

THE OPPORTUNITY IN SPECIAL EDUCATION

Because the world is ambiguous, a field of endeavor—whether a natural science, a social science, or a social profession—must have a way of unrandomizing complexity to be productive. Like a scientific culture, a professional culture must have a paradigm or knowledge tradition, a socially constructed way of interpreting the world and acting upon it. Although the field of special education can never escape the need for a paradigm, its special relationship with society demands that special educators be reflective about their paradigm and its implications for individuals and the common good. Without a paradigm crisis, however, professional autonomy means that there is little to compel special educators to question their knowledge tradition. As in the natural and social sciences, a crisis in knowledge is a precondition for growth of knowledge and progress in the field of special education.

As we have seen, progress in the natural sciences requires the deconstruction and reconstruction of paradigms, a process that begins with the recognition of anomalies that, because the scientific community is so committed to the correctness of its paradigm, are exposed as a matter of course during normal science. However, because its multiple paradigm status and bureaucratic working conditions conceal and distort anomalies, the field of special education needs a way to bring its anomalies to the surface, to prompt the suspicion that something is amiss with the accepted knowledge tradition, thus setting the stage for its deconstruction. To be productive the profession of special education must have a paradigm; to be morally and politically viable in a democracy, it also must have a way to continuously deconstruct and reconstruct its knowledge, practices, and discourses.

Critical Pragmatism

Whether a crisis in special education leads to positive growth and renewal depends on the manner in which special educators reconstruct their professional knowledge, practices, and discourses. Reconstruction always involves pragmatic choices among alternative theories and practices, a process that can take one of two general forms: naive pragmatism or critical pragmatism. Naive pragmatism values functional efficiency, pure utility, or expediency. Although it questions professional models, practices, and tools, it unreflectively accepts the assumptions, theories, and metatheories in which they are grounded. As such, naive pragmatism "is socially reproductive, instrumentally and functionally reproducing accepted meanings and conventional organizations, institutions, and ways of doing things for good or ill" (Cherryholmes, 1988, p. 151). Conversely, critical pragmatism approaches decision making in a way that recognizes and treats as problematic the assumptions, theories, and metatheories behind professional models, practices, and tools; it accepts the fact that our assumptions, theories, and metatheories themselves require evaluation and reappraisal (see Cherryholmes, 1988; Skrtic, 1986, 1991a).

Critical pragmatism is premised on philosophical pragmatism, the progressive liberal form of postmodernism associated primarily with John Dewey historically, and today with philosophers such as Richard Rorty (1979, 1982, 1989, 1991), Richard Bernstein (1971, 1983, 1991), Cornel West (1989), Donald Davidson (1984), Hillary Putnam (1981, 1988), and W. V. O. Quine (1981). Pragmatism is a method for deconstructing and reconstructing social knowledge, practices, discourses, and institutions under conditions of uncertainty, conditions in which it is recognized that there are no independent, cognitive criteria for choosing among interpretations of the social world. Whereas the aim of modern social inquiry is to justify social practices and institutions by showing that they are based on a true representation of the social world, the goal of philosophical pragmatism is to reform social practices and institutions by reconciling them with moral ideals (Bernstein, 1971, 1991; Rorty, 1982, 1989, 1991). Pragmatism avoids the foundational question of representation by focusing on the consequences of knowledge, on the question of whether, if acted upon, a particular form of knowledge contributes to the practical realization of desirable social values. As William James (1907/1975) noted, pragmatism is

> a method of settling metaphysical disputes that otherwise might be interminable. Is the world one or many? – fated or free? – material or spiritual? – here are notions either of which may or may not hold good of the world; and disputes over such notions are unending. The pragmatic method in such cases is to try to interpret each notion by tracing its respective practical consequences. What difference would it practically make to anyone if this notion rather than that notion were true? . . . Whenever a dispute is serious, we ought to be able to show some practical difference that must follow from one side or the other's being right. (p. 28)

Like philosophical pragmatism, the goal of critical pragmatism is not certainty; it does not seek objective knowledge or monological truth. Rather, its goal is education, or self-formation; it is a pedagogical process of remaking ourselves by redescribing our practices, discourses, and institutions in alternative theoretical and metatheoretical languages (Gadamer, 1975). Pragmatism is premised on a continual search for "new and more interesting [ways] of expressing ourselves, and thus of coping with the world. From [this] educational . . . point of view, the way things are said is more important than the possession of truths" (Rorty, 1979, p. 359). Rorty (1979) referred to the project of finding new and better ways of describing ourselves as "edifying philosophy" (p. 378). Applied to the profession of special education, it is a mode of inquiry that constantly forces special educators to face the fact that what they think, do, say, write, and read as professionals is shaped by convention, thus helping them avoid the delusion that they can know themselves, their practices, their clients, "or anything else, except under optional descriptions" (1979, p. 379). More recently, Rorty (1989) noted that edifying philosophy is

> the same as the "method" of utopian politics or revolutionary science (as opposed to parlimentary politics or normal science). The method is to redescribe lots and lots of things in new ways, until you . . . tempt the rising generation to . . . look for . . . new scientific equipment or new social institutions. This sort of philosophy . . . works holistically and pragmatically. It says things like "try thinking of it this way"—or more specifically, "try to ignore the apparently futile traditional questions by substituting the following new and possibly interesting questions." (p. 9)

Place of Values

Whereas the critique of positivism and objectivism questions whether social inquiry can be value-free, antifoundationalism and pragmatism question whether it should be. Describing special education in new ways is concerned fundamentally with making choices among the possible knowledges or optional descriptions in which the field's practices and discourses could and should be grounded. And because there are no scientific rules for making these decisions objectively, values provide the criteria for judging the merit of our choices. As Dewey (1925/1981) noted with regard to such decisions:

> Selective emphasis, choice, is inevitable whenever reflection occurs. This is not an evil. Deception comes only when the presence and operation of choice is concealed, disguised, denied. (p. 34)

The field of special education must be concerned with the means *and* ends of its practices, both of which are influenced by values because, implicitly or explicitly, values shape special educators' perspective on society, social arrangements, and desirable educational and social outcomes, as well as their choice of theories to ground and justify their practices and discourses.

In addition to being explicit about the values that guide their choices, special educators must decide on which values they will promote. In this regard, pragmatists are democrats; they promote the democratic values of liberty, equality, justice, and, above all, community (Dewey, 1917/1981, 1931/1989). Indeed, Dewey once was described as "the first philosopher who tried to read democracy into the ultimate nature of things and social reform into the meaning of knowledge" (Feuer, 1959, p. 568). Dewey read democracy (and reform) into social existence because he valued democracy as more than a form of government. For him, democracy is primarily a method of social inquiry, "a mode of associated living, of conjoint communicated experience" (Dewey, 1916/1980, p. 93). Democracy is central to the pragmatist outlook because reconstruction through dialogical discourse relies on democratic participation. Referring to what he believed was the necessary reconstruction of social knowledge, practices, and institutions in the twentieth century, Dewey explained that, in its final actuality, reconstruction

> is accomplished in face-to-face relationships by means of direct give and take. Logic in its fulfillment recurs to the primitive sense of the word: dialogue. Ideas which are not communicated, shared, and reborn in expression are but soliloquy, and soliloquy is but broken and imperfect thought. (1927/1988, p. 371)

This is why education is so central in Dewey's thought: If democracy is about equal participation by all in the dialogical discourse of humankind, as he believed, education is the means by which we are prepared to enter the conversation (Dewey, 1899/1976, 1916/1980, 1927/1988, 1929–30/1988).

As an area of educational policy, special education must be concerned with more than technical issues. From the normative perspective of pragmatism, all social policy must be concerned primarily with moral transactions and social relations (see Gil, 1973; Titmuss, 1968). In reconstructing their practices and discourses under the pragmatist orientation, special educators must be explicit about what they believe is morally and politically right. Moreover, like all those who approach social policy from the pragmatist perspective, they must "probe and push the value assumptions" (Moroney, 1981, p. 84) that shape special education policy toward those that unite us (see Rein, 1970, 1976; Titmuss, 1968). As Boulding (1967) argued in this regard, above all, social policy should be concerned with building an "integrative system," one that "includes those aspects of social life that are . . . justified by some kind of appeal to . . . identity or community . . . to build the identity of a person around some community with which he is associated"

(p. 7). Identity must be central to social policy because its opposite, alienation, threatens community itself (Moroney, 1981, 1991). Moreover, because humans must learn to be democratic, social policy, and particularly education policy, must promote integrative systems because these are the types of institutional arrangements in which democratic identities, values, and communities are cultivated (Dewey, 1916/1980, 1929–30/1988; Guttman, 1987; Chapter 6).

METHODS OF DECONSTRUCTION AND RECONSTRUCTION

Pragmatism provides an epistemological framework and moral grounding for special education to address the philosophical and political implications of antifoundationalism. Moreover, the emergence of antifoundationalism itself has resulted in the production or rediscovery of a variety of methods for deconstructing and reconstructing social practices and discourses. Although there are other methods that can be used for this purpose (see Cherryholmes, 1988; Maxcy, 1991; Stanley, 1992), in the following sections I describe four that I have recommended elsewhere (see Skrtic, 1991a, 1995b) and that I am using in this book.[7] They include two modern methods of critical social analysis, *immanent critique* (see Antonio, 1981; Benhabib, 1986; Taylor, 1977) and *ideal types* (Mommsen, 1974; Weber, 1904/1949), and two postmodern methods, *deconstruction* (Derrida, 1972/1982a, 1972/1982b) and *genealogy* (Best & Kellner, 1991; Foucault, 1980b, 1983).

Immanent Critique and Ideal Types

Immanent critique is more than a method of social analysis; historically, it has been understood as the driving force behind social progress itself. As Kiel explains in Chapter 6, Hegel (1807/1977) described the history of Western civilization as the progressive development of human consciousness and self-consciousness, a process driven by the affinity of humans to reconcile their claims about themselves (ideals) with their actual social conditions (reality) (see also Benhabib, 1986; Kojeve, 1969; Taylor, 1977). As a method of social analysis, immanent critique is a means of exposing the contradictions between our claims and our conditions, between our values and practices. Moreover, immanent critique is a form of emancipatory social analysis; it seeks to free us from our present conditions, to transform the real into the ideal, by describing "what a social totality holds itself to be, and then confronting it with what it is in fact becoming" (Schroyer, 1973, pp. 30–31).

This book is an immanent critique of special education and, by implication, public education itself (see Chapter 10). I used the method of immanent critique in this chapter and Chapter 1 to expose the contradictions between the claims and conditions of the social professions, and I use it again in Chapter 3 to expose the contradictions between the ideals and actual practices of the field of special education. The remaining chapters also can be read as immanent critiques because, in one way or another, each of them confronts the reader with contradictions between the ideal and the real in special education. As alternative metatheoretical interpretations of special education and student disability, Chapters 4 through 6 force special educators to think about the field today and to imagine what it could and should be in the future. As theoretical critiques of special education and the notion of student disability, Chapters 7 through 10 confront special educators with optional descriptions of what special education has become in the twentieth century.

Immanent critique is a powerful form of criticism, but on its own it does not provide a way of identifying either the ideals or conditions associated with particular social phenomena. This requires Max Weber's (1904/1949) method of ideal types, an analytic device for characterizing social phenomena in terms of the cultural ideals that give them meaning. Weber believed that, properly construed, the social sciences are cultural sciences, disciplines that "analyze the phenomena of life in terms of their cultural significance" (Dall-mayr & McCarthy, 1977, p. 20). And because "knowledge of cultural reali-ty . . . is always knowledge from *particular points of view*" (Weber, 1904/1949, p. 81), he argued that, explicitly or implicitly, all social analysis "*must* use concepts which are precisely and unambiguously definable only in the form of ideal types" (p. 92). For him, the problem with social science is not the inherent subjectivity of the knowledge it produces, but the objectivist assumption that this knowledge actually portrays "the 'true' content and the essence of historical reality" (p. 94).

An ideal type is an exaggerated mental construct "formed by the one-sided *accentuation* of one or more points of view. . . . In its conceptual purity, this mental construct . . . cannot be found empirically anywhere in reality. It is a *utopia*" (Weber, 1904/1949, p. 90). Moreover, one ideal type is never sufficient. The more complex the phenomena of interest and thus "the more many-sided their cultural *significance*," Weber noted, "repeated attempts to discover ever *new* aspects of significance by the construction of new ideal-typical concepts is all the more natural and unavoidable" (p. 97). Ideal types are not true in an objectivist sense; they are exaggerated mental constructions, the value of which stems from their utility as expository devices, conceptual tools for analyzing the meaning and practical consequences of social and institutional practices (Dallmayr & McCarthy, 1977; Mommsen, 1974; Ritzer, 1983).

I used ideal types in Chapter 1 to characterize the objectivist and subjectivist conceptualizations of the professions and professional knowledge, and in this chapter to characterize modern social scientific thought. I use them again in Chapter 3 to characterize the special education knowledge tradition in terms of its underlying value assumptions, and I use my own and others' ideal types in Chapters 9 and 10 to expose the contradictions between the values and practices of special education and public education from an organizational perspective. Although Chapters 4 through 6 were not written expressly as ideal types, they can and should be read as such. Each of these chapters is an optional description of special education and the notion of student disability, a utopia that can be used to trace the practical consequences of grounding the field's practices and discourses in an alternative metatheoretical paradigm. Chapters 7 through 10 can and should be read as ideal types as well, as exaggerated heuristics for seeing what is worth keeping in the special education knowledge tradition and what, in the interest of students and society, needs to be dropped. The point in reading all of these chapters, then, is not to *believe* them but to *use* them to assess the practical consequences of seeing special education and student disability in different ways.

Deconstruction and Genealogy

Deconstruction (Derrida, 1972/1982a, 1972/1982b) and genealogy (Foucault, 1980b) are both antifoundational methods associated with the radical Continental form of postmodernism.[8] Derrida and Foucault reject modern knowledge outright, and thus the metatheoretical grounding of philosophy and, either explicitly (Foucault) or implicitly (Derrida), the social sciences and social professions. They are both "end-of-philosophy" metaphilosophers; they argue that philosophy has come to an end and that philosophers must do something different, something beyond philosophy. The difference is what they choose to do now that philosophy is over. Whereas Derrida has elected to "write metaphilosophical deconstructions of the history of philosophy" (Hoy, 1985, p. 59), Foucault "writes concrete histories of practical attempts to gather social and psychological knowledge" (p. 59), that is, concrete genealogies of the human sciences.

In his reading of Western philosophy, Derrida (1972/1982b) does not focus on the central ideas or arguments of philosophical texts. Instead, he is concerned with the margins of these texts, with what is not said, as well as with the rhetorical devices that are used to gloss over their contradictions, inconsistencies, and incompleteness. Whereas traditional analyses purport to enable us to read these texts, Derrida's object is to demonstrate that they are unreadable. Rather than "assuming the text succeeds in establishing its message, Derrida's strategy is to get us to see that it does not work. In short, he does not reconstruct the text's meaning, but instead deconstructs it" (Hoy, 1985, p. 44). For Derrida, a philosophical work would succeed if it represented a reality external to itself; deconstructing such texts "shows the failure of a work's attempt at representation and, by implication, the possibility of comparable failure by any such work, or by any text whatsoever" (Hoy, 1985, p. 44), including those of the social sciences and social professions (see Ryan, 1982).

Deconstruction implies that there are no limits on how a text can be read, and thus that a text cannot refer beyond itself to an independent reality. Derrida emphasized the "undecidability" of texts because deconstruction is a critique of objectivism and foundationalism, a critique of "the assumption in philosophy that a set of formal logical axioms can be constructed which provides a complete account of the truth or meaning of the world, as well as the related assumption that a single foundation . . . could be posited . . . into which everything in the world ultimately resolves itself" (Ryan, 1982, p. 16). Given the undecidability of texts, Derrida (1972/1982b) argued that philosophers should abandon the traditional project of interpretation and instead take up "dissemination," the project of illustrating through alternative interpretations or optional descriptions the fundamental illegibility of texts.

I used deconstruction in this and the previous chapter to expose the inconsistencies, contradictions, and silences in the objectivist view of the professions and the modern view of social knowledge, and I use it again in Chapter 3 to expose those contained in the special education knowledge tradition. In addition, I use the same approach in Chapters 9 and 10 to deconstruct special education as an institutional practice of public education and to deconstruct the institution of public education itself. Although the remaining chapters were not written expressly as deconstructions, they can and should be read as such because, as optional metatheoretical (Chapters 4 through 6) and theoretical (Chapters 7 through 10) descriptions of special education and student disability, they expose the inconsistencies, contradictions, and silences in the conventional outlook. Finally, this book should be thought of as an act of dissemination, a project aimed at illustrating through optional descriptions the fundamental illegibility of special education, and thus the need for special educators to read something more – the democratic values of liberty, equality, justice, community, participation, inclusion, and identity – into their deliberations about the nature and effects of the field's practices and discourses.

Foucault's metaphilosophical works emphasize the moral and political implications of antifoundationalism for the human sciences. Given his concern with disciplinary power, his genealogies are attempts to "foreground the material context of subject construction, to draw out the political consequences of 'subjectification,' and to help form resistances to subjectifying practices" (Best & Kellner, 1991, p. 47). As such, they focus on the knowledge traditions of the human sciences, on the "norms, constraints, conditions, conventions, and so on" (Dreyfus & Rabinow, 1983, p. 108) that guide and justify their disciplinary practices and discourses. A Foucauldian genealogy is "an *ascending* analysis of power, starting, that is, from its infinitesimal mechanisms, which each have their own history, their own trajectory, their own techniques and tactics" (Foucault, 1980b, p. 99).

In his genealogies, Foucault (1980b) searches for two kinds of knowledge. The first is knowledge that has been "buried and disguised in a functionalist coherence or formal systemisation" (p. 81). These are possible knowledges or optional descriptions such as those of the interpretivist, radical humanist, and radical structuralist paradigms, forms of knowledge that have been distorted and hidden from the human sciences because of the dominance of functionalism during the modern era. The second type of knowledge is what Foucault called "disqualified knowledge (such as that of the psychiatric patient, of the ill person, of the nurse, of the doctor . . . of the delinquent, etc.)" (1980b, p. 82). Here, Foucault is referring to the experiential knowledge of the client *and* the professional practitioner, "a whole set of knowledges that have been disqualified as inadequate . . . knowledges located low down on the hierarchy, beneath [what is presumed to be] the required level of cognition or scientificity" (p. 82). For Foucault, the experiential knowledges of clients and practitioners are essential because it is through "these local popular knowledges, these disqualified knowledges, that criticism performs its work" (p. 82).

I use Foucault's genealogical approach primarily in Chapter 3 to trace the development of the knowledge tradition that has shaped and justified special education practices and discourses in this century (see also Skrtic, 1986, 1988, 1991a, 1995b). My aim is to show that, far from objective knowledge of reality, the special education knowledge tradition is simply an historical artifact of the functionalist discourse on school failure that has dominated public education in the twentieth century. Chapters 4 through 10 should be read as buried knowledges, forms of knowledge that have been distorted and hidden from special educators beneath the apparent coherence of functionalism. Finally, Chapters 9 and 10 propose a vehicle to legitimize the discredited popular knowledges of special education practitioners and clients, a way to give them a voice in the necessary deconstruction and reconstruction of special education.

I began the process of deconstructing the special education (and education) knowledge tradition in Chapter 1 by deconstructing the traditional objectivist view of the professions, thus raising doubts in the reader's mind about the legitmacy of the process of professionalization. In this chapter I continued the process by exposing some of the inconsistencies, contradictions, and silences in modern social knowledge, thus calling into question the claim to legitimacy of the social sciences and, in turn, social professions such as special education and education. I also highlighted the epistemological and moral dilemma that antifoundationalism poses for special educators, and recommended pragmatism as a philosophical and moral grounding for addressing the crisis in the field. Finally, I described four methods for deconstructing and reconstructing the special education knowledge tradition and alerted the reader to the ways in which these methods are being used in this book.

In Chapter 3 I deconstruct special education as a professional practice by way of a genealogy that exposes the inconsistencies, contradictions, and silences in the knowledge tradition that has guided and justified the field's practices and discourses in the twentieth century. The remaining chapters provide optional metatheoretical (Chapters 4 through 6) and theoretical (Chapters 7 through 10) descriptions of special education and the notion of student disability. These chapters are meant to serve a dual purpose. On one hand, they continue the deconstruction of the special education knowledge tradition because, by redescribing special education and student disability from unconventional perspectives, they raise further questions about the conventional outlook. On the other hand, by providing the reader with optional theories and metatheories of special education and student disability, they also contribute substantively to the process of reconstructing the field's knowledge tradition for the future. Finally, Chapters 9 and 10 deconstruct schools as organizations and propose an alternative configuration that uses pragmatism as the central organizing principle, thus providing the institutional conditions in which the necessary deconstruction and reconstruction can take place.

This book was written to contribute to the deconstruction and reconstruction of special education and the twentieth-century notion of student disability. Its aim is to tempt the rising generation of special educators to look for new professional knowledge, practices, and discourses, ones that are more consistent with the ideal of serving the best educational and political interests of its clients and the democratic needs of society.

NOTES

1. Whereas to this point in the book I have used "objectivism" and "subjectivism" to refer to the two opposing modern philosophies of *natural* science, from here on in this chapter and, except where noted, in the remainder of the book the terms

"objectivism" and "subjectivism" are used to refer to the two opposing modern philosophies of *social* science (see Chapter 1, note 1). I should note here too that, historically, the modern social disciplines have characterized their project as one of using reason to improve society. Ranging from the philosophical project of Descartes, through the Enlightenment, to the social theory of Comte, Marx, Weber, and others, the theoretical discourses of the modern social disciplines "championed reason as the source of progress in knowledge and society, as well as the privileged locus of truth and the foundation of systematic knowledge. Reason was deemed competent to discover adequate theoretical and practical norms upon which systems of thought and action could be built and society could be restructured . . . to produce a just and egalitarian social order that would embody reason and social progress" (Best & Kellner, 1991, p. 2). The question with regard to the objectivism–subjectivism dichotomy, then, is whether the models and methods of natural science are adequate for carrying out the Enlightenment project of improving society through social or human inquiry. Although certain forms of modern subjectivism question "scientific" reasoning as a way of knowing (see Chapters 4 and 8) and the Enlightenment project itself (see Chapter 6), all forms of modern social knowledge view reason as the way to truth and social progress, as a foundation for improving the human condition (see below).

2. Ritzer does not equate the microscopic–macroscopic and order–conflict designations. Indeed, he made a point of using Gans's (1972) functionalist analysis of poverty to illustrate that functionalism *can be* used to expose fundamental social conflicts and contradictions. In this regard, one could also point to Farber (1968) as another example of a conflict-oriented functionalist analysis of, in this case, mental retardation. Nevertheless, the conservative bias in the way functionalism *has been* used historically is generally recognized (see Burrell & Morgan, 1979), even by Ritzer, as noted below. Also see Chapter 4 on the question of equating the microscopic–macroscopic and order–conflict designations, and Chapters 9 and 10 where I draw organization theory from all four paradigms to conduct a critical analysis of school organization and change.

3. A comprehensive treatment of the paradigm shifts in the social sciences is beyond the scope of this chapter (see, e.g., R. J. Bernstein, 1971, 1976, 1983; Burrell & Morgan, 1979; Giddens, 1974; Rorty, 1979, 1991). Thus, the discussion in the text is necessarily an oversimplification, intended merely to note the broad parameters of the shifts in paradigmatic commitment in order to highlight their implications for the social sciences and social professions.

4. A comprehensive treatment of the implications of these paradigm shifts is beyond the scope of this chapter (see R. J. Bernstein, 1971, 1976, 1983; Giddens, 1977; Outhwaite, 1987; Rorty, 1979, 1991). As in the case of the discussion of paradigm shifts (note 3), the discussion in the text is necessarily an oversimplification, intended merely to highlight some of the key implications for the social sciences and social professions.

5. Like "modernity" (Chapter 1, note 1), "postmodern" or "postmodernity" is an epochal term that refers to the period that allegedly follows the modern era, "allegedly" because there has been a great deal of controversy over whether modernity

has ended or simply taken a new form (see Giddens, 1990). Nevertheless, there is no question that, since at least the late 1960s, a series of socioeconomic and cultural transformations (e.g., an explosion of media and information technologies, a restructuring of capitalism, new cultural forms, political shifts and upheavals, and changes in the way we experience space and time) have occurred that require new forms of theorizing the social (see Best & Kellner, 1991; Giddens, 1990; Harvey, 1990). Broadly speaking, postmodernism refers to a variety of intellectual and political movements and cultural artifacts that can be distinguished from those of modernism. As used here, however, it refers more narrowly to a mode of social theorizing that, as opposed to the modern view that theory mirrors reality, is based on the antifoundational or "'perspectivist' and 'relativist' positions that theories at best provide partial perspectives on their objects, and that all cognitive representations of the world are historically and linguistically mediated" (Best & Kellner, 1991, p. 4). In addition, postmodern theorizing "rejects modern assumptions of social cohesion and notions of causality in favour of multiplicity, plurality, fragmentation, and indeterminacy . . . [and] abandons the rational and unified subject postulated by much modern theory in favour of a socially and linguistically decentered and fragmented subject" (Best & Kellner, 1991, pp. 4–5). Its alleged abandonment of the "rational and unified subject" is a key point of criticism of postmodernism because, for many, it signifies a rejection of the modern faith in reason and collective action as a way to social progress (see notes 1 and 7; Chapter 1, note 2). As we will see in the text, however, only certain forms of postmodern theorizing (see note 6) reject the possibility of social progress through rational social struggle.

     6. Saying that there are two forms of postmodernism is a vast oversimplification because, as Best and Kellner (1991) noted, "there is no unified postmodern theory, or even a coherent set of positions" (p. 2). Nevertheless, Antonio's (1989) "radical versus progressive" classification scheme is useful for highlighting the essential difference between the two dominant trends within postmodernism, which is a fundamentally different evaluation of modernism itself (see below). In this regard, see Burbules and Rice (1991, p. 397), who use "antimodernism" to characterize what Antonio refers to as radical Continental postmodernism.

     As an intellectual movement, philosophical pragmatism emerged in the United States and Europe between 1870 and 1900 as a *via media* or way between both the extreme epistemological positions of objectivism and subjectivism and the extreme sociological positions of regulation (order) and radical change (conflict) (Kloppenberg, 1986). Although methodologically I draw from both the American and European pragmatist traditions – Dewey in the United States and Max Weber in Europe (see below and Chapter 10) – substantively I emphasize the American tradition because, like postmodernism today, pragmatism has had different philosophical and political manifestations on either side of the Atlantic, giving rise to the political philosophy of progressivism in the United States and that of social democracy in Europe (see Kloppenberg, 1986; Chapter 10). In addition, I emphasize the American tradition because ultimately I want to recover Dewey's notion of progressive education, which, although grounded epistemologically and morally in philosophical pragmatism *per se*, is tied historically to the American cultural experience (see Chapter 10).

Although I will associate philosophical pragmatism primarily with Dewey, it should be noted that it originated with C. S. Peirce (1878/1934) and subsequently was expanded upon and championed by Dewey and William James (1907/1975). Dewey's version of pragmatism, which he called "instrumentalism," was first elaborated in *Studies in Logical Theory* (1903/1976). Generally speaking, "pragmatism is primarily a means of settling otherwise interminable metaphysical disputes by asking, 'What difference would it practically make to anyone if this notion rather than that notion were true?'" (James, 1907/1975, p. 28). As a method of social inquiry, pragmatism raises this relatively straightforward idea to the level of metatheoretical presuppositions and paradigms of modern social thought. My approach, which, following Cherryholmes (1988), I call "critical pragmatism" (see Skrtic, 1991b; below), combines the liberal progressive form of postmodernism and the insights of Derrida and Foucault, whose work, although ordinarily viewed as archetypical of radical Continental postmodernism, provides valuable critical resources for the progressive project (see Best & Kellner, 1991; Cherryholmes, 1988; Skrtic, 1991a; Stanley, 1992; notes 7 and 8; below). I expand the discussion of philosophical pragmatism in this chapter, relative to its implications for social inquiry and professional discourse, and again in Chapter 10, relative to Dewey's notion of progressive education and the idea of cultural transformation and social reconstruction through education.

7. Another approach that should be noted in this regard is "critical pedagogy," a form of radical social and educational theorizing within the field of curriculum theory. Although in the 1970s critical pedagogy had been grounded in what we have called the radical structuralist paradigm (e.g., Apple, 1979; Giroux, 1981), several of its leading figures shifted to the radical humanist paradigm in the early 1980s (e.g., Apple, 1982; Giroux, 1983) and, by the end of the decade, had begun to address the implications of postmodernism for their critical project (e.g., Giroux, 1988a; McLaren & Hammer, 1989). Concerned initially with the antifoundational or relativist epistemology of postmodernism and what they saw as its retreat from the emancipatory values of modernism, particularly the rejection of the "rational and unified subject" (see note 5), they now see it as a mode of theorizing with both "reactionary and progressive possibilities" (Giroux, 1988b, p. 6; McLaren & Hammer, 1989) (see above and note 6). Drawing on the progressive or "oppositional" form of postmodernism, Giroux (1988a) and others (e.g., Stanley & Whitson, 1990; Whitson, 1991) have called for reconstituting critical pedagogy by combining the best insights of both the modern and postmodern theoretical orientations. For an excellent treatment of the utility of postmodernism (and poststructuralism), neopragmatism, and social reconstructionism (see Chapter 10) for the emancipatory project of critical pedagogy, see Stanley (1992).

8. Given their central place in what we have called radical Continental postmodernism, the work of Derrida and Foucault initially was criticized as nihilistic and a threat to modern emancipatory values (e.g., Habermas, 1981, 1987). Indeed, even Foucault (1983) criticized Derrida for his apparent ambivalence toward the political implications of deconstruction. More recently, however, Derrida's method of deconstruction and Foucault's genealogical approach have been recognized as important

contributions to critical theorizing, as reappropriations and refinements of modernist values even though they are based on a rejection of modern knowledge (for reviews on this point, see Best & Kellner, 1991; Stanley, 1992).

REFERENCES

Althusser, L. (1969). *For Marx*. Hamondsworth, England: Penguin.

Antonio, R. J. (1981). Immanent critique as the core of critical theory: Its origins and developments in Hegel, Marx, and contemporary thought. *British Journal of Sociology, 32*(3), 330–345.

Antonio, R. J. (1989). The normative foundations of emancipatory theory: Evolutionary versus pragmatic perspectives. *American Journal of Sociology, 94*(4), 721–748.

Apple, M. W. (1979). *Ideology and curriculum*. London: Routledge & Kegan Paul.

Apple, M. W. (1982). *Education and power*. London: Routledge & Kegan Paul.

Apple, M. W. (1985). *Education and power*. London: Routledge & Kegan Paul.

Barnes, B. (1982). *T. S. Kuhn and social science*. New York: Columbia University Press.

Barnes, B. (1985). Thomas Kuhn. In Q. Skinner (Ed.), *The return of grand theory in the human sciences* (pp. 83–100). Cambridge: Cambridge University Press.

Barone, T. E. (1992). On the demise of subjectivity in educational inquiry. *Curriculum Inquiry, 22*(1), 25–38.

Baudrillard, J. (1983). *Simulations* (P. Foss, P. Patton, & P. Beitchman, Trans.). New York: Semiotext(e).

Benhabib, S. (1986). *Critique, norm, and utopia: A study of the foundations of critical theory*. New York: Columbia University Press.

Berger, P. L., & Luckmann, T. (1967). *The social construction of reality*. New York: Doubleday.

Bergner, J. T. (1981). *The origin of formalism in social science*. Chicago: University of Chicago Press.

Bernstein, B. (1971). *Class, codes and control: Vol. 1. Theoretical studies towards a sociology of language*. London: Routledge & Kegan Paul.

Bernstein, R. J. (1971). *Praxis and action: Contemporary philosophies of human activity*. Philadelphia: University of Pennsylvania Press.

Bernstein, R. J. (1976). *The restructuring of social and political theory*. Philadelphia: University of Pennsylvania Press.

Bernstein, R. J. (1983). *Beyond objectivism and relativism: Science, hermeneutics, and praxis*. Philadelphia: University of Pennsylvania Press.

Bernstein, R. J. (1991). *The new constellation*. Cambridge: Polity Press.

Best, S., & Kellner, D. (1991). *Postmodern theory: Critical interrogations*. New York: Guilford Press.

Boulding, K. (1967). The boundaries of social policy. *Social Work, 12*, 3–11.

Bourdieu, P. (1977). *Outline of a theory of practice* (R. Nice, Trans.). Cambridge: Cambridge University Press.

Burbules, N. C., & Rice, S. (1991). Dialogue across differences: Continuing the conversation. *Harvard Educational Review, 61*(4), 393–416.

Burrell, G., & Morgan, G. (1979). *Sociological paradigms and organizational analysis.* London: Heinemann.

Caputo, J. D. (1987). *Radical hermeneutics: Repetition, deconstruction, and the hermeneutic project.* Bloomington: Indiana University Press.

Cherryholmes, C. H. (1988). *Power and criticism: Poststructuralist investigations in education.* New York: Teachers College Press.

Chomsky, N. (1959). [Review of Skinner's "Verbal Behavior"]. *Language, 35,* 26–58.

Clark, R. (1971). *Einstein: The life and times.* New York: Avon Books.

Dallmayr, F. R., & McCarthy, T. A. (1977). *Understanding and social inquiry.* Notre Dame, IN: University of Notre Dame Press.

Davidson, D. (1984). Inquiries into truth and interpretation. Oxford: Oxford University Press.

Davidson, D. (1986). A coherence theory of truth. In E. LePore (Ed.), *Truth and interpretation: Perspectives on the philosophy of Donald Davidson* (pp. 307–319). Oxford: Blackwell.

Derrida, J. (1982a). *Dissemination* (B. Johnson, Trans.). London: Athlone Press. (Original work published 1972)

Derrida, J. (1982b). *Margins of philosophy* (A. Bass, Trans.). Chicago: University of Chicago Press. (Original work published 1972)

Dewey, J. (1976). The school and society. In J. A. Boydston (Ed.), *John Dewey: The middle works, 1899–1924* (Vol. 1, pp. 1–109). Carbondale: Southern Illinois University Press. (Original work published 1899)

Dewey, J. (1976). Studies in logical theory. In J. A. Boydston (Ed.), *John Dewey: The middle works, 1899–1924* (Vol. 2, pp. 239–375). Carbondale: Southern Illinois University Press. (Original work published 1903)

Dewey, J. (1980). Democracy and education. In J. A. Boydston (Ed.), *John Dewey: The middle works, 1899–1924* (Vol. 9, pp. 1–370). Carbondale: Southern Illinois University Press. (Original work published 1916)

Dewey, J. (1981). The need for a recovery of philosophy. In J. J. McDermott, *The philosophy of John Dewey* (pp. 58–97). Chicago: University of Chicago Press. (Original work published 1917)

Dewey, J. (1981). Experience and nature. In J. A. Boydston (Ed.), *John Dewey: The later works, 1925–1953* (Vol. 1, pp. 1–326). Carbondale: Southern Illinois University Press. (Original work published 1925)

Dewey, J. (1982). Reconstruction in philosophy. In J. A. Boydston (Ed.), *John Dewey: The middle works, 1899–1924* (Vol. 12, pp. 77–201). Carbondale: Southern Illinois University Press. (Original work published 1920)

Dewey, J. (1988). The public and its problems. In J. A. Boydston (Ed.), *John Dewey: The later works, 1925–1953* (Vol. 2, pp. 235–372). Carbondale: Southern Illinois University Press. (Original work published 1927)

Dewey, J. (1988). The quest for certainty. In J. A. Boydston (Ed.), *John Dewey: The later works, 1925–1953* (Vol. 4, pp. 1–250). Carbondale: Southern Illinois University Press. (Original work published 1929)

Dewey, J. (1988). Individualism, old and new. In J. A. Boydston (Ed.), *John Dewey: The later works, 1925–1953* (Vol. 5, pp. 41–123). Carbondale: Southern Illinois University Press. (Original work published 1929–30)

Dewey, J. (1989). The development of American pragmatism. In H. S. Thayer (Ed.), *Pragmatism: The classic writings* (pp. 23–40). Indianapolis: Hackett. (Original work published 1931)

Dreyfus, H. L., & Rabinow, P. (1983). *Michel Foucault: Beyond structuralism and hermeneutics.* Chicago: University of Chicago Press.

Farber, B. (1968). *Mental retardation: Its social context and social consequences.* Boston: Houghton Mifflin.

Ferguson, P. M. (1987). The social construction of mental retardation. *Social Policy, 18*(1), 51–56.

Feuer, L. (1959). John Dewey and the back to the people movement. *Journal of the History of Ideas, 20,* 545–568.

Foucault, M. (1973). *Madness and civilization: A history of insanity in the age of reason.* (R. Howard, Trans.). New York: Vintage/Random House. (Original work published 1961)

Foucault, M. (1973). *The order of things: An archaeology of the human sciences.* New York: Vintage/Random House. (Original work published 1966)

Foucault, M. (1975). *The birth of the clinic: An archeology of medical perception* (A. M. Sheridan Smith, Trans.). New York: Vintage/Random House. (Original work published 1963)

Foucault, M. (1979). *Discipline and punish: The birth of the prison* (A. M. Sheridan Smith, Trans.). New York: Vintage/Random House. (Original work published 1975)

Foucault, M. (1980a). *Power/knowledge: Selected interviews and other writings, 1972–1977* (C. Gordon, Ed. and C. Gordon, L. Marshall, J. Mepham, & K. Soper, Trans.). New York: Pantheon Books.

Foucault, M. (1980b). Two lectures. In M. Foucault, *Power/knowledge: Selected interviews and other writings, 1972–1977* (C. Gordon, Ed. and C. Gordon, L. Marshall, J. Mepham, & K. Soper, Trans.; pp. 78–108). New York: Pantheon Books.

Foucault, M. (1983). The subject and power. In H. L. Dreyfus & P. Rabinow (Eds.), *Michel Foucault: Beyond structuralism and hermeneutics* (pp. 208–226). Chicago: University of Chicago Press.

Gadamer, H. G. (1975). *Truth and method* (G. Barden & J. Cumming, Eds. and Trans.). New York: Seabury Press.

Gage, N. L. (1989). The paradigm wars and their aftermath: A "historical" sketch of research on teaching since 1989. *Educational Researcher, 18*(7), 4–7.

Gans, H. (1972). The positive functions of poverty. *American Journal of Sociology, 78,* 275–289.

Geertz, C. (1983). *Local knowledge: Further essays in interpretive anthropology.* New York: Basic Books.

Giddens, A. (1974). *New rules of sociological method.* London: Hutchinson.

Giddens, A. (1977). *Studies in social and political theory.* London: Hutchinson.

Giddens, A. (1981). *A contemporary critique of historical materialism*. London: Macmillan.

Giddens, A. (1990). *The consequences of modernity*. Cambridge: Polity Press.

Gil, D. (1973). *Unraveling social policy*. Cambridge: Schenkman.

Giroux, H. A. (1981). *Ideology, culture, and the process of schooling*. Philadelphia: Temple University Press.

Giroux, H. A. (1983). Theories of reproduction and resistance in the new sociology of education: A critical analysis. *Harvard Educational Review, 58*(3), 257, 293.

Giroux, H. A. (1988a). Border pedagogy in the age of postmodernism. *Journal of Education, 170*(3), 162–181.

Giroux, H. A. (1988b). Postmodernism and the discourse of educational criticism. *Journal of Education, 170*(3), 5–30.

Guba, E. G. (Ed.). (1990). *The paradigm dialog*. Newbury Park, CA: Sage.

Guttman, A. (1987). *Democratic education*. Princeton, NJ: Princeton University Press.

Habermas, J. (1970). *Toward a rational society* (J. J. Shapiro, Trans.). Boston: Beacon Press. (Original work published 1968)

Habermas, J. (1971). *Knowledge and human interests* (J. J. Shapiro, Trans.). Boston: Beacon Press. (Original work published 1968)

Habermas, J. (1981). Modernity versus postmodernity. *New German Critique, 22*, 3–14.

Habermas, J. (1987). *Lectures on the philosophical discourse of modernity*. Cambridge, MA: MIT Press.

Harvey, D. (1990). *The condition of postmodernity: An enquiry into the origins of cultural change*. Cambridge, MA: Blackwell.

Hegel, G. W. F. (1977). *Phenomenology of spirit*. Oxford: Clarendon Press. (Original work published 1807)

Held, D. (1980). *Introduction to critical theory*. Berkeley and Los Angeles: University of California Press.

Heshusius, L. (1982). At the heart of the advocacy dilemma: A mechanistic world view. *Exceptional Children, 49*(1), 6–13.

Hoy, D. (1985). Jacques Derrida. In Q. Skinner (Ed.), *The return of grand theory in the human sciences* (pp. 41–64). Cambridge: Cambridge University Press.

Iano, R. P. (1986). The study and development of teaching: With implications for the advancement of special education. *Remedial and Special Education, 7*(5), 50–61.

Iano, R. P. (1987). Rebuttal: Neither the absolute certainty of prescriptive law nor a surrender to mysticism. *Remedial and Special Education, 8*(1), 52–61.

James, W. (1975). Pragmatism. In F. Burkhardt, F. Bowers, & I. K. Skrupskelis (Eds.), *William James: Pragmatism and the meaning of truth* (pp. 1–166). Cambridge, MA: Harvard University Press. (Original work published 1907)

Jay, M. (1973). *The dialectical imagination*. Boston: Little, Brown.

Kloppenberg, J. T. (1986). *Uncertain victory: Social democracy and progressivism in European and American thought, 1870–1920*. New York: Oxford University Press.

Kojeve, A. (1969). *Introduction to the reading of Hegel*. New York: Basic Books.

Kuhn, T. S. (1962). *The structure of scientific revolutions* (1st ed.). Chicago: University of Chicago Press.

Kuhn, T. S. (1970). *The structure of scientific revolutions* (2nd ed.). Chicago: University of Chicago Press.

Kuhn, T. S. (1977). *The essential tension: Selected studies in scientific tradition and change.* Chicago: University of Chicago Press.

Lévi-Strauss, C. (1963). *Totemism.* Boston: Beacon Press.

Lincoln, Y. S., & Guba, E. G. (1985). *Naturalistic inquiry.* Beverly Hills, CA: Sage.

Lyotard, J.-F. (1984). *The postmodern condition: A report on knowledge.* Minneapolis: University of Minnesota Press. (Original work published 1979)

Marcuse, H. (1964). *One-dimensional man.* Boston: Beacon Press.

Masterman, M. (1970). The nature of a paradigm. In I. Lakatos & A. Musgrave (Eds.), *Criticism and the growth of knowledge* (pp. 59–89). Cambridge: Cambridge University Press.

Maxcy, S. J. (1991). *Educational leadership: A critical pragmatic perspective.* New York: Bergin & Garvey.

McLaren, P., & Hammer, R. (1989). Critical pedagogy and the postmodern challenge: Toward a critical postmodernist pedagogy of liberation. *Educational Foundations, 3*(3), 29–62.

Mead, G. H. (1934). *Mind, self, and society: From the standpoint of a social behaviorist* (C. W. Morris, Ed.). Chicago: University of Chicago Press.

Mommsen, W. J. (1974). *The age of bureaucracy: Perspectives on the political sociology of Max Weber.* New York: Harper & Row.

Morgan, G., & Smircich, L. (1980). The case for qualitative research. *Academy of Management Review, 5,* 491–500.

Moroney, R. M. (1981). Policy analysis within a value theoretical framework. In R. Haskins & J. J. Gallagher (Eds.), *Models for analysis of social policy: An introduction* (pp. 78–101). Norwood, NJ: Ablex.

Moroney, R. M. (1991). *Social policy and social work: Critical essays on the welfare state.* New York: Aldine de Gruyter.

Outhwaite, W. (1987). *New philosophies of social science: Realism, hermeneutics and critical theory.* London: Macmillan.

Peirce, C. S. (1931–35). *Collected papers of Charles Sanders Peirce* (C. Hartshorne & P. Weiss, Eds.). Cambridge, MA: Harvard University Press.

Peirce, C. S. (1934). How to make our ideas clear. In C. Hartshorne & P. Weiss (Eds.), *Collected papers of Charles Sanders Peirce* (Vol. 5, pp. 257–258). Cambridge, MA: Harvard University Press. (Original work published 1878)

Philp, M. (1985). Michel Foucault. In Q. Skinner (Ed.), *The return of grand theory in the human sciences* (pp. 65–81). Cambridge: Cambridge University Press.

Putman, H. (1981). *Reason, truth, and history.* Cambridge: Cambridge University Press.

Putman, H. (1988). *Reality and representation.* Cambridge, MA: MIT Press.

Quine, W. V. O. (1981). Pragmatists' place in empiricism. In R. J. Mulvaney & P. M. Zeltner (Eds.), *Pragmatism: Its sources and prospects* (pp. 21–40). Columbia: University of South Carolina Press.

Rein, M. (1970). *Social policy: Issues of choice and change.* New York: Random House.

Rein, M. (1976). *Social science and public policy.* New York: Penguin.

Ricoeur, P. (1981). *Paul Ricoeur: Hermeneutics and the human sciences* (J. B. Thompson, Ed. and Trans.). Cambridge: Cambridge University Press.

Ritzer, G. (1980). *Sociology: A multiple paradigm science*. Boston: Allyn & Bacon.

Ritzer, G. (1983). *Sociological theory*. New York: Knopf.

Ritzer, G. (Ed.). (1990). *Frontiers of social theory: The new syntheses*. New York: Columbia University Press.

Rorty, R. (1979). *Philosophy and the mirror of nature*. Princeton, NJ: Princeton University Press.

Rorty, R. (1982). *Consequences of pragmatism*. Minneapolis: University of Minnesota Press.

Rorty, R. (1989). *Contingency, irony, and solidarity*. New York: Cambridge University Press.

Rorty, R. (1991). *Objectivity, relativism, and truth: Philosophical papers* (Vol. 1). Cambridge: Cambridge University Press.

Ryan, M. (1982). *Marxism and deconstruction: A critical articulation*. Baltimore: Johns Hopkins University Press.

Saussure, F. (1966). *Course in general linguistics*. New York: McGraw-Hill.

Schroyer, T. (1973). *The critique of domination*. Boston: Beacon Press.

Skrtic, T. M. (1986). The crisis in special education knowledge: A perspective on perspective. *Focus on Exceptional Children, 18*(7), 1–16.

Skrtic, T. M. (1988). The crisis in special education knowledge. In E. L. Meyen & T. M. Skrtic (Eds.), *Exceptional children and youth: An introduction* (pp. 415–447). Denver: Love Publishing.

Skrtic, T. M. (1990a). Counter-hegemony: A radical's attempt to demystify special education ideology. [Review of *Radical analysis of special education: Focus on historical developments and learning disabilities*, by S. Sigmon]. *Contemporary Psychology, 35*(1), 54–55.

Skrtic, T. M. (1990b). Power/knowledge and the professions. In P. Leone (Ed.), *Understanding troubled and troubling youth* (pp. 7–12). Newbury Park, CA: Sage.

Skrtic, T. M. (1990c). Social accommodation: Toward a dialogical discourse in educational inquiry. In E. G. Guba (Ed.), *The paradigm dialog* (pp. 125–135). Newbury Park, CA: Sage.

Skrtic, T. M. (1991a). *Behind special education: A critical analysis of professional culture and school organization*. Denver: Love Publishing.

Skrtic, T. M. (1991b). The special education paradox: Equity as the way to excellence. *Harvard Educational Review, 61*(2), 148–206.

Skrtic, T. M. (1995a). The crisis in professional knowledge. In E. L. Meyen & T. M. Skrtic (Eds.), *Special education and student disability: Traditional, emerging, and alternative perspectives* (pp. 538–577). Denver: Love Publishing.

Skrtic, T. M. (1995b). The special education knowledge tradition: Crisis and opportunity. In E. L. Meyen & T. M. Skrtic (Eds.), *Special education and student disability: Traditional, emerging, and alternative perspectives* (pp. 609–672). Denver: Love Publishing.

Soltis, J. F. (1984). On the nature of educational research. *Educational Researcher, 13*(10), 5–10.

Stanley, W. B. (1992). *Curriculum for utopia: Social reconstructionism and critical pedagogy in the postmodern era*. Albany: State University of New York Press.

Stanley, W. B., & Whitson, J. A. (1990, October). Practical competence, human interest, and schooling. Paper presented at the annual meeting of the Conference on Curriculum Theory and Classroom Practice, Dayton, OH.

Taylor, C. (1977). *Hegel*. New York: Cambridge University Press.

Titmuss, R. (1968). *Commitment to welfare*. London: Allen & Unwin.

Weber, M. (1949). "Objectivity" in social science and social policy. In E. A. Shils & H. A. Finch (Eds. and Trans.), *The methodology of the social sciences* (pp. 49–112). New York: Free Press. (Original work published 1904)

West, C. (1989). *The American evasion of philosophy: A genealogy of pragmatism*. Madison: University of Wisconsin Press.

Whitson, J. A. (1991). *Constitution and curriculum: Semiotic analysis of cases and controversies in education, law, and social science*. London and Philadelphia: Falmer Press.

PART 2

Optional Metatheories of Special Education and Disability

CHAPTER 3

The Functionalist View of Special Education and Disability:
Deconstructing the Conventional Knowledge Tradition

Thomas M. Skrtic

A knowledge tradition is the hierarchy of presuppositions that guides and justifies the practices and discourses of communal enterprises such as the natural sciences (Kuhn, 1970), the social sciences (Barnes, 1982), and the social professions (Schön, 1983; Skrtic, 1986; Chapter 1). The hierarchy of presuppositions that constitutes the special education knowledge tradition includes the metatheories, theories, assumptions, models, practices, and tools that guide and justify what the field's applied scientists and professional practitioners think, do, say, read, and write as special educators. Each level of the hierarchy is defined and subsumed by the higher levels, and all levels ultimately are grounded in the metatheoretical presuppositions of the functionalist paradigm, the dominant mode of social theorizing in the modern era. In Part 1 my intent was to question the legitimacy of professional knowledge traditions. Here, I want to raise questions about the legitimacy of the special education knowledge tradition by deconstructing the hierarchy of functionalist presuppositions that has shaped the field's practices and discourses in this century.

By deconstructing the special education knowledge tradition, I hope to raise doubts about the legitimacy of the field's practices and discourses, doubts that will tempt the rising generation of special educators to develop new knowledge, practices, and discourses for the future. My ultimate goal is to clear the way for reconstructing special education in a manner that avoids its unintentional negative consequences, thereby reconciling the field's professional practices and discourses with the ethical ideal of serving the best educational and political interests of its clients and the democratic needs of society. The remaining chapters provide optional metatheoretical (Chapters 4 through 6) and theoretical (Chapters 7 through 10) descriptions of special education and the notion of student disability; such descriptions are intellectual resources for assessing the educational, political, and moral consequences of alternative ways of grounding the field's knowledge, practices, and discourses.

I deconstruct the special education knowledge tradition by presenting a genealogy of the field and its practices and discourses. However, given special education's relationship to the broader profession of education, and the role it has played historically as an institutional practice of public education, I begin the discussion with a brief genealogy of the knowledge, practices, and discourses of the subfields of general education and educational administration.[1] In the first section below I show that both the profession and institutional practice of special education are products of the functionalist view of education and school failure that has been dominant in the twentieth century (also see Skrtic, 1987, 1988b, 1991a, 1991b). In the next section I locate the metatheoretical grounding of special education's knowledge tradition in the most extreme objectivist region of the functionalist paradigm and consider the social consequences of such a paradigmatic outlook. Finally, I conclude the chapter with a discussion of the way the field of special education has responded to criticism of its practices and discourses, which I use to reinforce and extend my arguments in Chapter 2 about pragmatism as a method for deconstructing and reconstructing special education.

FUNCTIONALIST EDUCATION

I begin this section by considering how the functionalist worldview shaped the way the problem of school failure has been conceptualized in this century, a conceptualization that produced the profession and the institutional practice of special education. Then I consider this phenomenon more closely by reviewing the actual functionalist practices and discourses of general education and educational administration that give rise to the need for a field like special education within the institution of public education.[2]

Two Discourses on School Failure

As the dominant mode of social theorizing in the modern era, functionalism is the interpretation of social reality that grounds the knowledge, practices, and discourses of the social professions (Glazer, 1974; Schön, 1983). This includes the social profession of education, of course, and the various fields within it, including general education (Bowles & Gintis, 1976; Feinberg & Soltis, 1985; Giroux, 1981), educational administration (Foster, 1986; Griffiths, 1983, 1988), and special education (Heshusius, 1982; Iano, 1986;

Skrtic, 1986). We know from Chapter 2 that the functionalist or micro-objective paradigm is grounded in the sociology of regulation, takes a micro-scopic view of social reality, and approaches social science from an objectivist point of view. Given its realist ontology and deterministic view of human nature, functionalism assumes a single social reality to which humans react mechanistically. Moreover, given its positivist epistemology and preference for nomothetic methodologies, it assumes that, by employing the methods of the natural sciences, social science can, over time, represent this reality objectively and thus predict and control the way humans react to it. To-gether, then, the metatheoretical presuppositions of functionalism yield a view of social reality in which the current arrangement of society is assumed to be functional and thus indispensable, if not inherently correct.

Functionalism presupposes that social reality is objective, inherently or-derly, and rational, and thus that social and human problems are pathological (Foucault, 1954/1976; Ritzer, 1980). As such, the dominance of the func-tionalist worldview institutionalized the mutually reinforcing theories of *orga-nizational rationality* and *human pathology* in society and in public education (see below). As a result, when industrialization, immigration, and compul-sory school attendance brought into school large numbers of students who were difficult to teach in traditional classrooms, the problem of school failure was reframed as two interrelated problems—inefficient (nonrational) organi-zations and defective (pathological) students. This distorted the problem of school failure by largely removing it from the general education discourse and compartmentalizing it into two separate but mutually reinforcing discourses on school failure. The first discourse was in the developing field of educational administration, which, in the interest of maximizing the efficiency of school organizations, was compelled to rationalize its practices and discourses ac-cording to the precepts of "scientific management," an approach to adminis-tration designed to increase the efficiency of industrial mass production firms (see Callahan, 1962; Chapter 9; below). The second discourse on school failure was in the new field of special education, which emerged as a means to remove and contain the most recalcitrant students, in the interest of main-taining order in the new rationalized school plant (Lazerson, 1983; Sarason & Doris, 1979).

As we know from Chapter 1, the practices and discourses of the social professions are shaped by presuppositions grounded in particular bodies of disciplinary knowledge. They are also shaped by prevailing social norms. That is, as members of a professional community, persons who have been educated and socialized as professionals engage in practices and discourses that are shaped by the presuppositions contained in a body of disciplinary or social scientific knowledge. However, because professionals are also members of society, their practices and discourses are shaped as well by the common beliefs and assumptions contained in social norms. For present purposes, we can think of presuppositions grounded in disciplinary knowledge as being *explicit*, and those grounded in social norms as *implicit*. Moreover, the two types of presuppositions are related in that the disciplinary knowledge that is produced by social science research informs and over time changes norms and practices in society (Giddens, 1990). Given the dominance of functionalism in the social sciences, the functionalist theories of human pathology and organizational rationality are more than social science theories; in the modern world, they have become social norms. As such, the theories of human pathology and organizational rationality ground the practices and discourses of the fields of general education, educational administration, and special education in both explicit and implicit ways.

Because their knowledge tradition is grounded in scientific management, educational administrators explicitly presuppose that school organizations are rational (Clark, 1985; Griffiths, 1983), and, given the social norm of human pathology, they implicitly presuppose that school failure is pathological (see Skrtic, 1991a, 1991b).[3] Conversely, special education's knowledge tradition is grounded in psychology and biology (medicine) (see Mercer, 1973; Skrtic, 1986; below), which means that special educators explicitly presuppose that school failure is pathological, and, given the social norm of organizational rationality, implicitly presuppose that school organizations are rational (Skrtic, 1987, 1988b, 1991a; Chapter 9). The knowledge tradition of general education is grounded in psychology *and* scientific management (Cherryholmes, 1988; Spring, 1980), which means that its practices and discourse explicitly presuppose that school organizations are rational and that school failure is a pathological condition (Oakes, 1985; Skrtic, 1991a).

Taken together, these theoretical and normative presuppositions yield four mutually reinforcing assumptions that guide and justify the practices and discourses of all three fields and thus of the institution of public education as a whole. Synthesizing the work of a number of authors (Bogdan & Kugelmass, 1984; Cherryholmes, 1988; McNeil, 1986; Oakes, 1985; Sirotnik & Oakes, 1986; Skrtic, 1991a, 1991b; Spring, 1980), these assumptions are that

1. School failure is a (psychologically or sociologically) pathological condition that students have.
2. Differential diagnosis (i.e., homogeneous classification by ability or need) is an objective and useful practice.
3. Special programming (e.g., in-class ability grouping, curricular tracking, and segregated and pull-out special needs programs) is a rationally conceived and coordinated system of services that benefits diagnosed students.

4. Progress in education (i.e., greater academic achievement and efficiency) is a rational-technical process of incremental improvements in conventional diagnostic and instructional practices.

The four assumptions are derived from the two functionalist theories noted above: the first two from the theory of human pathology, and the last two from the theory of organizational rationality. Moreover, rather than a corrective or way of questioning these theories and assumptions (and thus the educational models and practices that are derived from them), educational inquiry actually reinforces them. This is so because educational inquiry is premised on the same functionalist presuppositions as those from which the theories and assumptions are derived. For present purposes, the most important of these presuppositions is functionalism's positivist epistemology.

Historically, inquiry in general education (Cherryholmes, 1988; Giroux, 1981), educational administration (Foster, 1986; Griffiths, 1983, 1988; Maxcy, 1991), and special education (Poplin, 1987; Skrtic, 1986) has been dominated by positivist methodologies. As we know from Chapter 1, the nineteenth-century version of positivism assumes that empirical observation yields objective knowledge of reality, "facts" that are unaffected by the observer's explicit or implicit theories. And although the Popperian (1959) version of positivism recognizes that humans make sense of the world through theories that affect their interpretation of the phenomena they are trying to observe, it assumes too that the objectivity of scientific inquiry ultimately rests upon an appeal to the facts (see Churchman, 1971; Mitroff & Pondy, 1974). Given their grounding in positivism, then, research in the fields of general education, educational administration, and special education is a form of naive pragmatism (Cherryholmes, 1988; Skrtic, 1991a; Chapter 2), an approach to inquiry that analyzes the nature and effects of schooling without questioning the assumptions, theories, and metatheories in which it is grounded. The problem with this approach is that it is "socially reproductive, instrumentally and functionally reproducing accepted meanings and conventional organizations, institutions, and ways of doing things for good or ill" (Cherryholmes, 1988, p. 151). This reproduces the status quo in all three fields, which reinforces the four assumptions and, ultimately, reaffirms the functionalist theories of organizational rationality and human pathology in the field of education and in society at large.

The institutional practice of special education is an artifact of the functionalist quest for rationality, order, and certainty in public education, a quest that is both intensified and further legitimized by the institutional practice of educational administration (see Maxcy, 1991; Skrtic, 1988b; Chapter 9). The existence of special education distorts the anomaly of school failure by objectifying it as student disability, thus eliminating it as an occasion for educators to question their conventional practice. As we know from Chapter 2, this is a problem because the uncertainty caused by anomalies is a precondition for progress and growth of knowledge in paradigm-bound communal endeavors such as the natural sciences (Kuhn, 1970), social sciences (Barnes, 1982), and social professions (Schön, 1983; Skrtic, 1986). Redefining school failure as student disability prevents the profession of education from entering into a productive confrontation with uncertainty, the very sort of confrontation that it needs in order to move beyond its functionalist knowledge tradition.

The problem in special education and educational administration has been that, although both fields have experienced enough uncertainty to call their knowledge, practices, and discourses into question on several occasions (Griffiths, 1983, 1988; Skrtic, 1991a; Chapter 9; below), they have lacked a method for addressing their problems of practice critically (Foster, 1986; Maxcy, 1991; Skrtic, 1986, 1991a; Tomlinson, 1982). The problem in general education is more fundamental, however. Not only has it lacked a method of critical discourse (Cherryholmes, 1988; Giroux, 1981, 1983; Sirotnik & Oakes, 1986), it largely has been prevented from having to confront uncertainty altogether, precisely because of the objectification of school failure as student disability (Skrtic, 1991a; Chapter 9). Thus, the problem in the profession of education generally is that the functionalist distortion of school failure as student disability eliminates it as an anomaly and thus as an opportunity to call the prevailing knowledge tradition into question. Ultimately, this prevents the profession of education (and the public) from seeing that schooling in America is inconsistent with the democratic ideals upon which public education's claim to legitimacy is premised. That is, it prevents us from seeing that our practices are inconsistent with the normative proposition that, in a democracy, public education must be both excellent and equitable. [4]

Functionalist Education Practices and Discourses

As the dominant framework for social theorizing in the modern era, functionalism has had different manifestations in the various social science disciplines, two of which are particularly important for present purposes: functionalist sociology and functionalist psychology. Functionalist sociology is important because it embodies the functionalist theory of organizational rationality applied to society and social institutions such as education. As we know from Chapter 2, the sociological functionalist views society as being composed of interrelated parts, each of which is functional because it contributes to the maintenance of the other parts and thus of the system as a whole. Because the parts of society are always changing, and these changes lead to sympathetic changes in other parts of the system, change from the functionalist perspective is essentially an orderly, continuous, and integrated process rather than a disorderly, discontinuous, and disintegrative one (Burrell & Morgan, 1979). In the extreme, functionalists argue that all of parts of society are functional and thus indispensable to the system. This outlook leads to the conservative bias that all current aspects of society should continue to exist, which has the effect of limiting the possibility of fundamental change (Ritzer, 1980).

Functionalist psychology is important because it is the explicit disciplinary grounding of the profession of education. Two branches of functionalist psychology are particularly relevant in this regard: psychological behaviorism, which in the twentieth century has dominated education's conceptualization of curriculum and instruction (Giroux, 1981; Stanley, 1992); and experimental psychology, which underwrites education's psychometric approach to assessment and evaluation (Cherryholmes, 1988). The manifestation of functionalism in education is largely a product of both psychological and sociological functionalism, which of course are themselves shaped by the metatheoretical presuppositions of the functionalist paradigm, and thus by the theories of human pathology and organizational rationality. These presuppositions have shaped virtually every aspect of public education in this century, including the accepted view of knowledge itself, which in turn has influenced the common conceptualization of curriculum, instruction, and learning (see Cherryholmes, 1988; Feinberg & Soltis, 1985; Freire, 1970, 1973; Giroux, 1981).

Given its realist ontology and positivist epistemology (see Chapter 2), functionalism views knowledge as certain and objective, as a monological body of objective facts about a single reality that is independent of humans' apprehension of it. As such, curriculum from the functionalist perspective is largely a matter of codifying this knowledge in the form of a rationalized or task-analyzed hierarchy of higher- and lower-order facts and skills (Cherryholmes, 1988). Given its realist ontology and deterministic view of human nature, the functionalist view of learning is premised on psychological behaviorism, on the idea that learning occurs as a function of humans' reaction to the environmental contingencies of an objective reality (see below). Combining functionalism's views of learning and knowledge yields a conceptualization of instruction premised on the application of a systematic technology of behavioral procedures for knowledge and skill acquisition.

Given the functionalist interpretation of knowledge, curriculum, and instruction, the role of the teacher is conceptualized as that of a technician who organizes the codified knowledge for efficient presentation and arranges the environmental contingencies to reward and punish desirable and undesirable responses. As such, the role of the learner is that of a passive receiver of factual material and skill training under the conditions imposed by appropriate environmental contingencies (Giroux, 1981; Heshusius, 1986). Learning, then, is understood as "an accumulation of pieces of knowledge and bits of skill . . . [which are] placed in learners' heads through practice and appropriate rewards" (Resnick & Klopfer, 1989, p. 2).

The same functionalist assumptions underwrite the approach to evaluation in schools, as well as the view of the function of schooling itself (see Feinberg & Soltis, 1985; Giroux, 1981; Skrtic, 1988a). The positivist orientation of functionalist educational psychology yields psychometrics, a quantitative approach to evaluation that serves two functions. First, through the use of standardized ability testing, students are grouped into relatively homogeneous tracks for efficient delivery of instruction. Second, standardized achievement tests are used to evaluate student acquisition of the knowledge and skills contained in the rationalized curriculum. Ability testing is assumed to serve the interest of organizational efficiency by reducing student variability within tracks (Oakes, 1985); achievement testing is assumed to serve the interest of economic efficiency by providing a means of credentialing graduates for efficient assignment to occupational roles in business and industry (Meyer & Rowan, 1978). From the functionalist outlook, the function of schooling in society is similar to that of industrial psychology in business and industry; that is, the efficient slotting of workers into occupational roles in the economy (Spring, 1980).

The way schools are organized and managed conforms to the functionalist outlook as well. Given the functionalist view of the nature and function of schooling, the formal structure of such a system takes on the configuration of a "machine bureaucracy"; that is, the pyramid-shaped, top-down structure of formal control relations that is common to mass production firms in business and industry (Callahan, 1962; Haber, 1964; Mintzberg, 1979). Although I will have much more to say about the nature and implications of this organizational configuration in Chapter 9, at this point we can understand it as a centralized hierarchy of formal authority relations, which, in conjunction with scientific management, is assumed to be the most efficient way of organizing and managing schools relative to their primary functions—that is, codifying objective knowledge, implementing behavioral technologies, and awarding credentials. Applied to schools, the goal of scientific management is to ensure teacher-proof and learner-proof instruction through standardization of curricular content, instructional procedures, personnel roles, and student classifications, as well as the enforcement of these standards through direct supervision and competency testing of students and, more recently, teachers (Callahan, 1962; Mintzberg, 1979; Chapter 9).

The management of planned change in such a system follows the procedures that are used to change industrial machine bureaucracies. The assumption is that school organizations are like machines that can be fine-tuned in a rational-technical manner through increased standardization of work processes and outcomes, further specification of professional roles and student classifications, and closer supervision of personnel and clients (House, 1979; Wolcott, 1977; Wise, 1979). Change is viewed as fine tuning the existing system, rather than changing it in more fundamental ways, or replacing it altogether. From this perspective, change is simply a matter of creating a more efficient machine bureaucracy (Cuban, 1989; Skrtic, 1988b, 1991a; Chapter 10).

Educational accountability from the functionalist perspective amounts to the legal-bureaucratic control of personnel, work processes, and student classifications and outcomes (Martin, Overholt, & Urban, 1976; Skrtic, 1991a; Wise, 1979, 1988). This mode of accountability is based on standardization of services and outcomes, and is aimed at efficiency of operation and equal treatment of clients. However, accountability premised on equality of treatment through standardization of services and outcomes produces a routinized system that, given the inevitability of client variability, is too rigid to accommodate students whose needs do not correspond to the standardized routines. This creates the need for various "special needs" programs, that is, programs that are designed to serve students whose needs are "special" by virtue of the fact that they do not fall within the scope of the organization's conventional instructional models, practices, and tools. As we will see below and in Chapter 9, although these programs are intended to, and in a narrow political sense actually do, serve the interests of students with special educational needs, they largely act to protect the legitimacy of the system by deflecting the problem of school failure onto the students, their parents, or society at large (see Skrtic, 1987, 1991a, 1991b). This is accomplished administratively by formally identifying recalcitrant students as either economically disadvantaged, culturally and/or linguistically different, or educationally handicapped or gifted, and subsequently removing them from the system, for all or part of the school day, by assigning them to one of several categorical special needs programs, such as Chapter 1 or bilingual, migrant, gifted, or special education.

FUNCTIONALIST SPECIAL EDUCATION

Special education is a more extreme version of functionalist education, more extreme in both an objectivist and a microscopic sense. Special education's disciplinary grounding in psychology and biology (see below) yields an approach to diagnosis and instruction that is premised on diagnostic-prescriptive teaching and behavioristic theory (Bogdan & Knoll, 1988; Skrtic, 1986). Diagnostic-prescriptive teaching is the attempt to design instructional programs on the basis of test performance, using one of two approaches: ability training or task analysis. Given special education's inability to develop a psychometric technology for actualizing the ability training model, however, the preference in the field has been for the task analysis approach (Salvia & Ysseldyke, 1981).

The task analysis version of diagnostic-prescriptive teaching is based on the application of behavioristic theory to instruction in specific knowledge and skills (Bogdan & Knoll, 1988). Relatively complex instructional goals are selected from the general education curriculum and task analyzed further into subskills, which are taught using a more systematic application of behavioral procedures for skill acquisition. This more advanced form of behavioral technology is commonly referred to as "systematic instruction," an approach that conceptualizes the special education teacher as even more of a technician than the general education teacher (see, e.g., Haring, 1978; White & Haring, 1976). Systematic instruction is premised on applied behavior analysis and thus ultimately is grounded in the psychological behaviorism of B. F. Skinner (1953, 1957, 1971). Special education applied researchers justify grounding the field's practices and discourses in applied behavior analysis because it is scientific, that is, premised on

> the experimental analysis of behavior, which, as a scientific discipline, sought to find a systematic interpretation of human behavior based on generalized principles, or laws, of behavior. The goal of this search for laws of behavior was much the same as in any other branch of science—to make reliable predictions. The development of behavior analysis has been rigorously scientific, beginning with basic laboratory research and slowly generalizing the results to social situations. (Haring, 1978, p. 21)

Metatheoretically, the Skinnerian form of psychological behaviorism that underwrites special education's diagnostic and instructional practices and discourses is located in the extreme objectivist region of the functionalist paradigm. Referring to their four-paradigm matrix of modern social scientific knowledge (see Chapter 2), Burrell and Morgan (1979) noted that

> Skinner's perspective is a highly coherent and consistent one in terms of the four strands of the subjective–objective dimension of our analytical scheme. Ontologically, his view is firmly realist; epistemologically, his work is the archetype of positivism; his view of human nature reflects a determinism of an extreme form; [and] the highly nomothetic methodology reflected in his experimental approach is congruent with these other assumptions. (p. 103)

Thus, the knowledge tradition that has guided and justified special education practices and discourses in this century is an extreme form of functionalism (see also Heshusius, 1982; Iano, 1987; Poplin, 1987; Skrtic, 1986; Tomlinson, 1982).

As in the profession of education generally, special education's grounding in functionalism means that the guiding assumptions behind its professional models, practices, and tools are premised on the theories of human pathology and organizational rationality. Drawing on the work of a number of authors (Bogdan & Knoll, 1988; Bogdan & Kugelmass, 1984; Heshusius, 1982; Iano, 1987; Poplin, 1987; Rist & Harrell, 1982; Skrtic, 1986; Tomlinson, 1982), and restating the assumptions about school failure presented above, special education practices and discourses are premised on the following four assumptions, the first two derived from the theory of human pathology and the last two from the theory of organizational rationality:

1. Student disability is a pathological condition.
2. Differential diagnosis is objective and useful.
3. Special education is a rationally conceived and coordinated system of services that benefits diagnosed students.
4. Progress in special education is a rational-technical process of incremental improvements in conventional diagnostic and instructional practices.

Given these assumptions, progress in special education is conceptualized in terms of using rational-technical means to improve and extend its diagnostic and instructional models, practices, and tools. As we will see below, P.L. 94–142, the Education for All Handicapped Children Act of 1975 (EHA; now the Individuals with Disabilities Education Act), is the actualization of this notion of progress in the field (also see Chapters 9 and 10). When it was enacted, the law was perceived as an advanced technology, an improved model of special education diagnostic and instructional practices and tools (see Abeson & Zettel, 1977; Gilhool, 1989; Turnbull, 1986).

Given its functionalist knowledge tradition, special education's sense of itself as a profession is premised on an implicitly functionalist version of the liberal ideology of benevolent humanitarianism. As Tomlinson (1982) noted in this regard:

> the way in which children are categorized out of . . . mainstream education and into special education is generally regarded as enlightened and advanced, and an instance of the obligation placed upon civilized society to care for its weaker members. Special education is permeated by an ideology of benevolent humanitarianism, which provides [the] moral framework within which professionals . . . work. (p. 5)

True to both the functionalist and liberal ideologies, the field's conceptualization of an effective and equitable system of education assumes the inevitability of the status quo in public education, while at the same time seeks progress in the form of quantitative and bureaucratic solutions to educational inequities (see Skrtic, 1991a; Chapter 9; below). In effect, the field of special education calculates progress toward an effective and just educational system in terms of identifying more students as disabled and securing for them and their parents more rights, resources, and participation within the general education system. Ultimately, these outcomes are to be achieved rationally through scientific advances in technology, and bureaucratically through procedural compliance with the rules of the EHA and, as we will see below, the logic of the mainstreaming model.

The need for a profession and institutional practice of special education in public education is an unintentional negative consequence of the functionalist practices and discourses of the fields of general education and educational administration, a product of the functionalist interpretation of education and school failure that has shaped public education in the twentieth century. By relating special education to these practices and discourses, and focusing on its institutional role within public education, my intent has been to show that, far from being a rational and just response to the problem of school failure and special educational needs, special education is a social artifact, an unintentional consequence of functionalism, the worldview that has guided and justified the profession and institution of education historically. There is nothing true or inherently correct about the special education knowledge tradition; it is an historically situated social construction. Had the profession of education been grounded in a different discipline or in one of the other paradigms of modern knowledge, special education would be something other than what it is today. Indeed, had the profession of education been grounded in a different paradigm, the need for special education might not have emerged at all.

SPECIAL EDUCATION'S RESPONSE TO CRITICISM

Historically, there have been two types of criticism of special education theory and practice—*practical* criticism, which focuses exclusively on the field's models, practices, and tools; and *theoretical* criticism, which also criticizes models, practices, and tools but, more important, does so by criticizing the theories and guiding assumptions upon which they are premised. Whereas practical criticism has been mounted by special education clients, advocates, and professionals, until recently theoretical criticism has come largely from the social sciences. As we will see, however, an important development in the

1980s has been the emergence of a theoretical discourse within the field of special education.

Practical Criticism

Of the two types of criticism, practical criticism has been more apparent to the field and has had a greater impact on the way special education is actually practiced. Special education emerged from practical criticism of public education at the turn of the century (Lazerson, 1983; Sarason & Doris, 1979), and the way it is practiced today is a response to criticism of previous twentieth-century special education models, practices, and tools. Although episodes of practical criticism and change can be traced over the entire history of the field, two are particularly important for present purposes. The first episode is the "mainstreaming" debate, which occurred in the 1960s and early 1970s, a period in which the field's traditional special classroom model was criticized and subsequently replaced with the mainstreaming model. The second episode, what I will call the "inclusion" debate, began in the 1980s with sharp criticism of the mainstreaming model and arguments for a more integrated or inclusive approach to special education programming.

The Mainstreaming Debate. During the civil rights movement of the 1960s, parents and special education advocates and professionals criticized the field's traditional model of segregated classrooms and schools for being racially biased, instructionally ineffective, and psychologically and socially damaging (Blatt & Kaplan, 1966; Dunn, 1968; Johnson, 1962). This round of practical criticism led to a series of legal and legislative victories that culminated in the EHA, which redefined special education by mandating a free, appropriate public education for all students with disabilities in the least restrictive environment (LRE). Although the law did not mention "mainstreaming," the mainstreaming or "continuum of services" model (Deno, 1970; Dunn, 1973; Reynolds, 1962) became the "legal preference" for complying with the law's LRE principle (Turnbull & Turnbull, 1978, p. 149).

The EHA and mainstreaming changed special education practice by changing the field's structural relationship to general education (see Chapter 9) and by extending to students and their parents certain constitutional rights and procedural safeguards, including the right to education or treatment, participation in decision making, and due process of law. The EHA did not end critical commentary on special education practice; public debate and legal action over the meaning of "appropriate education" and "least restrictive environment" have continued until today (see Turnbull, 1993). The point is that the changes brought about by the EHA and mainstreaming resulted from practical criticism – moral, legal, and political arguments against the spe-

cial classroom model (Ballard-Campbell & Semmel, 1981; Biklen, 1985) –
not arguments against the theoretical knowledge and guiding assumptions in
which the field and its practices are grounded (Skrtic, 1986, 1988a).

The Inclusion Debate. The first round of practical criticism largely sub-
sided in the mid-1970s with enactment of the EHA and broad adoption of
the mainstreaming model. Although these measures were presumed to be
solutions to the problems associated with the special classroom model (Abeson & Zettel, 1977; Dunn, 1968; Turnbull & Turnbull, 1978), the inclusion
debate emerged in the early 1980s when some of the leading figures in the
field began to question the ethics and efficacy of the EHA and mainstreaming
(e.g., Lipsky & Gartner, 1987; Pugach & Lilly, 1984; Reynolds & Wang,
1983; Stainback & Stainback, 1984b; Will, 1984, 1986).[5] Referring to a
common body of implementation research (see Gartner & Lipsky, 1987;
Heller, Holtzman, & Messick, 1982; Wang, Reynolds, & Walberg, 1987),
they argued, in effect, that the EHA and mainstreaming had created virtually
the same problems as the special classroom model – racial, cultural, and linguistic bias, instructional ineffectiveness, and psychological and social damage
(see Skrtic, 1988b, 1991a).

The critics of the current system of special education argue for more or
less abandoning the classification system of the EHA and the mainstreaming
model. As an alternative, they propose the inclusive education or inclusion
model of special education programming, which is premised on restructuring
the separate general and special education systems into a new "unitary" system
in which, depending on the particular reform proposal, some, most, or all
students with special educational needs are educated in general education
classrooms on a full-time basis (see Chapter 10). The opponents of inclusion
question the wisdom and feasibility of this approach on the grounds that,
given the apparent inflexibility of general education classrooms, abandoning
the EHA and the pull-out approach of mainstreaming could lead to a loss of
hard-won rights and resources and, in the worst case, a return to the unac-
ceptable conditions that existed before the EHA and mainstreaming (Kauffman, 1988, 1989, 1991; Kauffman, Gerber, & Semmel, 1988).[6] Although
there is opposition to the inclusion model, even the defenders of the EHA
and mainstreaming agree that there are fundamental problems with the current system of special education that need to be corrected (see Fuchs &
Fuchs, 1991; Skrtic, 1991a, 1991b).

I present an in-depth discussion of the proponents' and opponents'
positions on the wisdom and feasibility of the inclusion model in Chapter 10.
For present purposes, however, the implication to be drawn from the inclusion debate on the question of the ethics and efficacy of the current system is
that, rather than resolving the special education problems of the 1960s, the

EHA and mainstreaming merely reproduced them in the 1980s and 1990s (see Skrtic, 1987, 1988b, 1991a; Chapter 9).

The Problem with Practical Criticism

The inclusion debate parallels the mainstreaming debate in several important ways. First, in both cases the ethics and efficacy of special education practices are criticized and a new approach is proposed. In the 1960s, the target of criticism was the special classroom model, and mainstreaming emerged as the solution; today, mainstreaming is under attack, and the inclusion model is being advocated as the solution. Second, in both cases the new approach draws opposition and the field is divided. Although there was some opposition to mainstreaming (e.g., Keogh & Levitt, 1976; MacMillan & Semmel, 1977), that debate was far less divisive than the current one because mainstreaming is less ambitious than inclusion and, moreover, there was far less to lose in the 1960s in terms of established rights and resources.

The third parallel between the mainstreaming and inclusion debates is that both of them take place during a period of apparent reform in general education. In the 1960s, Dunn (1968) argued that mainstreaming was a real possibility because it was consistent with what he called the "American Revolution in Education" (p. 10), which was his term for the introduction of more powerful instructional technologies (e.g., individualized instruction, teaching machines) and more flexible instructional practices (e.g., team teaching, open classrooms). In the current debate, the proponents of inclusion are making the same argument relative to the school restructuring movement and the availability of what they see as more powerful instructional and diagnostic practices, such as cooperative learning, collaborative consultation, and curriculum-based assessment (see Lipsky & Gartner, 1989; Pugach & Lilly, 1984; Stainback, Stainback, & Forest, 1989; Wang, Reynolds, & Walberg, 1986).

The fourth and most important parallel between the mainstreaming and inclusion debates explains the first three: Both debates are forms of naive pragmatism. As we know from Chapter 2, the problem with naive pragmatism as a method for resolving problems of professional practice is that, although it questions models, practices, and tools, it unreflectively accepts the assumptions, theories, and metatheories that stand behind them. As such, rather than resolving these problems, naive pragmatism merely reproduces them in a new form (Cherryholmes, 1988; Skrtic, 1991a, 1991b). The EHA and mainstreaming reproduced the special education problems of the 1960s in the 1980s because criticism stopped at the special classroom model and its associated practices and tools; it did not question the assumptions, theories, and metatheories in which they are grounded. As a result, the new models, practices, and tools introduced under the EHA and mainstreaming were premised on the same functionalist theories of human pathology and organizational rationality, and thus on the same four assumptions noted above about the nature of disability and diagnosis and special education and progress (Skrtic, 1986, 1988b). What is so troubling today is that the inclusion debate is largely following the same pattern as the mainstreaming debate. It, too, is a form of naive pragmatism that criticizes current special education models, practices, and tools without explicitly criticizing the theories and assumptions that stand behind them (see Skrtic, 1987, 1988b, 1991a).[7] The danger here, of course, is that, rather than resolving the special education problems of the twentieth century, the inclusion debate will simply reproduce them in the twenty-first century.

Fortunately, however, there is an important difference between the mainstreaming and inclusion debates, which, if capitalized upon, may mitigate against the possibility of yet another round of criticism that reproduces old problems in a new form. During the mainstreaming debate, the field of special education had no meaningful way to interpret the negative empirical evidence on the ethics and efficacy of the special classroom model, and thus no way to conceptualize the sources of the problems other than defaulting implicitly to functionalist theories and assumptions. In the end, mainstreaming emerged as the solution to these problems, not because it was conceptually sound but because, given the field's functionalist grounding, it appeared to be the right thing to do (Ballard-Campbell & Semmel, 1981; Biklen, 1985; Skrtic, 1986). The difference today is that an array of conceptual resources are available for interpreting the negative empirical evidence on the ethics and efficacy of the EHA and mainstreaming. This is so because a theoretical discourse has emerged within the field of special education, one that appropriates critical insights from the social sciences and applies them to past and current problems of special education practice.

THEORETICAL CRITICISM OF SPECIAL EDUCATION

Like practical criticism, theoretical criticism questions the ethics and efficacy of special education models, practices, and tools, but does so by criticizing the theoretical knowledge and guiding assumptions upon which they are premised. Whereas practical criticism is an empirical critique of the field's models, practices, and tools, theoretical criticism is a critique of its grounding theories and assumptions. The advantage is that, rather than interpreting empirical data by defaulting implicitly to the field's traditional theories and assumptions, theoretical criticism explicitly questions the legitimacy of the theories and assumptions themselves, and on this basis proposes alternative theories, both as a way to interpret empirical data and as an alternative grounding for the field's models, practices, and tools. Prior to the emergence of the theoretical discourse within the field of special education, theoretical criticism came from external sources, largely from the social sciences. And because the new internal theoretical discourse is largely a reappropriation of the external theoretical discourse, I begin the discussion of theoretical criticism by reviewing the social sciences' case against special education.

The External Theoretical Discourse

The arguments that social scientists have made against the profession and institutional practice of special education are based on one of three interrelated claims: that special education is atheoretical; that it confounds theory; or that it is based on the wrong theory (see Skrtic, 1986). The atheoretical claim is that the field of special education operates in the absence of a guiding theory, that its practices and discourses are simply guided by the four assumptions about the nature of disability, diagnosis, special education, and progress noted above (see, e.g., Bogdan & Kugelmass, 1984; Rist & Harrell, 1982; Tomlinson, 1982). This does not mean that there are no theories behind special education's guiding assumptions. Rather, the atheoretical claim refers to the unconscious, and thus acritical, nature of these assumptions, and not whether they are grounded in theory (see Skrtic, 1991a).

The second claim is that the special education knowledge tradition confounds theories. The most notable example of this type of criticism is Mercer's (1973) explanation of the way biological and psychological theories of deviance are confounded within the clinical perspective of mental retardation. Derived from medicine and psychology, the clinical perspective contains two contrasting theories of normality: the pathological model from medicine (biology) and the statistical model from psychology. The pathological model is bipolar and evaluative. It defines normal/abnormal according to the presence or absence of observable biological processes: those that interfere with life are "bad" (pathology); those that enhance it are "good" (health). The statistical model defines normal/abnormal in terms of variance above or below a population mean and is evaluatively neutral. Whether being above or below a mean on an attribute is good or bad is a social definition.

According to Mercer (1973), both models are used to define mental retardation—the pathological model for assessing biological symptoms and the statistical model for assessing behavioral manifestations, which are not comprehensible within the pathological model. Although some instances of mental retardation are associated with observable patterns of biological symptoms (syndromes), and are thus comprehensible under the pathological model, the vast majority of individuals labeled mentally retarded show no biological signs. In these instances, a low score on an intelligence (IQ) test is accepted as a symptom of pathology, a conceptual transposition that turns behavioral patterns into pathological signs.

> The implicit logic that underlies this transformation is as follows: Low IQ = "bad" in American society: a social evaluation. "Bad" = pathology in the pathological model. Therefore, low IQ = pathology. Thus, IQ, which is not a biological manifestation but is a behavioral score based on responses to a series of questions, becomes conceptually transposed into a pathological sign carrying all of the implications of the pathological model. (Mercer, 1973, pp. 5–6)[8]

The third type of theoretical criticism rests on the claim that the special education knowledge tradition is based on the wrong theory, or that it relies too narrowly on theory derived from the disciplines of psychology and biology (e.g., Farber, 1968; Goffman, 1961, 1963; Gould, 1981; Lemert, 1967; Scott, 1969; Szasz, 1961). By their very nature, these disciplines place the root cause of deviance within the person, excluding from consideration causal factors that lie in social and political processes external to the individual. Social scientists who make this claim view diagnostic and instructional models based solely on theories derived from the behavioral and biological sciences as superficial because they do nothing to assess or alter the social context of "disability." From this perspective, disability is viewed as a social construction (Biklen, 1977; Bogdan, 1974; Braginsky & Braginsky, 1971; Davis, 1963; Goffman, 1961, 1963; Gubrium, 1975; Lemert, 1967; Scheff, 1966; Scott, 1969; Szasz, 1961; Taylor & Bogdan, 1977; Wiseman, 1970), and special education in industrialized societies as an arm of education that creates powerless groups (see Barton & Tomlinson, 1984; Farber, 1968; Sarason & Doris, 1979; Smith, 1985; Tomlinson, 1982; Chapters 2, 5, and 7).

Although theoretical criticism of special education from outside the field has been available since at least the 1960s, it has had virtually no effect on the field's practices and discourses (Bogdan & Kugelmass, 1984), or on its guiding assumptions and theories (Skrtic, 1986, 1988a, 1991a). One problem, of course, is that unorthodox perspectives such as these tend to be overlooked in professional education. Anything that might question or offer an alternative to the profession's established knowledge tradition is avoided (Barnes, 1982; Kuhn, 1970; Chapter 2). Moreover, even when special education professionals are confronted with theoretical criticism, they ordinarily have difficulty accepting and using it. Theoretical criticism is difficult for special educators to accept because it questions their taken-for-granted assumptions about themselves, their clients, and their practices and discourses. It is difficult for them to use because it is presented in theoretical languages that fall outside the logic of special education's functionalist knowledge tradition.

Although special educators cannot deny that theoretical criticism is scientific, they tend to ignore it because, given their commitment to the field's established knowledge tradition, it appears to be irrelevant or, at best, ill-informed (see Skrtic, 1986, 1991a; below).

Internal Theoretical Discourse

The critical discourse that has emerged within the field of special education is largely a reappropriation of the theoretical insights of the external discourse (see, e.g., Bogdan & Knoll, 1988; Bogdan & Kugelmass, 1984; Carrier, 1983; Ferguson, 1987; Heshusius, 1982, 1986; Iano, 1986, 1987; Janesick, 1988; Poplin, 1984, 1987; Sigmon, 1987; Skrtic, 1986, 1988a; Sleeter, 1986; Tomlinson, 1982). By their very nature, the internal critiques make the case, implicitly or explicitly, that the field of special education is atheoretical, or acritical in the sense noted above. In addition, most of them draw on the confounded theory argument to make a case against special education's overreliance on biological theories of deviance (the "medical model") and its inappropriate use of functionalist or reductionist approaches to curriculum, instruction, assessment, and research (see Bogdan & Kugelmass, 1984; Heshusius, 1982, 1986; Iano, 1986, 1987; Poplin, 1984, 1987; Sigmon, 1987). Finally, each of the internal critiques is a version of the wrong theory claim. In effect, each one argues against special education's grounding in functionalism and makes a case for an alternative grounding in a different paradigm, as illustrated in Figure 3.1.

Like the mainstreaming debate, the inclusion debate is important because it is empirical; it questions the legitimacy of special education's models, practices, and tools in the language of the field and in terms of its own standards, which makes it comprehensible to the members of the special education community. However, because empirical data can be interpreted in a variety of ways, depending on the explicit or implicit theory of the interpreter (Harré, 1981; Hesse, 1980), the field's atheoretical (acritical) orientation means that special educators must default conceptually to their traditional theories and assumptions to interpret the meaning of the empirical evidence put forth in the inclusion debate, just as they did in the mainstreaming debate. This is naive pragmatism; rather than resolving problems of special education practice, it reproduces them in a new form.

The theoretical discourse is important because it is critical; it questions the field's implicit theories and assumptions and proposes a number of alternative theories for grounding the field's practices and discourses. The advantage of a theoretical discourse is that it recognizes that altering practices and discourses in ways that do not reproduce old problems requires altering the theories and assumptions upon which they are based. As illustrated in Figure

FIGURE 3.1. The Theoretical Discourse in Special Education

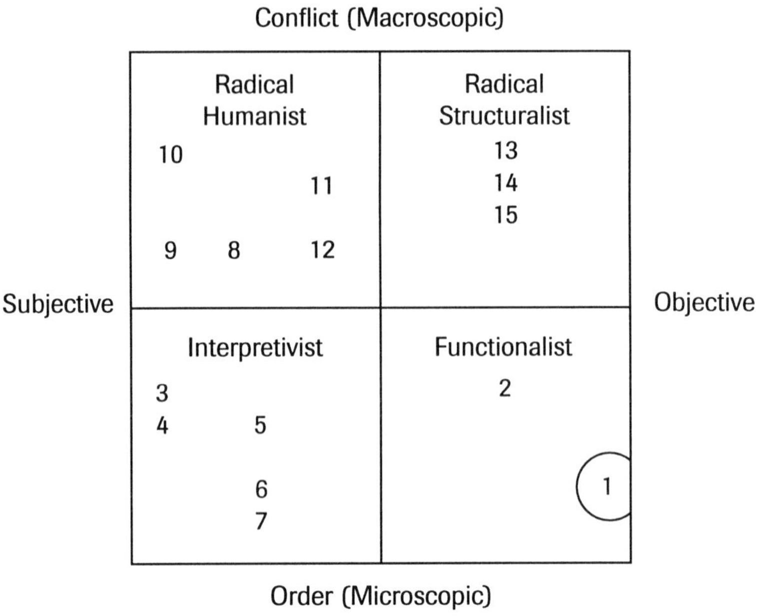

Conflict (Macroscopic)

Radical Humanist	Radical Structuralist
10	13
11	14
	15
9 8 12	
Interpretivist	Functionalist
3	2
4 5	
6	1
7	

Subjective   Objective

Order (Microscopic)

1 = Conventional knowledge tradition	9 = Iano (1986, 1987)
2 = Farber (1968)	10 = Kiel (Chapter 6)
3 = Heshusius (1982, 1986)	11 = Tomlinson (1988)
4 = Poplin (1984, 1987)	12 = Sigmon (1987)
5 = Ferguson (1987)	13 = Carrier (1983)
6 = Bogdan and Knoll (1988)	14 = Tomlinson (1982)
7 = Biklen (1985)	15 = Sleeter (1986)
8 = Janesick (1988)	

Source: Adapted from T. M. Skrtic, 1991, *Behind Special Education: A Critical Analysis of Professional Culture and School Organization*, p. 120, Denver: Love Publishing.

3.1, the general trend in the internal theoretical discourse is away from functionalism and into the other three paradigms, paralleling developments in the social sciences (see Chapter 2). The advantage is that the internal discourse provides special educators with optional descriptions of the nature and effects of its practices and discourses from all four paradigms of modern social scientific thought (see Skrtic, 1990a, 1995b). In principle, these optional descriptions provide the field with an array of conceptual resources for deconstructing and reconstructing its professional knowledge, practices, and discourses. If the internal discourse is to help the field of special education resolve its problems of practice, however, it must resolve three problems of its own: the problems of incomprehensibility, of foundationalism, and of disqualified knowledge.

The Problem of Incomprehensibility

Because the internal theoretical discourse is being carried out largely by special educators, it has been more difficult for the field to ignore. Nevertheless, its impact on the field has been minimal because, like the external theoretical discourse, it questions taken-for-granted assumptions and is presented in unfamiliar theoretical languages. The difference is that, because the internal theoretical discourse cannot be ignored as irrelevant or ill-informed, it has been condemned as unscientific and misleading at best (e.g., Lloyd, 1987; Simpson & Eaves, 1985; Ulman & Rosenberg, 1986), and rude, ideological, and dangerous at worst (Carnine, 1987; Forness & Kavale, 1987; Kavale & Forness, 1987).

For example, the field reacted to Heshusius's (1982) argument for grounding special education practices and discourses in the holistic orientation of the interpretivist paradigm (rather than the mechanistic worldview of the functionalist paradigm) by dismissing it entirely as unscientific superstition (see Ulman & Rosenberg, 1986). Of course, this is to be expected because, given their functionalist grounding, Heshusius's critics naturally evaluated her proposal exclusively on the basis of functionalist presuppositions about the nature of reality, knowledge, and inquiry, which, given the objectivist logic of functionalism, they took to be the only criteria that exist. Another example is the way the field characterized Sleeter's (1986) radical structuralist critique of the learning disabilities classification as "ideological rhetoric . . . a distorted account of history" (Kavale & Forness, 1987, p. 7), one that is dangerous in that it "may be taken seriously because of its . . . . ready appeal to egalitarian 'instincts' and [its] warping of reality" (Kavale & Forness, 1987, p. 7). Given functionalism's realist ontology and microscopic (order) view of society, Sleeter's critics naturally read her macroscopic (conflict) interpretation as a dangerous distortion of reality.

Together, the problems of naive pragmatism and theoretical incomprehensibility create a situation in which the practical criticism of the inclusion debate is comprehensible *but* acritical, whereas the theoretical discourse that special educators need to avoid reproducing their problems is critical *but* incomprehensible to the field. One way to respond to this situation is to combine the field's empirical evidence on the ethics and efficacy of its practices with the critical insights of the theoretical discourse, creating an expanded discourse in special education that is both critical *and* comprehensible to the field. The advantage of such a discourse is that it would make available for theoretical and critical analysis the empirical evidence produced by the field itself, according to its conventional assumptions and in its traditional language (see Skrtic, 1991b; Chapter 10).

Although an expanded discourse of this sort is necessary, it is not sufficient to understand and resolve past and current problems of special education practice. This is so because, although the theoretical discourse is *critical*, it is not *pragmatic*. It is critical because it questions the field's theoretical grounding and provides alternative theories for interpreting data and conceptualizing solutions. It is not pragmatic, however, because it does not solve the problem of choosing among the various theories that are put forth in the theoretical discourse. To be critical *and* pragmatic the expanded discourse must not only look behind special education practice to expose its unquestioned theories and assumptions, it must also look behind the various theories themselves to expose the metatheoretical presuppositions in which they are grounded. To be critical and pragmatic at a metatheoretical level, the expanded discourse must be antifoundational; it must provide a way to choose among alternative theoretical interpretations of special education and disability under conditions in which the "truth" of any particular interpretation cannot be established. The problem with the new theoretical discourse in special education is that it is foundational.

The Problem of Foundationalism

As we know from Chapter 1, the subjectivist view of science is that, rather than a rational-technical process that produces objective knowledge, it is a nonrational-cultural undertaking that yields different kinds of knowledges, depending on the frame of reference of the observer. Given the relationship between the social sciences and the social professions, this means that, far from being objective knowledge about social reality, the theoretical knowledge that guides and justifies special education's professional practices and discourses is subjective knowledge based on an historically situated and, at best, temporarily valid frame of reference. Although subjectivism means that there is nothing inherently true about special education's functionalist knowledge tradition, antifoundationalism means that there is nothing inherently false about it either. Indeed, the question of the adequacy of the special education knowledge tradition is not whether functionalism is true or false, but whether it serves the best interests of the field's clients and of society. In this sense, the problem that special education faces today is that the professional models, practices, and tools that flow from its functionalist assumptions, theories, and metatheories have been shown to be ineffective at best and harmful at worst, first during the mainstreaming debate and again during the inclusion debate.

Given that its functionalist knowledge tradition is neither true nor effective, the field of special education is compelled intellectually and ethically to reconstruct its knowledge tradition in a way that ensures that the best interests of its clients and society are being served. Of course, antifoundationalism means that the field has no way to establish the cognitive authority of any other theoretical perspective or disciplinary orientation as a grounding for its knowledge tradition. Here again, however, the question is not whether any particular theoretical or disciplinary grounding is true or false, but whether the professional practices and discourses that flow from it promote the best interests of special education clients and of society. And, because there is no cognitively certain way to decide on a grounding, the criteria for making such a determination must be based on values (see Chapter 2; below). If special educators are to reconstruct their knowledge tradition in a way that avoids its past and current inadequacies, they must have a method of discourse that is empirical, critical, and pragmatic. I will expand upon what I mean by "empirical" below. At this point, however, I want to consider the reasons why the method of discourse must be critical and pragmatic, cognitively and normatively.

The theoretical discourse on special education is critical because it questions the field's theoretical grounding. However, the problem with the theoretical discourse is that it is foundational. Although it provides the field with an array of optional descriptions of special education and disability, and thus a variety of possible knowledges for grounding the field's practices and guiding its research, each theoretical critique is a version of the wrong theory claim. Implicitly or explicitly, each alternative theoretical perspective argues against special education's traditional theoretical (and disciplinary) grounding in the functionalist paradigm and makes a case for an alternative theoretical grounding in one of the other paradigms of modern social scientific thought (refer to Figure 3.1 and Chapters 4 through 6). Thus, although the theoretical discourse is critical, it is not pragmatic because it does not solve the problem of choosing among the various theories and disciplinary orientations that it puts forth. To be critical and pragmatic, the method of discourse that special educators need in order to reconstruct their knowledge tradition must be critical on two levels. It must be critical with respect to both the *theories* that ground its practices *and* the metatheoretical *paradigms* that ground the theoretical interpretations that are proposed as alternatives. And, of course, to be critical and pragmatic at a metatheoretical level, the method of discourse that special educators need in order to reconstruct their knowledge tradition must be antifoundational.

As we know from Chapter 2, under the antifoundational view of knowledge there are no independent foundational criteria for judging knowledge claims, and thus no cognitively certain way to interpret the social world. From this perspective, the "truth" about the social world is understood in terms of an ongoing conversation, a radically open, normative dialogue among many paradigmatic and theoretical voices (Bernstein, 1983, 1991; Rorty, 1979, 1989). Thus, the problem of foundationalism is a problem of voice, or in Foucault's (1980) terms a problem of uncovering "buried knowledge," the possible knowledges or optional descriptions that have been distorted and hidden from special educators because of their functionalist outlook. But moral philosophers like Dewey (1916/1980, 1927/1988) and Foucault are concerned with more than theoretical knowledge (see Chapter 2). They also want to give a voice to what Foucault (1980) called "disqualified knowledges"; they want to democratize discourse by including the experiential knowledges of clients and professional practitioners, because it is through "these local popular knowledges . . . that criticism performs its work" (p. 82).

The Problem of Disqualified Knowledge

I suggested above that the field of special education can address the problems of naive pragmatism and theoretical incomprehensibility by combining its empirical evidence on the effects of its practices with the critical insights of the theoretical discourse, thus creating an expanded discourse that is both critical and comprehensible to the field. Although such a discourse is necessary for critically reconstructing the special education knowledge tradition, it is insufficient for two reasons. As we have just seen, one reason that combining empirical evidence and theoretical insights is insufficient is that special education's theoretical discourse is foundational and thus not pragmatic. The second reason stems from the inadequacy of empirical knowledge itself.

As a nomothetic method grounded in the functionalist paradigm, empirical research seeks objective truth largely through systematic protocols, standardized instruments, and various forms of quantitative data analysis (see Chapter 2; below). Interpretivist methods, such as ethnography (Erickson, 1973), participant observation (Bogdan & Biklen, 1982), and naturalistic inquiry (Lincoln & Guba, 1985; Skrtic, 1985; Skrtic, Guba, & Knowlton, 1985), generally use emergent protocols, nonstandardized instruments, and various forms of qualitative analysis. They are concerned with intersubjective truth, that is, with the way humans construct meaning as a guide to action in particular social contexts. In the field of education the difference between functionalist and interpretivist methods initially was cast in terms of the type of data favored by each approach, which in the 1970s and early 1980s gave rise to the so-called "quantitative–qualitative debate" (Smith & Heshusius, 1986, p. 4; Firestone, 1990; Howe, 1988). However, the quantitative–qualitative distinction is superficial because, by emphasizing type of data it glosses over the fact that each type of research produces a different type of knowledge. The distinction between functionalist and interpretivist methods is better cast as the difference between empirical knowledge—*etic*, outsider or researcher-driven—and phenomenological knowledge—*emic*, insider or participant-driven (see Lincoln & Guba, 1985). Whereas empiricism conceives of truth as objective knowledge based on a consensus among researchers on the meaning of a data set, interpretivism defines it as intersubjective knowledge based on a consensus among research participants on the meaning of a social context (Skrtic, 1990c).

Although initially the quantitative–qualitative debate asked the foundational question of whether functionalism or interpretivism is the correct grounding for educational inquiry, today the view (at the margins, at least) is that both types of research are essential in educational decision making (see Firestone, 1990; Howe, 1988; Sirotnik & Oakes, 1986; Skrtic, 1990c, 1991a). Nevertheless, the historical dominance of functionalism has meant that, for most of this century, the decision-making process in public education has been dominated by experts, educational researchers at the applied science level of the profession (see Chapter 1). Calls for greater use of interpretivist methodologies began in the 1960s (Bogdan & Biklen, 1986) and have continued with increasing intensity throughout the quantitative–qualitative debate, in both general education (e.g., Lincoln & Guba, 1985; Sirotnik & Oakes, 1986) and special education (e.g., Poplin, 1987; Skrtic, 1985; Stainback & Stainback, 1984a). The perceived value of these methods is that they consider the nature and effects of educational practices from the multiple perspectives of research participants, which include the perspectives of education clients (students, parents, advocates) and educational practitioners, thus giving them a voice in the decision-making process (see below; Chapter 10).[9]

I raise the issue of the inadequacy of a solely empirical approach to educational inquiry to extend my argument that, to be comprehensible to special educators, the expanded discourse for critically reconstructing the special education knowledge tradition must be empirical (as well as critical and pragmatic). At this point I can say that the discourse must be comprehensible to special education professionals at both the applied science and practitioner levels of the field, as well as to special education clients and advocates. As such, to be methodologically and politically viable, the discourse must be based on empirical *and* phenomenological knowledge of the nature and effects of special education practices. Although I will have more to say about the voice of professional practitioners below, I want to conclude the present discussion by noting that including the voice of special education clients in the critical discourse necessarily requires redefining them as "consumers."

Consumer is an economic construct that implies that individuals have the capacity to know best what is good for them. The notion of a client is an artifact of the traditional objectivist view of the professions; it implies that professionals "know better what is good for the client than the client himself" (Schein, 1972, p. 9). The objectivist view has meant that the relationship between professionals and their clients in this century has taken the form of a monologue, the familiar one-way conversation in which professionals diagnose and prescribe and clients simply accept their pronouncements on faith (Bledstein, 1976; Schein, 1972; Chapter 1). By calling this view into question, however, subjectivism and antifoundationalism have given currency to the idea that the traditional professional–client *monologue* should be transformed into a professional–consumer *dialogue*, a more democratic process in which professionals share decision-making power with those who consume their services (Collins, 1979; Freidson, 1988; Schein, 1972; Chapter 10). If the field of special education is to deconstruct and reconstruct its knowledge tradition in a way that avoids its unintentional negative consequences, it must have a method of discourse that is empirical and phenomenological, theoretically critical, and intellectually and morally pragmatic.

PRAGMATISM AS A MODE OF SPECIAL EDUCATION PRACTICE AND DISCOURSE

Critical pragmatism is a method of social analysis grounded in the tradition of philosophical pragmatism, the progressive form of postmodernism (see Chapter 2). As an antifoundational approach to social inquiry, critical pragmatism (hereafter simply pragmatism) seeks edification rather than monological truth; it is a pedagogical process for deconstructing and reconstructing social and institutional practices and discourses by redescribing them in alternative theoretical and metatheoretical languages (Gadamer, 1975; Rorty, 1979, 1991). It is a radically democratic and participatory form of dialogical social inquiry in which all knowledges are accepted or rejected on the basis of their consequences for realizing social values rather than whether they are true in a foundational sense (Bernstein, 1983, 1991; Rorty, 1979, 1989). Whereas the aim of modern social inquiry is to justify social practices and institutions by showing that they are based on a true representation of the social world, pragmatism seeks to change social practices and institutions by reconciling them with traditional democratic ideals (Bernstein, 1971, 1991; Rorty, 1982, 1989).

Although in Chapter 2 I discussed pragmatism as a method of social analysis, it also can be used as a mode of professional practice and discourse, one premised on continually evaluating and reappraising the practical consequences of a profession's knowledge, practices, and discourses by critically assessing them and the assumptions, theories, and metatheories in which they are grounded (see Cherryholmes, 1988; Skrtic, 1991a). If the field of special education is to deconstruct and reconstruct its knowledge tradition in a way that avoids its unintentional negative consequences, it must reconstitute itself as a community of critical inquiry, and I am suggesting that the mode of inquiry should be pragmatism, drawing on the methods of immanent critique, ideal types, deconstruction, and genealogy discussed in Chapter 2 (see also Cherryholmes, 1988; Maxcy, 1991; Skrtic, 1991a, 1991b; Stanley, 1992; Chapter 10).

As a mode of professional practice and discourse, pragmatism entails two ongoing and interrelated critical activities: *critical practice*, or "continual movement between construction of a practice, which justifies why things are designed as they are, and deconstruction of that practice, which shows its incompleteness and contradictions" (Cherryholmes, 1988, pp. 96–97); and *critical discourse*, or "continual movement between the constitution of a methodology designed to [construct and deconstruct practices] and subsequent criticism of that approach" (p. 97). Applied to the profession of special education, pragmatism is a way for special educators to continually evaluate and reappraise the practical consequences of what they do (critical practice), as well as to continually evaluate and reappraise how they carry out such critical appraisals of their practices (critical discourse) (see Skrtic, 1991a). And, of course, the goal is not to justify special education practices and discourses by showing that they are based on a true representation of the world; it is to change them by reconciling them with what special education professionals *and* consumers believe is right.

The value of pragmatism as a mode of special education practice and discourse is that it provides special educators with a way to avoid the delusion that they can know themselves and their practices or the educational and political interests of their consumers except under optional descriptions. And while I am recommending critical pragmatism as a mode of professional discourse in the field of special education, I do so with the understanding that special educators need more than a method of discourse to deconstruct and reconstruct their knowledge tradition. They need adequate conditions of discourse as well, a topic I will return to in Chapters 9 and 10.

NOTES

1. Deconstructing the special education knowledge tradition is complicated by the fact that special education is composed of several subfields organized around categories of exceptionality or disability. Although each subfield has a somewhat unique knowledge tradition that reflects the presumed differences among the traditional categories of exceptionality, behind these surface differences each subfield nevertheless subscribes to a more or less common foundation of professional knowledge. My aim is to deconstruct this common foundation of knowledge, which is what I am referring to as the special education knowledge tradition.

2. Although school psychology plays an important role in public education, particularly in special education student classification, I do not include it in the present analysis. For a separate treatment, see Skrtic (1990b).

3. In Chapter 9 I argue that the assumption that school failure is pathological is, in effect, an explicit presupposition in the discourse of educational administration.

4. The idea that public education in a democracy should be both excellent and equitable is based on the Jeffersonian concept of meritocracy (see Ford, 1904; Greer, 1972; Chapter 10), which I am treating as a minimum requirement. Drawing on the discussion of the place of values in critical pragmatism in Chapter 2 (also see Chapter 9), I provide an expanded view of the requirements for democratic education in Chapter 10. See MacPherson (1974) on various forms of liberal democracy, and Soltis (1993) on the relationship between forms of democracy and approaches to schooling.

5. The inclusion debate began as the "regular education initiative" in the early 1980s and evolved into the inclusion or "full inclusion" movement by the end of the decade (for reviews, see, e.g., Davis, 1989; Fuchs & Fuchs, 1991, 1994; Goetz & Sailor, 1990; Skrtic, 1988b, 1991a; Stainback & Stainback, 1992). A more comprehensive treatment of the debate and the principal inclusive education reform proposals is presented in Chapter 10 (also see Skrtic, 1991a, 1991b, 1995a, 1995b).

6. For additional criticism of the inclusive education model, see, for example, Anderegg and Vergason (1988); Braaten, Kauffman, Braaten, Polsgrove, and Nelson (1988); Bryan, Bay, and Donahue (1988); Bryan, Bay, Lopez-Reyna, and Donahue (1991); Council for Children with Behavioral Disorders (1989); Gerber (1988a, 1988b); Hallahan, Kauffman, Lloyd, and McKinney (1988); Hallahan, Keller, McKinney, Lloyd, and Bryan (1988); Keogh (1988); Lloyd, Crowley, Kohler, and Strain (1988); McKinney and Hocutt (1988); Schumaker & Deshler (1988); Vergason and Anderegg (1989); Walker and Bullis (1991). For a review and critique of the these and other criticisms of inclusion, as well as of the main inclusive education reform proposals, see Skrtic (1991a, 1991b) and Chapter 10.

7. In Chapter 10, we will see that, in their arguments for and against the current system and the inclusion approach, the proponents and opponents of inclusion impli-

cate school organization in the problem of school failure (see also Skrtic, 1991a, 1991b). In this sense, the inclusion debate is less naive than the mainstreaming debate because, by arguing in effect that the problem of school failure lies largely outside the student in the organizational context of schooling, the inclusion debate is an *implicit* critique of special education's grounding assumptions and thus a rejection of the functionalist theories of human pathology and organizational rationality. However, the participants in the debate do not *explicitly* recognize the connection between practices, assumptions, and theories. As a result, neither the reform proposals of the inclusion proponents nor the counterproposals of the opponents resolve the problems that are identified in the debate (see Skrtic, 1987, 1988b, 1991a; Chapters 9 and 10).

8. Although Mercer limited her criticism to the special education disability classification of mental retardation, the same type of criticism has been leveled with respect to the classifications of learning disabilities (Rist & Harrell, 1982; Schrag & Divorky, 1975) and emotional disturbance (Algozzine, 1976, 1977; Apter, 1982; Hobbs, 1975; Rhodes, 1970; Ross, 1980; Swap, 1978), which, together with mental retardation, represent the majority of all students identified as handicapped under the EHA (see Gerber & Levine-Donnerstein, 1989; United States Department of Education, 1988).

9. Operating under interpretivist principles, a number of policy analysts (e.g., Jennings, 1987; Kelly & Maynard-Moody, 1993; Lindblom, 1990), program evaluators (e.g., Guba & Lincoln, 1989; Sirotnik, 1991), and implementation researchers in general education (Gitlin, 1990; Sirotnik & Oakes, 1986) and special education (Skrtic, 1985, 1990c, 1991a; Skrtic, Guba, & Knowlton, 1985) are arguing for a dialogical approach to inquiry premised on enabling "disenfranchised groups to participate in the decision making process" (Gitlin, 1990, p. 446). Nevertheless, the problems of incomprehensibility and foundationalism and the nature of professional induction (see Chapters 2 and 3) raise serious questions about whether interpretivist methodologies alone can fully represent the interests of research participants (see Barone, 1992; Lather, 1991; Chapters 9 and 10).

REFERENCES

Abeson, A., & Zettel, J. (1977). The end of the quiet revolution: The Education for All Handicapped Children Act of 1975. *Exceptional Children, 44*(2), 115–128.

Algozzine, B. (1976). The disturbing child: What you see is what you get? *Alberta Journal of Education Research, 22*, 330–333.

Algozzine, B. (1977). The emotionally disturbed child: Disturbed or disturbing? *Journal of Abnormal Child Psychology, 5*(2), 205–211.

Anderegg, M. L., & Vergason, G. A. (1988). An analysis of one of the cornerstones of the regular education initiative. *Focus on Exceptional Children, 20*(8), 1–7.

Apter, S. J. (1982). *Troubled children, troubled systems*. New York: Pergamon Press.

Ballard-Campbell, M., & Semmel, M. (1981, August). Policy research and special education: Research issues affecting policy formation and implementation. *Exceptional Education Quarterly*, pp. 59–68.

Barone, T. E. (1992). On the demise of subjectivity in educational inquiry. *Curriculum Inquiry, 22*(1), 25–38.

Barnes, B. (1982). *T. S. Kuhn and social science.* New York: Columbia University Press.

Barton, L., & Tomlinson, S. (Eds.). (1984). *Special education and social interests.* London: Croom Helm.

Bernstein, R. J. (1971). *Praxis and action: Contemporary philosophies of human activity.* Philadelphia: University of Pennsylvania Press.

Bernstein, R. J. (1983). *Beyond objectivism and relativism: Science, hermeneutics, and praxis.* Philadelphia: University of Pennsylvania Press.

Bernstein, R. J. (1991). *The new constellation.* Cambridge: Polity Press.

Biklen, D. (1977). Exclusion. In B. Blatt, D. Biklen, & R. Bogdan (Eds.), *An alternative textbook in special education* (pp. 135–151). Denver: Love Publishing.

Biklen, D. (1985). *Achieving the complete school: Strategies for effective mainstreaming.* New York: Columbia University Press.

Blatt, B., & Kaplan, F. (1966). *Christmas in purgatory.* Boston: Allyn & Bacon.

Bledstein, B. J. (1976). *The culture of professionalism: The middle class and the development of higher education in America.* New York: Norton.

Bogdan, R. (1974). *Being different: The autobiography of Jane Fry.* New York: Wiley.

Bogdan, R., & Biklen, S. (1982). *Qualitative research for education: An introduction to theory and methods.* Boston: Allyn & Bacon.

Bogdan, R., & Knoll, J. (1988). The sociology of disability. In E. L. Meyen & T. M. Skrtic (Eds.), *Exceptional children and youth: An introduction* (pp. 449–477). Denver: Love Publishing.

Bogdan, R., & Kugelmass, J. (1984). Case studies of mainstreaming: A symbolic interactionist approach to special schooling. In L. Barton & S. Tomlinson (Eds.), *Special education and social interests* (pp.173–191). London: Croon Helm.

Bowles, S., & Gintis, H. (1976). *Schooling in capitalist America.* New York: Basic Books.

Braaten, S. R., Kauffman, J. M., Braaten, B., Polsgrove, L., & Nelson, C. M. (1988). The regular education initiative: Patent medicine for behavioral disorders. *Exceptional Children, 55*(1), 21-27.

Braginsky, D., & Braginsky, B. (1971). *Hansels and Gretels.* New York: Holt, Rinehart & Winston.

Bryan, T., Bay, M., & Donahue, M. (1988). Implications of the learning disabilities definition for the regular education initiative. *Journal of Learning Disabilities, 21*(1), 23–28.

Bryan, T., Bay, M., Lopez-Reyna, N., & Donahue, M. (1991). Characteristics of students with learning disabilities: The extant database and its implications for educational programs. In J. W. Lloyd, N. N. Singh, & A. C. Repp (Eds.), *The regular education initiative: Alternative perspectives on concepts, issues, and models* (pp. 113–131). Sycamore, IL: Sycamore Publishing.

Burrell, G., & Morgan, G. (1979). *Sociological paradigms and organizational analysis.* London: Heinemann.

Callahan, R. E. (1962). *Education and the cult of efficiency: A study of the social forces that have shaped the administration of public schools*. Chicago: University of Chicago Press.

Carnine, D. (1987). A response to "False standards, a distorting and disintegrating effect on education, turning away from useful purposes, being inevitably unfulfilled, and remaining unrealistic." *Remedial and Special Education, 8*(1), 42–43.

Carrier, J. G. (1983). Masking the social in educational knowledge: The case of learning disability theory. *American Journal of Sociology, 88*(5), 948–974.

Cherryholmes, C. H. (1988). *Power and criticism: Poststructuralist investigations in education*. New York: Teachers College Press.

Churchman, C. W. (1971). *The design of inquiry systems*. New York: Basic Books.

Clark, D. L. (1985). Emerging paradigms in organizational theory and research. In Y. S. Lincoln (Ed.), *Organizational theory and inquiry: The paradigm revolution* (pp. 43–78). Beverly Hills, CA: Sage.

Collins, R. (1979). *The credential society*. New York: Academic Press.

Council for Children with Behavioral Disorders. (1989). Position statement on the regular education initiative. *Behavioral Disorders, 14*(3), 201–208.

Cuban, L. (1989). The "at-risk" label and the problem of urban school reform. *Phi Delta Kappan, 70*(10), 780–784, 799–801.

Davis, F. (1963). *Passage through crisis*. Indianapolis: Bobs-Merrill.

Davis, W. E. (1989). The regular initiative debate: Its promises and problems. *Exceptional Children, 55*(5), 440–446.

Deno, E. (1970). Special education as developmental capital. *Exceptional Children, 37*(3), 229–237.

Dewey, J. (1980). Democracy and education. In J. A. Boydston (Ed.), *John Dewey: The middle works, 1899–1924* (Vol. 9, pp. 1–370). Carbondale: Southern Illinois University Press. (Original work published 1916)

Dewey, J. (1988). The public and its problems. In J. A. Boydston (Ed.), *John Dewey: The later works, 1925–1953* (Vol. 2, pp. 235–372). Carbondale: Southern Illinois University Press. (Original work published 1927)

Dunn, L. M. (1968). Special education for the mildly retarded—Is much of it justifiable? *Exceptional Children, 35*(1), 5–22.

Dunn, L. M. (1973). *Exceptional children in the schools: Special education in transition*. New York: Holt, Rinehart & Winston.

Erickson, F. (1973). What makes school ethnography "ethnographic"? *Council on Anthropology and Education Newsletter, 4*(2), 10–19.

Farber, B. (1968). *Mental retardation: Its social context and social consequences*. Boston: Houghton Mifflin.

Feinberg, W., & Soltis, J. F. (1985). *School and society*. New York: Teachers College Press.

Ferguson, P. M. (1987). The social construction of mental retardation. *Social Policy, 18*(1), 51–56.

Firestone, W. A. (1990). Accommodation: Toward a paradigm-praxis dialectic. In E. G. Guba (Ed.), *The paradigm dialog* (pp. 105–124). Newbury Park, CA: Sage.

Ford, P. L. (Ed.). (1904). *Thomas Jefferson, works*. New York: Knickerbocker Press.

Forness, S. R., & Kavale, K. A. (1987). Holistic inquiry and the scientific challenge in special education: A reply to Iano. *Remedial and Special Education, 8*(1), 47–51.

Foster, W. (1986). *Paradigms and promises: New approaches to educational administration.* Buffalo, NY: Prometheus Books.

Foucault, M. (1976). *Mental illness and psychology.* Berkeley: University of California Press. (Original work published 1954)

Foucault, M. (1980). Two lectures. In M. Foucault, *Power/knowledge: Selected interviews and other writings, 1972–1977* (C. Gordon, Ed. and C. Gordon, L. Marshall, J. Mepham, & K. Soper, Trans.; pp. 78–108). New York: Pantheon Books.

Freidson, E. (1988). *Professional powers: A study of the institutionalization of formal knowledge.* Chicago: University of Chicago Press.

Freire, P. (1970). *Pedagogy of the oppressed* (M. B. Ramos, Trans.). New York: Herder & Herder.

Freire, P. (1973). *Education for critical consciousness.* New York: Continuum.

Fuchs, D., & Fuchs, L. S. (1991). Framing the REI debate: Abolitionists versus conservationists. In J. W. Lloyd, N. N. Singh, & A. C. Repp (Eds.), *The regular education initiative: Alternative perspectives on concepts, issues, and models* (pp. 241–255). Sycamore, IL: Sycamore Publishing.

Fuchs, D., & Fuchs, L. S. (1994). Inclusive schools movement and the radicalization of special education reform. *Exceptional Children, 60*(4), 294–309.

Gadamer, H. G. (1975). *Truth and method* (G. Barden & J. Cumming, Eds. and Trans.). New York: Seabury Press.

Gartner, A., & Lipsky, D. K. (1987). Beyond special education: Toward a quality system for all students. *Harvard Educational Review, 57*(4), 367–390.

Gerber, M. M. (1988a). Tolerance and technology of instruction: Implications for special education reform. *Exceptional Children, 54*(4), 309–314.

Gerber, M. M. (1988b). Weighing the regular education initiative: Recent calls for change lead to slippery slope. *Education Week, 7*(32), 36, 28.

Gerber, M. M., & Levine-Donnerstein, D. (1989). Educating all children: Ten years later. *Exceptional Children, 56*(1), 17–27.

Giddens, A. (1990). *The consequences of modernity.* Cambridge: Polity Press.

Gilhool, T. K. (1989). The right to an effective education: From *Brown* to P.L. 94–142 and beyond. In D. K. Lipsky, & A. Gartner (Eds.), *Beyond separate education: Quality education for all* (pp. 243–253). Baltimore: Paul H. Brookes.

Giroux, H. A. (1981). *Ideology, culture, and the process of schooling.* Philadelphia: Temple University Press.

Giroux, H. A. (1983). Theories of reproduction and resistance in the new sociology of education: A critical analysis. *Harvard Educational Review, 58*(3), 257, 293.

Gitlin, A. D. (1990). Educative research, voice, and school change. *Harvard Educational Review, 60*(4), 443–466.

Glazer, N. (1974). The schools of the minor professions. *Minerva, 12*(3), 346–364.

Goetz, L., & Sailor, W. (1990). Much ado about babies, murky bathwater, and trickle-down politics: A reply to Kauffman. *Journal of Special Education, 24*(3), 334–339.

Goffman, E. (1961). *Asylums: Essays on the social situation of mental patients and other inmates.* Garden City, NY: Doubleday/Anchor Books.

Goffman, F. (1963). *Stigma: Notes on the management of spoiled identity.* Englewood Cliffs, NJ: Prentice Hall.

Gould, S. J. (1981). *The mismeasure of man.* New York: Norton.

Greer, C. (1972). *The great school legend: A revisionist interpretation of American public education.* New York: Basic Books.

Griffiths, D. E. (1983). Evolution in research and theory: A study of prominent researchers. *Educational Administration Quarterly, 19*(3), 201–221.

Griffiths, D. E. (1988). Administrative theory. In N. J. Boyan (Ed.), *Handbook of research on educational administration* (pp. 27–51). New York: Longman.

Guba, E. G., & Lincoln, Y. S. (1989). *Fourth generation evaluation.* Newbury Park, CA: Sage.

Gubrium, J. (1975). *Living and dying at Murray Manor.* New York: St. Martin's Press.

Haber, S. (1964). *Efficiency and uplift: Scientific management in the progressive era, 1890–1920.* Chicago: University of Chicago Press.

Hallahan, D. P., Kauffman, J. M., Lloyd, J. W., & McKinney, J. D. (1988). Introduction to the series: Questions about the regular education initiative. *Journal of Learning Disabilities, 21*(1), 3–5.

Hallahan, D. P., Keller, C. E., McKinney, J. D., Lloyd, J. W., & Bryan, T. (1988). Examining the research base of the regular education initiative: Efficacy studies and the adaptive learning environments model. *Journal of Learning Disabilities, 21*(1), 29–35, 55.

Haring, N. G. (1978). *Behavior of exceptional children: An introduction to special education.* Columbus, OH: Merrill.

Harré, R. (1981). The positivist-empiricist approach and its alternative. In P. Reason & J. Rowan (Eds.), *Human inquiry: A sourcebook of new paradigm research* (pp. 3–17). New York: John Wiley.

Heller, K., Holtzman, W., & Messick, S. (1982). *Placing children in special education: A strategy for equity.* Washington, DC: National Academy of Sciences Press.

Heshusius, L. (1982). At the heart of the advocacy dilemma: A mechanistic world view. *Exceptional Children, 49*(1), 6–13.

Heshusius, L. (1986). Paradigm shifts and special education: A response to Ulman and Rosenberg. *Exceptional Children, 52*(5), 461–465.

Hesse, M. (1980). *Revolutions and reconstructions in the philosophy of science.* Bloomington: Indiana University Press.

Hobbs, N. (1975). *The futures of children: Categories, labels, and their consequences.* San Francisco: Jossey-Bass.

House, E. R. (1979). Technology versus craft: A ten year perspective on innovation. *Journal of Curriculum Studies, 11*(1), 1–15.

Howe, K. R. (1988). Against the quantitative–qualitative incompatibility thesis, or dogmas die hard. *Educational Researcher, 17*(8), 10–16.

Iano, R. P. (1986). The study and development of teaching: With implications for the advancement of special education. *Remedial and Special Education, 7*(5), 50–61.

Iano, R. P. (1987). Rebuttal: Neither the absolute certainty of prescriptive law nor a surrender to mysticism. *Remedial and Special Education, 8*(1), 51–56.

Janesick, V. J. (1988). Our multicultural society. In E. L. Meyen & T. M. Skrtic (Eds.), *Exceptional children and youth: An introduction* (pp. 519–535). Denver: Love Publishing.

Jennings, B. (1987). Interpretation and the practice of policy analysis. In F. Fisher & J. Forester (Eds.), *Confronting values in policy analysis: The politics of criteria* (pp. 128–152). Newbury Park, CA: Sage.

Johnson, G. O. (1962). Special education for the mentally handicapped–A paradox. *Exceptional Children, 29*(2), 62–69.

Kauffman, J. M. (1988). Revolution can also mean returning to the starting point: Will school psychology help special education complete the circuit? *School Psychology Review, 17*, 490–494.

Kauffman, J. M. (1989). The regular education initiative as Reagan–Bush education policy: A trickle-down theory of education of the hard-to-teach. *Journal of Special Education, 23*(3), 256–278.

Kauffman, J. M. (1991). Restructuring in sociopolitical context: Reservations about the effects of current reform proposals on students with disabilities. In J. W. Lloyd, N. N. Singh, & A. C. Repp (Eds.), *The regular education initiative: Alternative perspectives on concepts, issues, and models* (pp. 57–66). Sycamore, IL: Sycamore Publishing.

Kauffman, J. M., Gerber, M. M., & Semmel, M. I. (1988). Arguable assumptions underlying the regular education initiative. *Journal of Learning Disabilities, 21*(1), 6–11.

Kavale, K. A., & Forness, S. R. (1987). History, politics, and the general education initiative: Sleeter's reinterpretation of learning disabilities as a case study. *Remedial and Special Education, 8*(5), 6–12.

Kelly, M., & Maynard-Moody, S. (1993). Policy analysis in the post-positivist era: Engaging stakeholders in evaluating the Economic Development Districts program. *Public Administration Review, 53*(2), 135–142.

Keogh, B. K. (1988). Improving services for problem learners: Rethinking and restructuring. *Journal of Learning Disabilities, 21*(1), 19–22.

Keogh, B. K., & Levitt, M. L. (1976). Special education in the mainstream: A confrontation of limitations? *Focus on Exceptional Children, 8*(1), 1–11.

Kuhn, T. S. (1970). *The structure of scientific revolutions* (2nd ed.). Chicago: University of Chicago Press.

Lather, P. (1991). Deconstructing/deconstructive inquiry: The politics of knowing and being known. *Educational Theory, 41*(2), 153–173.

Lazerson, M. (1983). The origins of special education. In J. G. Chambers & W. T. Hartman (Eds.), *Special education policies: Their history, implementation, and finance* (pp. 15–47). Philadelphia: Temple University Press.

Lemert, E. (1967). *Human deviance, social problems, and social control.* Englewood Cliffs, NJ: Prentice-Hall.

Lincoln, Y. S., & Guba, E. G. (1985). *Naturalistic inquiry.* Beverly Hills, CA: Sage.

Lindblom, C. E. (1990). *Inquiry and change: The troubled attempt to understand and shape society.* New Haven: Yale University Press.

Lipsky, D. K., & Gartner, A. (1987). Capable of achievement and worthy of respect: Education for handicapped students as if they were full-fledged human beings. *Exceptional Children, 54*(1), 69–74.

Lipsky, D. K., & Gartner, A. (Eds.). (1989). *Beyond separate education: Quality education for all.* Baltimore: Paul H. Brookes.

Lloyd, J. W. (1987). The art and science of research on teaching. *Remedial and Special Education, 8*(1), 44–46.

Lloyd, J. W., Crowley, E. P., Kohler, F. W., & Strain, P. S. (1988). Redefining the applied research agenda: Cooperative learning, prereferral, teacher consultation, and peer-mediated interventions. *Journal of Learning Disabilities, 21*(1), 43–52.

MacMillan, D. L., & Semmel, M. I. (1977). Evaluation of mainstreaming programs. *Focus on Exceptional Children, 9*(4), 1–14.

MacPherson, C. B. (1974). *The life and times of liberal democracy.* Oxford: Oxford University Press.

Martin, D. T., Overholt, G. E., & Urban, W. J. (1976). *Accountability in American education: A critique.* Princeton, NJ: Princeton Book Company.

Maxcy, S. J. (1991). *Educational leadership: A critical pragmatic perspective.* New York: Bergin & Garvey.

McKinney, J. D., & Hocutt, A. M. (1988). The need for policy analysis in evaluating the regular education initiative. *Journal of Learning Disabilities, 21*(1), 12–18.

McNeil, L. M. (1986). *Contradictions of control: School structure and school knowledge.* New York: Methuen/Routledge & Kegan Paul.

Mercer, J. (1973). *Labeling the mentally retarded: Clinical and social system perspectives on mental retardation.* Berkeley: University of California Press.

Meyer, J. W., & Rowan, B. (1978). The structure of educational organizations. In M. W. Meyer (Ed.), *Environments and organizations* (pp. 78–109). San Francisco: Jossey-Bass.

Mintzberg, H. (1979). *The structuring of organizations.* Englewood Cliffs, NJ: Prentice-Hall.

Mitroff, I. I., & Pondy, L. R. (1974). On the organization of inquiry: A comparison of some radically different approaches to policy analysis. *Public Administration Review, 34*(5), 471–479.

Oakes, J. (1985). *Keeping track: How schools structure inequality.* New Haven, CT: Yale University Press.

Poplin, M. S. (1984). Toward an holistic view of persons with learning disabilities. *Learning Disabilities Quarterly, 7*(4), 290–294.

Poplin, M. S. (1987). Self-imposed blindness: The scientific method in education. *Remedial and Special Education, 8*(6), 31–37.

Popper, K. R. (1959). *The logic of scientific discovery.* New York: Harper & Row.

Pugach, M., & Lilly, M. S. (1984). Reconceptualizing support services for classroom teachers: Implications for teacher education. *Journal of Teacher Education, 35*(5), 48–55.

Resnick, L. B., & Klopfer, L. E. (1989). *Toward the thinking curriculum: Current cognitive research.* Alexandria, VA: Association for Supervision and Curriculum Development.

Reynolds, M. C. (1962). A framework for considering some issues in special education. *Exceptional Children, 28*(5), 367–370.

Reynolds, M. C., & Wang, M. C. (1983). Restructuring "special" school programs: A position paper. *Policy Studies Review, 2*(1), 189–212.

Rhodes, W. C. (1970). A community participation analysis of emotional disturbance. *Exceptional Children, 36*(5), 309–314.

Rist, R., & Harrell, J. (1982). Labeling and the learning disabled child: The social ecology of educational practice. *American Journal of Orthopsychiatry, 52*(1), 146–160.

Ritzer, G. (1980). *Sociology: A multiple paradigm science.* Boston: Allyn & Bacon.

Rorty, R. (1979). *Philosophy and the mirror of nature.* Princeton, NJ: Princeton University Press.

Rorty, R. (1982). *Consequences of pragmatism.* Minneapolis: University of Minnesota Press.

Rorty, R. (1989). *Contingency, irony, and solidarity.* New York: Cambridge University Press.

Rorty, R. (1991). *Objectivity, relativism, and truth: Philosophical papers, volume 1.* Cambridge: Cambridge University Press.

Ross, A. O. (1980). *Psychological disorders of children* (2nd ed.). New York: McGraw-Hill.

Salvia, J., & Ysseldyke, J. E. (1981). *Assessment in special and remedial education.* Boston: Houghton Mifflin.

Sarason, S. B., & Doris, J. (1979). *Educational handicap, public policy, and social history.* New York: Free Press.

Scheff, T. J. (1966). *Being mentally ill: A sociological theory.* Chicago: Aldine.

Schein, E. H. (1972). *Professional education.* New York: McGraw-Hill.

Schön, D. A. (1983). *The reflective practitioner: How professionals think in action.* New York: Basic Books.

Schrag, P., & Divorky, D. (1975). *The myth of the hyperactive child.* New York: Pantheon Books.

Schumaker, J. B., & Deshler, D. D. (1988). Implementing the regular education initiative in secondary schools: A different ball game. *Journal of Learning Disabilities, 21*(1), 36–42.

Scott, R. (1969). *The making of blind men.* New York: Russell Sage Foundation.

Sigmon, S. B. (1987). *Radical analysis of special education: Focus on historical development and learning disabilities.* London: Falmer Press.

Simpson, R. G., & Eaves, R. C. (1985). Do we need more qualitative research or more good research? A reaction to Stainback and Stainback. *Exceptional Children, 51*(4), 325–329.

Sirotnik, K. A. (1991). Critical inquiry: A paradigm for praxis. In E. C. Short (Ed.), *Forms of curriculum inquiry* (pp. 243–258). New York: State University of New York Press.

Sirotnik, K. A., & Oakes, J. (Eds.). (1986). *Critical perspectives on the organization and improvement of schooling.* Boston: Kluwer-Nijhoff Publishing.

Skinner, B. F. (1953). *Science and human behavior.* New York: Free Press.

Skinner, B. F. (1957). *Verbal behavior.* New York: Appleton-Century-Crofts.

Skinner, B. F. (1971). *Beyond freedom and dignity*. New York: Knopf.

Skrtic, T. M. (1985). Doing naturalistic research into educational organizations. In Y. S. Lincoln (Ed.), *Organizational theory and inquiry: The paradigm revolution* (pp. 185–220). Beverly Hills, CA: Sage.

Skrtic, T. M. (1986). The crisis in special education knowledge: A perspective on perspective. *Focus on Exceptional Children, 18*(7), 1–16.

Skrtic, T. M. (1987). An organizational analysis of special education reform. *Counterpoint, 8*(2), 15–19.

Skrtic, T. M. (1988a). The crisis in special education knowledge. In E. L. Meyen & T. M. Skrtic (Eds.), *Exceptional children and youth: An introduction* (pp. 415–447). Denver: Love Publishing.

Skrtic, T. M. (1988b). The organizational context of special education. In E. L. Meyen & T. M. Skrtic (Eds.), *Exceptional children and youth: An introduction* (pp. 479–517). Denver: Love Publishing.

Skrtic, T. M. (1990a). Counter-hegemony: A radical's attempt to demystify special education ideology. [Review of *Radical analysis of special education: Focus on historical developments and learning disabilities*, by S. Sigmon]. *Contemporary Psychology, 35*(1), 54–55.

Skrtic, T. M. (1990b, August). School psychology and the revolution in modern knowledge. Paper presented at the annual meeting of the American Psychology Association, Boston.

Skrtic, T. M. (1990c). Social accommodation: Toward a dialogical discourse in educational inquiry. In E. G. Guba (Ed.), *The paradigm dialog* (pp. 125–135). Newbury Park, CA: Sage.

Skrtic, T. M. (1991a). *Behind special education: A critical analysis of professional culture and school organization*. Denver: Love Publishing.

Skrtic, T. M. (1991b). The special education paradox: Equity as the way to excellence. *Harvard Educational Review, 61*(2), 148–206.

Skrtic, T. M. (1995a). The organizational context of special education and school reform. In E. L. Meyen & T. M. Skrtic (Eds.), *Special education and student disability: Traditional, emerging, and alternative perspectives* (pp. 729–791). Denver: Love Publishing.

Skrtic, T. M. (1995b). The special education knowledge tradition: Crisis and opportunity. In E. L. Meyen & T. M. Skrtic (Eds.), *Special education and student disability: Traditional, emerging, and alternative perspectives* (pp. 609–672). Denver: Love Publishing.

Skrtic, T. M., Guba, E. G., & Knowlton, H. E. (1985). *Interorganizational special education programming in rural areas: Technical report on the multisite naturalistic field study*. Washington: National Institute of Education.

Sleeter, C. E. (1986). Learning disabilities: The social construction of a special education category. *Exceptional Children, 53*(1), 46–54.

Smith, D. J. (1985). *Minds made feeble: The myth and legacy of the Kallikaks*. Rockville, MD: Aspen.

Smith, J. K., & Heshusius, L. (1986). Closing down the conversation: The end of the quantitative–qualitative debate among educational inquirers. *Educational Researcher, 15*(1), 4–12.

Soltis, J. F. (1993). Democracy and teaching. *Journal of Philosophy of Education, 27*(2), 149–158.

Spring, J. (1980). *Educating the worker-citizen: The social, economic, and political foundations of education*. New York: Longman.

Stainback, S., & Stainback, W. (1984a). Broadening the research perspective in special education. *Exceptional Children, 50*(5), 400–409.

Stainback, S., & Stainback, W. (1984b). A rationale for the merger of special and regular education. *Exceptional Children, 51*(2), 102–111.

Stainback, S., & Stainback, W. (1992). Schools as inclusive communities. In W. Stainback & S. Stainback (Eds.), *Controversial issues confronting special education: Divergent perspectives* (pp. 29–44). Baltimore: Paul H. Brookes.

Stainback, S., Stainback, W., & Forest, M. (1989). *Educating all students in the mainstreaming of regular education*. Baltimore: Paul H. Brookes.

Stanley, W. B. (1992). *Curriculum for utopia: Social reconstructionism and critical pedagogy in the postmodern era*. Albany: State University of New York Press.

Swap, S. (1978). The ecological model of emotional disturbance in children: A status report and proposed synthesis. *Behavioral Disorders, 3*(3), 156–186.

Szasz, T. S. (1961). *The myth of mental illness*. New York: Hoeber-Harper.

Taylor, C. (1977). *Hegel*. New York: Cambridge University Press.

Taylor, S., & Bogdan, R. (1977). A phenomenological approach to "mental retardation." In B. Blatt, D. Biklen, & R. Bogdan (Eds.), *An alternative textbook in special education* (pp. 193–203). Denver: Love Publishing.

Tomlinson, S. (1982). *A sociology of special education*. London: Routledge & Kegan Paul.

Tomlinson, S. (1988). Why Johnny can't read: Critical theory and special education. *European Journal of Special Needs Education, 3*(1), 45–58.

Turnbull, H. R. (1986). *Free appropriate public education: The law and children with disabilities*. Denver: Love Publishing.

Turnbull, H. R. (1993). *Free appropriate public education: The law and children with disabilities*. Denver: Love Publishing.

Turnbull, H. R., & Turnbull, A. P. (1978). *Free appropriate public education: Law and implementation*. Denver: Love Publishing.

Ulman, J. D., & Rosenberg, M. S. (1986). Science and superstition in special education. *Exceptional Children, 52*(5), 459–460.

United States Department of Education, Office of Special Education and Rehabilitative Services. (1988). *Annual report to Congress on the implementation of the Education for All Handicapped Children Act*. Washington, DC: Author.

Vergason, G. A., & Anderegg, M. L. (1989). Save the baby! A response to integrating the children of the second system. *Phi Delta Kappan, 71*(1), 61–63.

Walker, H. M., & Bullis, M. (1991). Behavior disorders and the social context of regular class integration: A conceptual dilemma? In J. W. Lloyd, N. N. Singh, & A. C. Repp (Eds.), *The regular education initiative: Alternative perspectives on concepts, issues, and models* (pp. 75–93). Sycamore, IL: Sycamore Publishing.

Wang, M. C., Reynolds, M. C., & Walberg, H. J. (1986). Rethinking special education. *Educational Leadership, 44*(1), 26–31.

Wang, M. C., Reynolds, M. C., & Walberg, H. J. (Eds.). (1987). *Handbook of special education: Research and practice, Vol. 1. Learner characteristics and adaptive education.* Oxford: Pergamon Press.

White, O. R., & Haring, N. G. (1976). *Exceptional teaching: A multimedia training package.* Columbus, OH: Merrill.

Will, M. C. (1984). Let us pause and reflect—But not too long. *Exceptional Children, 51*(1), 11–16.

Will, M. C. (1986). Educating children with learning problems: A shared responsibility. *Exceptional Children, 52*(5), 411–416.

Wise, A. E. (1979). *Legislated learning: The bureaucratization of the American classroom.* Berkeley: University of California Press.

Wise, A. E. (1988). The two conflicting trends in school reform: Legislated learning revisited. *Phi Delta Kappan, 69*(5), 328–333.

Wiseman, J. (1970). *Stations of the lost.* Englewood Cliffs, NJ: Prentice Hall.

Wolcott, H. F. (1977). *Teachers versus technocrats: An educational innovation in anthropological perspective.* Eugene, OR: Center for Educational Policy and Management.

CHAPTER 4

The Interpretivist View of Special Education and Disability:
The Value of Telling Stories

Philip M. Ferguson and Dianne L. Ferguson

Let us begin with a story. We have a 22-year-old son named Ian. In a lot of ways Ian is a typical young adult: he has (in our humble opinion) terrible taste in music, which of course he likes to demonstrate at a volume that shakes the walls along with our composure. He goes through tubs of industrial-strength Clearasil, fighting a never ending battle against acne. He has a winning smile that he knows exactly how to use to get what he wants from his parents. As it happens, he is also labeled as severely retarded with spastic quadriplegia and a vision impairment. He does not walk, and what little language he does have is often hard to understand. But lists of attributes and labels, no matter how long, do not completely describe Ian for us. Neither can only one story, but it is a place to start.

Several years ago, we went to see the movie "Rainman" and took Ian with us. It happened to be January 1, New Year's Day, when we went. Now, one of the skills Ian has is to keep track of the date with incredible reliability. For the current month or the one immediately following, you can ask him what day of the week a certain date will fall on and Ian will tell you with amazing quickness and accuracy. However, he cannot handle the year change without some help. So we spent a lot of that New Year's Day doing a drill with Ian about it being 1989, not 1988. Of course, we overdid it and pretty quickly Ian was muttering at every chance: "It's 1989, January 1st, 1989." So, anyway, we went to see "Rainman" that night. Those of you who have seen the movie may remember how one of the things Dustin Hoffman's character keeps doing whenever anyone asks about his mother is to repeat a line that began something like: "Yes, my mother died on October 10, 1956. It was a dark and rainy day . . . " Well, the first time Hoffman said it in the movie, we could feel Ian jerk up in his wheelchair. We knew what was coming but were powerless to stop it. He looked at us with that winning smile and then informed everyone in our general vicinity: "It's *1989*; it's *1989*, January 1, *1989*." For the rest of the movie, every time Dustin did his routine, Ian pitched in with his correction. For Ian, this was clearly the best part of the movie. He probably thought it was some clever test we had arranged to see if he had, in fact, learned the year change that we had worked on all day. Everyone else probably wondered if Dustin Hoffman was making a guest appearance in the theater. We kept wanting to stand up and explain to everyone what was going on.

That is an example of one type of story. If we told you more, and told them well, you would gradually come to form your own image of who Ian is, and who we are as well. For us, the story says something about what it means to live with Ian, what he teaches us, and all sorts of other things. When people ask us what it is like to live with a son who is severely retarded, we might just tell them that story. It is just as likely, if people asked us what it meant to be an interpretivist, that we also might respond with a story. Indeed, the interpretivist paradigm is basically about letting people tell their stories.

Over the past several years of trying to teach alternative research methods to graduate students in special education, we have tried many approaches and techniques to wean the students from their comfortable but restrictive reliance on the functionalist worldview described in Chapter 3. Increasingly we have come to believe that for most of these students, the best way for them to gain a quick appreciation of the interpretivist paradigm as a valid approach to the study of social reality is to convince them of the value of telling stories. There is an important distinction here, however. It is not just the stories whose value the students must appreciate; the *telling* of the story is equally important. For it is only in "the telling" that both a speaker and a listener become implicit collaborators in giving meaning to that which is told. That is where interpretation comes in. We tell our stories to interpret our lives for other people. Upon hearing them, other people interpret our interpretations. All individuals, all families, have their own particular stories. However, it is our telling of our own stories that best reveals how we really make sense of our world: which stories we choose to tell about life with Ian, which remain private; what words we use, what labels we endorse; who is in the audience to interpret our choices.

One way to characterize the research methodology associated with the interpretivist paradigm is simply as the systematic collection and analysis of the stories people tell about how they interpret reality. Functionalists—at least when they are acting as functionalists—tend not to like stories. For one thing, the metaphor comes from the humanities, not the hard sciences. More generally, however, the problem for functionalists is that stories have too much particularity about them. They do not control variables very well.

Stories are slippery and individualistic, subjective and judgmental. And all of that is precisely why the interpretivists favor stories. The poet Yeats once said that he "liked a little seaweed" in his definition of water. Letting people tell their own stories, in their own voice, in their own words, is how interpretivist social science tries to keep the seaweed in our understanding of reality.

LOCATING INTERPRETIVISM

The notion of telling stories gains us an entree into the interpretivist paradigm. It is important not to stop there. The power of stories needs to be firmly grounded in a more explicit discussion of the theoretical assumptions of interpretivism. The specific implications of the paradigm for special education and the experience of disability need to be outlined. The remainder of our discussion on interpretivism then will proceed as follows. First, after a brief reminder of interpretivism's location within the metatheoretical matrix laid out by Skrtic in Chapter 2 and elsewhere (Skrtic, 1986, 1991), we will establish a bit of the philosophical heritage of the interpretivist worldview. We then will run quickly through an all too sketchy review of some of the key tenets of interpretivism and contrast them with the functionalist paradigm. We then will shift the discussion more directly to the implications of interpretivism for the understanding of disability and special education. Finally, we will offer some concluding thoughts about the value of interpretivism as a guiding framework for the pursuit of social justice for people with disabilities and their families.

Subjectivism

Certainly, in terms of the general philosophy of science dimension that Skrtic has extended from the work of Burrell and Morgan (1979), interpretivism would fall on the subjectivist side of things. However, it is important to recognize that this metatheoretical categorization of interpretivism is made from outside the assumptions of the paradigm itself. That is, viewing interpretivism's approach to such basic components of a philosophy of science as ontology, epistemology, human agency, and methodology as essentially subjectivist is useful mainly in distinguishing it from the basic approach to the same issues adopted by both functionalism and structuralism. If one wants to summarize a functionalist philosophy of science as objectivist, then one also might summarize interpretivism's philosophy of science as subjectivist or relativist. However, we will argue along the line taken by several interpretivists (Eisner, 1991; Patton, 1990) that if one moves from external comparison of separate paradigms to an internal examination and understanding of interpretivism on its own terms, then the label of subjectivism can be intellectually misleading.[1]

Microscopic Social Analysis

A similar caution must apply to the description of interpretivism along the other dimension of social theory. Along this dimension, interpretivism's phenomenological emphasis on individual perspective and experience would clearly identify it as having a "micro" focus. Again, such a categorization may be useful by way of contrasting interpretivism with the "macro" analyses of structuralists or humanists. Indeed, it also may reveal unnoticed commonalities between interpretivism's emphasis on descriptive detail and functionalism's clinical analysis. However, from within the paradigm itself, the focus on the individual perspective is not so much a choice among options as an ineluctable reliance on individual human beings as the ultimate source of organization and change in any social setting. From the interpretivist perspective, individuals are not "cultural dopes" passively pushed along by social structures and collective determinism.

Interpretivism emphasizes description rather than intervention, and in that sense might be said to emphasize order over conflict; the status quo over change.[2] However, description itself can be reformative if it gives voice to those not usually asked to describe anything. Complete description challenges power, because an important part of being powerful is the ability to limit description, to define the terms, to set the agenda. In its emphasis on complete description of individual cases, interpretivism eventually challenges inequity by legitimating the perspective of those on the bottom of society as well as those on the top. We will return to this theme at the end of our remarks.

Some Tenets of Interpretivism

Let us try to move now to a more internal discussion of interpretivism. What is life like if one tries to approach it from inside the assumptions of this paradigm? Before trying to make that shift, however, we must enter some careful caveats about our exposition. First, it will be too short. Limitations of space will require us to capsulize philosophical arguments that others, smarter than we, have spent lifetimes considering. Our goal is to entice more than to explain.

A second caveat is even more important to note. Interpretivism is not monolithic. There are many versions, many variations. Proponents of this general worldview cannot even agree on what to call the paradigm. Naturalism, conventionalism, constructionism, holism, are all names that other scholars prefer for positions that resemble what we are here calling interpretivism. In terms of methodology associated with this paradigm, the labels can be even more confusing. Qualitative research, ethnography, ethnomethodology, naturalistic inquiry, hermeneutics, are all terms for different ways of gathering and analyzing information about the world that have evolved within the interpretivist paradigm, or at least within the more broadly framed subjectivist tradition. Adherents of one or another of these schools of thought would probably present the paradigm differently than we do (see Chapter 8). That diversity betokens a resistance to standardization that is itself one of the hallmarks of interpretivist thinking. It also makes it more difficult to describe.

Philosophical Heritage of Interpretivism

The diversity within interpretivism reflects the richness of the philosophical traditions upon which it draws. Certainly, important elements of American pragmatism can be found in certain components of interpretivism, especially within the branch of interpretivism known as symbolic interactionism and associated with the work of George Herbert Mead (1934). This is suggestive for those of us in education, of course, because it immediately connects interpretivism with Dewey's influential approach to the purpose of schooling in a democratic society. Two other important philosophical traditions for interpretivistic social science may be less familiar to scholars and practitioners in the field of education generally, and in special education in particular. These are phenomenology and (for lack of a better term) Wittgensteinian relativism. Let us say a few words about these two intellectual sources to try to establish a general orientation to the world that interpretivism assumes.

Many interpretivists, especially those who uphold versions of interpretivism such as ethnomethodology (Garfinkel, 1967; Heritage, 1987) or phenomenography (Marton, 1988), characterize themselves as broadly affiliated with something called phenomenology. You often might hear such interpretivists refer to themselves and their research methods as taking a "phenomenological approach" to a particular topic or issue. Most often associated with the writings of the early-twentieth-century philosopher Edmund Husserl (1931/ 1969, 1954/1970), phenomenology has been taken in many different directions by subsequent interpreters. One of the major influences on interpretivist social science is the evolution of the phenomenological perspective developed by Alfred Schutz (1962; Heritage, 1987). There is much to be said about this association between interpretivism and phenomenology, and we can give only the barest of outlines here.

A phenomenological approach to a particular topic or issue implies a basic attention—not to things themselves, out there, in the objective world—but to things *as experienced*, as perceived, as intended, by individuals. As summarized in one textbook on qualitative research:

> The phenomenologist views human behavior, what people say and do, as a product of how people define their world. The task of the phenomenologist and, for us, the qualitative methodologist, is to capture this process of interpretation. . . . The phenomenologist attempts to see things from other people's point of view. (Taylor & Bogdan, 1984, pp. 8–9)

A classic example of phenomenology from the study of religion may suffice to explain the difference this can make. Rudolf Otto was one of the first theologians to apply the principles of phenomenology to the study of religion. The result was that, unlike traditional theologians, Otto did not write a book about the nature of God, or the evidence for God's existence, but a study of the phenomenon of divinity. The English translation of his book was titled *The Idea of the Holy* (Otto, 1923/1958) but more aptly might have been called, "The *Experience* of the Holy." Phenomenology led Otto to ask a different question, one thought to be more answerable than some definitive statement about reality and God's place in it. Instead, Otto presented an account of how people in widely different contexts experienced something they interpreted as divine, holy, supreme. The reality behind those experiences was "bracketed," if you will, or neither endorsed nor challenged by the investigator. One does not begin with a search for God, but a search for God's believers. If Otto had been in special education instead of theology, one can surmise that his book might have been about "the experience of disability" rather than "the nature of mental retardation."

There are similarities between the phenomenological approach to reality and that associated with a type of Anglo-American philosophy broadly labeled linguistic analysis. Instead of continuing to ask questions directly about ontology and metaphysics in the tradition of Western philosophy since the Presocratics, linguistic philosophers in the first half of the twentieth century (and most notably in England) advocated a shift in focus to the study of how we use language to talk about such things in the first place. Thus, to continue the theological theme, linguistic approaches would change the question from the traditional one of "Does God exist?" to the different question of "What does it mean for someone to say 'God does exist'?" Instead of asking about the reality, the point of philosophy was to understand how people spoke about reality.

Now, perhaps even more than phenomenology, linguistic analysis has taken some divergent (even oppositional) paths. In the final analysis, however, the philosophical path associated with Ludwig Wittgenstein strikes us as the most useful for understanding interpretivism. Wittgenstein was a strange figure in recent philosophy. He was born in Vienna; wrote in German; taught at Cambridge; published only one book in his lifetime, which is considered perhaps the definitive statement of logical positivism (Wittgenstein, 1921/

1961); and then spent the rest of his life refuting that defense. His most influential book, *Philosophical Investigations* (1958b), is a posthumously published analysis of how all of us interpret reality according to the various "language games" we all play, and the "forms of life" in which we share those games (Wittgenstein, 1958a).

Wittgenstein used to ask his students a question: What is left if I subtract the fact of my arm going up from the act of my raising my hand? The answer, of course, is that everything remains that makes the act meaningful. The mere physical movement has no purpose, no intention, no meaning without my agency. It is only as an individual's act within the context of an interaction that hand raising becomes an interpretable – that is, a perceivable – event. At one of his Cambridge lectures, Wittgenstein summarized his argument with a phrase that is perhaps the closest to a one-sentence slogan for his approach to philosophical questions: "Don't ask for the meaning, ask for the use" (cited in Wisdom, 1965, p. 87). That is, don't ask for the essence, don't ask for the controlled study; ask for the context, the interpretation, the example, the case. The point is similar to that made by the phenomenologists. It is not that the physical event or object is not "real," but simply that we can never approach it outside of some particular perspective, a language game with certain rules rather than others. True insight comes with the recognition that there is no such thing as a bare fact; facts always come clothed in the wardrobe of social assumptions.

One can see the connection with American pragmatism, in this emphasis on the individual case, as well. Long before Wittgenstein's plea for a focus on practice, William James said that the study of religion and religious experience required an impatience with abstractions that obscured the example and thus clouded understanding. James warned of the dangers of the "precise definition." Using government as an example he made an argument that any interpretivist would endorse.

> The man [sic] who knows governments most completely is one who troubles himself least about a definition which shall give their essence. Enjoying an intimate acquaintance with all their particularities in turn, he would regard an abstract conception in which these were unified as a thing more misleading than enlightening. (James, 1902/1958, p. 39)

Four Tenets of Interpretivism

Whether one relies on Husserl, Wittgenstein, or James for the intellectual grounding of interpretivism, certain central tenets of the paradigm can be outlined. In keeping with our discussion, however, we hasten to add that these cannot be taken as the "essence" or "nature" of some abstract thing called interpretivism. Just as interpretivists encourage researchers to turn to the examples, the instances, of whatever they are studying so that it may be understood in terms of people's actual experience, so must we encourage readers who wish to understand interpretivism to turn to examples of people actually doing it.

We will review four tenets or themes often found in examples of interpretivist inquiry. Regard them as "family resemblances" rather than essential components. These are ways one might recognize two or more interpretivists as related to each other. While the individual features overlap, some distant cousins might look very different from each other. Some of these have already been mentioned in passing, and none of them can be fully explored here.

Reality Is Constructed and Intentional. This is simply the point of Wittgenstein's question that we just described. Another way of putting the same point is that reality is always a process of social construction. People act in response to the "meanings" of a situation to them. However, those meanings are not inherent in the object or event. Meanings are socially constructed. The value of telling stories is that this is how one discovers what the social constructions are. Indeed, what we mean by the term "story" is simply one person's, or one group's, social construction of "what happened."

In most cases, one of two situations holds with regard to social construction. First, everyone often agrees so completely on a particular social construction that no one notices any longer that it is, in fact, a construction and not the actual thing or event. An example might be the accepted greeting behavior of smiling and waving my hand as someone approaches. Only when this behavior is interpreted as something other than a friendly hello am I reminded that "meaning it" as a greeting is a construction of my intentions, not an objective feature of my physical movements. The second situation is where one person's or group's particular social construction of an event or object holds sway over other people's constructions. In this situation there is not so much a consensus of interpretation as there is a dominance of one over others. Think of what it "meant" to be "female," say, 20 years ago. There was a dominant social construction of what was and was not feminine or female, but this does not mean that there were not always many women who had very different interpretations, different social constructions. It was just that no one ever asked them to tell their stories.

Splitting Subject and Object Is Impossible. Once within the assumptions of the interpretivist paradigm it becomes misleading to think of it as subjectivist. At the heart of the interpretivist paradigm is a fundamental challenge to the subjective–objective or mental–physical dualism embedded in Western culture at least since the time of Descartes. If everything is unavoidably subjective, then the dichotomy itself becomes misleading. Indeed, such a dichotomy between subject and object, knower and known, is itself a construction of the functionalist paradigm, which is then forced upon the other paradigms as a way of defining themselves in words the functionalists will understand. The preferable way would be for functionalists to learn another language game, one in which objectivity literally made no sense. In the interpretivist paradigm, to speak of choosing subjectivity is analogous to a fish discussing its choice of water over land.

Splitting Fact and Value Is Impossible. This is the ethical corollary of the epistemological tenet about subjectivism and objectivism. Not only are facts the products of social constructions; their production never occurs in a moral vacuum. Many physical scientists recognize this better than social scientists. Regardless of whether they choose to do so, few physicists today would argue that working on the "Starwars" project (or the Strategic Defense Initiative) is a morally neutral action. Logical positivism holds that "you can't imply ought from is." Objective reality, in other words, has no inherent ethical implications. No accumulation of factual premises will ever justify a moral conclusion. Insofar as science is about the accumulation of facts, then morality has no place in the process. This contention is harder to make today because our century has seen the logical extreme of this approach to science in Hitler's Germany. Again, however, the point to note for the interpretivist paradigm is not simply to reverse the argument and contend that you can imply ought from is. Rather, as with the epistemological unity of subject and object, the ethical stance of interpretivism is that you can not separate facts and values at all. Facts do not simply imply values; they are values.

The Goal of Research Is Understanding. The goal of research within the functionalist paradigm is to describe, predict, and control. Because of interpretivism's fundamental belief in the multiple realities of social construction, prediction and control become questionable. The linear approach of cause–effect is replaced by a much more holistic understanding of how things change over time. Instead of "describe, predict, and control," the goal of interpretivist research might better be summarized as "describe, interpret, and understand." Moreover, the understanding sought is a kind of empathic process whereby one tries to approximate the perspective of others (although not uncritically). At least since the work of Max Weber, interpretivists have adopted the German word *Verstehen* to convey this deeper, fuller sense of understanding. However, it is also important to note that interpretivism's emphasis on empathy and understanding is not simply an excuse for sloppy research. Interpretivistic research is not simply the collection of poignant vignettes or supportive anecdotes, a kind of "warm and fuzzy" approach to research. Interpretive research, properly done, is just as systematic, just as rigorous, as the best statistical analyses one can find.

THE IMPORTANCE OF QUESTIONING:
INTERPRETIVISM, DISABILITY, AND SPECIAL EDUCATION

So, how does all this fit with disability, special education, and schooling reform? What implications might the interpretivist perspective have for us? Perhaps some of the implications have already struck you as obvious. Let us mention a few of the ones that best illustrate the potential value of the interpretivist paradigm to those in the disability community whose stories rarely are told. We will organize our comments by talking first about what the interpretivist paradigm teaches us about the importance of questions, and then what differences these ideas might hold for special education.

Asking Different Questions

The first, and perhaps most fundamental, implication for special education has to do with what we understand about disability itself. Or, perhaps more accurately, "What are the questions about disability that we should be asking?" The usual question would be something like, "What is disability; what is its nature?" Our description of the basic tenets of interpretivism, however, suggests a different question as the starting point. Instead of asking, "What is disability?" interpretivists are more likely to ask, "What is the experience of disability?" Remember Wittgenstein's slogan: "Don't ask for the meaning, ask for the use" (cited in Wisdom, 1965, p. 87). That is, ask for the context, the social construction through which social reality takes shape. Interpretivism maintains that disability is not a fact—an entity—whose nature is just waiting to be discovered. Disability is rather an experience waiting to be described or, more precisely, a multitude of experiences waiting to be described.

Perhaps the most telling illustration of the different answers you get when you ask different questions is captured in the events of 1973, when the "official" definition of mental retardation was changed by lowering the IQ score that was needed to qualify (Grossman, 1973). As the story goes, with a stroke of Herbert Grossman's pen, thousands of people became normal; "cured," as it were, not by changing *things* or *facts*, but by changing the socially agreed-upon rules that identify some people as mentally retarded and others as not. What is mental retardation? It is what the American Association on Mental Deficiency (now the American Association on Mental Retardation, an interesting change in labeling in itself) says it is.

That last point is important. The interpretivist perspective teaches us that the social construction of disability, in this case, is more than just the social rule. It is also the actions of applying the rule. What is important about the Grossman story is the "stroke of the pen." With that *act*, people became normal. We have other examples in our society of this kind of "power-speak." At the end of a wedding ceremony, for example, when the minister or justice of the peace utters the words, "I now pronounce you husband and wife," he or she is not just saying something, but doing something as well. The saying of the phrase, in that context, by that person, *makes* the couple married. It is both a verbal signal and an official act.

Similarly, when at the end of an assessment report a school psychologist speaks (or writes) the words, "This child has an IQ of 62," he or she also does something more than just utter some words. The statement by that person, in that context, *makes* the child mentally retarded. In a very real social sense, the child was not so until those words were spoken. As a consequence, the child's experience of life, and of schooling, changes. What it means to be a student is different from what it means to be a student who is mentally retarded, even when the child can read the same words, remember the same math facts, and survive even better on the same mean streets. It is that new life story that the interpretivist paradigm teaches us to value and discover. Sometimes, in fact, the field of special education has responded to these realizations about the power and meaning of social constructions. Consider, for example, the shift in preferred usage from "mongolism" to "Down Syndrome." These words, both official labels at different times, ostensibly refer to exactly the same physical residuum, yet connote vastly different social constructions about the significance of that physical beginning.

Asking Questions Differently

The interpretivist paradigm not only urges us to ask different questions, but also prompts us to ask questions differently. Let us explain by turning to an example of cognitive disability that would seem to be particularly hard for this paradigm to encompass. Consider for a moment persons with very severe or profound mental impairments. The vulnerability of a social constructivist approach to understanding the experience of disability emerges in precisely those instances where culture seems beside the point; where physiology has gone so far awry that it threatens to overwhelm the social context. The very epistemology of the interpretivist paradigm assumes that we humans are agents in the social interpretation of our world, rather than mere reactors to our confrontations with an unchanging world of facts that are "out there," in the "real world."

The challenge of profound retardation for interpretivism is precisely how close it seems to come to the absence of agency. It is not just that the passivity often is enforced by limbs that do not move, or environmental barriers that trap the individual physically. One reason for the relative scarcity of interpretivist research with individuals with profound retardation and multiple handicaps is the difficulty in conceiving the social world of someone whose experience of concepts and communication is so uncertain for us. The relativity of language seems a woefully inadequate explanation.

We are offered a way out of this conceptual *cul de sac*, however, in the logic of cultural hermeneutics—one of the methodological occupants of the interpretivist paradigm. Depending more on a literary metaphor, cultural hermeneutics treats a social setting or process as a "text" (Ricouer, 1981; Chapter 2). What its practitioners do is try to discover what a particular text means. Just as with literary criticism, part of determining the meaning of a "social text" is finding out what the authors of that text intended it to mean. That is never enough, however. The meaning of a social text belongs as well to the text itself, and must be determined anew by all those who "read" it. Now, just as with real books, social texts often have multiple authors. People with severe retardation do not need to have any explicit communicative skills (written, oral, or gestural) to have participated as coauthors, if you will, for the various social texts being interpreted, for example, in special education. Even if some of them do not noticeably interpret the experience for themselves, in any strong sense of human agency, by telling their own stories, the social text remains—containing their contribution—for others to interpret. People do not have to "talk" to tell their stories, and many authors never read their own work.

It is with these examples, where you start stretching the notion of human agency, that the interpretivist paradigm allows you to ask questions differently. We do not want to overstate this: Interpretivist methods are most directly and obviously applicable with people who can tell their own stories, in their own words. Nonetheless, there are stories to be discovered within the text for those who learn to ask questions differently. At times, the way to ask questions differently is not to ask questions at all, but simply to look; to see the experience. At other times, asking questions differently means not asking questions of oneself—reflective questions—but to listen to the questions that others are asking, or to admit different information as answers to one's questions. In our own work, for example, we are learning to approach the puzzling behavior of some people as personal answers to some unheard questions. Operating as such, the teacher's task is to try to discover the questions he or she should be asking, in a kind of special education version of the *Jeopardy* game show.

REDIRECTING SPECIAL EDUCATION: TWO EXAMPLES

Interpretivism changes how we approach disability. Special education is one of the main organizational contexts through which our society officially approaches children with disabilities. It should not be surprising, then, that interpretivistic special education would dramatically redirect some of its approaches. We will examine some of these new directions of interpretivistic special education by sharing two examples—family transitions and teacher work groups. The examples also will illustrate two primary methodological procedures used in interpretivist research.

Family Transitions

The field of special education lately has become absorbed with transitions, especially the transition from school to work and adult life. Its interest in the problem of transition emerged quite recently as an act of self-reflection and evaluation of traditional practices. Has it worked? Has special education's new emphasis on transition made a difference? Do students achieve a more satisfactory life as a consequence of the field's specialized efforts? Although "transition" quickly became the adjective of choice for trendy professionals, the field's efforts have been guided by its functionalist understanding of transition as an objective, chronological process in which the appropriate course of action seems certain. Special educators now write "individual transition plans" during "transition planning meetings." These meetings are staffed by a "transition team" and led by a "transition specialist," who is guided in her or his duties by a "transition manual" that reveals the mysteries of the "transition process." Of course, there has been little improvement in the degree to which students get and keep jobs. Perhaps the best that can be said is that special educators are documenting their failure more thoroughly. Moreover, given the logic of functionalism, the field has begun to ask and answer the question, "How can transition proceed more smoothly?" a question that can lead to only one type of transition story.

The interpretivist paradigm suggests we ask a different question, one focused on discovering the stories of those who experience "transition" directly: parents and young adults. Over the past few years, we have talked with parents of young adults with severe disabilities about their perspectives on the events surrounding their children leaving school and/or turning 21 (Ferguson, Ferguson, & Jones, 1988). Using open-ended interview techniques, we created what some have called "topical oral histories" (Matthews, 1986, p. 11) for 15 families. These stories amended the professionalized version of the transition picture. For example, we found that these families did not experience *the* transition process, but at least three distinct transition processes that often occurred simultaneously. Only one of these, the one we named "bureaucratic transitions," might be thought of as most similar to what professionals usually mean by transition. Families also experienced their own "family transitions" as they negotiated the challenges and disruptions created by changes in daily routines and schedules, and the demands of the new and exotic world of adult services, all mixed up with the personal struggles of understanding the meaning of "adulthood" for a person who at this stage required even greater parental involvement, advocacy, and support.

As is common with interpretivist research, these initial findings have led us to probe more deeply into areas and perceptions that we had initially overlooked as too obvious or basic. What it means to "be an adult" and how one "becomes" an adult turned into essential questions that went beyond matters of mere chronology or physical maturity. It also has led us to explore how human service professionals and adults with disabilities interpret the status of adulthood, in addition to the perspective of parents (Ferguson & Ferguson, 1993).

Teacher Work Groups

In a different sphere of our research that involves working with teachers before and after they acquire certification, we (and our colleagues) have faced quite different questions. Perhaps the most troubling of these is how to close the gap between "preferred" and "current" practices. The story behind the gap is a familiar one by now. As academic educators we spend our time solving educational problems. We write elegant proposals for the federal funding that allows us to design our models, test our theories, and validate our new and improved practices. Then we produce desktop-published manuals and hold a series of inservice programs, aided by overheads, videotapes and performance standards. We do all of this only to be left with the question: Why don't teachers seem to be able to implement our best practices?

Guided by the interpretivist paradigm, we asked some different questions of the teachers in Oregon: How do you enjoy your work? What would you like to change about what you do? What would help you do that? What is *your* story? After visiting and talking with teachers, and watching and listening to them ask questions about their students, their work, and their professional growth, we found that most of the teachers knew all about "best practices" (Ferguson, 1989; Ferguson, 1994). They read journals and went to conferences, only to generate task lists that were never accomplished because it seemed that every item required somebody else – usually an administrator – to do something first. What they needed was a way to be permitted to act, to create their own interpretation of change toward better practices that would lead them to actions that might be professionally satisfying instead of stultifying.

Once we began to listen to these teachers' stories, we changed the focus of our efforts. Instead of inservice modules, programmed texts, and model fidelity checklists, we began to help teachers find their own problems, together, through informal teacher work groups. Now, rather than telling teachers what they should be doing differently, we are helping them learn to ask and answer their own questions. Currently we are working with about 108 teachers and 4 principals in 19 work groups across 5 states, who collectively support nearly 871 students with severe handicaps. They are discovering the problems they have in common and collectively creating the solutions that fit their own contexts. In the process, they have acquired a new power to take control of changes in their own classrooms and professional lives. As we noted above, it is not just the stories, but the *telling* of them that is important.

INTERPRETIVISM AND SOCIAL JUSTICE

So, finally, let us come full circle. Given what we have said, what is interpretivism's contribution to the pursuit of social justice for people with disabilities and their families? For us, the ultimate test of a paradigm always must be how it helps make life better for devalued individuals and groups. Asking this question about the interpretivist paradigm returns us to where we began: What is the value of telling stories? Although we cannot begin here to answer this question adequately, we will mention two ways that we believe telling stories – in the expanded sense of the interpretivist paradigm – can contribute to a more just and equitable society.

First, the stories being told can have a reformative effect by virtue of their content. Letting people who lived for years in the large, segregated institutions tell of their experiences has been one of the most powerful arguments for deinstitutionalization during the past 20 years in our country. Letting parents describe their experiences and perspectives about raising their children with severe disabilities in the community, in the local school, with other children, has been one of the primary forces toward integrated, inclusionary education. The very emphasis of interpretivism on micro-level description exalts the specific, the contextual, the local, the individual; in short, all that can be so easily flattened out in the more abstract structural analyses of world systems and ideologies. Ironically, perhaps, it is this commitment to completeness of description within interpretivism that allows it to create the firmest foundation for social change. As the bumper sticker says: Think globally, act locally. It begins with the individual.

This reformative effect of stories is related to a second, empowering effect of simply getting to tell one's stories. Interpretivism empowers devalued individuals and groups within our society by giving them a voice. Indeed, interpretivism can empower even groups such as teachers by legitimizing their credibility and authenticity of perspective through simple arrangements such as work groups. Certain individuals within our society have almost always gotten to tell their stories more often, to more people, with fewer questions than have other individuals. Able-bodied, white males come to mind as one such group of individuals whose stories have had a lot of telling. That imbalance allows an impression of unanimity about things that quickly transforms a social construction into a biological destiny. Interpretivism empowers by challenging that monologue. Equally important, interpretivism empowers by connecting people together to hear each other's stories. In advocacy circles, this is called networking. Interpretivism pursues social justice one story at a time.

So, let us tell our stories: recognize them as legitimate. Listen to the stories of others; appreciate them as additions, not as contradictions. And most important, proclaim the value of those whose stories so often go untold.

NOTES

Portions of this chapter have been published previously, in a somewhat different version, in Ferguson, Ferguson, and Taylor (1992).

1. See Skrtic's explanation of his use of the term "subjectivism" in Chapter 1 (note 1) and Chapter 2 (note 1). Also see Kiel's discussion of "social interpretivism" in Chapter 6.

2. Also see Skrtic's caveat on the relationship between microscopic social analysis and the sociology of regulation or order perspective in Chapter 2 (note 1).

REFERENCES

Burrell, G., & Morgan, G. (1979). *Sociological paradigms and organizational analysis*. London: Heinemann.

Eisner, E. W. (1991). *The enlightened eye: Qualitative inquiry and the enhancement of educational practice*. New York: Macmillan.

Ferguson, D. L. (1989). *Teacher work groups: Getting a little help from your friends*. Eugene: University of Oregon, Specialized Training Program.

Ferguson, D. L. (1994). Magic for teacher work groups. *Teaching Exceptional Children, 27*(1), 42–47.

Ferguson, P. M., & Ferguson, D. L. (1993). The promise of adulthood. In M. Snell (Ed.), *Instruction of students with severe disabilities* (4th ed., pp. 588–607). New York: Merrill.

Ferguson, P. M., Ferguson, D. L., & Jones, D. (1988). Generations of hope: Parental perspectives on the transitions of their severely retarded children from school to adult life. *Journal of the Association for Persons with Severe Handicaps, 13,* 177–186.

Ferguson, P. M., Ferguson, D. L., & Taylor, S. J. (Eds.). (1992). *Interpreting disability: A qualitative reader*. New York: Teachers College Press.

Garfinkel, H. (1967). *Studies in ethnomethodology*. Englewood Cliffs, NJ: Prentice-Hall.

Grossman, H. J. (1973). *Manual on terminology and classification in mental retardation*. Washington, DC: American Association on Mental Deficiency.

Heritage, J. C. (1987). Ethnomethodology. In A. Giddens & J. H. Turner (Eds.), *Social theory today* (pp. 224–272). Stanford: Stanford University Press.

Husserl, E. (1969). *Ideas: General introduction to pure phenomenology* (W. R. B. Gibson, Trans.). New York: Humanities Press. (Original work published 1931)

Husserl, E. (1970). *The crisis of European sciences and transcendental phenomenology: An introduction to phenomenological philosophy* (D. Carr, Trans.). Evanston, IL: Northwestern University Press. (Original work published 1954)

James, W. (1958). *The varieties of religious experience: A study in human nature*. New York: New American Library. (Original work published 1902)

Marton, F. (1988). Phenomenography: A research approach to investigating different understandings of reality. In R. R. Sherman & R. B. Webb (Eds.), *Qualitative research in education: Focus and methods* (pp. 141–161). Philadelphia: Falmer Press.

Matthews, S. H. (1986). *Friendships through the life course: Oral biographies in old age*. Newbury Park, CA: Sage.

Mead, G. H. (1934). *Mind, self, and society: From the standpoint of a social behaviorist* (C. W. Morris, Ed.). Chicago: University of Chicago Press.

Otto, R. (1958). *The idea of the holy: An inquiry into the non-rational factor in the idea of the divine and its relation to the rational* (J. W. Harvey, Trans.). New York: Oxford University Press. (Original work published 1923)

Patton, M. Q. (1990). *Qualitative evaluation and research methods* (2nd ed.). Newbury Park, CA: Sage.

Ricouer, P. (1981). *Hermeneutics and the human sciences* (J. B. Thompson, Ed. and Trans.). Cambridge: Cambridge University Press.

Schutz, A. (1962). *Collected papers: Vol. 1. The problem of social reality* (M. Natanson, Ed.). The Hague: Martinus Nijhoff.

Skrtic, T. M. (1986). The crisis in special education knowledge: A perspective on perspective. *Focus on Exceptional Children, 18*(7), 1–16.

Skrtic, T. M. (1991). *Behind special education: A critical analysis of professional culture and school organization*. Denver: Love Publishing.

Taylor, S. J., & Bogdan, R. (1984). *Introduction to qualitative research methods: The search for meanings* (2nd ed.). New York: Wiley.

Wisdom, J. (1965). *Paradox and discovery.* New York: Philosophical Library.

Wittgenstein, L. (1958a). *Preliminary studies for the "philosophical investigations" generally known as the blue and brown books.* New York: Harper.

Wittgenstein, L. (1958b). *Philosophical investigations* (3rd ed., G. E. M. Anscombe, Trans.). New York: Macmillan.

Wittgenstein, L. (1961). *Tractatus logico-philosophicus* (D. F. Pears & B. F. McGuinness, Trans.). New York: Routledge & Kegan Paul. (Original work published 1921)

CHAPTER 5

The Radical Structuralist View of Special Education and Disability:
Unpopular Perspectives on Their Origins and Development

Sally Tomlinson

Radical structuralist theories are not popular in democratic societies. Such societies like to think they are relatively harmonious, ordered places organized around a consensus of values and working toward ideals of social justice and social progress. Radical structuralist theories question this vision of society and point out that, even in democracies, powerful social groups attempt to control and dominate weaker social groups and treat them differentially and unequally. Power struggles and conflicts, attempts at domination and resistance to these attempts, thus characterize such societies. This chapter attempts to demonstrate that, as much of what happens in social life is the product of conflict – power struggles between vested interests and attempts at domination – special education must not be regarded as an exception, and that special education policies and practices can be usefully analyzed from radical structuralist perspectives. The chapter concentrates on development of special education in Britain to illustrate the argument. One caveat to be entered at the outset is that the argument does not assume a conspiracy among dominant social groups who can unproblematically force their will or decisions upon weaker social groups. Power, as Lukes (1979) noted, is a complex concept, and the assumption that conflicts are always solved by the simple coercion of one group by another is not a true representation of social life.

CHARACTERISTICS OF THE RADICAL STRUCTURAL PARADIGM

The radical structural paradigm takes a large-scale or macroscopic, objective, and realist view of the social world, assuming that there is a real social world in which conflict, domination, and coercion predominate. Burrell and Morgan (1979) have pointed out that there have been and are many different theorists working within this paradigm who have different approaches to the study of social institutions, but all approaches have in common the belief that society is characterized by fundamental social, political, and economic conflicts, which have the potentiality, as they are worked through, to generate radical social change. Optimistic radical structuralists believe that if people can better understand the social structures and forces they live with, they will be better able to emancipate themselves from unfair discrimination and the influence of the powerful.

The founding intellectuals of this paradigm were Marx and Weber, whose work has subsequently provided the basis for two major conflict approaches to the study of social institutions and processes, and for a synthesis of conflict approaches. Marx was interested primarily in analyzing social conflict in terms of social class and the labor market (McLellan, 1971), and Weber in showing how dominant interest groups can shape social structures to their own ends and persuade other groups to accept resulting inequalities (Weber, 1904–05/ 1930). Marxist-oriented theorists in Europe divided into radical structuralists, for example, Althusser (1969), Poulantzas (1978), and Anderson (1976); and radical humanists, most notably perhaps the so-called critical theorists such as Habermas (1968/1971), Horkheimer (1947/1985), Gramsci (1971), and Marcuse (1964). Within the study of education Marxian theories have been used by Wexler (1977), Bowles and Gintis (1976), Giroux (1983), and Apple (1982) in the United States; Foucault (1973/1961) in France; and Tomlinson (1981), Whitty (1985), and Johnson (1991) in England. Bowles and Gintis (1976), for example, related the role of education to social selection in employment and attacked the role of "IQ testing" as a mechanism for legitimizing inequality between socioeconomic groups.

Weberian theories concentrate on the way in which conflicts can permeate all social institutions, not simply the labor market, and are often concerned with status and power (Dahrendorf, 1959; Rex, 1973). These theories indicate that structural inequalities are sustained by the development of ideologies, and other modes of legitimation, which means that dominant groups do not have to use force or coercion. If, for example, weaker groups accept the "legitimate authority" of superior groups, or if they can be "persuaded" to agree to unequal conditions, no overt coercion need be used. In education, Bourdieu and Passeron (1977), French conflict theorists, have argued that educational advancement or exclusion is controlled by ostensibly fair, meritocratic testing, but that the education system demands a cultural competence during test procedures, which it does not itself provide. An advantage is thus given to families who possess "cultural capital" and can pass it on to their children. Social class and cultural reproduction thus become linked, as test "failures" are assigned to lower social groups, who are persuaded that the failure "was their own fault," without any further need for coercion.

Radical structuralist perspectives also can analyze the structures of power and the way power often is exercised by secrecy, nonaccountability, persuasion, and control of resources, as well as by overt coercion. In the twentieth century the service of professionals has become essential to the state, in terms of legitimating the treatment of certain groups of potentially "troublesome" people, such as the clients of special education. The radical structuralist paradigm, when applied to education as a social institution, can show that education systems and their parts do not develop in an evolutionary or adaptive manner – they develop out of conflicts; power struggles, especially over scarce resources; and covert and overt coercion. Winners and losers emerge not so much because of individual merit or deficit, but because they belong to groups who have, or lack, access to power and modes of legitimation. Weaker social groups can be symbolically coerced, for example, by professionals, into accepting decisions that they would, if things were equal, prefer not to accept.

Critique of Other Paradigms

It can be asked why structural approaches are more useful in explaining social and educational phenomena than are functionalist or interpretivist approaches. Functionalist perspectives, the most popular basis for educational research, have limited value in analyzing events in education and special education, although most research in both fields has been carried out from this perspective. Functionalist-oriented research usually has assumed that educational developments automatically constitute progress and are in the best interests of the students concerned, and that the only problems lie in the implementation of new developments. Dominant concerns with functionalist perspectives are those of order, balance, and equilibrium in society (Parsons, 1952). Research and literature on special education from a functionalist perspective have been concerned with how persons considered disabled or special "fit in" to society, and with documenting the extent and type of disability and techniques and practices for "dealing with," managing, and providing for them. A major problem with this approach is that it is based on consensus in society being the normal state of affairs; conflict cannot be explained except in terms of deviance, and it is assumed that professionals are working in a benevolent and humanitarian manner for the good of their clients. The functionalist approach views the clients of special education as a social problem that can be dealt with by professional teamwork and the "right resources," rather than viewing all special educational activity as a sociological problem to be explained. The approach usually denies clients their version of "what is going on" and unproblematically accepts that professionals really do know best (see Skrtic, 1991; Chapter 3).

A variety of interpretivist and phenomenological approaches in sociology are available to ask questions about education and special education (see Chapter 4). These perspectives have proved extremely useful as an explanatory tool at a microscopic level. Phenomenologists stress the way in which social reality is the creation of social participants, and that social categories and social knowledge are not given or natural, but are socially constructed. The application of interpretivist approaches has opened up wider empirical possibilities, as researchers are able to consider as problematic such issues as labeling, classifying, and categorizing students, and interactions between teachers and students, professionals and clients.

However, there are problems posed by purely interpretivist analyses of social situations. The paradigm tends to situate people in a microscopic structure and has difficulty placing encounters in a macroscopic framework. Some interpretivist and phenomenological approaches attempt to eliminate references to structure altogether by reducing the social to a series of negotiated intersubjective encounters, and there is no doubt that the "problem of dualism" (Archer, 1979, p. 9) remains an outstanding sociological problem. Following Weber (1930), whose work comprised an attempt to chart a path leading from understanding individual behavior to the analysis of process and structure, twentieth-century sociologists have tended to divide into those who study groups and institutions and those who study actors and small-scale situations. The micro–macro distinction is very real, and much sociological research represents a pragmatic acceptance of dualism and the use of very different kinds of theorizing and methodology, according to the size of the problem under investigation. Interpretivist or phenomenological approaches can reduce the possibility of the social context exerting any influence or constraint on the interaction. Conversely, some macro-sociologists can be accused of ignoring the way in which individuals endow the social world with conscious meaning and then reinterpret with others new structures of meanings so that, as Sharp and Green (1975) proposed, "the subtle texture of meaning constitutes social reality" (p. 222). Sharp and Green in England and Bogdan and Kugelmass (1984) in the United States are sociologists who have successfully managed to relate micro-interactions in school settings to wider social structures.

RADICAL STRUCTURALIST PERSPECTIVES IN SPECIAL EDUCATION

Radical structuralist perspectives in special education are concerned with a macro-analysis of the relationship of special education to other parts of the educational system and to other institutions, notably the economy. The perspectives also can be used to examine the interests of the different groups concerned with the "special," the power and resources they command, the beliefs, ideologies, and rationalizations they employ to legitimate their practices, and the ways their practices and decisions affect their relatively powerless clients.

Thus, in Britain, as in other advanced technological societies, special education can be analyzed as part of a political response to a crucial dilemma facing education systems in late-twentieth-century technological societies. The dilemma is centered around restructuring the education–training system to deal with the increasing number of young people who are defined as unable or unwilling to participate in a system primarily directed toward producing academic and technical elites. Achievements in "normal" schooling are becoming more important in gaining any sort of employment or income above subsistence level or making any impact on the wider society. The expansion of special education is closely linked to the question of what sort of preparation for a future life should be offered to a large social group who are likely to be partially or permanently unemployed, and thus from a traditional industrial society perspective, not economically profitable or "useful" to society. As special education expands, it is providing both a rationale and a justification for at least a part of this group. Although presented in ideological terms as catering to the "needs" of students, the expansion of special education can be regarded as the result of rational action on the part of those who control and direct education and training, as they restructure the education system to fit the needs of a postindustrial, technologically based society.

The expansion of special education in England can be linked, via structural analysis, to the disappearing youth labor market during the 1970s. Up to that time the vocational and educational programs aimed at those with special educational needs assumed an endpoint of possible unskilled or semi-skilled employment. During the 1980s and early 1990s, programs for the "special" are largely a political response to the problem of dealing with larger numbers of young people who, despite new vocational initiatives, probably will never acquire permanent employment. The expansion of postsecondary special programs to embrace larger numbers of young people may provide both a rationale and a justification for the subsequent economic position of this group. In 1982 I suggested that "to have received a special education, with its historic stigmatic connotations, even a non-recorded special education in an integrated setting, may be regarded unfavorably by potential employers" (Tomlinson, 1982, p. 177). In 1995 this may be just as accurate, although the role of special education in preparing numbers of young people for a workless future, or one of sporadic, low-skilled employment, needs considerable research and analysis.

Radical structuralist perspectives on special education also can illustrate the mechanism by which the "clients" of special education – usually the parents of children identified as disabled–come to accept the judgment that their child is "not normal." It already has been noted that the service of professionals is now essential to the state. Larson (1977) has asserted that professional judgments exert a form of ideological control over people, with the expertise of professionals being used to validate what are, in fact, forms of social control. Without the mystique of professional judgments–particularly psychological assessments–it is doubtful whether many parents would accept that their children had "special needs," which ordinarily means that they are excluded from a fully typical education. The techniques of professional persuasion usually work by encouraging reluctant parents to allow their children to be placed in special education, but enforceable procedures are, in England, built into the law to back up professional views. The enforceable procedures have always made it difficult for professionals to claim that their assessment decisions were based on purely objective criteria and motivated by humanitarian concern. However, professionals seldom mention to parents, in their initial consultations, that coercion is available if persuasion fails.

The Origins of Special Education

The expansion of special education programs also can be linked to the need to provide an education for "normal" students unimpeded by students who are troublesome, in the widest possible sense. From structuralist perspectives it is possible to regard the development of special education as a "safety valve" for the rest of the system. This can be illustrated by a brief examination of the origins of special education in both Britain and the United States.

The origins of special education in Britain, particularly for those with moderate learning difficulties and behavioral problems, lies in the development, from 1870, of a mass elementary education system that necessitated the recognition of pupils who could not function satisfactorily within the system. How to define such pupils posed a problem, and the changing terminology of defect, disability, handicap, retardation, or special needs is an indication that such terms are social constructs developed within particular historical contexts. By the 1880s, children who were "weak and feeble-minded" were causing concern in the newly established elementary schools. Children who before education was made compulsory had functioned socially and often economically at an adequate level were found to be educationally deficient. Payment by results, a system whereby teachers obtained remuneration based on the educational success of their pupils, was singled out as a problem for pupils and teachers, and a Commission chaired by Lord Egerton was set up in 1885 to examine what had become the problem of the blind, deaf, dumb, and feeble-minded. The setting up of his Commission was frankly for economic and social control reasons, for as Lord Egerton put it:

The blind, the deaf, dumb and educable classes of imbeciles if left uneducated become not only a burden to themselves, but to the state. It is in the interests of the state to dry up . . . the minor streams which must ultimately swell to a great torrent of pauperism. (Egerton Commission, 1889, p. 1)

In 1889 the Egerton Commission recommended the separation of such pupils from "ordinary scholars in public elementary schools," and it was largely the "feeble-minded" and badly behaved who formed the clientele for the first special classes and schools set up in large cities in the 1890s. Some schools developed a "standard zero" class for children who could not reach adequate levels of what now would be called "test performance"–an inspector noting in 1897 that of "every 70 children in the standard one, 25 are almost entirely ignorant, they misbehaved, truanted and learned nothing" (Pritchard, 1963, p. 43). The social origins of pupils with learning and behavioral difficulties are traceable to the needs of ordinary schools to separate their problem pupils in order to promote the interests of other pupils within a competitive education system. In the process it was the children and their families who were labeled as deficient and problematic, rather than the social, educational, and economic structures. The 1988 Education Act allows children with "statements of Special Educational Needs" and other children to be permanently or temporarily disapplied from following the national curriculum and assessment with other students.

A similar situation occurred in the United States, as Lazerson (1983) has documented. In the 1890s compulsory school attendance laws had brought into public schools large numbers of children who were difficult to teach and manage, students who disrupted the education of "normal" pupils. Elizabeth Farrell, the first director of "ungraded" or special classes in New York City, noted that the establishment of the first special classroom in 1899 was not grounded in any educational theory, but was simply meant to contain "the odds and ends of a large school . . . . over-age children, so-called naughty children, dull and stupid children" (cited in Lazerson, 1983, p. 20). In 1924, Wallin, after observing special classrooms in Washington, DC, argued that

In the regular grades the feeble-minded and subnormal represent, as it were, an unassimilated accumulation of human clinkers, ballast, drift wood, or derelicts which seriously retards the rate of progress of the entire class and which often constitutes a positive irritant to the teacher and other pupils. (cited in Lazerson, 1983, p. 23)

Special education became a means of controlling potentially deviant pupils and reducing possible criminal and immoral behavior–a particular fear in the early part of the twentieth century when the influence of the eugenics movement[1] was at its height–and also of ensuring that "normal" pupils received adequate schooling. In both Britain and the United States it was, and continued to be, the poor, Black, and foreign-born who were more likely to be regarded as retarded and deviant. Lazerson (1983, p. 33) has noted that the children of wealthy and middle-class parents were not regarded as a "social menace" or as potential economic problems, and thus were not regarded as candidates for special education. The same was true in Britain, where Tredgold (1908) noted that

> Throughout the country there are hundreds of feeble-minded persons, many of them gentlefolk by birth. . . . They take up simple hobbies like poker-work, stamp collecting and cabinet making, and enter into the ordinary social amusements of their class. (p. 175)

The application of radical structuralist perspectives to an analysis of the origins of special education certainly can indicate that special education was perhaps more a solution to problems of social order than a way of "doing good" for children with special educational needs.

The Expansion of Special Education in Britain

As special education expanded in twentieth-century Britain, policy makers and practitioners developed a legitimating ideology of benevolent humanitarianism and charitable provision. This ideology became so firmly entrenched that it became difficult to suggest other possible motives or to challenge the notion that developments were "for the good" of the students. In 1973, a committee of inquiry into the "Education of Handicapped Children and Young People" was set up by Mrs. Margaret Thatcher, then Education Minister, under the chair of Dame (later Baroness) Warnock (Department of Education and Science, 1978). The Warnock Committee, representing a variety of professional and administrative interests, regarded special education as an unproblematic "good" and presented its origins as follows:

> As with ordinary education, education for the handicapped began with individual and charitable enterprise. There followed in time the intervention of government, first to support voluntary effort and make good deficiency through state provision, and finally to create a national framework of public and voluntary agencies to see that all children, whatever their disability, received a suitable education. (Department of Education and Science, 1978, p. 8)

In fact, the development of special education may have been intended to "do good" to mainstream pupils rather than those with special educational needs. Special education developed by seeking out more and more children considered to be incapable of "normal" education and placing them in administrative categories for which differential provision was made. The categories developed from two in 1886 to 11 in 1945.

Spectre and Kitsuse (1977) have suggested that where there is competition between groups who have vested interests in defining weaker social groups, the labels applied will be those of the winning group. The development of particular categories of exceptionality in Britain was the result of struggle between medical, psychological, and educational personnel, and there were winners and losers. Dyslexia and autism, for example, were never recognized as statutory educational categories of disability, although they were recognized under a Health Act in 1970. Other categories suggested by various interest groups, but never given any legal status, were the neuropathic child, the inconsequential child, the psychiatrically crippled child, the clumsy child, the hyperactive child, the attention-span deficient child, the child with severe lethargy, and a variety of others.

By the late 1970s, making provision in separate schools for the expanding number of pupils categorized as handicapped or having a "disability of body or mind" had become too expensive, and there was strong pressure from egalitarians to include all children within a comprehensive education system. The Warnock Committee in 1978 recommended the abolition of statutory categories of handicap, and this was realized through the 1981 Special Education Act. However, descriptive labels were retained and old categories were renamed—for example, "maladjusted" became "emotionally and behaviorally disturbed," or EBD. The Warnock Committee recommended that children with disabilities and learning difficulties be known as children with special educational needs, and this concept has become an ambiguous and tautological rationalization for the expansion of special education programs. In particular, more pupils are now considered to have mild learning difficulties (MLD) and as EBD, and these are overwhelmingly the children of working-class or ethnic minority parentage.

The excessive placement of Black and other minority pupils in special education has been a focus for comment in both Britain and the United States (Cooper, Upton, & Smith, 1991; Maheady, Towne, Algozzine, Mercer, & Ysseldyke, 1990; Tomlinson, 1982). Black and other minority pupils in Britain have been overrepresented in the MLD and EBD categories. Cooper and coauthors (1991) have suggested that "by placing such groups in a marginalized and stigmatized sector of the education system, the present and future stability of the status quo is, to some extent, protected from the challenge posed by these groups" (p. 78).

Despite a rhetoric of integration, the numbers of pupils segregated in special schools and units has remained the same as before the 1981 Education Act (around 2% of the total school population), although the chances of being "statemented" as in need of special provision and segregated vary considerably from one local education authority to another. Many more pupils in mainstream schools, up to 20% of the total school population, are now targeted for special classes, special support, or special programs. Research in Britain, as in the United States, demonstrates a familiar and understandable reluctance on the part of teachers to deal with children with learning and behavioral problems in ordinary classrooms without a good deal of support. "Integration" in Britain is likely to remain problematic, given the tasks and expectations imposed on teachers in an increasingly competitive education system, which is moving away from an egalitarian, comprehensive principle.

The 1988 Education Act requires that all students be tested at ages 7, 11, 14, and 16, with test results being published, and that all children follow programs of study in the 10 subjects of the national curriculum. In addition, parental choice of school is increased, and schools can choose to "opt-out" of local authority control and become grant-maintained by central government. Debates center on how far students with special educational needs should have their curriculum "modified" (as allowed for in the Act); whether they should be exempt from testing; whether their test scores will depress overall school scores, causing parents of "normal" students to withdraw their children from "low-score" schools; whether grant-maintained schools will refuse pupils with special needs to keep up good test records; and whether the provisions of the Act will create the conditions for a return to segregated special education programs. Such debates can be understood only within conflict perspectives. Consensus views and humanitarian motivation have become, in the 1990s, conspicuously absent from debates on the future provision for the expanded number of students considered to have special educational needs.

CONCLUSIONS

Those who analyze social events from optimistic radical structuralist perspectives are committed to the belief that progress in emancipating the powerless from their social position is possible, and that the condition for radical change can be created by a conflict analysis that demonstrates to social participants "what is really going on." But conflict theorists are also familiar with situations in which, after struggles and conflicts, a truce or compromise can involve moving goalposts, and that this can result in the less powerful being no better off. Thus, prior to 1981 Black parents in Britain successfully campaigned to prevent their children from being categorized as "educationally subnormal," only to find that after 1981 they were being reclassified as MLD or as EBD.

Teachers who have attempted to change their practices so that more students with special needs could remain in mainstream classes, now find that they are expected to teach and test to higher standards and to be more publicly accountable, and that resources for helping such students are being redirected to more able students. However, conflict theorists are also familiar with the notion of contradiction, or what has been described as "system conflict." There is much evidence that, in special education, parts of the system are in continued conflict with each other—interprofessional conflicts, resource conflicts, parental–professional conflicts, legal conflicts—and that conflict resolution can, on occasion, be beneficial. For example, the activity of the "disability rights" movement in the United States and other countries has led to demands by people with disabilities in Britain for antidiscrimination legislation and an end to derogatory labeling.

There is, in special education as in all other social institutions, a tendency to inertia and to favor the status quo. For example, with regard to special education in Britain, I wrote in 1982 that, "when challenged, the education system will defend itself by reverting to innate individualistic explanations stressing the pupils' deficiencies" (Tomlinson, 1982, p. 162), and Sleeter (1986) and Sigmon (1987) have repeated this view for education in the United States. For example, Sigmon has written that

> The regular education community runs the risk of becoming increasingly unwilling or unable to cope with those who are divergent from some average expectation for social and academic performance in schools. (1987, p. 101)

The challenge for conflict theorists working from radical structuralist perspectives is to continue to demonstrate that explanations in terms of negative properties such as disability, deficiency, or inability are saying more about the groups who control the social, economic, and political structures of society than about anything else. Structuralist perspectives are unpopular in special education; they suggest ways of looking at events and practices that are often uncomfortable for professionals and administrators. But, by moving to levels of structural analysis, it becomes possible to ask broader questions about the aims, forms, and ideologies in special education, and thus to work toward positive change.

NOTE

1. Eugenics is the attempt to improve the inherited qualities of a race or breed through the science of genetics (English & English, 1958). The eugenics movement was founded by Sir Francis Galton and enthusiastically promoted in the United States by H. H. Goddard, whose book, *The Kallikak Family* (1912), fostered efforts to sterilize persons with mental retardation and helped to justify their segregation from society.

REFERENCES

Althusser, L. (1969). *For Marx*. Hamondsworth, England: Penguin.

Anderson, P. (1976). *Considerations on western Marxism*. London: Verso.

Apple, M. (1982). *Education and power*. London: Routledge & Kegan Paul.

Archer, M. S. (1979). *The social origins of education systems*. London: Sage.

Bogdan, R., & Kugelmass, J. (1984). Case studies of mainstreaming: A symbolic inter-actionist approach to special schooling. In L. Barton & S. Tomlinson (Eds.), *Special education and social interests* (pp. 173–191). London: Croom-Helm.

Bourdieu, P., & Passeron, J. (1977). *Reproduction in education, society, and culture*. London: Sage.

Bowles, S., & Gintis, H. (1976). *Schooling in capitalist America*. New York: Basic Books.

Burrell, G., & Morgan, G. (1979). *Sociological paradigms and organizational analysis*. London: Heinemann.

Cooper, P., Upton, G., & Smith, C. (1991). Ethnic minority and gender distribution among staff and pupils in facilities for pupils with emotional and behavioral difficulties in England and Wales. *British Journal of Sociology of Education, 12*(1), 77–94.

Dahrendorf, R. (1959). *Class and class conflict in industrial society*. Stanford: Stanford University Press.

Department of Education and Science. (1978). *Special educational needs* (The Warnock report). London: H.M.S.O.

Egerton Commission. (1889). *Report of the regal commission on the blind, deaf, dumb and others of the United Kingdom*. London: H.M.S.O.

English, H. B., & English, A. C. (1958). *A comprehensive dictionary of psychological and psychoanalytic terms*. New York: Longmans, Green.

Foucault, M. (1973). *Madness and civilization: A history of insanity in the age of reason*. (R. Howard, Trans.). New York: Vintage/Random House. (Original work published 1961)

Giroux, H. A. (1983). *Theory and resistance in education: A pedagogy for the opposition*. South Hadley, MA: Bergin & Garvey.

Goddard, H. H. (1912). *The Kallikak family*. New York: Macmillan.

Gramsci, A. (1971). *Selections from the prison notebook*. (Q. Hoare & G. N. Smith, Eds. and Trans.). New York: International Publishers.

Habermas, J. (1971). *Knowledge and human interests* (J. J. Shapiro, Trans.). Boston: Beacon Press. (Original work published 1968)

Horkheimer, M. (1985). *Eclipse of reason*. New York: Continuum. (Original work published 1947)

Johnson, R. (1991). A new road to serfdom. In Education Group II (Ed.), *Education limited: Schooling, training and the New Right in England since 1979* (pp. 31–86). London: Unwin Hyman.

Larson, M. S. (1977). *The rise of professionalism*. Berkeley: University of California Press.

Lazerson, M. (1983). The origins of special education. In J. G. Chambers & W. T.

Hartman (Eds.), *Special education policies: Their history, implementation, and finance* (pp. 15–47). Philadelphia: Temple University Press.

Lukes, S. (1979). *Power: A radical view*. London: Macmillan.

Maheady, L., Towne, R., Algozzine, B., Mercer, J., & Ysseldyke, J. (1990). Minority representation: A case for alternative practice prior to referral. In S. B. Sigmon, *Critical voices on special education* (pp. 89–102). Albany: State University of New York Press.

Marcuse, H. (1964). *One-dimensional man*. Boston: Beacon Press.

McLellan, D. (1971). *The thought of Karl Marx*. London: Macmillan.

Parsons, T. (1952). *The social system*. New York: Free Press.

Poulantzas, N. (1978). *State, power, socialism*. London: New Left Books.

Pritchard, D. G. (1963). *Education and the handicapped in Britain, 1760–1960*. London: Routledge & Kegan Paul.

Rex, J. (1973). *Discovering sociology*. London: Routledge & Kegan Paul.

Sharp, R., & Green, A. (1975). *Education and social control*. London: Routledge.

Sigmon, S. B. (1987). *Radical analysis of special education: Focus on historical development and learning disabilities*. London: Falmer Press.

Skrtic, T. M. (1991). *Behind special education: A critical analysis of professional culture and school organization*. Denver: Love Publishing.

Sleeter, C. E. (1986). Learning disabilities: The social construction of a special education category. *Exceptional Children, 53*(1), 46–54.

Spectre, M., & Kitsuse, T. (1977). *Constructing social problems*. Los Angeles: Cummings.

Tomlinson, S. (1981). *Educational subnormality: A study in decision making*. London: Routledge & Kegan Paul.

Tomlinson, S. (1982). *A sociology of special education*. London: Routledge & Kegan Paul.

Tredgold, A. F. (1908). *A text-book of mental deficiency*. London: Balliere, Trindinal and Cox.

Weber, M. (1930). *The Protestant ethic and the spirit of capitalism*. London: Unwin. (Original work published 1904–05)

Wexler, P. (1977). *The sociology of education: Beyond inequality*. Indianapolis: Bobbs-Merrill.

Whitty, G. (1985). *Sociology and school knowledge*. London: Methuen.

CHAPTER 6

The Radical Humanist View of Special Education and Disability:
Consciousness, Freedom, and Ideology

Dwight C. Kiel

The paradigm of knowledge I will discuss in this chapter is often termed the radical humanist or simply the humanist paradigm. There are good reasons for this title, which we will explore shortly, but to make some clearer linkages with the other paradigms, I also will refer to the humanist paradigm as the "social interpretivist" view. Social interpretivists view the world from a macroscopic perspective – from a social, rather than simply an individual (interpretivist) or mechanical (functionalist), perspective. Thus, social interpretivists – humanists – are very sympathetic to the perspectives and many of the arguments of structuralists. However, social interpretivists, while approving of the macro-perspective of structuralists, disagree fundamentally with structuralists over the issue of the objectivity of analyses. Humanists do not believe that social analysis can be objective. Rather, humanists assert that the world is not known objectively, but is interpreted. Thus, we can see the humanist affinity for the interpretivist paradigm. Social interpretivists agree with interpretivists that knowledge is subjective. However, social interpretivists stress how knowledge is *inter*subjective – reality and knowledge are socially constructed in the ongoing dialogue among participants. Social interpretivists, then, view the world from a macro-perspective and from a subjectivist understanding of knowledge.

An important caveat, though, must be added at this point about the humanist perspective on knowledge. Humanists see in each of the other three paradigms important moments of insight – "moments of truth." I will turn to a fuller discussion of these moments of truth in other paradigms below, but I want to stress that humanists are paradigm pluralists. For humanists, no single paradigm has a patent on knowledge, and each makes its contributions to human understanding. Humanists are proud of their pluralism, although critics sometimes accuse them of acting like the fellow at lunch who doesn't order any food, but would just like a bite out of everyone else's sandwich.

SHARED ASSUMPTIONS IN THE HUMANIST PARADIGM

Humanists, despite their diversity, share four fundamental and interrelated beliefs that guide their analyses. The first belief is that the development of human consciousness and self-consciousness is a crowning achievement. The ability of humans to reflect on and to criticize their own thoughts and actions provides humans the opportunity to engage in ethical reflection and ethical action. Humans are the animals who can choose and can reflect and act on the choices made. Humans learn. Indeed, a goal of humanists is to provide environments where humans can make ethical choices without coercion and without ideological blinders. Humanists seek environments with high levels of "transparency." In other words, humanists seek environments where people can see more clearly the existing relations of power within society, the ideologies that mold social choices, and the likely outcomes of the actions that people choose.

For humanists, the emphasis on the development of consciousness and self-consciousness leads directly to a concern over ethical life and the proper environments for cultivating and improving the ethical reflection and action of humans.

The second belief shared by humanists, by social interpretivists, is the need to increase human freedom. Freedom from "unnecessary" constraints is essential if humans are to use and develop their ethical abilities. Practice in ethics does not make perfect, but it can and often does lead to improvement.

Two of the major constraints on human freedom in modernity are organizations and governments. Humanists are always suspicious of these two entities because of their abilities to coerce members and to cause them to sacrifice their integrity for the norms of these institutions. The response to the institutions of modernity by humanists has taken two paths. The first path has been a rejection of all institutions and governments: humanist anarchism. These humanists wish to rid the world of organizations and governments, because these entities are seen as inherently constraining and tyrannical. The second path, which most humanists trod, demands that organizations and governments meet highly democratic standards of operation, including the cultivation of democratic values and abilities. These humanists desire a social order that is the reflective product of human participants. They view organizations and governments as legitimate as long as they are created and run by citizens. They wish to replace the arbitrary power of tyrants (big and small) with a democratic authority where everyone is involved in reflecting on the social order. This reflection on the logic of collective action (mutually imposed constraints) must be accompanied, of course, by participation in the making of the rules (laws) for collective action. For these humanists freedom is the practice of choice within an order – a political and social order – that is chosen and run by all those within that order.

Both of these groups of humanists agree, though, that organizations and government are not the only threats to human freedom. Human freedom and self-realization are also threatened by dominant, yet many times subtle, ideologies that shape the choices humans make and thus lead not to social transparency, but to opaqueness. For humanists, ideologies are value schemata that emphasize the differences among people and allow injustices to be perpetrated self-righteously. Ideologies allow ethical decisions to be made with little or no ethical reflection. Ideologies do not clarify human responsibilities; they make opaque the ethical relationships among people. This, then, is the third shared belief of humanists: that dominant ideologies in societies restrict human development by causing a gap – sometimes a chasm – between appearance and reality.

This claim that ideologies create a disjuncture between appearance and reality may seem to be a strange claim coming from a paradigm that is subjectivist. Do not humanists also claim that reality is socially constructed? How can humanists talk about reality as opposed to appearances? Let me give an example to clarify the humanist argument on appearance and reality. After World War II, the ideology of "wife as second class citizen" was reinvigorated through TV, other forms of popular culture, and legal decisions. The subservient status of women was glorified, even by some women. The women's liberation movement sought to reveal the unequal power relations in many marriages and in society, and the debilitating effects on women of this ideology. The ideology of wife as second class citizen, which had masked these consequences by claiming to honor and respect women, was weakened as the relations between husband and wife were made more transparent. For humanists, one cannot force change in the relations of husband and wife, but one can and must make arguments that aid participants in removing the blinders and shackles of ideologies.

An important aside is in order. Does not such an approach lead to moral relativism? It does in fact lead to a type of moral relativism by humanists: a relativism that argues that in our moral judgments about actors, we acknowledge the conditions and the world in which these actors make ethical choices. My condemnation of slavery in ancient Greece is very mild compared with my condemnation of apartheid in modern South Africa. Chauvinistic actions by my father in 1957 might be regrettable, and occasionally deplorable, but these same actions in 1995 would be downright damnable. Thus, humanists do not take a relativistic flight from moral and ethical criticism. Rather, they take into account the access one has to arguments and views that expose the tyranny of ideologies.

The fourth belief that humanists share is that the Enlightenment was a two-edged sword. The Enlightenment, with its attacks on the mythologies and structures of the late Middle Ages, held out the promises of increased human freedom and of citizen participation. Rational and reasonable forms of thought and action would replace the superstitions and myths of seventeenth-century Western thought. Democratic and republican forms of government would replace the tyranny of monarchs. All this, of course, was applauded by humanists. However, the Enlightenment also was seen as responsible for four developments that humanists continue to criticize. First, the Enlightenment emphasis on science as a way to the truth fueled narrower and narrower scientific inquiries that increasingly lost connection with wider human interests. Science, especially the social sciences, did not ask questions that might engender needed reforms in society, but rather sought power by asking small "neutral" questions that could be answered "authoritatively" and "rigorously" by professional experts. One of the legacies of the Enlightenment, then, was a science severed from social life–human knowledge (science) and human interests (social life) were separated.

Second, while the Enlightenment attacked the myths of the ancient regimes, the old myths soon were replaced with equally debilitating ideologies. One set of shackles was discarded, only to be replaced by new shackles.

Third, the old structures of hierarchy and domination were supposed to give way to democratic and participatory social organizations, yet the large modern nation-state has, at best, extremely remote forms of citizen control over government (interest group activity and occasional voting) and organizations that are typically hierarchical, bureaucratic, and nonparticipatory.

Fourth, the Enlightenment, which freed humans from the old mythologies, produced the ideology of utilitarianism. Utilitarianism, in all its forms, encourages those in its spell to see the world as a set of objects for human consumption, use, and abuse. Nature is degraded as humans view forests as lumber warehouses and rivers as pollution disposal devices. Fellow citizens are degraded as humans view each other as objects and as means to personal ends. Furthermore, utilitarianism in an age of capitalism and the large nation-state leads to extremely dangerous results for workers, who are viewed as units of production power, and leads to callous attitudes toward citizens, who often are viewed as units of military power. Utilitarianism and capitalism invade the organizations of modern societies and produce organizations founded on efficiency, productivity, quantitative results, and the "bottom line."

Humanists, then, view the Enlightenment as problematic. It is a two-edged sword, for it cuts both ways. The Enlightenment promises greater human freedom and more social transparency, but it often has not delivered on those promises.

We can see how the four shared beliefs of humanists are interrelated. Consciousness needs freedom to learn and develop. Ideologies are the modern versions of intellectual shackles. The Enlightenment held out the promise of increased human freedom, greater citizen participation, and more social transparency, but it has delivered feebly, according to humanists. Humanists are still seeking an ethical life in a community of citizens who are self-conscious and free. In this community citizens could draw on the insights and knowledges of reasonable and concerned scientists and citizens.

TRADITIONS AND DIRECTIONS IN THE HUMANIST PARADIGM

The major figure in the history of humanism, of social interpretivism, is G. W. F. Hegel (1770–1831). Hegel in his masterpiece, *Phenomenology of Spirit* (1807/1977), presented the history of Western civilization as the progressive development of human consciousness and self-consciousness. Human self-consciousness progressed because humans try to reconcile their claims about themselves (appearance) with existing social relations (reality). Yet, Hegel insisted that his work was not based on an objectivist foundation. Hegel's method for critically revealing the disjuncture between appearance and reality was the immanent critique. An immanent critique exposes how the claims of humans do not correspond to their life conditions (see Chapter 2). It is the type of critique that self-conscious humans find most troubling, because it points out that they are not living up to their own standards. An immanent critique does not bring in outside standards, but instead demands that actors reflect on the disjuncture between the standards and norms they claim to live by and the existing social relations. Reflection by the actors when they are accused of this disjuncture may not lead to change: The actors may state that their claims have been misunderstood (bad analysis by the accuser) or they may blind themselves to the disjuncture by assuming an ideological position (at the extreme they may become ideologues).

However, the immanent critique can bring about change. It weighs in the minds of self-conscious actors and can force, over time, the actors to change their existing social relations or to change their claims. A political example and an individual example can help clarify this idea of immanent critique. The immanent critique is often used in court cases. Lawyers will argue that the law (or Constitution) guarantees in the abstract equal treatment before the law to all citizens, but that in practice there are huge inequalities. The defendant's right to an attorney in criminal cases was not recognized by many states in the United States until the 1960s with the Supreme Court decision in *Gideon* v. *Wainwright* (1963). The expansion of rights in this area occurred when denial of an attorney came to be seen as undermining the claim about "equality before the law." Moreover, as everyone involved in special education should be well aware, the expansion of rights for students with disabilities in the United States–the right to education and treatment, least restrictive alternative, and due process of law in educational and place-ment decisions–depended on developing and sustaining immanent critiques (see Tweedie, 1983).

At the individual level immanent critiques also can work well. In fact, they can be quite galling. The failure to live up to one's own standards of conduct and norms of action, especially when pointed out by someone else, is always troubling. If I proclaim myself an animal lover, but routinely kick my dog, I probably should be more reflective in the first place. But when I am confronted by the disjuncture between my claims and my actions I am now under a heavier ethical obligation. I must change either my claims or my actions, or explain how the magical powers of my very soft and instructive foot have contributed to my dog's welfare. The immanent critique, at the very least, forces a more reflective consideration of one's values and actions. The immanent critique is one that works on self-conscious individuals who can reflect on ethical life.

Hegel's contributions to the social interpretivist paradigm are many, but the immanent critique is one of his most important. The immanent critique allows for critical leverage without having to rest on an objectivist foundation. Humanists will still focus on their concerns for freedom, ethical reflection, and democracy, but they will try to promote those values through the use of the immanent critique. The humanist reliance on the persuasive power of immanent critiques creates antagonism to humanists on two fronts. Radical structuralists accuse humanists of being mere reformers, and very slow re-formers at that. Supporters of the status quo find humanists irksome because they keep pointing out the discrepancies in the contemporary situation. Hu-manists usually are seen either as ineffective tweekers of the public conscience or as interfering superegos who will not leave "well enough" alone.

Within the humanist tradition four general directions have been taken since the death of Hegel. The group that has remained closest to the structur-alist paradigm are the critical theorists. These scholars' thoughts grew out of a Marxian tradition. While they accept much of Marx's criticism of capitalism, they are much more skeptical than Marx of science and the Enlightenment. Furthermore, they are particularly interested in how the ideology of the Enlightenment has separated science and knowledge from human interests. The major works in critical theory, the titles of which reveal their concerns, are Max Horkheimer's *Eclipse of Reason* (1947/1985) and Jurgen Habermas's

Toward a Rational Society (1968/1970) and *Knowledge and Human Interests* (1968/1971).

The humanist perspective closest to the interpretivist paradigm is existentialism. Indeed, many existentialists would place themselves within the interpretivist paradigm. Their concern with the question of "Being"–"What does it mean to be?"–leads existentialists to focus on self-consciousness and perception at the individual level. But existentialists often move from this individual focus to a larger inquiry about the social construction of self-consciousness and perception. Thus, these existentialists move to the issues of ideology and structure. Two examples of existentialists who are within the humanist paradigm are Jean-Paul Sartre and Simone deBeauvoir. Sartre explored the questions of self-consciousness and perception and the issues of freedom and ethics in his work *Being and Nothingness* (1943/1969). Simone deBeauvoir, in *The Second Sex* (1949/1953), exposed some of the ideologies of sexism that were so deeply held by Western individuals and societies that they often were not even subject to reflection and concern. She pursued the problems of ethical life in modernity in her work *The Ethics of Ambiguity* (1947/1949).

A third direction taken by some humanists is humanist anarchism. Anarchists, as stated earlier, make a radical assault not only on ideologies, but on most, if not all, social and political organizations. They wish to tear down those intellectual and physical structures that bring out the worst in humans and that contribute to the inequalities and brutality of, and in, the modern state. Emma Goldman, in *Anarchism and Other Essays* (1917), critiqued the ideologies and structures of capitalism and sexism. Ivan Illich, in *Deschooling Society* (1971), assaulted the U.S. school system for creating the ideology that schools and teachers alone can teach, and for contributing to the ideology that excellence is measured by the ever-increasing consumption of tangible products.

A fourth direction taken by humanists is one concerned particularly with the orderly construction of democratic politics and organizations. Two contemporary "democratic humanists" in political science are William E. Connolly and Jean Bethke Elshtain. Connolly, in *Appearance and Reality in Politics* (1981), illustrated how liberalism includes ideologies set up to exclude certain types of people–"others"–from political dialogue and power. Elshtain, in *Public Man, Private Woman* (1981), showed how Western thought and society have carved out public and political space for men and secured a private and familial role for women, to the detriment of the wholeness of both sexes.

The most well-known, and certainly most prolific, scholar in the democratic humanist tradition is John Dewey (1859–1952). Dewey has been claimed by many paradigms, but his major works, especially on education, are democratic humanist pieces of inquiry. In *The School and Society* (1899/ 1910) and *Democracy and Education* (1916/1946) Dewey sought to promote an educational system and curriculum that would prepare students to be reflective, autonomous, and ethical citizens in a democratic society (see Chapter 10). For Dewey, schools were institutions for preparing citizens for the continual learning experience of being a self-conscious citizen concerned with ethical thought and action. Democracies were the best practice grounds for ethical citizens, and schools must prepare students to take advantage of these practice grounds, for they would come of age as citizens. Indeed, all four humanist directions support democratic societies, because democracies promote ethical development and personal freedom. Furthermore, democracies, which arrive at social truths through discourse among subjects–through intersubjective communication–recognize that there are not objective answers to the most important questions of social life. A world that is socially constructed should be constructed as democratically as possible.

THE HUMANIST CONCEPTUALIZATION OF EDUCATION

Given the humanist commitment to democratic politics and society, humanists' views on education largely reflect those of Dewey. Education must prepare the democratic citizen for ethical participation in society. Obviously, humanists do not have many positive comments on elementary and, especially, secondary schools in the United States. The most serious problem is that schools do not develop exactly those characteristics and abilities necessary for reflective citizens in a democracy. First, schools, rather than encouraging individual autonomy, stifle it. Students are taught that information flows in one direction in the school–from the expert down to the learner. Knowledge is imparted in the imperative case: as a command. This diminishes the reflection and critical abilities of students and prepares them for authoritarian structures of work and politics rather than democratic structures. It discourages students from individual inquiry and from learning from peers. Schools prepare students to take orders, to dismiss their peers' intelligence, and to view learning as a monopoly of the schools.

Second, students–future citizens–find, in their introduction to a public organization, a school where participation and public efficacy are limited, if not denigrated. Students soon realize that there is little space for public-regarding activities, and that the organization they must live in rewards them for docility and for private, not public, interests. Students soon learn one of their most important organizational lessons in the United States: Public organizations are not designed with the client in mind. Schools encourage what our society encourages: a turn from public-regarding action and public participation to private-regarding behavior and private satisfactions.

Third, given these first two debilitating aspects of education, students are not prepared for the ethical dialogue and ethical decision making necessary in a democracy. Moral dialogue is replaced with the imperative monologue. Ethical decision making is denied or limited to superficial arenas. Dewey desired schools that would progressively increase the democratic abilities and personal autonomy of students soon to be citizens. He would be appalled at how schools have been organized to create docile workers waiting for commands.

Education, then, is a window on the relations in, and ideologies of, society. For humanists, the goal of education is not simply the mastery of facts and the disciplining of bodies, but the development of ethical pro-cesses—of reflection, discourse, and participatory action—in students. The right answer is much less important than the cultivation of ethical abilities. As Callahan (1962) has shown, schools in the United States, draped in the democratic values of Dewey, but practicing the bureaucratic monologues of debilitation, are obvious targets for the immanent critiques of humanists.

HUMANIST CONCEPTUALIZATION OF SPECIAL EDUCATION AND DISABILITY

Humanists pose three questions about special education and disability in industrialized nations. The first question is, "What are the consequences for special education of relying primarily on the functionalist paradigm for the diagnosis and education of students with disabilities?" This question leads to two secondary questions: "Are the categories of disability used to enable students or to disempower them?" "Is the knowledge generated by special education research tied to human interests or to the interests of researchers who have separated the problem of knowledge from political, economic, and social questions?" Humanists, given their view of the Enlightenment and science as problematic, will remain suspicious of the functionalist paradigm, which they see as an extremely narrow and fragmented view of knowledge.

A second question humanists pose, given their view of education gener-ally, is, "How does education shape the idea of disability for special educa-tion?" Education must find a place for those students who do not fit into the system, regardless of the reasons. Thus, one of the difficulties of special education is dealing with students whose chief "disability" is an inability to meet the disciplinary standards and the docility requirements of the education system. For humanists, the failure of a student to meet the organizational demands of education suggests that the failure may be located in the organization and not in the student (see Skrtic, 1991; Chapter 9). Too often, special education finds itself taking on the responsibilities of a bureaucratized educational system.

A third question posed by humanists is closely related to the second question: "How does society shape the idea of disability for special education?" Two avenues of exploration are available here. First, many disabilities are not recognized as such in different societies or even in the same societies over time. For example, in the United States the change from an agrarian society to an industrial society "revealed" new types of disabilities. And more "disabilities" are being "revealed" in the transition from an industrial society to a postindustrial society (see Sleeter, 1986; Chapters 5 and 7). Behind the modern school lies, not a commitment to a truly pluralistic society with many choices of lifestyle, but a drive for producing homogeneous students ready for a society marked by ever-increasing homogeneity. Second, we constantly should be examining how we can structure our society to increase the autonomy of persons with disabilities. Consider, for example, the long, torturous, and ongoing battle over the issue of transportation. Industrialized societies certainly have the resources to be much more enhancing of personal autonomy and inclusive in their politics. Many "disabilities" are the result of political, economic, and social choices, not of dramatic personal deficiencies. For humanists, the social construction of reality and the potential for democratic reconstruction of society open up the possibility for an increasingly enabled world. A positive sign for humanists has been the recent gains made by persons with disabilities in the United States to enhance their political power.

HUMANISM AND SOCIAL PROGRESS

From a humanist perspective social progress, and progress in special education, cannot follow a predetermined blueprint. Humanists seek freer, self-enhancing, and transparent social relations in democratic settings. In these democratic settings, humanists endorse a politics of inclusivity–a politics that includes citizens rather than categorizing them for the purpose of differentiation and disempowerment.

The major danger of maintaining the status quo in education is that we are not cultivating the types of humans necessary to meet the demands of ethical dialogue and democratic participation. In special education the danger of the status quo is that the focus will be on "revealing" new categories of disability without engaging in a critique of the educational and social systems that help create and maintain disabilities. For humanists, wary of the "truth" of science, the question concerning the status quo is, "Will experts one day 'reveal' that all of us are disabled?" If so, will any of us be prepared for the rigors of democratic life?

HUMANISM AND PARADIGMATIC PLURALISM

For humanists, no single paradigm can provide all the answers for social progress. Humanists see strengths and weaknesses in each of the other three paradigms of knowledge. Drawing once again on Hegel, humanists seek to expose both the flaws and the "moments of truth" in alternative methods and interpretations.

The most serious criticism that humanists level at the functionalist paradigm is that in practice methodology determines ontology. By this, humanists mean that the methods of empiricism, especially microscopic quantitative analyses, determine for the researcher the world that exists. Rather than asking important social questions, researchers allow available methodology, even with its recognized limitations, to shape the questions that they will pursue. Science and human interests are severed when research is guided by methodology rather than by social issues and theoretical questions.

A second criticism by humanists of the functionalist paradigm is that it too often turns the real into the ideal – the "is" into the "ought." In political science the most glaring example of this has come in functionalist research on voting in the United States. One of the conclusions of the extensive research on voting was that about 45% of the electorate did not vote in national elections and did not care about the outcome of the elections (Berelson, Lazarsfield, & McPhee, 1954). These results, of course, did not square with the ideal of democracies, which political scientists had been taught must have high levels of participation by interested citizens. Rather than questioning whether there were political, economic, and/or social reasons for low voter turnout and high levels of apathy, the leading researchers argued that the ideal was unreal and dangerous. They claimed the existing situation was to be preferred over the ideal, because it made "democracy" safer if many were uninterested and acquiescent! Furthermore, they argued that the existing situation should be declared the ideal form of democracy! Functionalists too often turn the real into the ideal.

However, the functionalist paradigm does produce valuable knowledge about causal relations, measurement techniques, and verification problems. For humanists, functionalist techniques are necessary for good analyses. These techniques, though, must not determine the questions asked and the knowledge produced.

The humanist views on interpretivist and radical structuralist paradigms are not surprising given the humanist paradigm's position in the four-paradigm matrix of modern knowledge. Humanists view interpretivists as having understood the important role of the actor and self-consciousness in analyses. However, humanists emphasize the social construction of the self and, thus, the interaction with others as central in analyses. It is through social interaction that ideologies can be revealed and discarded. The self-understanding of the actor is important from the humanist view (the use of the immanent critique depends on self-conscious actors reflecting on their world), but for humanists the self-understanding of the actor is not sacrosanct. Knowledge is a discursive process—a discourse with others—in which we are all open to new views. The participant's self-understanding is necessary in this discourse, but it is not authoritative.

From the humanist perspective, interpretivists err by overemphasizing the authority of the self-understanding of the actor, but radical structuralists err by underemphasizing the self-understanding of the actor. Humanists argue that the structuralists' view that consciousness and self-consciousness are determined by structures, especially economic structures, ignores the freedom of humans to reflect creatively on their social world and to alter that world. Humanists desire to persuade humans to enlarge the scope of freedom, but fear that some radical structuralists would rather force actors to be free. Humanists seek to alter structures by first changing humans' self-understandings. Structuralists seek to alter humans' self-understandings by first changing structures.

Structuralists, though, are seen by humanists as emphasizing correctly how economic structures can shape and maintain ideologies. Structuralists remind humanists that the world is not just a world of discourse and ideas, but a world of material conditions that thwart human emancipation. Furthermore, both structuralists and humanists share a macro-perspective on social understanding that recognizes the connections among social relations, structures, and ideologies.

The humanist paradigm advocates inclusivity in both its politics and research. Indeed, it seeks to illustrate the connection between human interests and human knowledge in this inclusivity. The assault on the ideologies that shackle human freedom, and that differentiate to divide and sever knowledge from human interests, needs the aid of all four paradigms.

POSTSCRIPT ON POSTMODERNISM

While the other three paradigms have their criticisms of the humanist perspective, humanists have been most troubled by criticisms from postmodernists, scholars who claim to have moved out of (or above) the four paradigms we have examined (see also Chapter 2). Major names in the postmodern movement are Jacques Derrida (1978/1979), Jean-Francois Lyotard (1979/1984), and Michel Foucault. Two of the most accessible and interesting postmodern works are Foucault's *Madness and Civilization* (1961/1973) and *Discipline and Punish: The Birth of the Prison* (1975/1979). Foucault attempts in his works to illustrate that what have been seen as progressive achievements in the humanitarian treatment of people identified as different (e.g., the insane and the criminal) have been neither always progressive nor always emancipatory. We all have been taught about instances when eager reformers and/or scientists have engaged in behavior that they thought was progressive and that we see as antihumanitarian and regressive. Foucault's criticism goes much deeper, though, for he argues that in our treatment of the different – the "other" – in modern societies, we have regularly used the "other" to gain knowledge about how to discipline and train all citizens. Our knowledge, according to postmodernists, is a result of power relations in society, and if we wish to see the techniques of power and discipline that eventually will be deployed throughout society, we should look to our treatment and control of those we identify as different and in need of treatment.

I cannot lay out the extensive postmodern agenda in this short a space. There are, though, four major postmodernist themes that touch directly on the issues we have been discussing here and in Part 1 of this book. First, postmodernists claim that all four paradigms still cling to an Enlightenment idea of knowledge. Even the subjectivist paradigms are, according to postmodernists, built on the idea that behind appearances there is still the true and the real. Humanists and radical structuralists err, claim postmodernists, when both assume that once the unequal power relations in society are overcome there will be true knowledge and social transparency. For the postmodernists, knowledge is a product of power – power and knowledge are always linked. Behind the appearances in society are more appearances, not the real.

Second, postmodernists argue that all four paradigms, given their simplistic views of knowledge, misunderstand power in modern societies. For postmodernists, power is not something that flows in only one direction. They are particularly critical of humanists and radical structuralists who think that power is always best understood as existing within an exploiter–exploited relationship. Postmodernists assert that power flows in many directions and that we all are caught within the ever-increasing webs of power in society. The professions are a major part of these webs of power as they increase control over more and more people's lives and refine techniques to discipline and control citizens.

Third, citizens are open to the power of professions because professional knowledge/power is aimed at the self-conscious modern human. It does not require external force to control the reflective citizen; rather, the reflective citizen is controlled by the internalization of the norms of the disciplinary professions. The subjectivist paradigms, the interpretivists and the radical humanists, praise a self-consciousness that postmodernists view as a sophisticated form of social control.

Fourth, postmodernists do not assign responsibility for these developments to power-hungry professionals, ruthless capitalists, or evil politicians, because all have been caught up in the creation and the results of the modern power/knowledge linkage. Even the most superficially powerful person, professional or otherwise, is caught in the webs of power of modern society and is, in a postmodernist sense, a self-consciousness open to self-discipline.

This may all sound rather pessimistic. Are we all not trapped, then, in a world of appearances and power where reform may lead simply to more control and treatment? For postmodernists, though, their analyses offer new critical and social possibilities. For they demand a rethinking of our ideas of progress, of the very categories of difference that we construct and the world we choose to live in. For postmodernists, since there is no real, true world to get to, we have the ethical obligation of choosing which world of appearances we wish to create. Postmodernists argue that if "reality" is radically socially constructed, then let us be the architects, rather than the spectators, in that construction.

REFERENCES

Berelson, B. R., Lazarsfield, P. F., & McPhee, W. N. (1954). *Voting: A study of opinion formation in a presidential campaign*. Chicago: University of Chicago Press.

Callahan, R. E. (1962). *Education and the cult of efficiency: A study of the social forces that have shaped the administration of public schools*. Chicago: University of Chicago Press.

Connolly, W. E. (1981). *Appearance and reality in politics*. New York: Cambridge University Press.

deBeauvoir, S. (1949). *The ethics of ambiguity* (B. Frechtman, Trans.). New York: Philosophical Library. (Original work published 1947)

deBeauvoir, S. (1953). *The second sex* (H. M. Parshley, Trans.). New York: Knopf. (Original work published 1949)

Derrida, J. (1979). *Spurs/eperons* (B. Harlow, Trans.). Chicago: University of Chicago Press. (Original work published 1978)

Dewey, J. (1910). *The school and society*. Chicago: University of Chicago Press. (Original work published 1899)

Dewey, J. (1946). *Democracy and education: An introduction to the philosophy of education*. New York: Macmillan. (Original work published 1916)

Elshtain, J. B. (1981). *Public man, private woman: Women in social and political thought*. Princeton, NJ: Princeton University Press.

Foucault, M. (1973). *Madness and civilization: A history of insanity in the age of reason* (R. Howard, Trans.). New York: Vintage/Random House. (Original work published 1961)

Foucault, M. (1979). *Discipline and punish: The birth of the prison* (A. M. Sheridan Smith, Trans.). New York: Vintage/Random House. (Original work published 1975)

Gideon v. *Wainwright*, 372 U.S. 335 (1963).

Goldman, E. (1917). *Anarchism and other essays.* New York: Mother Earth.

Habermas, J. (1970). *Toward a rational society: Student protest, science and politics* (J. J. Shirpiro, Trans.). Boston: Beacon Press. (Original work published 1968)

Habermas, J. (1971). *Knowledge and human interests* (J. J. Shapiro, Trans.). Boston: Beacon Press. (Original work published 1968)

Hegel, G. W. F. (1977). *Phenomenology of spirit.* Oxford: Clarendon Press. (Original work published 1807)

Horkheimer, M. (1985). *Eclipse of reason.* New York: Continuum. (Original work published 1947)

Illich, I. (1971). *Deschooling society.* New York: Harper & Row.

Lyotard, J. F. (1984). *The postmodern condition: A report on knowledge.* Minneapolis: University of Minnesota Press. (Original work published 1979)

Sartre, J.-P. (1969). *Being and nothingness: An essay on phenomenological ontology.* London: Methuen. (Original work published 1943)

Skrtic, T. M. (1991). *Behind special education: A critical analysis of professional culture and school organization.* Denver: Love Publishing.

Sleeter, C. E. (1986). Learning disabilities: The social construction of a special education category. *Exceptional Children, 53*(1), 46–54.

Tweedie, J. (1983). The politics of legalization in special education reform. In J. G. Chambers & W. T. Hartman (Eds.), *Special education policies: Their history, implementation, and finance* (pp. 48–73). Philadelphia: Temple University Press.

PART 3

Optional Theories of Special Education and Disability

Radical Structuralist Perspectives on the Creation and Use of Learning Disabilities

Christine E. Sleeter

Social science research and theory invariably are grounded, either explicitly or implicitly, in a paradigm that presupposes the nature of reality, human social behavior, knowledge, and method. The paradigm defines what questions are worth asking, how one goes about answering them, and what sorts of evidence contribute to worthwhile or convincing answers. According to Popkewitz (1984):

> The very search for scientific reasoning reflects commitments which go beyond the coherence of findings or methods. Underlying the practice of social research are assumptions about society. These assumptions refer to the nature of social control, order, and responsibility. Far from being neutral, inquiry is a human activity which involves hopes, values, and unresolved questions about social affairs. (p. 1)

As Skrtic (1986) has pointed out, special education research and theory have been grounded almost exclusively in the functionalist paradigm, which "seeks to provide rational explanations of social affairs using an approach to science premised in the tradition of logical positivism" (p. 11).

In 1986, I published an article in *Exceptional Children* offering an interpretation of the history of learning disabilities grounded in the radical structuralist paradigm (Sleeter, 1986; see also Sleeter, 1987). It has met with numerous reactions from special educators, ranging from great enthusiasm (Sigmon, 1988), to disinterest (Zigmond, 1985), to strong condemnation (Kavale & Forness, 1987; see Chapter 3). I wish to use this opportunity to discuss the theoretical reasoning behind the thesis offered in that article and to suggest additional questions following from both the paradigm and my own research.

CONFLICT THEORY AND THE RADICAL
STRUCTURALIST PARADIGM

According to Burrell and Morgan (1979), the radical structuralist paradigm assumes "that contemporary society is characterized by fundamental conflicts which generate radical change through political and economic crises" (p. 34). It is concerned mainly with finding "explanations for the radical change, deep-seated structural conflict, modes of domination and structural contradiction which its theorists see as characterizing modern society" (p. 17). Rather than viewing society as essentially unified, harmonious, and continuously progressing, radical structuralists view it as inherently conflictual. Unequal groups struggle to control resources, and some groups dominate and oppress others. The goal of radical structuralism is to promote social change by explaining how domination and oppression arise and are perpetuated in society. Conflict theory is the major theoretical orientation within the radical structuralist research tradition.

As Tomlinson explained in Chapter 5, the intellectual forbearers of the radical structuralist paradigm are Marx and Weber, whose work provides the basis for two major approaches to conflict theory within the radical structuralist research tradition. The first approach, grounded in classical Marxism, locates the main source of structural inequality in the economic structure and material relations determined by the economy. This approach to conflict theory has been applied to education by theorists such as Apple (1979), Bowles and Gintis (1976), and Wexler (1977). The roots of the second, more diffuse approach to conflict theory can be traced roughly to Weber's (1924/1947, 1922/1978) theory of unequal status groups and to Dahrendorf's (1959) treatment of power. This approach locates structural inequality in ideological as well as, or in place of, material relations and focuses on forms of social inequality other than economic. In the field of education, the reproduction of cultural inequality has been explored by Bourdieu and Passeron (1977) and Collins (1979). In addition, conflict-oriented theories of racism and race relations have been developed, for example, by Ogbu (1978), Omi and Winant (1986), and Asante (1987); and gender relations have been analyzed from this perspective by theorists such as Barrett (1980), Grumet (1988), Pagano (1990), and Spender (1982). Theorists such as these do not at all view themselves as members of a cohesive school of thought, but they do share adherence to the main assumptions of conflict theory and rejection of the economy as the main or only source of social stratification and domination. However, there are other culture-oriented conflict theorists who, operating largely from the radical humanist paradigm (and referring to themselves as critical theorists rather than conflict theorists), link economic structures with questions of power and representation (Giroux, 1983; Giroux & Mc-Laren, 1989; McCarthy, 1990; Nicholson, 1990).

Before discussing how I used conflict theory to understand the development of learning disabilities, let me briefly summarize its main premises (see Sleeter & Grant, 1988, for a more complete discussion). First, a major premise of any sociological theory is that human behavior is organized on a group basis more than on an individual basis, with major social groupings centering around family, geographic proximity, level of wealth, religion, and culture. This premise is different from that guiding psychology or biology, which underlies most research and theory in special education (Mercer, 1973; Skrtic, 1986), and which holds that human behavior derives mainly from characteristics of individuals. Applied to learning disabilities, this premise would lead to questions about how groups of people have created and used the category of learning disabilities, rather than about what characteristics of individuals make them members of the category.

A second premise of conflict theory is that groups struggle with each other for control over resources, particularly scarce resources. Further, the more scarce and desired a resource, the more intense the struggle and the more important to the struggle group membership becomes. In most cases, one can identify groups that dominate such struggles. This premise would direct a researcher to identify resources that, at a given point in time, are viewed as desirable and scarce (such as jobs, wealth, political power, land) and to identify groups competing for them.

A third premise is that, in order to solidify, extend, and legitimate their control, dominant groups structure social institutions to maintain or increase their own advantage, doing so in a way that will be perceived as fair and legitimate by most of society. According to Michels (1959), "Every human power seeks to enlarge its prerogatives. He [or she] who has acquired power will almost always endeavor to consolidate it and to extend it" (p. 207). Applied to special education, this premise suggests the examination of policies to determine who created them, who benefits most from them, how new policies are made to appear legitimate and fair, and who may be put at a disadvantage by new policies. Policies and practices are not simply to be accepted at face value, but should be examined in light of the vested interests they may be furthering.

Finally, a fourth premise is that opposition and resistance, in various forms, are natural responses of oppressed people and provide entree to social change. Opposition may be overt and visible, or it may be private. It may be directed consciously toward social change, or it may take the form of destructive rebellion, withdrawal from "acceptable" social conventions, withdrawal from obvious membership in an oppressed group (such as "passing" for white), and so forth (see Giroux, 1983). In special education this premise could direct a researcher to examine how people with disabilities respond to their oppression (an excellent source for such an examination is the publication *Disability Rag*) or how other social groups placed at a disadvantage by special education policies react.

CONFLICT THEORY AND THE DEVELOPMENT OF LEARNING DISABILITIES

Hallahan and Cruickshank (1973) and Wiederholt (1974) have presented histories of the development of learning disabilities that have been fairly well accepted within the field and cited frequently in learning disabilities textbooks (Sleeter, 1986). These histories have been couched within the medical model for understanding the development of social policy. Essentially, the historic interpretation of both sources is that learning disabilities are a real, objective phenomenon within a small percentage of the population, a human pathology that only recently has been discovered and researched. Schools, in attempting to serve all children as fairly as possible, responded to pressure by parents, physicians, and other advocates of children with learning disabilities by creating programs to serve them.

The medical model has come under considerable attack in the past few years (e.g., Kavale & Forness, 1985a) and is being replaced mainly by the behavioral model for understanding and remediating learning "deficiencies." While Kavale and Forness (1985b) have argued that the behavioral model represents a different paradigm from the medical model, both share the same functionalist assumptions that learning disabilities are a real phenomenon, children with this disorder are different in meaningful ways from "normal" children, schools attempt to serve all children fairly, and special education programs and policies represent attempts to do so. Behaviorism has generated a different set of practical "solutions" to a specific set of educational problems than has the medical model, but the basic framing of what constitutes a problem, how one investigates it, and what sorts of solutions are acceptable has remained the same. Regardless of which model one subscribes to, learning disabilities are viewed as a problem within individuals, one that is treatable through programs that attempt to change the individual to fit the demands of what is assumed to be a rational system of education in a good society.

My approach to understanding learning disabilities, based on conflict theory, proceeded quite differently. I began by questioning whether learning disabilities are a real, objective phenomenon. During my own experience as a learning disabilities teacher, while simultaneously completing a master's degree in the field, I was troubled by the discrepancy between my understanding of my students and what the literature said learning disabilities are. The only things my students seemed to have in common were that they were failing most of their other classes, primarily due to severe reading difficulties, and that they were able to score at least 90 on an IQ test. During that time I also began to reflect on the racial composition of special education classes and other programs. I previously had been trained to work in inner-city schools and had spent a year substitute teaching in a metropolitan school district. During that year I came to expect to see learning disabilities classes populated mainly by white males, whereas remedial classes and classes for students with behavioral disorders and mental retardation seemed disproportionately minority. While I did not count children or record my observations, I developed the impression that there was some relationship between the race of a child and the program in which he or she was placed.

These observations led me to questions that conflict theory provides a way of addressing. Some of my work elsewhere (e.g., Sleeter & Grant, 1988), as well as the work of others (e.g., McLaren, 1989), synthesizes data on the extent to which our society continues to be stratified on the basis of race, social class, and gender. Various theorists have offered race (e.g., Omi & Winant, 1986), social class (e.g., Bowles & Gintis, 1976), and gender (e.g., Barrett, 1980) as major social divisions that structure competition for power, wealth, and control.

Over the past 20 years a sizable body of literature has developed, using ethnography as an important research tool, showing how schools reproduce stratification based on race and social class (e.g., Anyon, 1981; Everhart, 1983; Grant & Sleeter, 1986; Harry, 1992; Oakes, 1985; Rist, 1970, 1978; Sleeter, 1992). What this research shows is that many educational policies and practices are shaped in part by conflicting interests among various racial and social class groups, and usually operate in ways that benefit those who are white and wealthy more than those who are of color and/or poor.

One such practice, which relates directly to special education, is how students are grouped for instruction. Consistently, low-income students and students of color are disproportionately represented in lower tracks and ability groups and in many special education programs, while students who are white and middle or upper class are disproportionately placed in upper tracks and ability groups and in programs for the gifted. Studies of tracking and grouping have found that placement in groups often depends in part on ascribed student characteristics, students in lower groups rarely achieve upward mobility, and instruction in lower groups is qualitatively different and often inferior to instruction in upper groups (e.g., Collins, 1988; Oakes, 1985; Rist, 1970; Rosenbaum, 1976). As a result, students in upper groups (and in programs for the gifted), who are disproportionately white and middle to upper class, leave school better prepared to compete for entry into universities and higher paying occupations than students in lower groups, who are disproportionately of color and/or poor.

The studies noted above do not specifically address the special education category of learning disabilities. However, they raise questions about whose interests the learning disabilities track has served, and, if one does not accept the premise that learning disability is an objective condition of individuals, questions about how and why the category was created in the first place.

The learning disabilities category was "born" at the first meeting of the Association for Children with Learning Disabilities in 1963. Rather than investigating medical and psychological research that preceded its birth, as did Wiederholt (1974) and Hallahan and Cruickshank (1973), I chose to investigate the social conditions prior to 1963 that might have led certain groups to create a new category of student disability. Conflict theory provides some guidance here, arguing that social changes result from competition over scarce resources. The more scarce a given resource, the more intense the struggle among competing groups and thus the more important group membership becomes. Immediately preceding 1963, what had become scarce, leading to increased group competition?

Two major events had occurred in the 1950s that had a great impact on schools: the Supreme Court ruling in *Brown* v. *Board of Education* in 1954 and the launching of Sputnik in 1959. Black Americans have always struggled for access to resources enjoyed by white Americans, such as jobs, housing, and education. I will not review the history of that struggle here, but simply note that following World War II large numbers of blacks migrated to northern cities in search of these resources. The *Brown* decision, ruling that "separate" is not "equal" and is no longer legal, dissolved the legitimacy of laws and many practices whites had used to restrict black access to America's resources. In schools, this meant that black children were able to compete in much larger numbers than before with white children for access to the best instruction. Both Tyack (1974) and Kirp (1982) have documented how schools in New York and the California Bay Area, respectively, responded by resegregating black and Hispanic children into various remedial programs, purportedly on the basis of their being further behind than white children and therefore having different educational needs. However, by the late 1950s and early 1960s, the influx of black people into northern cities and of black children into white schools caused whites to perceive a threat to their domination over access to the better jobs and the best educational resources.

The launching of Sputnik fueled a different sort of competition, but one that converged with that brought about by the *Brown* decision. Sputnik led to a crisis in the competition that had been building since World War II between U. S. and Soviet business and military interests for control over raw materials and access to world markets. According to Hodgson (1976), World

War II left U. S. business with the problem of how to redirect wartime manufacturing and how to employ returning veterans. The approach business adopted was to produce a greatly increased volume of consumer goods at low prices. At the same time, the military establishment remained strong, attempting both to prevent another war as well as to protect America's access to foreign raw materials, goods, and markets. Both developments placed pressures on schools. Due to increased automation, the white collar labor market expanded much more rapidly than the blue collar labor market, causing business to pressure schools to push students to attain increasingly higher levels of achievement. In addition, the military criticized schools for their failure to produce scientists that would help America in its continued military development.

Sputnik created a symbol that enabled the business and military establishments to rally the American public behind specific school reforms. The resources viewed as in danger of becoming increasingly scarce were markets, cheap raw materials, and power in the international arena. The popular press of the day spelled out the crisis and the perceived solutions very clearly (see Sleeter, 1986, 1987). The proposed reforms included: (1) making elementary reading instruction more rigorous, (2) testing student achievement on the basis of higher and uniform standards while ending the practice of social promotion, (3) grouping students by ability, and (4) assigning the most capable teachers to the top students. These reforms, all of which were implemented to some degree, made access to the best instruction, a high school diploma, and subsequent employment at higher salaries more dependent on a student's reading level than previously had been the case. While these resources themselves had not become more scarce, including Americans of color among those who could compete for them reconstituted the competition.

If white middle- to upper-class people are viewed as a dominant group, what effects would these developments have on them? Members of this and other groups, of course, would want to ensure that their children tested well enough on achievement tests, especially on reading tests, to be placed in the top groups and thus to receive the best instruction and preparation for college. But, historically, white middle- to upper-class people had dominated educational and social positions of power, including school administration and school boards (Spring, 1982), as well as state and federal legislatures and the professions. This gave them the power to change the rules of social institutions in ways that maintained or increased their advantage, as well as to develop mechanisms that convinced most of society that the changes were fair and legitimate. From the perspective of conflict theory, the question to ask is: How did members of the white middle to upper class make certain that the reforms they wanted in public education would be instituted, thus ensuring that their children would continue to enjoy the best access to quality instruction, in spite of both the *Brown* decision and the tougher standards?

Members of the white middle to upper class employed a combination of strategies to achieve these ends, including instituting systems for grouping students for differential instruction, reconstituting the curriculum, and redefining intelligence, which formed the basis for IQ and other standardized tests. During the late 1950s, four categories existed in schools for grouping low-achieving students and "explaining" their low achievement: mentally retarded, slow learner, emotionally disturbed, and culturally deprived. Disproportionate numbers of lower-class and minority students were placed in all four of these categories (Bloom, Davis, & Hess, 1965; Dunn, 1963; Shaw & McKay, 1942), thus resegregating them for differential instruction on the basis of curricular content and tests that were designed to appear fair and neutral to most educators and members of the public.

At the same time, a small number of white middle- and upper-class parents faced a problem: Their own children were unable to keep up with escalated reading standards and, as a result, were (or were in danger of) being categorized as slow, retarded, or disturbed. The new category of learning disabilities, which at that time was cast in medical terms such as congenital word blindness, developmental alexia, specific dyslexia, minimal brain injury, and psychoneurological learning disorder, provided an alternative explanation and way of grouping these children. The idea already existed within the fields of medicine and psychology that minimal brain injury retards some learning functions of otherwise normal children, although supporting research was rather sparse and specific theories about the exact nature of the problem were somewhat contradictory. But it was more advantageous for these white parents to use this idea than it was for them to do nothing. Indeed, it explained their children's difficulties in a way that designated their intelligence and emotional state as normal, and did not blame their home background or the school reforms for their problems.

In fact, the creation of the learning disabilities classification helped to deflect attention away from questions that might have been taken very seriously at that time (and still should be taken seriously). Do children from low-income and minority backgrounds enter school "behind" their white middle-class counterparts, or simply with a different fund of knowledge and skills? (This argument has raged for at least 2 decades, but in practice still tends to be resolved according to the cultural deprivation thesis; see Sleeter & Grant, 1988.) Is it ethical to stratify children for differential education and subsequent differential life opportunities (see Oakes, 1985)? Is it ethical for the United States to treat the rest of the world as a source of raw materials, cheap labor, and markets for domestic business interests? Rather than dealing with basic questions such as these, however, parents, physicians, psychologists, and educators merely focused on ways to protect and remediate children who seemed to be afflicted with learning disabilities but who otherwise were "normal."

The learning disabilities category was created mainly by parent organizations, and in its first few years was used largely to serve low-achieving white students from economically advantaged backgrounds (Franks, 1971; Sleeter, 1986; White & Charry, 1966). By definition, students so classified were intellectually normal or superior, and they enjoyed whatever advantages, in the form of higher expectations, accrue to students who are white, middle class or above, and frequently from families with actively supportive parents.

According to many conflict theorists, oppressed groups react to developments that oppress them. And one certainly can see active resistance on the part of black and Hispanic parents (and educators) to the placement of their children in programs that thwart their ambitions for achievement. Due in part to their pressure, the category of culturally deprived was disbanded, and the IQ cutoff score for identification as mentally retarded was lowered from one to two standard deviations below the mean (Grossman, 1973). In addition, the proportion of students of color in classes for the mentally retarded declined somewhat, while, at the same time, increasing numbers of students of color began to be placed in classes for the learning disabled (Tucker, 1980). (The same data are not kept for student family income level, nor did the same struggle occur on the part of low-income whites, since the lower and working classes have never achieved the extent of political and grassroots organization that racial minority groups have.) This suggests that learning disabilities increasingly has been used as a preferred category for placing low-achieving students, although it also suggests that in many school districts the category probably is no longer serving the same protective function as it did when it was first created.

By the late 1980s, the learning disabilities classification was being used somewhat differently from state to state (and probably from school district to school district), depending on the racial and ethnic mix of students and the array of programs available. Nationally in 1987, white and African American students were slightly overrepresented in learning disabilities programs, whereas Asian American students were underrepresented, and Hispanic and Native American students were represented proportionally. But in many states, as the proportion of total school enrollment represented by African American, Hispanic, or Native American students rose, so too did the disproportionate placement of these students in classes for students classified as learning disabled and educable mentally retarded (Harry, 1992). Thus, depending on local factors, the learning disabilities classification may serve as a protective category for low-achieving white students or as a more "acceptable" classification than mental retardation or emotional disturbance for students of color who are experiencing school difficulties. In addition, as Trueba (1989) illustrated, learning disability classes sometimes become repositories for immigrant students whose low achievement results from the stress of cultural and linguistic incompatibility created by the inflexibility of conventional instructional practices in general education classrooms.

IMPLICATIONS

This discussion suggests implications for future work. Several questions about learning disabilities need to be investigated. For example, to what extent is the learning disabilities classification increasingly serving as a protective device for white middle- and upper-class college students, especially in an era in which general remedial and developmental support services are being reduced? Given current demographic trends in learning disabilities classification, whose interests are being served by the category? How are students so classified viewed and treated as compared with other students? If the learning disabilities classification is abandoned or severely limited, as some are advocating (e.g., Algozzine & Ysseldyke, 1983), whose interests will be served, and what new practices will be developed to replace the functions that the category currently serves? A variety of research methodologies are recommended for investigating such questions, including ethnographic case studies as well as literature analyses, demographic analysis, and surveys.

Conflict theory also needs to be applied to analyzing other special education categories. The category of emotional disturbance is waiting to be examined from a conflict theory perspective; so far it has received surprisingly little attention, although Kugelmass (1987) has published an excellent ethnography raising important questions about its use. In Wisconsin there is movement to establish a category for so-called "grey area" children; this could be examined profitably through conflict theory.

The present analysis questions much of what occurs in both special education and general education policy and practice. It does not have simple implications for change within the context of conventional educational structures and practices. What it does suggest is that schools are political institutions that, contrary to what most Americans would like to believe, do not serve all children equally. It reaffirms the need to deal directly with racism and classism at a broad social level, as well as to support practices that treat all students fairly and celebrate differences as normal and desirable rather than deviant.

Finally, this analysis suggests that those who are learning disabled, while they certainly have some learning difficulties, may not be members of a discrete category in the same way as those who are deaf or blind. Questioning the legitimacy of the learning disabilities category, however, does not negate the very real difficulties that some students experience in school because of the unreasonable expectation that all students read at a particular grade level at a particular time in order to learn. Requirements for learning as well as for participating in society might be made less dependent on the attainment of certain time-bound reading levels. Those who experience difficulties might well organize and press for changes that would open up learning and other opportunities to people like themselves. This is not meant to be antiliteracy; literacy is a valuable skill that other skills cannot duplicate. But learning history content, for example, should not depend mainly on one's ability to read a textbook at a certain grade level; understanding directions on medicine bottles should not depend mainly on the ability to decipher fine print. Those who experience problems because of difficulties with reading are in the best position to tell the rest of society what changes might serve their interests.

REFERENCES

Algozzine, B., & Ysseldyke, J. (1983). Learning disabilities as a subset of school failure: The oversophistication of a concept. *Exceptional Children, 50*(3), 242–246.

Anyon, Y. (1981). Elementary schooling and distinctions of social class. *Interchange, 12*(2–3), 118–132.

Apple, M. W. (1979). *Ideology and curriculum*. London: Routledge & Kegan Paul.

Asante, M. K. (1987). *The Afrocentric idea*. Philadelphia: Temple University Press.

Barrett, M. (1980). *Women's oppression today*. London: Verso Books.

Bloom, B. S., Davis, A., & Hess, R. (1965). *Compensatory education for the culturally deprived*. New York: Holt, Rinehart & Winston.

Bourdieu, P., & Passeron, J. (1977). *Reproduction in education, society, and culture*. London: Sage.

Bowles, S., & Gintis, H. (1976). *Schooling in capitalist America*. New York: Basic Books.

Burrell, G., & Morgan, G. (1979). *Sociological paradigms and organizational analysis*. London: Heinemann.

Collins, J. (1988). Language and class in minority education. *Anthropology and Education Quarterly, 19*(4), 299–326.

Collins, R. (1979). *The credential society*. New York: Academic Press.

Dahrendorf, R. (1959). *Class and class conflict in industrial society*. Stanford: Stanford University Press.

Dunn, L. M. (1963). *Exceptional children in the schools*. New York: Holt, Rinehart & Winston.

Everhart, F. (1983). *Reading, writing and resistance*. Boston: Routledge & Kegan Paul.

Franks, D. J. (1971). Ethnic and social status characteristics of children in EMR and LD classes. *Exceptional Children, 37*(7), 537–538.

Giroux, H. A. (1983). *Theory and resistance in education: A pedagogy for the opposition*. South Hadley, MA: Bergin & Garvey.

Giroux, H. A., & McLaren, P. (Eds.). (1989). *Critical pedagogy, the state, and cultural struggle*. Albany: State University of New York Press.

Grant, C. A., & Sleeter, C. E. (1986). *After the school bell rings*. Basingstoke, England: Falmer Press.

Grossman, H. J. (1973). *Manual on terminology and classification in mental retardation*. Washington, DC: American Association on Mental Deficiency.

Grumet, M. R. (1988). *Bitter milk*. Amherst: University of Massachusetts Press.

Hallahan, D. P., & Cruickshank, W. M. (1973). *Psychoeducational foundations of learning disabilities*. Englewood Cliffs, NJ: Prentice-Hall.

Harry, B. (1992). *Cultural diversity, families, and the special education system*. New York: Teachers College Press.

Hodgson, G. (1976). *American in our time*. Garden City, NY: Doubleday.

Kavale, K. A., & Forness, S. R. (1985a). *The science of learning disabilities*. San Diego: College Hill Press.

Kavale, K. A., & Forness, S. R. (1985b). Learning disability and the history of science: Paradigm or paradox? *Remedial and Special Education, 6*(4), 12–23.

Kavale, K. A., & Forness, S. R. (1987). History, politics, and the general education initiative: Sleeter's reinterpretation of learning disabilities as a case study. *Remedial and Special Education, 8*(5), 6–12.

Kirp, D. L. (1982). *Just schools*. Berkeley: University of California Press.

Kugelmass, J. W. (1987). *Bias, behavior and handicaps*. New Brunswick, NJ: Transaction Books.

McCarthy, C. (1990). *Race and curriculum*. London: Falmer Press.

McLaren, P. (1989). *Life in schools*. New York: Longman.

Mercer, J. (1973). *Labeling the mentally retarded: Clinical and social system perspectives on mental retardation*. Berkeley: University of California Press.

Michels, R. (1959). *Political parties: A sociological study of the oligarchial tendencies of modern democracies* (E. Paul & C. Paul, Trans.). New York: Dover.

Nicholson, L. J. (1990). *Feminism/postmodernism*. New York: Routledge, Chapman & Hall.

Oakes, J. (1985). *Keeping track: How schools structure inequality*. New Haven, CT: Yale University Press.

Ogbu, J. U. (1978). *Minority education and caste: The American system in cross-cultural perspective*. New York: Academic Press.

Omi, M., & Winant, H. (1986). *Racial formation in the United States*. New York: Routledge & Kegan Paul.

Pagano, J. A. (1990). *Exiles and communities: Teaching in the patriarchal wilderness*. Albany: State University of New York Press.

Popkewitz, T. S. (1984). *Paradigm and ideology in educational research*. London: Falmer Press.

Rist, R. C. (1970). Student social class and teacher expectations in ghetto education. *Harvard Educational Review, 40*(3), 411–451.

Rist, R. (1978). *The invisible children: School integration in American society*. Cambridge, MA: Harvard University Press.

Rosenbaum, J. (1976). *Making inequality*. New York: Wiley.

Shaw, C. R., & McKay, H. D. (1942). *Juvenile delinquency and urban areas*. Chicago: University of Chicago Press.

Sigmon, S. B. (1988). Remarks on the Kavale and Forness "case study." *Remedial and Special Education, 9*(3), 57.

Skrtic, T. M. (1986). The crisis in special education knowledge: A perspective on perspective. *Focus on Exceptional Children, 18*(7), 1–16.

Sleeter, C. E. (1986). Learning disabilities: The social construction of a special education category. *Exceptional Children, 53*(1), 46–54.

Sleeter, C. E. (1987). Why is there learning disabilities? A critical analysis of the birth of the field in its social context. In T. S. Popkewitz (Ed.), *The formation of school subjects: The struggle for creating an American institution* (pp. 210–238). London: Falmer Press.

Sleeter, C. E. (1992). *Keepers of the American dream*. London: Falmer Press.

Sleeter, C. E., & Grant, C. A. (1988). *Making choices for multicultural education: Five approaches to race, class, and gender*. Columbus, OH: Merrill.

Spender, D. (1982). *Invisible women: The schooling scandal*. London: Writers and Readers Publications.

Spring, J. (1982). *American education* (2nd ed). New York: Longman.

Trueba, H. T. (1989). English literacy acquisition: From cultural trauma to learning disabilities in minority students. In B. J. R. Shade (Ed.), *Culture, style, and the educative process* (pp. 49–70). Springfield, IL: Charles C. Thomas.

Tucker, J. A. (1980). Ethnic proportions in classes for the learning disabled: Issues in nonbiased assessment. *Journal of Special Education, 14*(1), 93–105.

Tyack, D. B. (1974). *The one best system*. Cambridge, MA: Harvard University Press.

Weber, M. (1947). *The theory of social and economic organization*. (T. Parsons, Ed.; A. M. Henderson & T. Parsons, Trans.). Glencoe, IL: Free Press. (Original work published 1924)

Weber, M. (1978). *Economy and society*. (G. Roth & C. Wittich, Eds.; E. Fischoff, H. Gerth, A. M. Henderson, F. Kolegar, C. W. Mills, T. Parsons, M. Rheinstein, G. Roth, E. Shils, & C. Wittich, Trans.) (Vols. 1–2). Berkeley: University of California Press. (Original work published 1922)

Wexler, P. (1977). *The sociology of education: Beyond inequality*. Indianapolis: Bobbs-Merrill.

White, M. A., & Charry, J. (1966). *School disorder, intelligence, and social class*. New York: Teachers College Press.

Wiederholt, J. L. (1974). Historical perspectives on the education of the learning disabled. In L. Mann & D. Sabatino (Eds.), *The second review of special education*. Philadelphia: Journal of Special Education Press.

Zigmond, N. (1985, April). Discussant comments in the session, Special education placements and programs: Sociological issues. Paper presented at the annual meeting of the American Educational Research Association, Chicago.

CHAPTER 8

Holism and Special Education:
There Is No Substitute for Real Life Purposes and Processes

Lous Heshusius

> *Researcher: What do you think about school?*
> *Jake: Boring. Everytime do lines. Have to do eighty thousand lines. Lots of spelling words.*
> *Researcher: What do you think about speech help (from speech pathologist)?*
> *Jake: Do lots of letters and spelling in Ms. E's class. Me no like doing that. Play tic-tac-toe and money games with you.*
> *Researcher: Is that work?*
> *Jake: Yeh.*
> *Researcher: What's different then?*
> *Jake: Fun here. Not fun in my classroom. Boring. Not do nothing. Just do work. Write. Write. Write. Do lines then throw them out. Do more. (Gould, 1988, p. 16)*

> *I am beginning to suspect all elaborate and special systems of education. They seem to me to be built upon the supposition that every child is a kind of idiot who must be taught to think. . . . Let (the child) come and go freely, let him touch real things and combine his impressions for himself, instead of sitting indoors at a little round table, while a sweet-voiced teacher suggests that he build a stone wall with his wooden blocks, or make a rainbow out of strips of coloured paper, or plant straw trees in bead flower pots. Such teaching fills the mind with artificial associations that must be got rid of, before the child can develop independent ideas out of actual experiences.*
> *—Anne Sullivan (in Keller, 1903, p. 319)*

This we know: All things are connected like the blood that unites us. We did not weave the web of life. We are merely a strand in it. Whatever we do to the web, we do to ourselves.
—*Chief Seattle*

Even a cursory overview of today's literature in a wide array of disciplines reveals that we are groping for an entirely different understanding of life. The dominant worldview, or paradigm, as I will use the term here, by which we have made sense out of life for the past 3 to 4 centuries, is collapsing all around us, and in us; in our relationship to each other, to knowledge, to the planet, and in our dawning awareness that our minds have been separated from our bodies, emotions, and spiritual needs, resulting in unprecedented levels of alienation and lack of coherence. The once powerful metaphors and assumptions that have guided our lives since the rise of Western science in the sixteenth and seventeenth centuries are now seen as no longer adequate to explain the nature of reality and of our place within "it," or to explain the ways in which we think we can come to know something. These metaphors and assumptions are referred to by different names. Within special education, for instance, Iano (1986) has used the term "natural science paradigm," while Poplin (1988a) used the term "reductionistic paradigm," and elsewhere I adopted the terms "mechanistic" (1982) and "Newtonian" (1989a) paradigm.

THE CONCEPT OF PARADIGM

I am using the concept of paradigm in its broadest sense, drawing from the literature on new paradigm thinking.[1] From this perspective, it should *not* be confused with theory, model, or strategy (meanings often given to the word paradigm, also in special education; see Heshusius, 1989a, 1989b). The word paradigm as used here refers to an interrelated set of beliefs and values about the nature of reality as well as the nature of knowledge (in other words, beliefs and values by which we allow each other to decide that something counts as real and by which we allow each other to say that we know something . . . and be believed!). This set of beliefs and values further includes procedures, models, and theories that flow coherently from these beliefs and values. It includes agreements about criteria for both problem selection and problem evaluation. All this is to say that what constitutes a "problem" in one paradigm may not even be recognized as a problem in another. Or what "works" within one set of paradigmatic beliefs and values may be seen as not relevant in another.

Paradigms, then, draw the parameters of what is seen as possible and worthwhile (see Battista, 1982; Jantsch, 1980; Schwartz & Ogilvy, 1979). Thus, answers to the paradigmatic questions (What counts as real, and How are we allowed to claim knowledge?) are *human agreements*. It is not the case that God appeared one day, and that he or she gave us, once and for all, the right answers to paradigmatic questions. The fathers of the scientific revolution (I don't think there were any mothers, which is significant), giants like Galileo, Descartes, Newton, Bacon, and Locke, certainly tried hard to find a place for God in their increasingly rational and mathematical images of reality, when they thought of God as the "chief mathematician of the universe" (LeShan & Margenau, 1982, p. 246). At the same time, however, they took the construction of knowledge *out* of the authority of the church and put it *into* the authority of their newly found methodological and mathematical rationality.

CONTEMPORARY DISCONTENT WITH THE MECHANISTIC PARADIGM

As we are approaching the twenty-first century, the Newtonian, mechanistic paradigm is no longer providing genuine meaning for our lives. As historian of science Morris Berman (1984) stated pointedly, the fundamental issues confronted by any civilization, or by any person in her or his life, are issues of *meaning*. Our loss of meaning, he said, expressed in the split between fact and value that characterizes the modern era we still live in, is rooted in the scientific revolution of the sixteenth and seventeenth centuries, which gave rise to a mechanistic interpretation of life (for interdisciplinary discussions of the breakdown of mechanistic thought, see, e.g., Berman, 1984, 1989; Capra, 1982; LeShan & Margenau, 1982; Merchant, 1980). The mechanistic, Newtonian way of appropriating reality has been tremendously successful for technology but is now widely acknowledged as inadequate for philosophy of science and the sociology of knowledge, including for an understanding of human individual and social behavior, and, therefore, for an understanding of schooling and learning.

Oliver and Gershman (1989) poignantly summarized the situation by pointing directly to the mechanistic worldview, which they call the "bits and pieces worldview," as responsible for the many bizarre contradictions in human behavior today. These include, they noted, discoveries that have greatly reduced infant mortality and childhood disease while children everywhere die of famine and malnutrition; the release of atomic energy while the entire world lives with the possibility of nuclear war and nuclear mistakes; the development of abundant foods while the earth, air, and water are poisoned by the chemicals used to sustain that very abundance. "Progress" has occurred piecemeal, ignoring the whole. We can no longer call it unqualified progress. Oliver and Gershman, as have many other scholars, went on to explain that these contradictions are *not interpretable* within the framework of their own meaning system. In other words, there is no way to understand the causes of these contradictions or to find solutions while guided by the fundamental assumptions of mechanistic thought, for mechanistic thought *itself* is the problem and, therefore, do what it will, it can only extend its tunnel vision and cause more contradictions. We do not have a technological crisis. We have a conceptual and perceptual crisis that can be solved only by shifting our paradigmatic framework at its most fundamental level, by shifting the very fabric of thought, feeling, and somatic awareness.

In education, too, the mechanistic worldview has led to bizarre contradictions through its belief in the possibility of objectivity, its emphasis on fragmentation, its view of learning as mastery of small pieces of information, its obsession with quantification and measurement, its insistence on "finding" direct relationships between "variables," and its normative, competitive, and ranking mode of viewing differences. These assumptions have given rise to a range of remedial and special programs, of which special education, of course, makes up the largest part. Skrtic (1991) has incisively analyzed such programs as institutionalized attempts to cover up general education's failure.

In terms of their instructional and assessment practices, special education programs too have been informed largely by mechanistic assumptions, as witnessed in a seemingly never ending array of remedial worksheets, workbooks, and programmed materials. There always seem to be still more "prerequisites" that need to be mastered before going on to the real thing. The mechanistic imagination has created a bottomless well of them. The real thing keeps being postponed. In that manner, real, genuine meaning for learning, which is a bit "messier" and cannot be put under external control, does not have to be dealt with (for detailed discussions of mechanistic-reductionistic beliefs and their specific impact on special education theory and practice, see Heshusius, 1982, 1989a, 1989b; Iano, 1986, 1987; Poplin, 1987, 1988a).

While at the *academic level* in education, these mechanistic constructs have increasingly been criticized, and entirely different metaphors and assumptions for instruction and assessment have been proposed (see, e.g., Crowell, 1989; Doll, 1986; Heshusius, 1989a, 1991; Oliver, 1990; Oliver & Gershman, 1989; Sawada, 1986; Sawada & Caley, 1985; Sloan, 1984), the *practice* of education in public schooling still reflects largely "old" paradigm thinking. And while there is a "sense of desperation" in the national and state reports on the precarious state of education in the United States and Canada (see Lipsky & Gartner, 1989; Miller, 1988; Oliver & Gershman, 1989), the *pedagogical* recommendations these reports provide reflect more of the same mechanistically informed attempts at remediating poor outcomes of school-ing: more homework, more testing, more school hours, more school days. Efforts at school reform, with few exceptions, are resulting, as Brown (1991) observed, in schools that function as "better oiled" machines, but still as machines (see also Darling-Hammond, 1990). Most schools, with the best intentions, conceive of better pedagogy as more of the same, or a slightly different version of the same (while thinking they have engaged in fundamen-tal change). Educators, as everyone else, are caught in the mechanistic world-view, the assumptions of which most of us are not even aware of. We have grown up with it. It requires a deliberate, conscious effort to become aware of its parameters and underlying assumptions before real, fundamental change at a paradigmatic level can occur.

The bizarre contradictions in education and special education caused by the "bits-and-pieces" paradigm can be seen when special education programs increase and increase, while dropout rates also increase and increase; when more testing is seen as a solution to our problems (since testing, mechanisti-cally speaking, is thought to be very precise through its standardization, quantification, and ranking procedures), while our students see the tests as useless, artificial, and irrelevant; when 4- and 5-year-olds, who need a nurtur-ing environment for their young bodies and minds, can fail kindergarten; when we preach equity and equality, while students from ethnicities other than white are disproportionately placed in special education classes on the basis of a particular view of learning and schooling by which they are judged and found wanting; when we see students as deficient and/or deviant, while their actual motivation for not performing in school often is resistance to the alienating school culture; when we demand more school hours, more "time on task," and more homework, while students call school "dead time." There are always exceptions, of course, but I do not think I am drawing an exagger-ated picture: Ample accounts of schooling support my statements (e.g., Brown, 1991; Goodlad, 1984; Shanker, 1989).

Out of the pervasive discontent with the mechanistic worldview, holistic thought has emerged providing an entirely different understanding of life, that is, an entirely different set of assumptions by which to understand the nature of reality and our place within it. With regard to education, we see some manifestations of holistic thought, mostly at the elementary level. Whole language, peace education, and global education at least are not strange terms any longer, although they typically are engaged in as "subjects" rather than being an integral part of a holistic understanding of education as a whole. Occasionally, one finds an emphasis on somatic awareness through forms of yoga or autogenic activities to establish (or rather re-establish) the body–mind integrity we lost under mechanistic thought. But the latter is still very rare. Teachers who engage in forms of holistic education have to deal with contradictory demands such as standardized testing, rigid grading practices, fragmentation of time, and externally prescribed and fragmented curricula, all of which make a holistic conception and practice of education impossible.

RESISTANCE TO FUNDAMENTAL CHANGE
IN SPECIAL EDUCATION

To date, special education has been particularly resistant to fundamental change. Instruction and assessment, with an occasional exception, continue to feature filling-in-the-blank kinds of exercises, endless worksheets, out-of-context spelling exercises, drill on out-of-context tasks, and the Dolch words, again and again. Diagnostic testing data and "intervention programs" as prescribed by these data, largely continue to constitute the formal information used to make placement and "programming" decisions. Yet these practices are based on outdated beliefs inherent in the mechanistic paradigm, such as knowing as mastery of components, measurement as the exclusive means of knowing, the idea of additive and linear progress, and the view of the learner as reactive (meaning active only in reaction to the teacher's curriculum, questions, etc.). All ignore the use of personal, somatic, social, and cultural meaning and context as *starting points* for learning and teaching. With few exceptions, one runs into these deadly rational pedagogical and assessment practices when visiting special education classes. Increasingly, one meets teachers, however, who do not *want* to engage in these meaningless activities, but not infrequently they are told by their special education supervisors that they have to.

While both general and special education have their roots in mechanistic thought, there may be a number of reasons for what seems to be the relatively greater difficulty in letting go of outdated paradigmatic beliefs in special education as compared with general education. One of the reasons, I believe, is what I like to refer to as "the stronger dose" formula: Given that learning has been understood to come about through mechanistic assumptions, the logical response *dictated* by the mechanistic paradigm, when youngsters do not perform as well as they are expected to, is application of the same assumptions but in a more intense manner, or in greater doses. If learning occurs by breaking down content into pieces of information to be mastered, then the size of the pieces for students who do not learn well in school must be broken down even further. We have not applied the principle well enough. When learning means drill and practice, for special education youngsters it must mean more drill and practice. Traditional medicine operates in the same manner. If the cold or the infection does not go away, take more and/or a stronger dose of antibiotics (instead of rest, changing nutrition, changing one's life style, etc.). The "stronger dose" framework manifests itself when educators say with regard to holistic principles in education: "That is fine for regular kids, but not for special needs kids. They need structure."

A beautiful example of the incorrrect reasoning involved in the "stronger dose" framework can be gleaned from comparing Itard's training of Victor, the wild boy of Aveyron, to Anne Sullivan's education of Helen Keller, who was blind, deaf, and mute.[2] Itard, a physician, whose thinking was informed by the standard mechanistic conception of what it meant to be scientific, followed a method that was a clear forerunner of applied behaviorism and behavior modification (Lane, 1976). He essentially incorporated into his training program all the assumptions I have indicated by the term "mechanistic." Itard's method was rational in the Cartesian, mechanical sense. It adhered to a component model, rendering the idea of progress sequential, additive, and controllable. Itard broke language down into its smallest components before handing these to Victor: speech sounds for speaking and isolated letters and words for reading. Again and again, he had Victor repeat the sounds and the words by having him match isolated words to the objects the words represented, using reinforcement, prompting, and fading procedures that later came to characterize behaviorism (Lane, 1976). There was some limited success in these exercises. However, Victor's mastery over some isolated pieces of language was never incorporated into communicative ability. Generalization never happened. The problem of generalization never occurred in Helen Keller's education: She simply was always learning in real life settings and for real life purposes.

Anne Sullivan never concerned herself with the teaching of isolated words or sounds, or isolated sentences (all of which would have created the problem of generalization, which can be viewed as a problem indigenous only to the mechanistic paradigm). From the very start, Anne Sullivan used complete phrases and sentences that were *directly* related to what she and Helen were doing together. *Helen's mind never became confused about what language was for.* It was to make meaning, to do important things together, to express understandings of real things and real events. Commenting on her methods, Anne Sullivan said:

> I see no sense in "faking" conversation for the sake of teaching language. It's stupid and deadening to pupil and teacher. If there is nothing in the child's mind to communicate, it hardly seems worthwhile to require him to write on the blackboard, or spell on his fingers, cut and dried sentences about "the cat", "the bird", "a dog". I have tried from the beginning to talk naturally to Helen and to teach her to tell me only things that interest her and ask questions only for the sake of finding out what she wants to know. When I see that she is eager to tell

me something, but is hampered because she does not know the words, I supply them and the necessary idioms, and we get along finely. (Keller, 1903, p. 382)

In Helen Keller's education, the somatic, emotional, and intellectual were never separated. It is telling that physicists Bohm and Peat (1987), in their book on wholeness in scientific thought, used Helen Keller's education as a striking example of holistic understanding of how one really comes to know something. They see genuine communication, metaphorical and creative perception, and the process of transformation through passion and insight (all of which characterize Helen Keller's learning and Anne Sullivan's teaching) as central to all acts of knowledge construction. Creative perception and free communication, Bohm and Peat (1987) stated, "are inseparably related, so that understanding and creation of knowledge arise as much in the flow of ideas between people as in the understanding of the individual alone" (p. 115). Real life meaning, then, was always *at the beginning* of Helen Keller's education, not projected as an end purpose, as is so strikingly the case in our schools, and particularly in special education's emphasis on remediation, practice, drill, and externally programmed progress. One must wonder what would have happened to Helen Keller if she had had to learn the Dolch words over and over, if her progress had been indicated on daily performance on isolated learning tasks, if her curriculum had consisted of lengthy sequences of prerequisite skills in programmed workbooks. I fear we might guess the answer.

Another reason for the greater difficulty in special education of letting go of outdated paradigmatic assumptions, is the field's initial grounding in the traditional medical model that largely conceptualizes difference as deviance or defect. The medical model focuses on direct treatment of what are seen as symptoms of the problem, assuming a causal relationship between symptoms and etiology of the hypothesized disease. The symptoms of a cold are treated (attacked) directly: typically by taking antibiotics (instead of rest, fresh air, change of life style, etc.). In education, the direct treatment of what are seen as learning problems leads to the practice of direct intervention, which of course was Itard's approach to Victor. Problems are attacked directly (just think of "word attack" skills). From a holistic understanding, such direct intervention or attack of symptoms is not justified, since the assumption of direct causal relationships between "symptoms" and hypothesized etiology is seen as incorrect and simplistic. Holistic health care will tell a patient with a lingering cold to rest, relax, eat differently, attend to stress, and the like, rather than directly "attack" the symptoms by prescribing more antibiotics. Holistic education likewise looks at what might be problematic and how to create a healthy learning environment with a far greater openness to the complexity and interdependency of all that might be involved.

Still another reason for the resistance to paradigmatic change in special education surely must lie in the marriage of legal mandates and behaviorism (the quintessential expression of mechanistic thought) with regard to assessment and instructional specifications in Public Law 94–142, The Education for All Handicapped Children Act. P.L. 94–142's prescriptions for assessment and instruction were developed in the heyday of behaviorism and can be seen as having legislated mechanistic instruction and assessment models. Teachers who do not want to engage their students and themselves in the contextless activities generated by mechanistic thought often are told by supervisors that they must because of legal mandates (see Heshusius, 1984).

From a new paradigm, holistic perspective, the crisis in special education, too, is not a crisis that can be solved within a "more of the same" framework dictated by mechanistic prescriptions. We do not have a crisis of efficiency. We have a paradigmatic crisis. A crisis of meaning. Our problems have outrun additive, linear, reductionistic, quantitative, and control solutions. Rather than trying forever to reduce complexity to simplicity through standardization of learning activities so we think we have control over learning, we will need to *tune into* complexity, to *re*introduce complexity and flexibility, to *re*introduce the centrality of novelty, creativity, and real life purpose to the act of learning, to *re*introduce the somatic and the emotional substrata that are so deeply involved in any act of learning, also for those children who do not do well in school. Again, Sullivan's approach to Helen Keller's education illustrates this view of life and learning even for the most difficult of learners. It further requires that we genuinely listen to children in schools and take their input deadly seriously.

This is no overly humanistic suggestion. Self-organization, self-regulation, inherent goal directedness, and immanent activity characterize all of life. If we want learners to learn in school, we *must* listen to how *they* view their situation. Albert Shanker (1989), president of the American Federation of Teachers, in his discussion of the publication of more than 20 interviews of high school students, commented on how students feel alienated and lost, and not connected to school life. They must *want* to come to school and learn, he stated; otherwise, no school reform, however ambitious, will improve student learning. He said, "It's hard to explain why we don't routinely ask kids–*especially kids in trouble*–about how to improve school" (p. 1; emphasis added).

THE EMERGENT HOLISTIC PARADIGM

It is important to keep in mind that a shift from mechanistic thought to holistic thought is not restricted to education. Education, in fact, lags behind the emergence of holistic thought as compared with other areas of study, including theoretical physics, ecology, biology, open systems theory, holistic medicine, and the study of the relationship between consciousness and brain function (e.g., Bohm & Peat, 1987; Briggs & Peat, 1984; Capra, 1982; Cousins, 1985; Griffin, 1988; LeShan & Margenau, 1982).

Terms other than "holistic" also are used to refer to assumptions largely similar to the ones I will briefly outline below. In education, Doll (1986), drawing from Prigogine's work (Prigogine & Stengers, 1984), spoke of a "new sense of order," translating into a "transformative curriculum" (p. 10); Crowell (1989) refers to "a new paradigm," "a new way of thinking," or "a new worldview" (p. 60); Poplin (1988b) speaks of the "constructivist/holistic" (p. 401) paradigm. While these authors do not necessarily agree fully with each other in all aspects, or stress different dimensions, the general *direction* is certainly the same, steering the metaphors by which we generate our thinking and language for theory and practice in education away from mechanistic thought and toward a view of life and learning that honors, among other characteristics, complexity, self-organization, self-regulation, and the centrality of novelty and creativity in the act of knowing, and points to ways of knowing other than the merely rational. What follows are brief descriptions of several key assumptions of the emergent, holistic paradigm and what they imply for educational thought.

The Epistemic Nature of Reality and Knowing

The nature of what counts as real and how we may know is understood to be epistemic; that is, there is nothing "out there" that is separate from our own construction of it. Reality is mind-dependent. In other words, *we* construct what we know. Who we are, with all our values, interests, and various needs, is part and parcel of what we come to construct as knowledge. Our knowledge emerges from it. In communal as well as in individual knowing, we cannot separate facts from values, or the observer from the observed, or the knower from the known, as the mechanistic paradigm told us it is possible to do. In education, our theories and research, and our diagnostic, assessment, and instructional practices do not have a life separate from our somatic, social, cultural, gender, and ethnic values, needs, and interests, but emerge from them. Just to mention one concrete example: Standard measurement procedures do not reflect something "real" out there, but present no more, and indeed no less, than a particular way we decided a long time ago would be a good way to construct knowledge. That decision was shaped by a particular set of social, cultural, and ideological values. There is absolutely nothing objective or sacred about any of the established procedures. This is not to say that established procedures are arbitrary. Not at all. What the epistemic nature of all knowing tells us is not that what we do is arbitrary or irrational, but that, however unconsciously, it represents our choices, contexts, values, needs, history, intentions, and desires, *and* that it could have been different. Many analyses exist, for example, that trace our obsession with measurement, prediction, and control to patriarchal, technological, and capitalist interests (e.g., Bordo, 1987; Highwater, 1981; Keller, 1985; Kubrin, 1981).

The recognition of the value-ladenness of all knowledge instantly puts morality and ethics at the center of what we do. Concern for the ethical consequences of our actions is, of course, not new. But the *explicit* recognition of the epistemic nature of all knowing casts a much more critical light on the ethical question by pointing to the inescapable fact that not only does what we do with our "findings" have ethical implications, but *our very ways of knowing* (our methods and procedures) are neither objective nor neutral; they rest on assumptions held to be true within the mechanistic paradigm, assumptions that in the past gave professional knowledge the edge of superiority over those we teach. As Bernstein (1983) stated, "Method is not neutral. It not only presupposes an understanding of what constitutes social and political life it has become a powerful factor in shaping (or rather misshaping) human life in the modern world" (p. 45). The realization of the value-laden nature of measurement and methodology means that we have to become more urgently aware of the personal, social, cultural, and political place our students have in *their* worlds, which should not be violated by our assessment and instructional constructs and procedures. The way *we* know can no longer claim the privilege of objective superiority.

The inextricable unity of value and fact, and of body, feeling, and mind, is also reflected by Bohm and Peat's (1987) summary of today's understanding of how the brain functions. "Intellect, emotion, and will cannot actually be separated," they stated, because the connection between thought, feeling, and will is so intimate that "there is no point at which one of them ends and the others begin" (pp. 218–219). As they stressed, this holds equally true for the scientist and the development of science.

Whole–Part–Whole Relationships

The nature of reality and of knowing is holistic. This does not mean that, starting with parts, all we have to do is attend to all possible parts in order to be holistic (a common misunderstanding). Nor does it mean doing away with "parts" (another common misunderstanding). Nor can holism be equated with humanism (still another common misunderstanding). Holism, rather, refers to a conception of life, and therefore also of education, that holds that the whole is more than the sum of the parts, is different from the sum of the parts, and *cannot be accounted for* or reduced to the sum of the parts. The holistic understanding of whole–part–whole relations turns the mechanistic position on its head: It is not the case that the dynamics of the whole can be understood from the properties of the parts, but rather that the properties of the parts can be understood *only* from the dynamics of the whole. Whole language, in its unadulterated form, is a fine example of the shift away from "parts" to whole–parts–whole relations. Within whole language, one does not do away with the "parts" but instead addresses the function they are meant to carry out in context to serve personal meanings and purposes. This alters the construct of the "skills" into that of meaningful functions and relations: The "parts" gain their meaning only within the dynamics of the whole. The mechanistic paradigm, on the other hand, holds that "parts" have an independent meaning of their own. They add up to the whole because the whole is not more than the sum of the parts. In special education, this is reflected, for instance, in isolated skill training, endless worksheets, remedial reading kits of some 300 reading skills, lengthy sequences of behaviors and strategies to be mastered, and other kinds of fragmentations and additive constructs.

Inherent Order Within Complexity

There is inherent order in all that exists. Nothing turns out to be random. Chief Seattle, as quoted at the beginning of this chapter, understood this perfectly. Inherent order cannot be externally forced, and where we try nevertheless, we create havoc. It is now a well-known fact that our planet is in the mess it is in because we have not attended to the inherent and complex order that exists in all that is. On the contrary, we have imposed the idea that "elements" are real and can be brought under our control, a view that has thwarted and upset the planet's internal, complex, purposive, and self-regulating order. This imposition has resulted in disastrous consequences for the planet, as we all know. Operating under mechanistic assumptions, we have taken external programming and control to be our mission.

Holistic educators would hold that lack of learning in school often occurs because of the same misconception about the nature of order. Most contemporary instructional and assessment practices continue to be shaped by the mechanistic belief in an external nature of order and control. Only that which takes place under conditions of external order is seen as real and as valid. In special education we typically act on the belief that even greater degrees of external order and control are necessary.

Change and Progress Are Transformative

Holism holds that change and progress, including human learning, are not additive, sequential, and linear, but occur through complex interactions at many interdependent levels. Change is transformative and is not under direct control. It occurs through immanent and goal-directed activity by the learner herself or himself within a specific context. When we learn, new knowledge is not just added to existing knowledge, but the act of learning transforms what we knew into something new. The past is linked to the present in a personal, social, and meaningful way; the body, the emotions, the intellect, and the will are *inextricably* connected. Meaning and context thus become crucial determiners of the very ability to learn and of learning outcomes.

An important characteristic of the transformative nature of change is the essential role of novelty. The role that novelty plays in transformation leads to the unpredictability of future events. Outcomes cannot be predicted from knowledge of initial conditions. We see this acknowledged across disciplines (Schwartz & Ogilvy, 1979). For educators it means that learning outcomes are not predictable from what and how we teach. (Which is *not* to say, to be sure, that our teaching makes no difference! Of course it does. It is only to say that there is no direct, predictable relationship.) If special educators were to take this seriously, it would mean, among other things, a fundamental rethinking of the immense efforts we now put into predictive testing, prestipulating measurable outcomes, and exerting tight, external control over curriculum and student performance, *as if* the future were under our control. We would pay far greater attention instead to the relevance and integrity of what we do with our learners at any given time.

Immanent Activity, Purposefulness, Goal-Directedness, Self-Organization, and Self-Regulation

In today's science, not just our brain and our planet, but even the universe is acknowledged as a self-organizing and goal-directed system (see Bohm, 1980; Bohm & Peat, 1987; Briggs & Peat, 1984; Jantsch, 1980). Self-organization, self-regulation, and inherent goal-directedness are central constructs for the holistic educator. Students *and* teachers cannot do anything else but make meaning in their own ways. Therefore, the *authenticity* of the learning and teaching experience becomes of immense importance. By authenticity is meant instruction that is directly relevant to the *student's* perception of relevancy, instead of instruction that is defined as mastery of skills that are "prerequisites" for real life. By authenticity in learning is meant learning for real purposes instead of exercises in learning. Perhaps no one expressed the difference more concisely than the child who asked his teacher: "When are we gonna stop readin' *reading* and start readin' *something*?" (cited in Weber, 1974, p. 83).

When we make students engage merely in exercises in learning, we can be sure that what they really are learning is something other than what we think we are making them learn. It is important, of course, to stress that the definition of authenticity cannot be owned by the textbook publisher, or by the programmer of curriculum, for then we are right back into mechanistic formulations and controls. It must be owned by the students' and teachers' minds and feelings.

Self-organization, self-regulation, and goal-directedness are also at the heart of the unpredictability of future behavior. For what is in between the initial conditions and the future behavior is guided by the self-organization, immanent meaning making, and goal-directedness of the person herself or himself. The impulse to learn, then, comes at the deepest level, always from *that which matters* to the person. And I submit that not much of what we typically ask students in special and remedial education to do really matters to them. Therefore, our typical instructional approaches will not easily set into motion real, authentic learning.

Seymour Sarason (in McKean, 1985) related how the light went on for him when, one morning, upon arriving at an institution for persons with mental retardation he learned that several residents, whom he had tested and had found wanting in intelligence, had escaped. Residents who had not been able to find their way out of a maze of paper had plotted their way out of a supervised institution! There is no substitute for real life purposes.

The Organism Is an Open, Living System, Always in Exchange with Its Environment and Its History

This assumption is, of course, of immense importance and becomes even more urgent when teachers and students are from different cultural, racial, ethnic, and linguistic communities that may adhere to different meanings about what schooling should be about, and may have different visions of what an educated person should be like. Gender, too, impacts on the view of what it means to come to know something (both cognitively and morally) and what it means to succeed or to fail. Given the continuing overrepresentation of cultural, racial, and linguistic minorities and of boys in special education, we must admit that we have not understood this principle well at all.

The social constructivist theory of human behavior, which holds that learning does not take place inside a person's head, but is largely a result of social and cultural interchanges with both persons and symbols, further reflects an "open system" understanding of learning. Frederick Erickson (1984), in his review of studies that view learning from this perspective, underscores the crucial importance of personal *ownership over problem formulation* for authentic learning to occur. We can see learning through personal ownership over problem formulation taking place very clearly in the years before school, when children learn many things at astonishingly rapid rates, because what they learn is almost always what they want to learn. A young child does not learn the word "donut" because someone tells her or him to learn it, or because it is the next step in a controlled vocabulary reading program, but because he or she wants a donut.

Taking ownership over problem formulation involves multiple value decisions that are of distinct human and cultural intent and meaning and that do not come into play when a child does the "same" problem in a workbook. We engage in the fallacy of reductionism when we assume that somehow these two conditions (authentic learning situations versus performance on predetermined, out-of-context, component tasks) are not different in any essential way. Subtracting 65 from 100 on a worksheet is *not* the same as knowing how much change to expect after buying a real candy bar from a real clerk in a real store. It is not just a matter of designing nice activities for children to do. We are concerned here with much more than that; namely, that the impulse for learning comes from that which matters to the person. Our entire emotional, somatic, cognitive, intuitive functioning operates as *a priori* and inextricable unity. While in the present school system, we cannot take our students routinely out of the school into real life, interesting, and meaningful learning situations, we definitely can bring real purpose and meaning from the real lives of our students (including ethnic, racial, gender, linguistic, and class dimensions) into our classrooms to form the basis of learning activities, particularly if we ask our students to help us do so.

Illustrations of Self-Organization, Intentionality, Purpose, and Goal-Directedness

The following is a page from a "kindergarten basal text" used in a qualitative research study by Polakov (1986) in which she focused on children's experience of literacy acquisition. Although I have used this illustration before, I would like to share it here because it so pointedly demonstrates, I believe, some of the differences between mechanistic and holistic understandings of what it means to learn to read.

> Little ant Big ant.
> Walk little ant, walk.
> Big ant hill.
> Walk to little ant hill.
> Walk to big ant hill.
> Funny little ant.
> Funny big ant. (cited in Polakov, 1986, p. 41)

Would you, the reader, know what the plot of the story was about if I were to ask you? Are you intrigued about what may happen on the next page? I am afraid that we all *know* what the next page is going to look like, and that we are not particularly intrigued about seeing it! Most would agree, I think, that this exercise in reading is rather disengaged from story line, disembedded from meaning, and disengaged from children's lives. I would also submit that it resembles many remedial materials that are used in special education. It was clearly programmed to teach certain words: "little" and "big." The word "funny" was introduced, and we can be sure that it will be printed several times on the next page whether it makes sense or not. This kind of "reading" illustrates the *idea* within the mechanistic paradigm (not the fact, but the idea) that we *can* program progress by forcing external, tightly sequentialized control over learning and teaching. It illustrates not the fact, but the idea, that progress is sequential and therefore is predictable and controllable, that learning equals adding components, that all children, regardless of their interests and backgrounds, will benefit from this approach, and that the entire exercise is not only desirable, but also objective and scientifically justified.

Listen now to what children think about all this and what they *actually* learn when *we* think that they are learning the new words "little" and "big."

Liz: The stories are too boring . . . they're so dumb and boring . . . and I hate those dopey books and the worksheets. . . . We have to sit there and do this and do that and worksheets all the time.

Polakov: What do you think kids could tell the people who write those books?

Liz: Tell the teachers not to get those books anymore.

Polakov: What books should the teachers get?

Liz: Get the books that are more interesting so kids will like to read the stories.

Polakov: Sasha, if you were the boss of the class, what would you change?

Sasha: I'd get the Ant and Bee books—'cos the story is fun and the kids read the red words and the big person reads the black words and they *both* read the story *together*. And it has much more pages. In kindergarten the books are dumb and there are little papers with the words on and you have to write them and it's *so* boring—I sit there and try and make up my own story out of the words so it's more interesting. (Polakov, 1986, p. 42)

When Polakov (1986) asked Liz how she knew how to read a story with rather difficult words in it, Liz said: "*'cos it's my favorite book*. I always know the words in my *favorite* books" (p. 42). When I read Liz's answer for the first time, I thought: Yes, indeed, why would you want to remember words from books you find dopey and boring. When Poplin (1988b) asked a student how he knew how to spell the word "horse" so well, he said (Poplin states, "in utter disgust at my naivity"): "Because I love them" (p. 410). As Poplin commented, passion and deep interest form the impulse for learning, not our stimulus–response management or external control of curriculum.

In a study on assessment, Rapkin (1987) inquired into the reasons for

answers children had just given to questions on a standardized word association test. Thirteen different relationships between the answers and the reasons for their answers emerged. The following are two examples from the
data of one such relationship, in which children gave the "wrong" answer
(according to the manual) to an association task but an answer that was
perfectly correct in terms of their personal construction of meaning, even
though the children knew the "right" answer as well.

DOWN   OLD   THIN   UP

The child had answered, "old and thin."

> Researcher: Can you tell me about that?
> Child: When they're old they're all so thin (touches his face).
> Researcher: You're showing me your face. Your face gets thin?
> Child: Ya.
> Researcher: Where have you seen that? Do you know anyone?
> Child: Ya, my grandfather . . . grandpa.
> Researcher: What about up and down? Do you think they go together, too?
> Child: Ya, 'cause some things go up and some go down . . . like opposites.

BOY   DOG   CRUMBLE   BARK

The child had answered, "boy and dog."

> Researcher: Can you tell me why?
> Child: 'Cause a dog is a boy's best friend.
> Researcher: Why is a dog a boy's best friend?
> Child: 'Cause if somebody was out walking past the dog and the dog runs after
>   the person and gets after him, when the boy says "Come here, dog," the
>   dog goes right back to him.
> Researcher: What about dog and bark?
> Child: Ya, 'cause a dog barks. (Rapkin, 1987, p. 14)

The test constructors viewed any deviation from the relationship they
had stipulated as a problem with "input organization." Studies like this one
show that the "wrong" answer can be perfectly right where it is the result of a
personal and often complex process the child goes through, linking the present (the test question) with her or his past, and that the child in fact may
know the more abstract answer as well. The study shows that real life experience and cognition are inextricably linked in the construction of knowledge
and that this does *not* represent a problem with input organization. The
problem, rather, lies in the fact that the test constructors separate cognition
from emotion and real life experience. It is really they who lack the ability to

de-center. From a holistic perspective, one could justly say that it is the test constructors who have a problem with "input organization."

What is crucial to stress here is that the most important answer *for the child*, the most "real" answer, emerges in a holistic manner: as a somatic, gender, and social-cultural construction and transformation of meaning. To mark answers "wrong" or "right" according to the manual (that is, according to our adult ways of rationalizing and taking apart knowledge) further illustrates unequal power relations in the construction of knowledge and a lack of understanding of how knowledge is constructed.

HOLISTIC LEARNING PRINCIPLES

The following is an evolving list of learning principles based on publications in special education by authors who are attempting to apply holism to instruction. They include, but are not limited to, publications by Church and Newman (1986), Dudley-Marling (1986), Goodman (1982, 1986), Heshusius (1989b), Poplin (1988b), Rhodes and Dudley-Marling (1988), Valencia and Pearson (1988), and Weaver (1982, 1988). This list of principles is certainly not exhaustive and could be put together in different ways.

Learning Is Immanently Active. The concept of the special needs student as a "passive learner" is a contradiction in terms and rather refers to a resistant learner. The processes of self-organization and self-regulation mean that the student is *always* learning and actively directing and regulating her/his learning, even if the teacher fails to notice it or cannot directly observe it. The student may do so in novel and unpredictable ways. Often, what the student is learning may not necessarily be what we have planned for her or him to learn. Immanent activity is not merely a characterization of cognition, but is grounded in and interwoven with the somatic and emotional substrata of our lives.

Learning Is Understanding Relations. Learning, from a holistic perspective, is coming to understand relationships and interdependencies: interdependency within self among what traditionally has been separated as intellectual life, emotional life, the life of the body, and our gender, social, and cultural lives; interdependency between self and other (an individual, a community, the planet); interdependency between self and knowledge; and interdependency between what we traditionally have separated as "subjects," fostering relational knowing instead.

Change and Progress Are Transformative. New meanings are not added but interact in complex and inherently personal/social ways with the past, drawing from cognition, bodily knowing, feeling, and will, in inextricable ways. This progress can be fostered, but cannot be externally programmed and controlled, because of the immanent activity in the person and the self-regulatory nature of learning.

Much Learning Occurs Through Social Exchanges with Persons and Symbols. Interactive and reflective teaching and learning are the preferred pedagogical approaches. Education occurs through engagement of the somatic and emotional substrata, through reflection, dialogue, the construction of questions, and personal, social, and cultural interpretations.

Assessment Equals Documentation of Authentic Learning Processes and Learning Outcomes. Assessment focuses on what students do over time in purposeful (to both student and teacher) learning activities in natural, interactive settings. We can no longer separate the question, "What does this learner need to learn?" from the question, "How does this learner construct meaning in a particular situation?" Authenticity characterizes learning for real purposes, not exercises in learning. Authenticity exists when meaning (in terms of the student's lived experience) is present at the start of the educational act, when instruction is grounded in it. It does not exist in the learning of isolated skills to be mastered. Meaning and purpose cannot be controlled or postponed.

A portfolio documentation of learning can come from many contexts, in and out of school, and can take many forms. Multiplicity of data from authentic learning situations constitutes assessment, not measures from tests or performance on controlled component tasks. Indicators of authentic learning and possible sources and ways to gather data for assessment include students' thoughts about what they read and what they do in school; students' dialogues with peers as they talk about their interpretation of text; students' summaries of readings; students' generated questions about the material learned; oral retelling of stories for meaningful purposes (e.g., retelling to young children); dialogue during writing conferences; reluctance to stop reading when the period is over; increased difficulty level in material selected; greater concentration during silent reading and greater impatience with disturbances; the quality of children's oral reading miscues; recall of past experiences in the construction of new meanings; dialectic journal writing approaches; generation of one's own math story problems; and the sharing with peers of favorite parts of learning activities and readings.

Errors Are Essential and Positive Activities and Should Never Be Punished. Errors should not be punished, even if only by counting them "wrong." They are not pieces of "wrong" information but rather constitute acts of meaning making. They are, as someone said, "wrong moves in the right direction, and therefore they are right moves." They provide great insights into students' thinking. Growth and errors, as Weaver (1982) stated, "Go hand in hand" (p. 443). She further suggested that we "take delight" in new kinds of errors that often appear when students learn new concepts, and see them for what they are: signs of progress.

Trust and Authenticity Between Teacher and Student Are Essential. This principle may be the most important and also the most self-evident one.

CONCLUSION

Ideally, then (ideally, because I am, of course, well aware of the resistance within existing special education structures), I am referring to a fundamentally different way of *thinking and feeling about thinking and feeling*, with regard both to ourselves and to our students, from what conventional theories in special education prescribe. All this is not "just theory." Holistic assumptions are manifested in practice by increasing numbers of teachers and principals in schools. Holistic principles within special education are found in increasing numbers of whole language special education classrooms. They are manifested in Anne Sullivan's teaching of Helen Keller, in the Vanier communities, and in many of the aspects of the Waldorf schools where, for both general and special education, the spiritual and artistic in the child are seen as the integrative forces.

Fundamental change will not be easy. There are already signs that holistic assumptions are being co-opted by the "old" but still dominant paradigm, when, for instance, whole language is turned into a nice and neat program of five or six steps to whole language, turning it right back into a mechanistic, fixed procedure. Or in the area of assessment, where the movement toward holistic scoring has co-opted the term "holistic," while, in fact, it has nothing to do with holistic understandings of body–mind–emotion interdependency, self-organization, and goal-directedness. The needed fundamental change does not have to do with producing another blueprint, which turns holistic thought into a mechanistically reconstructed "holism," or what Berman (1989) referred to as "cybernetic holism" (p. 306). Rather, it has to do with *being* with ourselves and with children in a different way altogether.

While this may sound idealistic, it seems increasingly clear that we have no choice. Even in politics, where characteristically short-term, material considerations and fragmented solutions, supposedly backed up by "hard data," are thoroughly shaped by mechanistic assumptions, "the end of the modern era" has been announced by none less than Vaclav Havel (1992), President of The Czech Republic. The reign of the ideas of objectivity and rationality is over, Havel said. Politicians must become people again, he went on to say, people who do not just look for a scientific and statistical representation of things but also trust real people, trust their own thoughts, their own feelings. The politician, Havel (1992) said, "must above all trust in his subjectivity as his principal link with the subjectivity of the world" (p. 1).

A cartoon I saw some time ago pictures two caterpillars talking to each other. Above them flutters a butterfly. One caterpillar, looking up at the butterfly, says to the other "No one is going to get me into one of those things!" We, too, may have no choice but to go through a metamorphosis, or else decay. The "bits and pieces worldview" we are so thoroughly used to can no longer interpret our educational problems for us, for it is itself the problem. We must become reacquainted with what Berman (1989) referred to as "embodied holism" (p. 306) (as contrasted to a cybernetic, mechanistic holism) that grounds us in the somatic and emotional substrata of our lives, so that learning may become again connected to how our real lives are lived.

NOTES

1. I am using the concept of paradigm in a way that is not consistent with the editor's general framework for this book. From my own studies in new paradigm thinking, I have come to see the world of knowledge construction within a two-paradigm perspective: The mechanistic and the emergent holistic paradigm, also referred to as the nonmechanistic, or just the "new" or "emergent" paradigm. I would see the four paradigms delineated by Skrtic rather as metatheories. The holistic paradigm incorporates humanistic and interpretivist dimensions but cannot be reduced to them. In other words, there is more to it. Therefore, there really would be no place for holism within Skrtic's four-paradigm perspective.

2. I am grateful to the late, eminent Dutch scholar Carl van Pareren, who pointed out to me the comparison between Itard's training of Victor and Helen Keller's education by Anne Sullivan in terms of paradigmatic differences. For those who read the Dutch language, a more elaborate comparison can be found in van Pareren (1984). As van Pareren also noted, drawing the comparison is not to attribute the differences in educational outcomes to the teachers' different approaches in an absolute sense. We do not know if Victor would have learned to really communicate had he had Sullivan as a teacher, although judging from Sullivan's spectacular success with Helen Keller we might speculate the results would have been better. Victor clearly showed intelligence and sought out human contact, both of which are necessary for the kind of success Sullivan accomplished in teaching Helen Keller. What we can say is that the likelihood is very great that Helen Keller would not have blossomed had her teacher used the methods Itard used on Victor.

REFERENCES

Battista, J. R. (1982). The holistic paradigm and general systems theory. In W. Gray, J. Fidler, & J. R. Battista (Eds.), *General systems theory and the psychological sciences* (Vol. I, pp. 209–210). Seaside, CA: Intersystems Publications.

Berman, M. (1984). *The reenchantment of the world.* New York: Bantam Books.

Berman, M. (1989). *Coming to our senses: Body and spirit in the hidden history of the West.* New York: Simon & Schuster.

Bernstein, R. J. (1983). *Beyond objectivism and relativism: Science, hermeneutics, and praxis.* Philadelphia: University of Pennsylvania Press.

Bohm, D. (1980). *Wholeness and the implicate order.* Boston: Routledge & Kegan Paul.

Bohm, D., & Peat, F. D. (1987). *Science, order, and creativity.* New York: Bantam Books.

Bordo, S. R. (1987). *The flight to objectivity: Essays on Cartesianism and culture.* Albany: State University of New York Press.

Brown, R. (1991). *Schools of thought. How the politics of literacy shape thinking in the classroom.* San Francisco: Jossey-Bass.

Briggs, D. P., & Peat, F. D. (1984). *Looking glass universe. The emerging science of wholeness.* New York: Simon & Schuster.

Capra, F. (1982). *The turning point: Science, society, and the rising culture.* New York: Simon & Schuster.

Church, S., & Newman, J. M. (1986). Danny: A case history of an instructionally induced reading program. In J. M. Newman (Ed.), *Whole language: Theory and practice* (pp. 169–179). Portsmouth, NH: Heinemann.

Cousins, N. (1985). *Nobel Prize conversations by Sir John Eccles, Roger Sperry, Ilya Prigogine, Brian Josephson.* Dallas: Saybrook.

Crowell, S. (1989). A new way of thinking: The challenge of the future. *Educational Leadership, 47*(1), 60–63.

Darling-Hammond, L. (1990). Achieving our goals: Superficial or structural reforms? *Phi Delta Kappan, 72*(4), 286–295.

Doll, W. E. (1986). Prigogine: A new sense of order, a new curriculum. *Theory into Practice, 25*(1), 10–16.

Doll, W. E. (1989). Complexity in the classroom. *Educational Leadership, 47*(1), 65–70.

Dudley-Marling, C. (1986). Assessing the written language development of learning disabled children: A holistic perspective. *Canadian Journal of Special Education, 2*(1), 33–43.

Erickson, F. (1984). School literacy, reasoning, and civility: An anthropologist's perspective. *Review of Educational Research, 54*(4), 525–546.

Goodlad, J. I. (1984). *A place called school: Prospects for the future.* New York: McGraw-Hill.

Goodman, K. S. (1982). Revaluing readers and reading. *Topics in Learning and Learning Disabilities, 1*(4), 87–93.

Goodman, K. S. (1986). *What's whole in whole language?* Richmond Hill, Ontario: Scholastic.

Gould, B. (1988). How do children perceive resource withdrawal for speech and language assistance? Unpublished paper, York University, Faculty of Education, Toronto.

Griffin, D. R. (Ed.). (1988). *The reenchantment of science*. Albany: State University of New York Press.

Havel, V. (1992, March 1). The end of the modern era. *New York Times* "OP-ED", p. 1.

Heshusius, L. (1982). At the heart of the advocacy dilemma: A mechanistic world-view. *Exceptional Children, 49*(1), 6–13.

Heshusius, L. (1984). Why would they and I want to do it? A phenomenological-theoretical view of special education. *Learning Disability Quarterly, 7*, 363–368.

Heshusius, L. (1989a). The Newtonian-mechanistic paradigm, special education, and contours of alternatives: An overview. *Journal of Learning Disabilities, 22*(7), 403–415.

Heshusius, L. (1989b). Holistic principles: Not enhancing the old but seeing a-new: A rejoinder. *Journal of Learning Disabilities, 22*(10), 595–602.

Heshusius, L. (1991). Education: What shall students take from it, to invent their futures? From the machine metaphor to new paradigm thinking. Paper presented at the Culverhouse Conference, The New Paradigms and Education, University of South Florida, Tampa.

Highwater, J. (1981). *The primal mind: Vision and reality in Indian America*. New York: New American Library.

Iano, R. P. (1986). The study and development of teaching: With implications for the advancement of special education. *Remedial and Special Education, 7*(5), 50–61.

Iano, R. P. (1987). Rebuttal: Neither the absolute certainty of prescriptive law nor a surrender to mysticism. *Remedial and Special Education, 8*(1), 52–61.

Jantsch, E. (1980). *The self-organizing universe: Scientific and human implications of the emerging paradigm of evolution*. Oxford: Pergamon Press.

Keller, E. F. (1985). *Reflections on gender and science*. New Haven, CT: Yale University Press.

Keller, H. (1903). *The story of my life*. New York: Doubleday, Page, & Company.

Kubrin, D. (1981). Newton's inside out! Magic, class struggle, and the rise of mechanism in the West. In H. Woolf (Ed.), *The analytic spirit: Essays in the history of science* (pp. 96–121). Ithaca, NY: Cornell University Press.

Lane, H. (1976). *The wild boy of Aveyron*. Cambridge, MA: Harvard University Press.

LeShan, L., & Margenau, H. (1982). *Einstein's space and van Gogh's sky: Physical reality and beyond*. New York: Macmillan.

Lipsky, D. K., & Gartner, A. (Eds.). (1989). *Beyond separate education: Quality education for all*. Baltimore: Paul H. Brookes.

McKean, K. (1985, October). Intelligence: New ways to measure the wisdom of man. *Discover, 6*(10), 25–41.

Merchant, C. (1980). *The death of nature*. New York: Harper & Row.

Miller, J. P. (1988). *The holistic curriculum*. Toronto: Ontario Institute for the Study of Education Press.

Oliver, D. (1990). Grounded knowing: A postmodern perspective on teaching and learning. *Educational Leadership, 78*(1), 64–69.

Oliver, D., & Gershman, K. W. (1989). *Education, modernity, and fractured meaning. Toward a process theory of teaching and learning.* Albany: State University of New York Press.

Polakov, V. (1986). On meaning making and stories: Young children's experience with texts. *Phenomenology and Pedagogy, 4*(3), 37–47.

Poplin, M. S. (1987). Self-imposed blindness: The scientific method in education. *Remedial and Special Education, 8*(6), 31–37.

Poplin, M. S. (1988a). The reductionist fallacy in learning disabilities: Replicating the past by reducing the present. *Journal of Learning Disabilities, 21*(7), 389–400.

Poplin, M. S. (1988b). Holistic/constructivist principles of the teaching/learning process: Implications for the field of learning disabilities. *Journal of Learning Disabilities, 21*(7), 401–416.

Prigogine, I., & Stengers, I. (1984). *Order out of chaos: Man's new dialogue with nature.* New York: Bantam Books.

Rapkin, S. (1987). Children's constructions of answers to test questions. Unpublished manuscript, York University, Faculty of Education, Toronto.

Rhodes, L. K., & Dudley-Marling, C. (1988). *Teaching reading and writing to learning disabled and remedial learners: A holistic perspective.* Portsmouth, NH: Heinemann.

Sawada, D. (1986). Spontaneous creativity in the classroom. *Journal of Humanistic Education and Development, 25*(1), 2–11.

Sawada, D., & Caley, M. T. (1985). Dissipative structures: New metaphors for learning in education. *Educational Researcher, 14*(3), 13–25.

Schwartz, P., & Ogilvy, J. (1979). *The emergent paradigm: Changing patterns of thought and belief* (Report 7, Values and lifestyle program). Menlo Park, CA: SRI International.

Shanker, A. (1989, October 22). What's wrong with schools? Ask the kids. *New York Times,* p. 1.

Skrtic, T. M. (1991). *Behind special education: A critical analysis of professional culture and school organization.* Denver: Love Publishing.

Sloan, D. (Ed.). (1984). *Toward the recovery of wholeness: Knowledge, education, and human values.* New York: Teachers College Press.

Valencia, S. W., & Pearson, P. D. (1988). Principles for classroom assessment. *Remedial and Special Education, 9*(1), 26–35.

van Pareren, C. P. (1984). *Ontwikkelend onderwijs.* Amersfoort, Netherlands: Acco.

Weaver, C. (1982). Welcoming errors as signs of growth. *Language Arts, 59*(5), 438–444.

Weaver, C. (1988). *Reading process and practice: From socio-psycholinguistics to whole language.* Portsmouth, NH: Heinemann.

Weber, J. K. (1974). *Yes, they can! A practical guide for teaching the adolescent slower learner.* Toronto: Methuen.

CHAPTER 9

Special Education and Student Disability as Organizational Pathologies:
Toward a Metatheory of School Organization and Change

Thomas M. Skrtic

Organizations are social tools, mechanisms that society uses to achieve goals that are beyond the reach of individual citizens (Parsons, 1960). In addition to doing things for society, however, organizations do things to society, undesirable things such as dominating the political process and causing alienation and overconformity (Argyris, 1957; Galbraith, 1967). But organizations have an even more pernicious effect on society: The nature and needs of organizations shape the very goals that society uses them to achieve (Allison, 1971; Scott, 1981). We seek "health" when we visit the hospital, but what we get is "medical care." Although we are encouraged to see these outcomes as synonymous, there may be no relation between them, or the relation may be negative; more care can result in poorer health (Illich, 1976). Like health, education is a social goal that is shaped by the medium of an organization. Society wants education, but what it gets is a particular kind of schooling, one that is shaped by the nature and needs of school organizations.

Although school organization should be an important topic in the field of education, until recently it received virtually no critical attention. Part of the problem is that for most of this century the question of school organization was left to the field of educational administration, which has tended to avoid research on the effects of schooling (Becker, 1983; Bridges, 1982; Erickson, 1977, 1979). A more serious problem, however, is that, even when educational administrators have studied schooling, they have taken an extremely narrow, functionalist view of schools as organizations. In this chapter I want to expand the view of schools as organizations by drawing on theories of organization and change that combine insights from each of the four paradigms of modern social scientific thought introduced in Part 1. I treat each theory as an ideal type, an exaggerated heuristic. Then I integrate the separate ideal types into a larger, more comprehensive metatheoretical heuristic, which I use in this chapter to deconstruct special education as an institutional practice of public education, and in Chapter 10 to deconstruct the institution of public education itself. To set the stage for my metatheoretical reading of school organization and change, I begin with a brief genealogy of the knowledge tradition of educational administration that shows why the field has been so tied to the functionalist outlook (also see Skrtic, 1988, 1991a, 1995; Tyack & Hansot, 1982; Chapter 3).

TWO DISCOURSES ON SCHOOL ORGANIZATION

The knowledge tradition of educational administration has been shaped by the broader discourse on organization, which is actually two discourses: the prescriptive and the scholarly. The prescriptive discourse is a purely functionalist undertaking, a form of naive pragmatism dominated by managers in business and industry who are concerned primarily with efficiency and thus with controlling people who work in organizations (Edwards, 1979; Chapter 2). The scholarly discourse emerged after World War II, when organization became an area of academic study in the social sciences, in what has become the multidisciplinary field of organization analysis (Scott, 1981). Although the scholarly discourse continues to be influenced by the needs of business and industry (Burrell & Morgan, 1979), it is concerned primarily with understanding the nature of organizations and their effects on people and society (Pfeffer, 1982). As we will see, the prescriptive discourse shaped the practices and discourses of educational administrators during the first half of the century and, following a failed attempt to ground the field in the scholarly discourse in the 1950s, largely has continued to do so until today.

The Prescriptive Discourse

Given its concern with efficiency, the prescriptive discourse gave rise to three schools of thought on organization and management during the first half of the twentieth century. The first school of thought was based on Fredrick Taylor's notion of "scientific management" (Taylor, 1911/1947), which is a detailed set of prescriptions for standardizing work processes in industrial organizations or factories (see Haber, 1964; Scott, 1981). It assumes that organizations are rational (prospective and purposeful or goal-directed) and yields the "machine bureaucracy" configuration, the familiar pyramid-shaped structure of formal control relations depicted in most organization charts (Mintzberg, 1979; below).[1] Although scientific management was meant for industrial organizations, during the progressive era it was vigorously promoted as a means of maximizing the efficiency of all organizations (Haber, 1964), particularly schools (Callahan, 1962). As a result, rather than social, moral, or instructional leaders, educational administrators became "experts in how to administrate and control organizations" (Spring, 1980, p. 100), treating schoolwork much like that of the factory (see Ayres, 1909; Bobbit, 1913).

Scientific management's lack of attention to the social dynamics of the workplace gave rise to its antithesis – the "human relations" approach to organization and management (Follett, 1924, 1940; Mayo, 1933; Roethlisberger & Dickson, 1939). In this view, an informal (social, cultural, or nonrational) structure of unofficial worker relations exists within the formal (rational) structure of organizations, the message for managers being that worker behavior is determined by the norms and value orientation of workers rather than the official specifications of the organization. Although on the surface managers, including educational administrators (see Campbell, 1971), began to pay greater attention to the social needs of workers, the human relations approach was short-lived, giving way to the third school of thought – Chester Barnard's (1938) synthesis of the rational and nonrational perspectives.

Barnard (1938; Simon, 1947) characterized organizations as essentially cooperative (rational) systems that can become uncooperative (nonrational) unless managers condition the behavior and attitudes of workers through training, indoctrination, and the manipulation of incentives. Ultimately, Barnard (1938) saw humans as inherently cooperative, regarding those who were "unfitted for co-operation" (p. 13) as "pathological cases, insane and not of this world" (Burrell & Morgan, 1979, p. 149). Although the human relations movement contained the seeds for what were to become nonrational-cultural theories of organization (see below), these insights were lost in Barnard's synthesis, which is a purely functionalist formulation (Burrell & Morgan, 1979). Barnard's approach to management became extremely influential in the prescriptive discourse (Perrow, 1972) and subsequently in educational administration (Campbell, Fleming, Newell, & Bennion, 1987; Griffiths, 1979).[2] Given the dominance of the prescriptive discourse, by mid-century the field of educational administration was firmly grounded in the mutually reinforcing functionalist theories of organizational rationality and human pathology (Clark, 1985; Griffiths, 1983; Skrtic, 1991a).

The Scholarly Discourse

The scholarly discourse on organization began with the English publication of Max Weber's theory of bureaucracy (Weber, 1922/1946, 1924/1947) in the late 1940s (Scott, 1981). Writing in German in the 1920s, Weber chronicled the advance of bureaucratic administration, focusing particularly on the way its rational legal authority relations were replacing more traditional (nonrational) forms. It is true, of course, that today "the terms bureaucracy and bureaucrat are epithets – accusations connoting rule-encumbered inefficiency and mindless overconformity" (Scott, 1981, p. 23), but when Weber's work first appeared the bureaucratic form was held in high regard within the prescriptive discourse, given its functionalist outlook. Although Weber meant to warn his readers of the negative effects of bureaucracy, the irony is that, given the functionalist orientation of the social sciences (see Chapter 2; below) and the prescriptive discourse, his ideal-typical analysis was misinterpreted by social scientists (Mommsen, 1974) and educational administrators (Clark, 1985) as endorsing bureaucracy as the "ideal" organizational structure, which further reinforced the functionalist theory of organizational rationality. As a result, the misreading of Weber's work spurred interest in that of Taylor and Barnard, among others, and together these works became the basis of the knowledge tradition in the field of organization analysis in the 1950s (Scott, 1981).

Forty years of theory building in organization analysis has produced what appears to be a bewildering array of competing and contradictory theories of organization (Pfeffer, 1982). One source of variability is the multidisciplinary character of the field of organization analysis (see Scott, 1981). A more important source, however, is that, given the multiple paradigm status of the social science disciplines, the field is also a multiparadigmatic intellectual endeavor. As such, the theories it has produced reflect the various modes of theorizing found in the social disciplines – functionalism, interpretivism, radical structuralism, and radical humanism (see Chapter 2; below). In the 1950s, however, when the field began to take form, organization analysis was a largely functionalist undertaking, given the functionalist grounding of the social sciences at that time, as well as the influence of Taylor and Barnard, and the misreading of Weber (Burrell & Morgan, 1979; Scott, 1981).

This is important for education because it was at this point that several leading professors of educational administration rejected the prescriptive discourse and proposed grounding the field's practices and discourses in the emerging scholarly discourse of organization analysis (see Griffiths, 1959, 1983). Given the initial grounding of organization analysis, of course, this meant that what was adopted from it was the functionalist mode of theorizing, an extremely narrow view of organization, which, although still dominant, has been radically enriched over the past 30 years by theoretical insights from the other three paradigms (see Burrell & Morgan, 1979; below).[3] Although there are professors of educational administration who have kept pace with these developments (e.g., Bates, 1980, 1987; Boyd & Crowson, 1981; Foster, 1986; Maxcy, 1991), most of the work on school organization in the field has been done from the functionalist perspective (see Clark, 1985; Foster, 1986; Griffith, 1983, 1988). As a result, educational administration remains today largely as it was in the 1950s (see Bates, 1980; Clark, 1985; Foster, 1986; Griffiths, 1988), firmly grounded in functionalism and thus in the theories of organizational rationality and human pathology.[4]

TOWARD A METATHEORY OF SCHOOL
ORGANIZATION AND CHANGE

Although the multiple paradigm status of organization analysis adds to the confusion in the field, it also provides a source of analytic clarity because the body of theory produced by the field can be understood in terms of the four modes of theorizing found in the social disciplines. As we know from Chapter 2, the four paradigms of modern social scientific thought are formed by the interaction of two dimensions of metatheoretical presuppositions: an objective–subjective dimension about the nature of science, and a microscopic–macroscopic or order–conflict (hereafter simply microscopic–macroscopic) dimension about the nature of society. Applying the conceptual framework to theories of organization (see Figure 9.1), the objective–subjective dimension corresponds to metatheoretical presuppositions about the nature of action in and by organizations, ranging from the extremes of *rational action* (prospective and purposeful or goal-directed) to *nonrational action* (emergent within an evolving system of meaning or culture) (see Pfeffer, 1982; Scott, 1981).

The microscopic–macroscopic dimension corresponds to metatheoretical presuppositions about the level at which organizational activity is most appropriately analyzed. *Individualist* theories of organization emphasize the microlevel of individuals and small groups and are concerned with organizing processes within organizations; *structuralist* theories emphasize the macrolevel of total organizations and are concerned primarily with organization structure (Pfeffer, 1982; Scott, 1981). Referring to Figure 9.1, we can think of all modern theories of organization as being grounded in one (or more) of the four paradigms of modern social scientific thought, the functionalist (micro-objective), interpretivist (micro-subjective), structuralist (macro-objective), or humanist (macro-subjective) modes of theorizing. Each mode of theorizing produces a fundamentally different way to understand organization and change because each is premised on a different set of metatheoretical presuppositions about the nature of action in or by organizations and the appropriate level at which organizational activity is analyzed (Burrell & Morgan, 1979; Morgan, 1983).

Because functionalism has been the dominant mode of theorizing in the

FIGURE 9.1. Four Paradigms of Modern Organization Theory

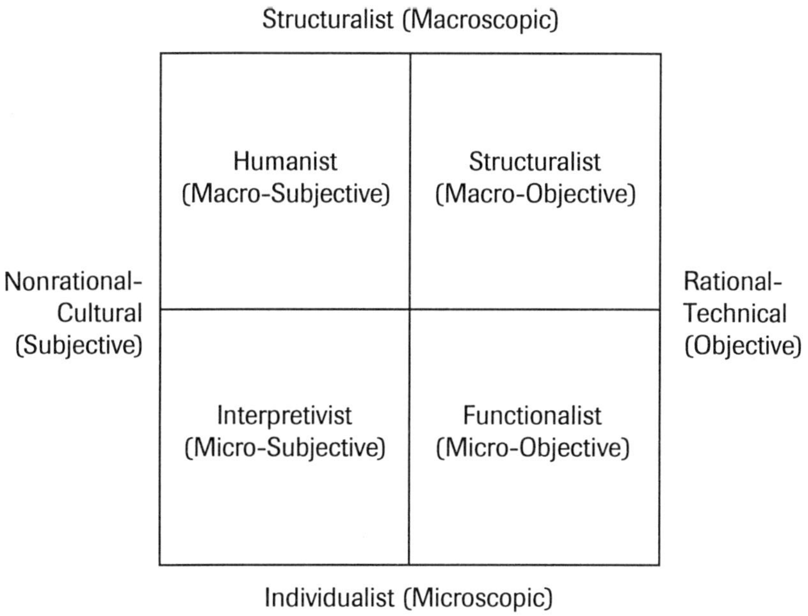

Structuralist (Macroscopic)

Humanist (Macro-Subjective)	Structuralist (Macro-Objective)
Interpretivist (Micro-Subjective)	Functionalist (Micro-Objective)

Nonrational-Cultural (Subjective) · Rational-Technical (Objective)

Individualist (Microscopic)

Source: Adapted from G. Burrell and G. Morgan, 1979, *Sociological Paradigms and Organizational Analysis*, p. 29, London: Heinemann Educational Books; J. Pfeffer, 1982, *Organizations and Organization Theory*, p. 13, Marshfield, MA: Pitman Publishing; and T. M. Skrtic, 1991, *Behind Special Education: A Critical Analysis of Professional Culture and School Organization*, p. 160, Denver: Love Publishing.

social sciences, most modern theories of organization are premised on the metatheoretical presuppositions of the micro-objective or functionalist paradigm. Over the past 30 years, however, there have been three shifts in emphasis that correspond to the paradigm shifts in the social sciences discussed in Chapter 2. The first shift took place in the 1960s within the rational perspective on action, from the micro-objective to the macro-objective paradigm (see Lawrence & Lorsch, 1967; Woodward, 1965). Two parallel shifts from the rational to the nonrational perspective on action occurred in the 1970s and 1980s—one at the individualist level of analysis, from the micro-objective to the micro-subjective perspective, and one at the structuralist level, from the macro-objective to the macro-subjective perspective (see Burrell & Morgan, 1979; Pfeffer, 1982; Scott, 1981).

As in the social sciences generally, one result of these shifts in perspective has been development of new theories of organization grounded in the other three paradigms, each of which previously had been underdeveloped in organizational studies (Burrell & Morgan, 1979; Scott, 1981). More significantly, beginning in the late 1970s, theories of organization began to appear that bridge paradigms, or combine theoretical insights from more than one paradigmatic perspective (see Skrtic, 1987, 1988; below). Methodologically, the trend in organization analysis, as in the social sciences generally, has been away from the traditional foundational perspective of one best paradigm or theory for understanding organizations, and toward the antifoundational approach of using multiple perspectives in a single analysis. Although historically discourse in the field of organization analysis had been dominated by the functionalist perspective and premised on the modern or foundational view of knowledge, by the 1980s it was characterized by theoretical and paradigmatic diversity, if not pluralism (Burrell & Morgan, 1979; Pfeffer, 1982; Scott, 1981), and at the margins by an antifoundational methodological orientation (see Morgan, 1983, 1986). Given these developments, today it is possible to study school organization and change dialogically by using multiple theories of organization within a single, antifoundational analysis (see Skrtic, 1987, 1988, 1991a).

Epistemological and Moral Framework

Because organization analysis is a multiple paradigm science with no foundational criteria for selecting the correct paradigm or theoretical construction (see Chapter 2), in the following analysis I combine theoretical perspectives on organization and change from each of the four paradigms of modern social scientific thought. Drawing on the antifoundational epistemology of pragmatism (see Dewey, 1929/1988; Peirce, 1931–35; Chapter 2), I treat the various theories of organization as ideal-typical constructions of organization theorists, constructions shaped by their value assumptions with respect to the metatheoretical dimensions of the analytic framework illustrated in Figure 9.1. By reading each theory as an ideal type and combining them dialogically, my aim in this chapter is to form a metatheoretical heuristic or "pragmatic ideal type" of school organization and change and to use it to deconstruct special education as an institutional practice of public education.

As a pragmatist, of course, I do not expect to construct the ultimate, "true" theory of school organization and change. Given the antifoundational epistemology of pragmatism, I am interested in selecting theories that are useful for reconciling the institutional practice of special education – and ultimately the institution of public education itself (Chapter 10) – with the ideal of serving the best educational and political interests of education consumers and the democratic needs of society. And because there are no scientific rules for making these theoretical decisions objectively, I use values to guide my choices. As Dewey (1925/1981) noted, the selective emphasis that is inevitable in such decisions "is not an evil. Deception comes only when the presence and operation of choice is concealed, disguised, denied" (p. 34). In this regard, I want to promote the democratic values of justice, liberty, equality, and community. Like Dewey (1917/1981, 1931/1989; Chapter 2), I want to read democracy and social reform into the very nature of school organization because, more than as a form of government, I value democracy as a method of social inquiry, "a mode of associated living, of conjoint communicated experience" (Dewey, 1916/1980, p. 93), and education as the means by which citizens are prepared to enter the conversation (Dewey, 1899/1976, 1927/1988, 1929–30/1988). Moreover, I want to read democracy into school organization because reconstructing social practices and institutions is achieved in democratic dialogue, "in face-to-face relationships by means of direct give and take" (Dewey, 1927/1988, p. 371). Reconstructing special education and public education requires more than a method of democratic discourse; it requires democratic organizational conditions as well.

Because education is the principal means of preparing citizens for democratic life, educational policy in a democracy must be concerned with moral transactions and social relations. In deconstructing the institutional practice of special education, I want to probe the value assumptions that have shaped it as a separate system in the twentieth century and push them toward those that will lead to an integrative system in the twenty-first century, one that is justified by an appeal to identity and community (Boulding, 1967; Chapter 2). Beyond its implications for special education consumers, I am concerned with identity because alienation, its opposite, threatens community itself (Moroney, 1981). Humans must learn to be democratic; educational policy that emphasizes an integrative system promotes the type of institutional arrangements in which democratic identities, values, and communities are cultivated (Dewey, 1916/1980, 1927/1988; Gutmann, 1987). Moreover, I will argue in Chapter 10 that the economic and political contingencies of the emerging postindustrial era make possible and require just such an integrative system of public education.

Theoretical Frames of Reference

For ease of presentation, I divide the theoretical territory into two frames of reference, the *structural* and the *cultural*, each of which includes two theoretical perspectives that bridge two or more of the four paradigms. The structural frame of reference includes *configuration theory* (Miller & Friesen, 1984; Miller & Mintzberg, 1983; Mintzberg, 1979, 1983), which bridges the micro-objective and macro-objective paradigms; and *institutional theory* (Meyer, 1979; Meyer & Rowan, 1977, 1978; Meyer & Scott, 1983), which bridges the macro-objective and macro-subjective paradigms (refer to Figure 9.1).[5] By combining institutional theory and configuration theory, we can understand traditional school organization as a two-structure bureaucratic configuration that is inherently nonadaptable at both the micro-level of professional practice and the macro-level of organization structure (see Skrtic, 1987, 1988, 1991a, 1995).

The two theoretical perspectives within the cultural frame of reference are what I will refer to as *paradigmatic* theories of organization (Brown, 1978; Golding, 1980; Jonsson & Lundin, 1977; Rounds, 1979, 1981), which bridge the macro-subjective and micro-subjective paradigms; and *cognitive* theories of organization (Weick, 1979a, 1979b, 1985), which bridge three paradigms—micro-subjective, macro-subjective, and macro-objective.[6] Combining cognitive and paradigmatic theories of organization provides a way to understand school organizations as corrigible systems of meaning. Together, the structural and cultural frames of reference highlight the sources of stability and change in school organizations.

STRUCTURAL FRAME OF REFERENCE

Every organized human activity gives rise to two fundamental and opposing requirements: the *"division of labor* into various tasks to be performed and the *coordination* of these tasks to accomplish the activity" (Mintzberg, 1983, p. 2). As such, the structure of an organization can be understood as "the sum total of the ways in which it divides its labor into distinct tasks and then achieves coordination among them" (Mintzberg, 1979, p. 2). The central idea in configuration theory is that organizations structure themselves into one of several regularly occurring configurations according to, among other things, the type of division of labor and means of coordination that they employ. Given their division of labor and means of coordination, traditional school organizations configure themselves as professional bureaucracies (Mintzberg, 1979), even though in this century they have been managed and governed as if they were machine bureaucracies (see Callahan, 1962; Weick, 1982a; above).

According to institutional theory, organizations like schools deal with this contradiction by maintaining two structures: a material structure that conforms to the technical demands of their work, and a normative structure that conforms to the social norms or cultural expectations of their institutional environments. By combining configuration theory and institutional theory, we can understand school organization in terms of two organizations, one inside the other, as it were. Their outer normative structure conforms to the machine bureaucracy configuration, the structure that educational administrators strive for because of their grounding in the prescriptive discourse of scientific management, and that society expects because of the social norm of organizational rationality. However, the inner material structure of school organizations conforms to the professional bureaucracy configuration, the structure that corresponds to the technical demands of their work.[7]

Differences Between the Machine and Professional Bureaucracy

Ultimately, the difference between the two configurations stems from the type of work that school organizations do, which is important because the nature of an organization's work limits managers' choices for dividing labor and achieving coordination. Organizations configure themselves as machine bureaucracies when their work is simple, that is, when it is certain enough to be *rationalized* into a series of relatively routine subtasks, each of which can be completely prespecified and done by a separate worker. Simple work can be coordinated by standardizing work processes through *formalization*, that is, by specifying precise rules for doing each subtask. Organizations configure themselves as professional bureaucracies when their work is too uncertain to be rationalized and thus formalized. Client-centered work, such as that of hospitals and schools, is uncertain because it requires judgment relative to applying general principles or theories to the particular and often variable needs of individual clients (see Schein, 1972). As such, division of labor in professional bureaucracies is achieved through *specialization*, a situation in which clients are distributed among the workers, each of whom specializes in the knowledge and skills presumed to be necessary to serve clients with a particular constellation of needs. Given a specialized division of labor, this type of work is coordinated through *professionalization*, that is, by standardizing the skills of the workers through intensive education and socialization carried out in professional schools (see Chapter 1).

The logic behind rationalization and formalization is premised on minimizing discretion and separating theory from practice. The theory behind the work in a machine bureaucracy rests with the engineers and technocrats; they do the thinking and the workers simply follow the rules. Conversely, specialization and professionalization are meant to increase discretion and to unite theory and practice in the knowledge and skills of the professional. In principle, professionals know the theory behind their work and have the discretion to adapt it to the actual needs of their clients (Mintzberg, 1979).

In practice, however, the standardization of skills is circumscribed in two ways. First, of course, it is circumscribed by the particular metatheoretical paradigm in which the profession's knowledge tradition is grounded (see

Chapters 1 and 2). Second, standardization of skills gives professionals a finite repertoire of standard practices that are applicable only to a limited set of contingencies or perceived client needs. As such, professional practice can be understood as a form of "pigeonholing" (Mintzberg, 1979, p. 374), a process in which the professional matches a presumed client need to one of the standard practices in his or her repertoire. Given adequate discretionary space (see below), there is room for some adjustment, but when clients have needs that fall on the margins or outside the professional's repertoire of standard practices, they must be either forced artificially into one of the available practices or sent to a different specialist, one who presumably has the appropriate standard practices (Perrow, 1970; Simon, 1977; Weick, 1976). We will see below that a fully open-ended process—one that seeks a truly creative solution to each unique need—requires a problem-solving orientation. In principle, of course, professionals know the theory behind their practices and have the discretion to adapt them. In practice, however, professionals are performers, not problem solvers. They perfect the standard practices in their repertoires; they do not invent new ones for unfamiliar contingencies. Instead of accommodating heterogeneity, they tend to screen it out by forcing their clients' needs into one of their standard practices, or by forcing them out of the professional–client relationship altogether (Segal, 1974; Simon, 1977).

Finally, an organization's division of labor and means of coordination shape the nature of the *interdependence* or "coupling" among its workers (March & Olsen, 1976; Thompson, 1967; Weick, 1976, 1982b). Because machine bureaucracies coordinate their work through rationalization and formalization, their workers are *tightly coupled*. Like links in a chain, they are highly dependent on one another in the unreflective and mechanistic sense implied by rule-governed behavior. In a professional bureaucracy, however, the workers are *loosely coupled* (Bidwell, 1965; Weick, 1976). Professionals are only minimally dependent on one another; they share common facilities and resources but do their work alone with their assigned clients. Coordination in a professional bureaucracy, a loose form of coordination at best, is achieved by everyone knowing roughly what everyone else is doing, given their common education and socialization (Mintzberg, 1979).

Managing Professional Bureaucracies
Like Machine Bureaucracies

Given the prescriptive discourse of educational administration and the social norm of organizational rationality, school organizations are managed and governed as if they were machine bureaucracies, even though the technical demands of their work configure them as professional bureaucracies. As such, schools are forced by managers (Weick, 1982a) and the public (Meyer & Rowan, 1978; Mintzberg, 1979) to adopt the management practices of the machine bureaucracy, particularly rationalization and formalization, even though they are ill-suited to the technical demands of complex work. In principle, the effect is that the professional bureaucracy configuration of schools is driven toward the machine bureaucracy configuration. As Weick (1982a) noted, when this occurs "effectiveness declines, people become confused, and work doesn't get done. That seems to be one thing that is wrong with many schools. They are managed with the wrong model in mind" (p. 673).

The most serious outcome of the drive toward machine bureaucracy is that it violates the discretionary logic of professionalization. Managing and governing schools as if they were machine bureaucracies misconceptualizes teaching as simple work that can be rationalized and formalized, which reduces teachers' discretion, thus minimizing the degree to which they can personalize their practices to the particular needs of their students. As Mintzberg (1979) noted, complex work cannot be formalized through rules and regulations, "except in misguided ways which program the wrong behaviors and measure the wrong outputs, forcing the professionals to play the machine bureaucratic game – satisfying the standards instead of serving the clients" (p. 377).

Fortunately, however, attempts to rationalize and formalize teaching do not work completely in schools because their formal, machine bureaucracy structure (where the rules and regulations are inscribed) is "decoupled" from the professional bureaucracy structure where the work is done (Meyer & Rowan, 1977, 1978). From the institutional perspective, schools' outer machine bureaucracy structure is largely a myth, an assortment of symbols and ceremonies that have little to do with the way the work is actually done. This decoupled, two-structure arrangement permits schools to do their work according to the localized judgments of teachers, while protecting their legitimacy by giving the public the appearance of the machine bureaucracy that it expects. As Meyer and Rowan (1977) explained, "Decoupling enables organizations to maintain standardized, legitimating, formal structures while their activities vary in response to practical considerations" (p. 357). But decoupling does not work completely either, because, from the configuration perspective, no matter how misguided they may be, rationalization and formalization require at least overt conformity (Mintzberg, 1979; cf. Dalton, 1959). Decoupling notwithstanding, managing and governing schools as if they were machine bureaucracies decreases professional thought and discretion, which in turn reduces even further the degree to which teachers can personalize their practices.

Professional Bureaucracies and Change

Even though they are different in these respects, machine and professional bureaucracies are similar in one important way: Both are premised on the principle of standardization, and thus both are inherently nonadaptable structures at both the micro-level of workers and the macro-level of organization structure. Because bureaucracies coordinate their work through standardization, they are performance organizations, structures configured to perfect the practices they have been standardized to perform. Of course, the standardization of skills is intended to allow for enough professional thought and discretion to accommodate client variability. But even with adequate discretionary space, there is a limit to the degree to which professionals can adjust their standard practices. A fully open-ended process of accommodation requires a problem-solving organization, a configuration premised on inventing new programs for unfamiliar client needs. But professional bureaucracies are performance organizations; they screen out heterogeneity by forcing their clients' needs into their existing practices, or by forcing them out of the system altogether (see Segal, 1974).

Because bureaucracies are performance organizations, they require a stable environment and, as such, are potentially devastated when they are forced to do something other than what they were standardized to do. Nevertheless, although it is a major undertaking, machine bureaucracies can change by restandardizing their work processes, a more or less rational-technical process of *re*rationalizing the work and *re*formalizing worker behavior. When their environments become dynamic, however, professional bureaucracies cannot respond by making rational-technical adjustments in their work because their coordination rests within each professional, not in their work processes. Nonetheless, because schools are managed and governed as if they were machine bureaucracies, attempts to change them typically follow the rational-technical approach (see Elmore & McLaughlin, 1988; House, 1979), which assumes that changes or additions to existing rationalization and formalization will result in changes in the way the work gets done. This fails to bring about the desired changes because the existing rationalization and formalization are located in the decoupled machine bureaucracy structure. However, because the changes require at least overt conformity, they act to extend the existing rationalization and formalization in schools, driving the organization further toward machine bureaucracy, thus reducing teacher thought and discretion even further, and leaving students with even less effective services. As in the case of management by rules, the inner professional bureaucracy structure of schools cannot be changed by adding more rules, except in the misguided way of putting even more pressure on teachers to play the machine bureaucracy game—satisfying the standards instead of serving the students.

Even though schools are nonadaptable structures, their status as public organizations means that they must respond to public demands for change. From the institutional perspective, schools deal with this problem by signaling the environment that a change has occurred, which creates the illusion that they have changed when in fact they remain largely the same (see Meyer, 1979; Rowan, 1980; Zucker, 1981). One way that schools signal change is by building symbols and ceremonies of change into their outer machine bureaucracy structure, which, of course, is decoupled from the actual work. Another important signal of change is the addition of "ritual" subunits, separate classrooms and programs, which, because they are "decoupled" from the rest of the organization, make any substantive reorganization of activity unnecessary (see Meyer & Rowan, 1977; Zucker, 1981). This is possible in schools because specialization and professionalization create precisely this sort of loose or decoupled interdependence within the organization. Like symbols and ceremonies of change, decoupled subunits relieve pressure for change while, at the same time, buffering the organization from the need to actually change.

The Adhocracy Configuration

As we have seen, professional bureaucracies are nonadaptable structures because they are premised on the principle of standardization, which configures them as performance organizations that perfect their existing standard practices. Adhocracies are the inverse of the bureaucratic form. They emerge in dynamic markets, extremely uncertain environments in which innovation and adaptation are essential for survival (Burns & Stalker, 1966; Woodward, 1965). As such, adhocracies are premised on the principle of innovation; they are problem-solving organizations that invent new practices for work that is so ambiguous and uncertain that the knowledge and skills for doing it are completely unknown (Pugh et al., 1963; Toffler, 1970). As Mintzberg (1979) noted with regard to the adhocratic configuration, "At the outset, no one can be sure exactly what needs to be done. That knowledge develops as the work unfolds. . . . The success of the undertaking depends primarily on the ability of the [workers] to adapt to each other along their uncharted route" (p. 3).[8] Given the extreme ambiguity of its work, the structure of an adhocracy "must be flexible, self-renewing, organic . . . a 'tent' instead of a 'palace'" (Mintzberg, 1979, p. 433). The advantage of an adhocratic configuration is that it

> exploits benefits hidden within properties that designers have generally regarded as liabilities. Ambiguous authority structures, unclear objectives, and contradictory assignments of responsibility can legitimate controversies and challenge tra-

ditions. . . . Incoherence and indecision can foster exploration, self-evaluation, and learning. (Hedberg, Nystrom, & Starbuck, 1976, p. 45)

According to Mintzberg (1979), the most well-known and successful example of an adhocracy is the National Aeronautics and Space Administration (NASA) during its Apollo phase in the 1960s. Given its mission to land an American on the moon by the end of the decade, it configured itself as an adhocracy because there were no established practices for manned space flight. NASA had to rely on its workers to invent these practices on an *ad hoc* basis, along their uncharted route to the moon, as it were. Although the Apollo Project employed professional workers, it could not use specialization and professionalization to divide and coordinate its work because there were no professional specializations that had perfected the knowledge and skills for doing the type of work that was required. Thus, division of labor and coordination of work within the Apollo Project were premised on *collaboration* and *mutual adjustment*, respectively.

Under the structural contingency of collaboration, division of labor is achieved by deploying professionals from various specializations on multidisciplinary project teams, a situation in which team members work collaboratively on the team's project and assume joint responsibility for its completion. Under mutual adjustment, coordination is achieved through informal communication among team members as they invent (and reinvent) novel problem solutions on an *ad hoc* basis, a process that requires them to deconstruct and reconstruct their conventional theories and practices relative to those of their colleagues and the team's progress on the task at hand (Chandler & Sayles, 1971; Mintzberg, 1979; Skrtic, 1991a; Chapter 10). Together, the structural contingencies of collaboration and mutual adjustment give rise to a *discursive coupling* arrangement that is premised on reflective problem solving through communication, and thus on the unification of theory and practice in the team of workers (see Burns & Stalker, 1966).

By contrast, during its Space Shuttle phase NASA has reconfigured itself as a professional bureaucracy (see Romzek & Dubnik, 1987), that is, as a performance organization that perfects a repertoire of standard launch and recovery practices, most of which were invented during its Apollo phase. The transformation from adhocracy to professional bureaucracy is a natural tendency that begins when uncertainty is reduced, as the organization's members begin to believe that they have solved their problems of practice, and thus that their current practices can be standardized as ready-made solutions for future use (see Mintzberg, 1979, 1983). The difference between the two configurations is that, faced with a problem, the adhocracy "engages in creative effort to find a novel solution; the professional bureaucracy pigeonholes it into a known contingency to which it can apply a standard [practice]. One engages in divergent thinking aimed at innovation; the other in convergent thinking aimed at perfection" (Mintzberg, 1979, p. 436).

Finally, under the organizational contingencies of collaboration, mutual adjustment, and discursive coupling, accountability in the adhocracy is achieved through a presumed community of interests, a sense among workers of a shared interest in a common goal. Under this form of accountability, responsibility flows from the workers' common concern for progress toward their mission, rather than an ideological identification with a professional culture (professional bureaucracy) or a formalized relationship with a hierarchy of authority (machine bureaucracy) (see Burns & Stalker, 1966; Chandler & Sayles, 1971; Romzek & Dubnick, 1987). Thus, rather than the *professional-bureaucratic* mode of accountability that emerges in the professional bureaucracy configuration (Martin, Overholt, & Urban, 1976; Meyer & Rowan, 1978; Wise, 1979), the organizational contingencies of the adhocracy give rise to a *professional-political* mode of accountability. Work is controlled by professionals who, although they act with discretion, are subject to sanctions that emerge within a political discourse among themselves and between them and their consumers (Burns & Stalker, 1966; Chandler & Sayles, 1971; Romzek & Dubnick, 1987; Skrtic, 1991a; Chapter 10).

CULTURAL FRAME OF REFERENCE

Cultural theories of organization are premised on the subjectivist idea that humans construct social reality through intersubjective communication (see Berger & Luckmann, 1967). Theorists who operate from the cognitive and paradigmatic perspectives think of organizations as bodies of thought, as schemas, cultures, or paradigms. They are concerned with the way people construct meaning and how this affects the way thought, action, and interaction unfold over time in organizations. The difference is that whereas cognitive theories emphasize the micro-processes through which workers construct their organizational realities, paradigmatic theories emphasis the macro-processes by which existing organizational realities shape the thought and action of workers. Together, cognitive and paradigmatic theories reflect the interactive character of the cultural frame of reference—people creating culture; culture creating people (Pettigrew, 1979).

Organizations as Paradigms

Paradigmatic theorists conceptualize organizations as paradigms or shared systems of meaning and are concerned with the ways existing socially constructed systems of meaning affect thought and action in organizations.

From Kuhn (1970) we know that a paradigm is a general guide to perception, a conceptual map for viewing the world (see Chapter 1). Applied to organizations, a paradigm is a system of beliefs about cause–effect relations and standards of practice and behavior. Regardless of whether the beliefs are accurate, the paradigm guides and justifies action by consolidating the organization's inherent ambiguity into an image of orderliness (Brown, 1978; Clark, 1972).

Organizational change from this perspective is similar to a Kuhnian (1970) paradigm revolution, that is, long periods of stability maintained by the self-reinforcing nature of the organizational paradigm (the long period of normal science), and occasional periods of change in which irreconcilable anomalies eventually undermine the paradigm's legitimacy (revolutionary science) (see Golding, 1980; Jonsson & Lundin, 1977; Chapter 1). Change is a slow and traumatic process in an organization because, once in place, the prevailing paradigm self-justifies itself by distorting contradictory information in support of the conventional view (Golding, 1980). Nevertheless, when sufficient anomalies build up to undermine and eventually overthrow the prevailing paradigm, a new one emerges and action proceeds again under the guidance of the new organizing framework (Golding, 1980; Jonsson & Lundin, 1977).

One way that anomalies are introduced into organizational paradigms is when values and preferences change in society. In this case, the paradigm falls into crisis because the social theory underlying it changes. To the degree that the new social values are inconsistent with the prevailing paradigm, however, resistance emerges in the form of political clashes and an increase in ritualized activity, which together act to reaffirm the paradigm that has been called into question (Lipsky, 1976; Perrow, 1978; Rounds, 1979; Zucker, 1977).

Another way that anomolies are introduced is through the availability of technical information that the current paradigm is not working, which can bring about a paradigm shift in one of two ways (Rounds, 1981). The first way is through a confrontation between an individual (or a small constituency group) who rejects the most fundamental assumptions of the current paradigm on the basis of information that the system is not working, and the rest of the organization's members who act in defiance of the negative information to preserve the prevailing paradigm. The second way is when an initially conservative action is taken to correct a generally recognized flaw in what otherwise is assumed to be a viable system. Here, the corrective measure exposes other flaws, which, when addressed, expose more flaws until enough of the system is called into question to prepare the way for a radical reconceptualization of the entire organization. In this scenario, what initially were conservative attempts to protect the system act to undermine it and ultimately usher in a new paradigm (Rounds, 1981).

Organizations as Schemas

From the cognitive perspective, an organization is a human schema, "an abridged, generalized, corrigible organization of experience that serves as an initial frame of reference for action and perception" (Weick, 1979a, p. 50). The difference in emphasis between the cognitive and paradigmatic perspectives is perhaps best captured in Weick's (1979a) assertion that "an organization is a body of thought thought by thinking thinkers" (p. 42). Like the paradigmatic theorists, Weick recognizes that organizational paradigms orient the thought and action of the people who subscribe to them, but he also accounts for "the important role that people play in creating the environments that impose upon them" (1979b, p. 5). The cognitive perspective bridges the micro- and macro-subjective perspectives by emphasizing the active and creative role that workers play in constructing and reconstructing organizational paradigms. Through activity, selective attention, consensual validation, and luck, people in organizations unrandomize streams of experience enough to form a "sensemaking map" (Weick, 1979a, p. 45) or paradigm of the territory. Of course, the paradigm is not the territory; it is only a *re*presentation of it. For Weick (1979a), however, "the map *is* the territory if people treat it as such" (p. 45). The point is that, accurate or not, organizational paradigms structure the field of action sufficiently so that members can initiate activity in it, out of which may emerge a workable order.

Organizational members' sampling of the environment, and thus the paradigms they construct, are shaped by prior beliefs and values, which act as filters through which they examine their experiences (Weick, 1979a, 1979b, 1985). Although this assertion is consistent with the paradigmatic perspective, by emphasizing action as the pretext and raw material for sense making, Weick actually bridges the structural and cultural frames of reference. According to Weick (1979a), activity in organizations is shaped by material structures like rationalization, formalization, specialization, and professionalization. These structural contingencies shape members' construction of reality because they influence the contacts, communication, and commands that members experience, which in turn affect the streams of experience, beliefs, values, and actions that constitute their organizational paradigms. Furthermore, the process works the other way as well: "Maps, beliefs, and thoughts that summarize actions, themselves constrain contacts, communication, and commands. These constraints constitute and shape organizational processes that result in structures" (1979a, p. 48). From the cognitive perspective, organization is a mutually shaping circularity of structure and culture. Depending on where one enters the circle, organization is a continuous, mutually shaping process in which structural contingencies shape the activities of organizational members, which in turn shape their value orientation and thus the nature of the paradigms they construct to make sense of the organization, that is, to interpret the very structural contingencies that shape their activities (see Weick, 1979b, 1985; Skrtic, 1995).

Although organization theorists have described schools as chaotic, unorganized, or anarchical systems (Cohen & March, 1974; Cohen, March, & Olsen, 1972), Weick (1985) suggested that "underorganized systems" (p. 106) is a more useful characterization. This is so, he argued, because, although school organizations are ambiguous and thus appear to be disorderly, there is some order, most of which is supplied by the schemas or paradigms that its members use to make sense of the organization and their experiences in it. This is an important point for Weick because it is the basis of his explanation of the nature of change in school organizations. From the structural frame of reference, ambiguity in school organizations stems from two sources—the loosely coupled form of interdependence among professionals, and the decoupled (or loosely coupled) relationship between their formal and informal structures—both of which minimize the potential for meaningful change (see above). Building on these structural insights, Weick (1979a, 1982b, 1985) noted a third type of loose coupling that pervades school organizations—a loose or indeterminate relationship between cause and effect—and used it to explain change from the cognitive perspective.

For Weick (1985), "a loosely coupled system is a problem in causal inference" (p. 121). Actors in such systems find it difficult to predict and actualize cause–effect relations because the relations are indeterminate or "intermittent, lagged, dampened, slow, abrupt, and mediated" (p. 121). Given these cognitive conditions, actors in loosely coupled, underorganized systems

> rely on trust and presumptions, are often isolated, find social comparison difficult, have no one to borrow from, seldom imitate, suffer pluralistic ignorance, maintain discretion, improvise, and have less hubris because they know the universe is not sufficiently connected to make widespread change possible. (Weick, 1985, p. 121)

A loosely coupled system is not a flawed system, however (Weick, 1982b). It is a social and cognitive response to ambiguity, "to constant environmental change, to the impossibility of knowing another mind, and to limited information-processing capabilities. Loose coupling is to social systems as compartmentalization is to individuals, a means to achieve cognitive economy and a little peace" (Weick, 1985, p. 121).

Given his cognitive interpretation of loosely coupled systems, Weick (1982b, 1985) used the ideas of superstitious learning (cf. Hedberg, 1981) and self-fulfilling prophecy (cf. Jones, 1977) to explain change in underorganized systems such as schools. Superstitious learning occurs when actors mistakenly see a change in the environment as the effect of their action (cause). As a result, they build into their paradigm or "cause map" (Weick, 1985, p. 124) the belief that they are able to change environments. Although this is an incorrect interpretation of what actually happened, Weick argued that, in malleable environments, acting on a mistaken belief can set in motion a sequence of activities that allows people to construct a reality in which the belief is true. In underorganized systems, an apparent efficacy can transform a superstitious conclusion into a "correct" perception.

> An original prophecy is incorrect and may result from a mistaken perception that an environmental outcome was caused by an individual action. Later, when the person acts as if the prophecy were correct, the prophecy can become correct and the environment becomes responsive to the individual action rather than to some other exogenous factor. Thus, the incorrect theory of action becomes self-correcting. It sets into motion a set of events that validate what was originally an invalid belief. (Weick, 1985, p. 124)

Ambiguity in underorganized systems is reduced when actors incorporate – rightly or wrongly – into their paradigms an inference about cause and effect. When they act on the inference as if it were true, a previously loose relationship between cause and effect becomes tightened and the uncertainty surrounding the effect is reduced. For Weick (1982b, 1985) confident action based on a presumption of efficacy reinforces the inference about efficacy stored in the paradigm. In short, people in ambiguous, underorganized systems can make things happen.

The inherent structural and cognitive ambiguity in loosely coupled, underorganized systems such as schools increases the extent to which action is guided by beliefs, values, and ideology (Weick, 1979a, 1982b, 1985). Those who can resolve ambiguity gain power because their beliefs and values affect what the organization is and what it can become. Moreover, when ambiguity is increased, it sets the stage for ideology and values to be reshuffled, for a paradigm shift in which the people best able to resolve the crisis gain power because their view of the world reconstitutes the organization. According to Weick (1985), the recognition of an important, enduring ambiguity – an unresolvable anomaly in the prevailing paradigm – is an occasion when an organization may redefine itself. Those who resolve the ambiguity for themselves and others implant a new set of values in the organization, a new set of relevancies and competencies and thus a source of innovation.

Ambiguity sets the occasion for organizations to learn about themselves and their environments and allows them to emerge from their crisis in confidence in a different form. And behind it all are people with ideas that are rooted in their values and vision of what can and should be. For Weick, the importance of presumptions, expectations, and commitments cannot be overestimated. Confident, forceful, persistent people, with their presumptions, expectations, and commitments, can span the breaks in loosely coupled, underorganized systems by encouraging interactions that tighten settings. "The conditions of order and tightness in organizations," Weick (1985) noted, "exist as much in the mind as they do in the field of action" (p. 128).

SPECIAL EDUCATION AS AN INSTITUTIONAL PRACTICE

In Chapter 3, my goal was to deconstruct special education as a professional practice. By exposing the inconsistencies, contradictions, and silences in the special education knowledge tradition, I tried to raise doubts in readers' minds about the legitimacy of the field's professional knowledge, practices, and discourses. Here, I want to deconstruct special education as an institutional practice of public education by reconsidering the four assumptions that have guided and justified its development and expansion within the institution of education over this century. As discussed in Chapter 3, the assumptions are that

1. Student disability is a pathological condition.
2. Differential diagnosis is objective and useful.
3. Special education is a rationally conceived and coordinated system of services that benefits diagnosed students.
4. Progress in special education is a rational-technical process of incremental improvements in conventional diagnostic and instructional practices.

In the discussion to follow I reconsider these assumptions from an organizational perspective, using the organizational insights developed above to ask whether the institutional practice of special education is a rational and just response to the problem of school failure.

The Nature of Disability and Diagnosis

From the structural frame of reference, schools are nonadaptable at the level of the professional because professionalization produces teachers with finite repertoires of standard practices matched to a limited set of predetermined student needs. This raises several questions relative to the nature of student disability and diagnosis, questions about the nature and source of these practices, as well as the way they are applied in schools. As we know from Chapter 1, the positivist model of professional knowledge assumes that professional practices are objective, the end result of a rational system of applied science grounded in objective social knowledge. However, because knowledge of social reality is always knowledge from a particular point of view, professional practices cannot be considered inherently correct (or incorrect) in an objective sense; they are merely social constructions, the customs and conventions of a professional culture grounded in a particular paradigm-bound knowledge tradition of disciplinary science. Assuming for the sake of argument that these practices are the most effective ones available relative to the contingencies for which they have been engineered, another question is whether they are the practices that teachers actually use in schools.

In Part 1 my argument about the nature of professional induction stopped at the level of the professional culture. At this point, I can extend it by introducing the idea that a profession actually is composed of two largely discontinuous subcultures, that is, in the field of education, the subculture of applied scientists who work in schools of education (or research labs and centers) and that of professional practitioners who work in public schools (see Elliott, 1975; House, 1974; Rudduck, 1977; Schön, 1983). Teachers leave their professional education programs with a repertoire of standard practices grounded in the customs and conventions of the applied science subculture. Upon entry into the public schools, however, they are inducted into a practitioner subculture that, faced with a different set of relevancies, has developed different customs and conventions and thus a different set of standard practices that have little to do with what they learned in their professional education programs (Dornbusch & Scott, 1975; Schempp & Graber, 1992).[9]

Although the structural frame of reference assumes that the practices teachers use in schools derive from professionalization, from this perspective we can think of the source of these standard programs as acculturation. Professional behavior in schools is governed by institutionalized cultural norms; things are done in certain ways in schools because they have always been done that way, and to do anything else would not make sense. Like all professional work, teaching is a ritualized activity that takes place in an institutionalized environment (Zucker, 1977, 1981). Teachers learn to teach by modeling other teachers such as their former public school teachers and those under whom they serve as student teachers, professionals who got their standard practices in the same way from previous models (Gehrke & Kay, 1984; Lortie, 1975; Schempp & Graber, 1992). Teaching practices are passed on from one generation of teachers to another within an institutionalized context. There is nothing rational or inherently correct or incorrect about them; they are simply artifacts of a professional subculture. What is important about these practices is whether they serve the best interests of students and society, a question that can be addressed by asking how they are applied in practice.

From the structural frame of reference, professional practice is a matter of pigeonholing a presumed client need into one of the standard practices in a repertoire of skills, a process that works until the client's needs do not match the skills that the professional has to offer. Although from the cultural frame of reference such an anomaly can lead to the construction of a new practice, a common problem associated with pigeonholing is that "the professional confuses the needs of his clients with the skills he has to offer them" (Mintzberg, 1979, p. 374). The problem of innovation at the level of the professional, or what Mintzberg called the "means–ends inversion" (p. 373), is rooted "in convergent thinking, in the deductive reasoning of the professional who sees the specific situation in terms of the general concept. In the professional bureaucracy this means that new problems are forced into old pigeonholes" (p. 375). Ultimately, pigeonholing preempts the need for problem solving and innovation in schools because, when the needs of the student do not match the teacher's repertoire of skills, the tendency is to force them artificially into one of the available standard practices. In principle, teachers know the theory behind their practices and have the discretion to adapt them. However, given the deductive and convergent nature of professional education (Chapter 1) and the misplaced rationalization and formalization in schools, teachers, like all professionals, are performers, not problem solvers. They tend to perfect the standard practice in their repertoires; they do not invent new practices for unfamiliar contingencies.

We can understand the means–ends inversion culturally by thinking of a teacher's repertoires of skills as a paradigm, a technology of standard practices premised on beliefs about cause–effect relations (Brown, 1978; Weick, 1979a). Regardless of whether the practices are effective, they persist because the paradigm guides and justifies the teacher's professional thought and action (Brown, 1978; Clark, 1972; Pfeffer, 1982). Once the paradigm is in place, it and its associated practices change very slowly because the self-justifying nature of the paradigm distorts instructional anomalies, making them consistent with the prevailing view (Jonsson & Lundin, 1977). Structurally, one source of distortion is professional pigeonholing, a process in which anomalies go unrecognized because of the deductive nature of professionalization. Another structural distortion arises from the relationship between professionalization and specialization, an organizational form of pigeonholing that occurs when a student's needs cannot be forced into any of the standard practices in a teacher's repertoire. Here, a potential anomaly is distorted by forcing the student out of the professional–client relationship altogether, and pigeonholing him or her into a new one with a different professional specialist who is presumed to have the standard practices the student needs (see Perrow, 1970; Simon, 1977; Skrtic, 1988, 1991a; Weick, 1976).

Both forms of pigeonholing simplify matters greatly in professional bureaucracies because they eliminate virtually all anomalies, thereby preempting the need for problem solving and innovation. In effect, professional pigeonholing distorts instructional anomalies by simply ignoring them. Organizational pigeonholing distorts them by turning instructional problems into jurisdictional problems, which are resolved by reassigning students to a different teaching specialization (see Skrtic, 1987, 1991a, 1991b). Pigeonholing is not a dysfunction of school organizations; professional bureaucracies are structured to screen out heterogeneity and uncertainty by forcing their clients' needs into the standard practices of one or another of their professional specializations. The problem of innovation in schools is that innovative problem solving requires inductive reasoning, that is, the induction of new general concepts or practices from particular experiences. As Mintzberg (1979) noted, "That kind of thinking is divergent—it breaks away from old routines or standards rather than perfecting existing ones. And that flies in the face of everything the professional bureaucracy is designed to do" (p. 375).

Structurally, schools are nonadaptable at the classroom level because professionalization ultimately results in convergent thinking. Given a finite repertoire of skills, students whose needs fall outside a teacher's standard practices must be forced into them, or forced out of general education classrooms and into the special education system (or one of the other special needs programs such as compensatory, bilingual, migrant, or gifted education). Moreover, the situation is compounded by the rational-technical approach to school management, which, by introducing unwarranted rationalization and formalization, reduces professional thought and discretion. This minimizes the degree to which teachers can personalize their standard practices, thus forcing more students into the special education system than otherwise would be the case.

The same phenomenon can be understood culturally by thinking of teachers' repertoires of skills as a paradigm of practice that persists because anomalies are distorted to preserve its validity. The principal distortion is the institutional practice of special education, which, by removing students from the general education system, prevents teachers from recognizing anomalies in their conventional paradigm of practice. Without anomalies, of course, there is no way for the professional culture to see that there is something amiss with its paradigm and associated instructional practices. This acts in a mutually reinforcing way to strengthen teachers' belief in both the validity of their conventional practices and the notion that school failure is a human pathology. Moreover, misplaced rationalization and formalization compound and further mystify the situation because they conflict with the values that ground the paradigm. This reduces professional thought and thus the degree to which general education teachers can personalize their practices, which forces more students into the special education system and further reinforces the view that conventional practices are valid and that students who fail to learn from them are pathological.

Whether we think of school organizations from the structural or the cultural frame of reference, the implication is that student disability is neither a pathological condition nor an objective distinction. School failure is an organizational pathology that results from the inherent structural and cultural characteristics of traditional school organizations. Being "handicapped" in school is a matter of not fitting the standard practices of the prevailing paradigm of a professional culture, the legitimacy of which is maintained and reinforced by the objectification of school failure as student disability through the institutional practice of special education.

The Nature of Special Education

As public organizations, schools must be responsive to what society wants them to be and do. Society is a constant source of pressure on schools in this respect, but when values and priorities in society change, additional demands are made that often require schools to change what they and their professionals are accustomed to doing (Mintzberg, 1979; Rounds, 1979). In some cases, schools are required to make incidental, add-on changes, which they are able to do quite easily because of their loosely coupled internal structure. In other cases, however, society demands more fundamental changes, ones that require professionals to do something other than what they were standardized (structural perspective) or acculturated (cultural perspective) to do.

Structurally, this is a problem for schools because of the convergent thinking and deductive reasoning of professionals. Culturally, it is a problem because the values that underwrite the demand that professionals do something different contradict the values of their prevailing paradigm of practice (Rounds, 1979, 1981). From the institutional perspective we know that schools deal with their inability to change through various forms of decoupling, such as simply adding decoupled programs and specialists. The greater significance of this form of decoupling is that it permits schools to respond to demands for fundamental change by converting them into incidental changes. That is, by adding separate programs and specialists to their existing operation, school organizations can respond to fundamental change demands without requiring their professionals to actually do anything fundamentally different.

The segregated special education classroom is the extreme case of this form of decoupling. Earlier in the century when society required schools to serve children from working-class and immigrant families, the special classroom model emerged to deal with students whose needs could not be accommodated within the standard practices of public education's prevailing paradigm (see Bogdan & Knoll, 1988; Lazerson, 1983; Sarason & Doris, 1979; Chapter 3). From an organizational perspective, the special classroom served as a legitimating device, a means for schools to signal the public that they had complied with the demand to serve a broader range of students, while at the same time allowing the schools to maintain their traditional paradigm of practice. Once special classrooms were created, they simply were decoupled from the rest of the school organization, thus buffering schools from the change demand by buffering their teachers from the need to change the way they actually taught. Indeed, this decoupled relationship between the general education system and the special classroom was one of the major criticisms of the special classroom model within the mainstreaming debate of the 1960s and 1970s (see Christophos & Renz, 1969; Deno, 1970; Dunn, 1968; Johnson, 1962; Chapter 3).

Another special education example is the overrepresentation of minority students in special classrooms, a problem that emerged in the 1960s (Chandler & Plakos, 1969; Dunn, 1968; Janesick, 1988; MacMillan, 1971; Mercer, 1973; Wright, 1967) following *Brown* v. *Board of Education* (1954), and that, in special education generally, has continued into the present (Cummins, 1989; Harry, 1992; Heller, Holtzman, & Messick, 1982; Rueda, 1989), even though P.L. 94–142, the Education for All Handicapped Children Act of 1975 (EHA) (now the Individuals with Disabilities Education Act) requires "racially and culturally nondiscriminatory testing and evaluation" (Turnbull, 1993, p. 85). From an organizational perspective, the overrepresentation of minority students in special classrooms and programs can be understood as a form of decoupling, a process in which school organizations use an existing decoupling device – the special classroom and the special education system *per se* – to maintain their legitimacy in the face of failing to meet the needs of disproportionate numbers of these students in general education classrooms.

Special education is not a rationally conceived system of services. From an organizational perspective, it is a legitimating device, a mechanism that school organizations use to cope with the change demands of their institutionalized environments. Moreover, special education is not a rationally coordinated system because, by design, it is decoupled from the general education system, as well as from the other special needs programs (see Reynolds & Wang, 1983; Reynolds, Wang, & Walberg, 1987), each of which has been added to traditional school organizations incidentally as values and priorities have shifted in society. I began this chapter by noting that the unintended consequence of using organizations to provide services to society is that the services are shaped by the nature and needs of the organizations themselves. From an organizational perspective, student disability and the institutional practice of special education are unintended consequences of traditional school organizations.

From a structural perspective, the institutional practice of special education is an organizational artifact that emerged to protect the legitimacy of a nonadaptable bureaucratic structure faced with the changing value demands of a dynamic democratic environment. Even though schools are nonadaptable structures, they maintain their legitimacy under dynamic social conditions by signaling the public that changes have occurred, which includes the addition of decoupled subunits like special education and the other special needs programs. Moreover, from a cultural perspective, the institutional practices of special education and special needs programs generally distort the anomaly of school failure and thus preserve public education's prevailing paradigm of practice, which ultimately reinforces the theories of organizational rationality and human pathology in the profession and institution of education and in society at large.

The Nature of Progress

As we know from Chapter 3, the EHA is premised on the assumption that progress in special education is a rational-technical process of incremental refinements in conventional practices. When it was enacted, the EHA (and mainstreaming) was perceived to be a refined model of special education diagnostic and instructional practices, one that resolved the ethical and efficacy problems associated with the segregated special classroom model (see Abeson & Zettel, 1977; Gilhool, 1989; Turnbull, 1986). Although special educators criticized the EHA and mainstreaming on practical grounds throughout the 1980s (see Chapter 3), in this section I want to consider them from an organizational perspective relative to the question of the nature of progress in the field.[10]

Structurally, the problem with the EHA is that it requires professional bureaucracies to function as adhocracies by treating them as if they were machine bureaucracies. The ends of the EHA are adhocratic. Given its procedural requirements of interdisciplinary assessment and programming, parent participation, individualized educational plans, and least restrictive placements (see Turnbull & Turnbull, 1978), the EHA requires schools to become problem-solving organizations in which teams of professionals collaborate among themselves and with their clients to invent personalized practices. At the same time, however, the means by which the EHA seeks to achieve this transformation are completely consistent with the rational-technical approach to change. The EHA assumes that schools are rational machine bu-reaucracies, organizations in which worker behavior is controlled through formalization and thus subject to modification through revision and exten-sion of existing rules and regulations (see Elmore & McLaughlin, 1982).

Moreover, because the ends of the EHA are adhocractic, they contradict the inner professional bureaucracy structure of schools, which has both struc-tural and cultural implications. The structural contradiction arises from the fact that, whereas the EHA requires a problem-solving organization in which professionals work together to invent personalized instructional practices, the inner professional bureaucracy structure of schools configures them as performance organizations in which professionals work alone to perfect the standard practices in their repertoires. In turn, this produces a cultural contra-diction, a conflict between the bureaucratic values that ground the perfor-mance-oriented paradigm of the professional culture and those that under-write the adhocratic or problem-solving orientation of the EHA. This is a problem because the contradiction in values leads to resistance in the form of political clashes that undermine the goal of collaboration, and an increase in ritualized activity that intensifies the problem of professionalization (perfor-mance of standard practices or problem solutions) and thus deflects the goal of personalization (interdisciplinary problem solving) (see Bogdan, 1983; Lortie, 1978; Martin, 1978; Moran, 1984; Patrick & Reschly, 1982; Singer & Butler, 1987; Skrtic, Guba, & Knowlton, 1985; Weatherley, 1979).

Because the means of the EHA are completely consistent with the outer machine bureaucracy structure of traditional school organizations, they ex-tend and elaborate the existing rationalization and formalization in schools. This creates two interrelated structural problems. The first problem is that more rationalization and formalization reduce professional thought and dis-cretion even further. This intensifies the problem of professionalization and thus reduces the possibility of personalization, which results in even more students whose needs fall outside the standard practices of teachers. And because many of these students must be forced into the special education system, the bureaucratic means of the EHA ultimately lead to ever-greater numbers of students identified as handicapped (see Gerber & Levine-Donnerstein, 1989; United States Department of Education, 1988). The second problem stems from the fact that the outer machine bureaucracy structure of schools is decoupled from their internal professional bureaucracy structure, which means that the additional rationalization and formalization associated with the EHA have little to do with the way teachers actually teach students with special educational needs (see below). Ultimately, not only do the bureaucratic means of the EHA produce more students who must be identified as handicapped, but at the same time the two-structure bureau-cratic configuration of schools largely deflects the law's adhocratic ends from students identified as handicapped, the very students the law is intended to benefit.

Nevertheless, because the EHA requires at least overt conformity, a number of symbols of compliance have emerged to signal the public that the intent of the law is being achieved. For example, the symbol of compliance for programs that serve students labeled severely and profoundly handicapped is the traditional decoupled subunit – the segregated special classroom. Like the special classrooms of the 1960s, these programs are simply added incidentally to the loosely coupled internal structure of schools and, to one degree or another, decoupled from the general education program and other special education programs. Indeed, the decoupled nature of these programs is a key point of criticism in the inclusion debate (Gartner & Lipsky, 1987; Stainback & Stainback, 1984, 1987; Chapter 3).[11] The symbol of compliance for most students in the EHA's high-incidence classifications of learning disabilities, emotional disturbance, and mild mental retardation is the special education resource room, a new type of decoupled subunit associated with the mainstreaming model. From an organizational perspective, the resource room is even more problematic than the traditional special classroom because it violates the logic of the division of labor, means of coordination, and form of interdependence in the professional bureaucracy configuration.

Under the mainstreaming model, the responsibility for implementing a student's individualized educational plan (IEP) is divided among one or more general education teachers and a special education resource teacher. This contradicts the specialized division of labor and professionalized means of coordination in schools because it requires that the student's instructional program be rationalized and assigned to more than one professional, which is justified implicitly on the assumption that the professionals will work collaboratively to implement the IEP in an integrated manner. But the collaboration required to integrate the student's IEP contradicts the logic of specialization and professionalization, and thus the form of interdependence among professionals in schools. In theory, a team of teachers working collaboratively in the interest of a single student for whom they share responsibility violates both the logic of loose coupling and the sensibility of the professional culture and thus should not be expected to occur as a generalized phenomenon in schools (Bidwell, 1965; Mintzberg, 1979; Weick, 1976). By design, there is no need for collaboration or mutual adjustment in schools because specialization and professionalization locate virtually all of the necessary coordination within the roles of individual specialists. In practice, if it occurs at all in schools, collaboration within or across specializations is at best rare, fleeting, and idiosyncratic (see Bishop, 1977; Lortie, 1975, 1978; Skrtic, Guba, & Knowlton, 1985; Tye & Tye, 1984). Mainstreaming and the IEP process require a collaborative division of labor and a means of coordination premised on mutual adjustment, and thus ultimately on the discursive coupling arrangement of the adhocracy configuration.

Although the EHA requires placements in the general education classroom to the maximum extent possible, students are identified as handicapped under the law precisely because they cannot be accommodated within the existing standard practices in these classrooms (see Skrtic, Guba, & Knowlton, 1985; Walker, 1987). Given the logic of specialization and the deductive reasoning of professionalization, mainstreaming for most of these students is largely symbolic and ceremonial (see Biklen, 1985; Skrtic, Guba, & Knowlton, 1985; Wright, Cooperstein, Reneker, & Padilla, 1982). Given the adhocratic ends of the EHA, it was intended to decrease the effects of student disability by increasing personalized instruction and general education integration. However, given its bureaucratic means and the bureaucratic nature of traditional school organizations, the EHA has resulted in an increase in the number of students classified as disabled (Gerber & Levine-Donnerstein, 1989; USDE, 1988), disintegration of instruction (Gartner & Lipsky, 1987; Walker, 1987; Wang, Reynolds, & Walberg, 1986, 1987), and a decrease in personalization in general education (Bryan, Bay, & Donahue, 1988; Keogh, 1988) and special education classrooms (Carlberg & Kavale, 1980; Skrtic, Guba, & Knowlton, 1985).

In Chapter 3, I deconstructed special education as a professional practice by exposing the inconsistencies, contradictions, and silences in the special education knowledge tradition. My aim was to raise doubts in readers' minds about the legitimacy of the field's practices and discourses by questioning the functionalist assumptions, theories, and metatheories in which they are grounded. In this chapter I questioned the legitimacy of special education from an organizational perspective. By exposing the inconsistencies, contradictions, and silences in the assumptions, theories, and metatheories that have guided and justified its development and expansion over this century, I deconstructed special education as an institutional practice of public education. In terms of the legitimacy of its grounding assumptions, special education cannot be considered a rational and just response to the problem of school failure. Moreover, as we will see in Chapter 10, the broader significance of deconstructing special education as an institutional practice is that it deconstructs the institution of public education itself, thus clearing the way for reconstructing it according to the ideal of public education in a democracy.

NOTES

1. The machine bureaucracy configuration actually resulted from the combination of scientific management and the so-called "principles of management" approach

to administration (Fayol, 1916/1949; Gulick & Urwick, 1937), which is premised on a detailed set of prescriptions (regarding, for example, the principles of "chain of command" and "span of authority") for bringing work under the formal control of managers. The synthesis of the notion of standardization of work processes (scientific management) with that of formal administrative authority (principles of management) yielded the machine model of organizational design and of management, both of which are premised on the notion of "man-as-machine" (Crozier, 1964; Mintzberg, 1979; Worthy, 1959).

2. Barnard's synthesis was imported into public education by way of the Getzels–Guba model of administration (Getzels & Guba, 1957), which is premised on Barnard's synthesis and subsequently became "the most successful theory in educational administration" (Griffiths, 1979, p. 50). In many of its essential features, total quality management (Deming, 1986) is also a synthesis of the rational and nonrational perspectives on organization and management. As an attempt to achieve efficiency and quality simultaneously by giving workers more of a voice in the control of work, total quality management is more of a synthesis than Barnard's approach or the Getzels–Guba model, but it falls far short of the "participatory" or "democratic" approaches to organization and management touched upon below and discussed more fully in the next chapter (see Chapter 10, note 15).

3. The leading professors of educational administration also urged the field to adopt positivism, which at that time was the dominant epistemology in the social sciences and thus in the field of organization analysis (see Griffiths, 1983; Chapter 2). Although the leading professors published several texts that attempted to appropriate the prevailing (functionalist) organizational and methodological insights of organization analysis into the field of educational administration (e.g., Campbell & Gregg, 1956; Coladarci & Getzels, 1955; Griffiths, 1959, 1964; Halpin, 1958), the idea of grounding their practices in theory never really captured the imagination of the professoriate or of practicing administrators, the vast majority of whom remained tied to the prescriptive discourse (see Campbell & Newell, 1973; Cunningham, Hack, & Nystrand, 1977; Halpin, 1970; Halpin & Hayes, 1977).

4. The most significant development in education relative to school organization was the emergence in the 1960s of a research tradition on educational change (see Elmore & McLaughlin, 1988; Skrtic, 1995). Over the past 30 years, the apparent inability to change schools in any meaningful way (Boyd & Crowson, 1981; Cuban, 1979) has forced educational change researchers to modify their perspective on change itself, a shift from an objectivist or rational-technical concern for the innovation to a subjectivist or nonrational concern for the culture of schools (see House, 1979), thus paralleling developments in the social sciences (see Chapter 2; below). The shift has provided new ways to understand schools as cultures and to influence practice through dialogical discourse (e.g., Bates, 1980, 1987; Foster, 1986; Gitlin, 1990; Lather, 1991; Maxcy, 1991; Sarason, 1982; Sirotnik & Oakes, 1986; Skrtic, 1985; Skrtic, Guba, & Knowlton, 1985). The problem, however, is that the new focus on culture and discourse pays too little attention to the material structure of schools and thus to the necessary organizational conditions of dialogical discourse (see Skrtic, 1991a; Chapters 3 and 10). In the analysis to follow I consider school organization and change dialogically, from both a structural and a cultural perspective within a

single antifoundational analysis (also see Skrtic, 1987, 1988, 1991a, 1991b, 1995; Skrtic & Ware, 1992).

5. Configuration theory synthesizes the individualists' concern for organizing processes with the structuralists' concern for organizational structure, under the analytical concept of organizational structur*ing* (see below). It is important for analyzing school organization because it provides several ideal-typical (see Chapter 2) organizational configurations that are particularly helpful for understanding the structure and functioning of traditional school organizations, as well as the structure implied in both the school restructuring movement in general education and the inclusive education movement in special education (see Skrtic, 1987, 1988, 1991a, 1995; Skrtic & Ware, 1992; Chapter 10; below). Institutional theory synthesizes the macro-subjectivist concern for normative or cultural structures and the macro-objectivist concern for material structures, under the analytic notion that all organizations maintain both types of structures. It is important for understanding the nature and functioning of school organizations, particularly how they respond to change demands (see Skrtic, 1987, 1988; Chapter 10; below).

6. By synthesizing macro-subjective and micro-subjective theories of organization, paradigmatic theories provide a way to understand the mutually shaping relationship between organizational cultures or paradigms and the thought and action of their members. They are important for understanding schools as cultures or systems of meaning and how such systems change (see Skrtic, 1987, 1988, 1991a, 1995). By synthesizing micro-subjective, macro-subjective, and macro-objective theories of organization, cognitive theories provide a means to understand the ways in which organizational members construct and reconstruct organizational paradigms, as well as the mutually shaping relationship between organizational structure and culture. They are important for understanding the relationship between structure and culture in schools and how both are formed and change (see Skrtic, 1987, 1988, 1991a, 1995; Skrtic & Ware, 1992; Chapter 10; below).

7. Except where noted otherwise, all of the material on configuration theory in this section (division of labor, coordination of work, interdependence among workers, and the implications of the machine bureaucracy, professional bureaucracy, and adhocracy configurations for management, adaptability, and accountability) is drawn from Mintzberg (1979, 1983), Miller and Mintzberg (1983), and Miller and Friesen (1984); all of the material on institutional theory (decoupled structures and subunits, and the implications of organizational symbols and ceremonies for school governance and educational reform) is drawn from Meyer and Rowan (1977, 1978), Meyer and Scott (1983), and Meyer (1979).

8. First recognized in the 1960s, this configuration was referred to originally as an "organic structure" (Pugh et al., 1963), and more recently as a "learning organization" (Senge, 1990). Mintzberg (1979) called it adhocracy, following Bennis and Slater (1964), who coined the term in *The Temporary Society*, and Alvin Toffler (1970), who popularized it in *Future Shock*.

9. Further evidence for the notion of decoupled subcultures can be found in the educational change literature. Given the objectivist view of the professions, it is assumed that teaching practices are updated as new, research-based procedures become available at the applied science level of the profession (see Chapter 1). But this

rarely occurs (see House, 1974, 1979); in most schools the methods of instruction and the curriculum itself are little different from what they were earlier in the century (Cuban, 1979).

10. Virtually all of the citations in this section are references to empirical and interpretive research findings that support my theoretical claims about organization and change. That is, in virtually all cases the author or authors cited in conjunction with an assertion have not made the assertion. The assertions are mine, based on the discussion of organization and change above, and they are supported by the empirical or interpretive research of the authors cited.

11. Because the needs of these students are beyond the standard practices of any single professional specialization and thus require an interdisciplinary approach, the efficacy of these programs depends on the will and capacity of local schools to provide the team of professionals that is required (see Biklen, 1985; McDonnel & McLaughlin, 1982; Noel & Fuller, 1985; Skrtic, Guba, & Knowlton, 1985). Beyond this, programs for students with severe to profound disabilities have had little to do with the operation of schools under the EHA, which is to be expected, of course, given the loosely coupled internal structure of school organizations.

REFERENCES

Abeson, A., & Zettel, J. (1977). The end of the quiet revolution: The Education for All Handicapped Children Act of 1975. *Exceptional Children, 44*(2), 115–128.

Allison, G. T. (1971). *Essence of decision: Explaining the Cuban missile crisis*. Boston: Little, Brown.

Argyris, C. (1957). *Personality and organization*. New York: Harper.

Ayres, L. P. (1909). *Laggards in the schools: A study of retardation and elimination in city school systems*. New York: Charities Publication Committee.

Barnard, C. I. (1938). *Functions of the executive*. Cambridge, MA: Harvard University Press.

Bates, R. J. (1980). Educational administration, the sociology of science, and the management of knowledge. *Educational Administration Quarterly, 16*(2), 1–20.

Bates, R. J. (1987). Corporate culture, schooling, and educational administration. *Educational Administration Quarterly, 23*(4), 79–115.

Becker, H. S. (1983). Studying urban schools. *Anthropology and Education Quarterly, 31*(2), 99–108.

Bennis, W. G., & Slater, P. L. (1964). *The temporary society*. New York: Harper & Row.

Berger, P. L., & Luckmann, T. (1967). *The social construction of reality*. New York: Doubleday.

Bidwell, C. E. (1965). The school as formal organization. In J. G. March (Ed.), *Handbook of organizations* (pp. 972–1022). Chicago: Rand McNally College Publishing.

Biklen, D. (1985). *Achieving the complete school: Strategies for effective mainstreaming*. New York: Teachers College Press.

Bishop, J. M. (1977). Organizational influences on the work orientations of elementary teachers. *Sociology of Work and Occupation, 4*, 171–208.

Bobbit, F. (1913). Some general principles of management applied to the problems of city school systems. In *The supervision of city schools: Twelfth yearbook of the National Society for the Study of Education, Part 1* (pp. 137–196). Chicago: University of Chicago Press.

Bogdan, R. (1983). Does mainstreaming work? is a silly question. *Phi Delta Kappan, 64*(6), 425–434.

Bogdan, R., & Knoll, J. (1988). The sociology of disability. In E. L. Meyen & T. M. Skrtic (Eds.), *Exceptional children and youth: An introduction* (pp. 449–477). Denver: Love Publishing.

Boulding, K. (1967). The boundaries of social policy. *Social Work, 12*, 3–11.

Boyd, W. L., & Crowson, R. L. (1981). The changing conception and practice of public school administration. In D. C. Berliner (Ed.), *Review of research in education* (pp. 311–373). Itasca, IL: F. E. Peacock.

Bridges, E. M. (1982). Research on the school administrator: The state of the art, 1967–1980. *Educational Administration Quarterly, 18*(3), 12–33.

Brown, R. H. (1978). Bureaucracy as praxis: Toward a political phenomenology of formal organizations. *Administrative Science Quarterly, 23*(3), 365–382.

Bryan, T., Bay, M., & Donahue, M. (1988). Implications of the learning disabilities definition for the regular education initiative. *Journal of Learning Disabilities, 21*(1), 23–28.

Burns, T., & Stalker, G. M. (1966). *The management of innovation* (2nd ed.). London: Tavistock Publications.

Burrell, G., & Morgan, G. (1979). *Sociological paradigms and organizational analysis.* London: Heinemann.

Callahan, R. E. (1962). *Education and the cult of efficiency: A study of the social forces that have shaped the administration of public schools.* Chicago: University of Chicago Press.

Campbell, R. (1971, August). NCPEA–Then and now. Paper presented at the meeting of the National Council of Professors of Educational Administration, University of Utah, Salt Lake City.

Campbell, R. F., Fleming, T., Newell, L. J., & Bennion, J. W. (1987). *A history of thought and practice in educational administration.* New York: Teachers College Press.

Campbell, R. F., & Gregg, R. T. (Eds.). (1956). *Administrative behavior in education.* New York: Harper & Brothers.

Campbell, R. F., & Newell, L. J. (1973). *A study of professors in educational administration: Problems and prospects of an applied academic field.* Columbus, OH: University Council for Educational Administration.

Carlberg, C., & Kavale, K. (1980). The efficacy of special versus regular class placement for exceptional children: A meta-analysis. *Journal of Special Education, 14*(3), 295–309.

Chandler, J. T., & Plakos, J. (1969). *Spanish-speaking pupils classified as educable mentally retarded.* Sacramento: California State Department of Education.

Chandler, M. D., & Sayles, L. R. (1971). *Managing large systems.* New York: Harper & Row.

Christophos, F., & Renz, P. (1969). A critical examination of special education programs. *Journal of Special Education, 3*(4), 371–380.

Clark, B. R. (1972). The organizational saga in higher education. *Administrative Science Quarterly, 17*, 178–184.

Clark, D. L. (1985). Emerging paradigms in organizational theory and research. In Y. S. Lincoln (Ed.), *Organizational theory and inquiry: The paradigm revolution* (pp. 43–78). Beverly Hills, CA: Sage.

Cohen, M. D., & March, J. G. (1974). *Leadership and ambiguity*. New York: Mc-Graw-Hill.

Cohen, M. D., March, J. G., & Olsen, J. P. (1972). A garbage can model of organizational choice. *Administrative Science Quarterly, 17*, 1–25.

Coladarci, A. P., & Getzels, J. W. (1955). *The use of theory in educational administration*. Stanford: Stanford University Press.

Crozier, M. (1964). *The bureaucratic phenomenon*. Chicago: University of Chicago Press.

Cuban, L. (1979). Determinants of curriculum change and stability, 1870–1970. In J. Schaffarzick & G. Sykes (Eds.), *Value conflicts and curriculum issues*. Berkeley, CA: McCutchan.

Cummins, J. (1989). A theoretical framework for bilingual special education. *Exceptional Children, 56*(2), 111–119.

Cunningham, L. L., Hack, W. G., & Nystrand, R. O. (Eds.). (1977). *Educational administration: The developing decades*. Berkeley, CA: McCutchan.

Dalton, M. (1959). *Men who manage*. New York: Wiley.

Deming, W. E. (1986). *Out of the crisis*. Cambridge, MA: MIT Press.

Deno, E. (1970). Special education as developmental capital. *Exceptional Children, 37*(3), 229–237.

Dewey, J. (1976). The school and society. In J. A. Boydston (Ed.), *John Dewey: The middle works, 1899–1924* (Vol. 1, pp. 1–109). Carbondale: Southern Illinois University Press. (Original work published 1899)

Dewey, J. (1980). Democracy and education. In J. A. Boydston (Ed.), *John Dewey: The middle works, 1899–1924* (Vol. 9, pp. 1–370). Carbondale: Southern Illinois University Press. (Original work published 1916)

Dewey, J. (1981). The need for a recovery of philosophy. In J. J. McDermott (Ed.), *The philosophy of John Dewey* (pp. 58–97). Chicago: University of Chicago Press. (Original work published 1917)

Dewey, J. (1981). Experience and nature. In J. A. Boydston (Ed.), *John Dewey: The later works, 1925–1953* (Vol. 1, pp. 1–326). Carbondale: Southern Illinois University Press. (Original work published 1925)

Dewey, J. (1988). The public and its problems. In J. A. Boydston (Ed.), *John Dewey: The later works, 1925–1953* (Vol. 2, pp. 235–372). Carbondale: Southern Illinois University Press. (Original work published 1927)

Dewey, J. (1988). The quest for certainty. In J. A. Boydston (Ed.), *John Dewey: The later works, 1925–1953* (Vol. 4, pp. 1–250). Carbondale: Southern Illinois University Press. (Original work published 1929)

Dewey, J. (1988). Individualism, old and new. In J. A. Boydston (Ed.), *John Dewey:*

The later works, 1925–1953 (Vol. 5, pp. 41–123). Carbondale: Southern Illinois University Press. (Original work published 1929–30)

Dewey, J. (1989). The development of American pragmatism. In H. S. Thayer (Ed.), *Pragmatism: The classic writings* (pp. 23–40). Indianapolis: Hackett. (Original work published 1931)

Dornbusch, S. M., & Scott, W. R. (1975). *Evaluation and the exercise of authority: A theory of control applied to diverse organizations*. San Francisco: Jossey-Bass.

Dunn, L. M. (1968). Special education for the mildly retarded – Is much of it justifiable? *Exceptional Children, 35*(1), 5–22.

Edwards, R. C. (1979). *Contested terrain: The transformation of the workplace in the twentieth century*. New York: Basic Books.

Elliott, J. (1975). *Objectivity, ideology, and teacher participation in educational research*. Norwich, England: University of East Anglia, Centre for Applied Research in Education.

Elmore, R. F., & McLaughlin, M. W. (1982). Strategic choice in federal education policy: The compliance–assistance trade-off. In A. Lieberman & M. W. McLaughlin (Eds.), *Policy making in education: Eighty-first yearbook of the National Society for the Study of Education* (pp. 159–194). Chicago: University of Chicago Press.

Elmore, R. F., & McLaughlin, M. W. (1988). *Steady work: Policy, practice, and the reform of American education*. Santa Monica, CA: Rand Corporation.

Erickson, D. A. (1977). An overdue paradigm shift in educational administration, or, how can we get that idiot off the freeway? In L. L. Cunningham, W. G. Hack, & R. O. Nystrand (Eds.), *Educational administration: The developing decades* (pp. 199–143). Berkeley, CA: McCutchan.

Erickson, D. A. (1979). Research on educational administration: The state-of-the-art. *Educational Researcher, 8*(3), 9–14.

Fayol, H. (1949). *General and industrial management*. Marshfield, MA: Pitman Publishing. (Original work published 1916)

Follett, M. P. (1924). *Creative experience*. London: Longmans and Green.

Follett, M. P. (1940). *Dynamic administration: The collected papers of Mary Parker Follett* (H. C. Metcalf & L. Urwick, Eds.). New York: Harper.

Foster, W. (1986). *Paradigms and promises: New approaches to educational administration*. Buffalo, NY: Prometheus Books.

Galbraith, J. K. (1967). *The new industrial state*. Boston: Houghton Mifflin.

Gartner, A., & Lipsky, D. K. (1987). Beyond special education: Toward a quality system for all students. *Harvard Educational Review, 57*(4), 367–390.

Gehrke, N. J., & Kay, R. S. (1984). The socialization of beginning teachers through mentor–protege relationships. *Journal of Teacher Education, 35*, 21–24.

Gerber, M. M., & Levine-Donnerstein, D. (1989). Educating all children: Ten years later. *Exceptional Children, 56*(1), 17–27.

Getzels, J. W., & Guba, E. G. (1957). Social behavior and the administrative process. *School Review, 65*, 423–441.

Gilhool, T. K. (1989). The right to an effective education: From *Brown* to P.L. 94–142 and beyond. In D. K. Lipsky & A. Gartner (Eds.), *Beyond separate education: Quality education for all* (pp. 243–253). Baltimore: Paul H. Brookes.

Gitlin, A. D. (1990). Educative research, voice, and school change. *Harvard Educational Review, 60*(4), 443–466.

Golding, D. (1980). Establishing blissful clarity in organizational life: Managers. *Sociological Review, 28,* 763–782.

Griffiths, D. E. (1959). *Administrative theory.* New York: Appleton-Century-Crofts.

Griffiths, D. E. (Ed.). (1964). *Behavioral science and educational administration*: Sixty-third yearbook of the National Society for the Study of Education, Part II. Chicago: University of Chicago Press.

Griffiths, D. E. (1979). Intellectual turmoil in educational administration. *Educational Administration Quarterly, 15*(3), 43–65.

Griffiths, D. E. (1983). Evolution in research and theory: A study of prominent researchers. *Educational Administration Quarterly, 19*(3), 201–221.

Griffiths, D. E. (1988). Administrative theory. In N. J. Boyan (Ed.), *Handbook of research on educational administration* (pp. 27–51). New York: Longman.

Gulick, L., & Urwick, L. (Eds.). (1937). *Papers on the science of administration.* New York: Institute of Public Administration, Columbia University.

Gutmann, A. (1987). *Democratic education.* Princeton, NJ: Princeton University Press.

Haber, S. (1964). *Efficiency and uplift: Scientific management in the progressive era, 1890–1920.* Chicago: University of Chicago Press.

Halpin, A. W. (Ed.). (1958). *Administrative theory in education.* Chicago: University of Chicago, Midwest Administration Center.

Halpin, A. W. (1970). Administrative theory: The fumbled torch. In A. M. Kroll (Ed.), *Issues in American education.* New York: Oxford University Press.

Halpin, A. W., & Hayes, A. E. (1977). The broken ikon, or What ever happened to theory? In L. L. Cunningham, W. G. Hack, & R. O. Nystrand (Eds.), *Educational administration: The developing decades* (pp. 261–297). Berkeley, CA: McCutchan.

Harry, B. (1992). *Cultural diversity, families, and the special education system: Communication and empowerment.* New York: Teachers College Press.

Hedberg, B. (1981). How organizations learn and unlearn. In P. C. Nystrom & W. H. Starbuck (Eds.), *Handbook of organizational design* (Vol. 1, pp. 3–27). New York: Oxford University Press.

Hedberg, B. L. T., Nystrom, P. C., & Starbuck, W. H. (1976). Camping on seesaws: Prescriptions for a self-designing organization. *Administrative Science Quarterly, 21*(1), 41–65.

Heller, K., Holtzman, W., & Messick, S. (1982). *Placing children in special education: A strategy for equity.* Washington, DC: National Academy of Sciences Press.

House, E. R. (1974). *The politics of educational innovation.* Berkeley, CA: McCutchan.

House, E. R. (1979). Technology versus craft: A ten year perspective on innovation. *Journal of Curriculum Studies, 11*(1), 1–15.

Illich, I. (1976). *Medical nemesis.* New York: Random House.

Janesick, V. J. (1988). Our multicultural society. In E. L. Meyen & T. M. Skrtic (Eds.), *Exceptional children and youth: An introduction* (pp. 519–535). Denver: Love Publishing.

Johnson, G. O. (1962). Special education for the mentally handicapped – A paradox. *Exceptional Children, 29*(2), 62–69.

Jones, R. A. (1977). *Self-fulfilling prophecies.* Hillsdale, NJ: Erlbaum.

Jonsson, S. A., & Lundin, R. A. (1977). Myths and wishful thinking as management tools. In P. C. Nystrom & W. H. Starbuck (Eds.), *Prescriptive models of organizations* (pp. 157–170). New York: Elsevier North-Holland.

Keogh, B. K. (1988). Improving services for problem learners: Rethinking and restructuring. *Journal of Learning Disabilities, 21*(1), 19–22.

Kuhn, T. S. (1970). *The structure of scientific revolutions* (2nd ed.). Chicago: University of Chicago Press.

Lather, P. (1991). Deconstructing/deconstructive inquiry: The politics of knowing and being known. *Educational Theory, 41*(2), 153–173.

Lawrence, P. R., & Lorsch, J. W. (1967). *Organization and environment: Managing differentiation and integration.* Boston: Graduate School of Business Administration, Harvard University.

Lazerson, M. (1983). The origins of special education. In J. G. Chambers & W. T. Hartman (Eds.), *Special education policies: Their history, implementation, and finance* (pp. 15–47). Philadelphia: Temple University Press.

Lipsky, M. (1976). Toward a theory of street-level bureaucracy. In W. D. Hawley, M. Lipsky, S. B. Greenberg, J. D. Greenstone, I. Katznelson, K. Orren, P. E. Peterson, M. Shefter, & D. Yates (Eds.), *Theoretical perspectives on urban politics* (pp. 196–213). Englewood Cliffs, NJ: Prentice-Hall.

Lortie, D. C. (1975). *Schoolteacher: A sociological study.* Chicago: University of Chicago Press.

Lortie, D. C. (1978). Some reflections on renegotiation. In M. C. Reynolds (Ed.), *Futures of education for exceptional students: Emerging structures* (pp. 235–243). Reston, VA: Council for Exceptional Children.

MacMillan, D. L. (1971). Special education for the mildly retarded: Servant or savant? *Focus on Exceptional Children, 2*(9), 1–11.

March, J. G., & Olsen, J. P. (1976). *Ambiguity and choice in organizations.* Bergen, Norway: Universitetsforlaget.

Martin, D. T., Overholt, G. E., & Urban, W. J. (1976). *Accountability in American education: A critique.* Princeton, NJ: Princeton Book Company.

Martin, E. (1978). Preface. In M. C. Reynolds (Ed.), *Futures of education for exceptional students: Emerging structures* (pp. iii–vi). Reston, VA: Council for Exceptional Children.

Maxcy, S. J. (1991). *Educational leadership: A critical pragmatic perspective.* New York: Bergin & Garvey.

Mayo, E. (1933). *The human problems of an industrial civilization.* New York: Macmillan.

McDonnell, L. M., & McLaughlin, M. W. (1982). *Education policy and the role of the states.* Santa Monica, CA: Rand Corporation.

Mercer, J. (1973). *Labeling the mentally retarded: Clinical and social system perspectives on mental retardation.* Berkeley: University of California Press.

Meyer, J. W., & Rowan, B. (1977). Institutionalized organizations: Formal structure as myth and ceremony. *American Journal of Sociology, 83*, 340–363.

Meyer, J. W., & Rowan, B. (1978). The structure of educational organizations. In M. W. Meyer (Ed.), *Environments and organizations* (pp. 78–109). San Francisco: Jossey-Bass.

Meyer, J. W., & Scott, W. R. (1983). *Organizational environments: Ritual and rationality.* Beverly Hills, CA: Sage.

Meyer, M. W. (1979). Organizational structure as signaling. *Pacific Sociological Review, 22*(4), 481–500.

Miller, D., & Friesen, P. H. (1984). *Organizations: A quantum view.* Englewood Cliffs, NJ: Prentice-Hall.

Miller, D., & Mintzberg, H. (1983). The case for configuration. In G. Morgan (Ed.), *Beyond method: Strategies for social research* (pp. 57–73). Beverly Hills, CA: Sage.

Mintzberg, H. (1979). *The structuring of organizations.* Englewood Cliffs, NJ: Prentice-Hall.

Mintzberg, H. (1983). *Structure in fives: Designing effective organizations.* Englewood Cliffs, NJ: Prentice-Hall.

Mommsen, W. J. (1974). *The age of bureaucracy: Perspectives on the political sociology of Max Weber.* New York: Harper & Row.

Moran, M. (1984). Excellence at the cost of instructional equity? The potential impact of recommended reforms upon low achieving students. *Focus on Exceptional Children, 16*(7), 1–11.

Morgan, G. (1983). *Beyond method.* Beverly Hills, CA: Sage.

Morgan, G. (1986). *Images of organization.* Beverly Hills, CA: Sage.

Moroney, R. M. (1981). Policy analysis within a value theoretical framework. In R. Haskins & J. J. Gallagher (Eds.), *Models for analysis of social policy: An introduction* (pp. 78–101). Norwood, NJ: Ablex.

Noel, M. M., & Fuller, B. C. (1985). The social policy construction of special education: The impact of state characteristics on identification and integration of handicapped children. *Remedial and Special Education, 6*(3), 27–35.

Parsons, T. (1960). *Structure and process in modern societies.* Glencoe, IL: Free Press.

Patrick, J., & Reschly, D. (1982). Relationship of state educational criteria and demographic variables to school-system prevalence of mental retardation. *American Journal of Mental Retardation, 86,* 351–360.

Peirce, C. S. (1931–35). *Collected papers of Charles Sanders Peirce* (C. Hartshorne & P. Weiss, Eds.). Cambridge, MA: Harvard University Press.

Perrow, C. (1970). *Organizational analysis: A sociological review.* Belmont, CA: Wadsworth.

Perrow, C. (1972). *Complex organizations: A critical essay.* New York: Scott, Foresman.

Perrow, C. (1978). Demystifying organizations. In R. C. Sarri & Y. Hasenfeld (Eds.), *The management of human services* (pp. 105–120). New York: Columbia University Press.

Pettigrew, A. M. (1979). On studying organizational cultures. *Administrative Science Quarterly, 24,* 570–581.

Pfeffer, J. (1982). *Organizations and organization theory.* Marshfield, MA: Pitman Publishing.

Pugh, D. S., Hickson, D. J., Hinnings, C. R., MacDonald, K. M., Turner, C., &

Lupton, T. (1963). A conceptual scheme for organizational analysis. *Administrative Science Quarterly, 8*(4), 289–315.

Reynolds, M. C., & Wang, M. C. (1983). Restructuring "special" school programs: A position paper. *Policy Studies Review, 2*(1), 189–212.

Reynolds, M. C., Wang, M. C., & Walberg, H. J. (1987). The necessary restructuring of special and general education. *Exceptional Children, 53*(5), 391–398.

Roethlisberger, F. J., & Dickson, W. J. (1939). *Management and the worker: An account of a research program conducted by the Western Electric Company, Hawthorne Works, Chicago.* Cambridge, MA: Harvard University Press.

Romzek, B. S., & Dubnick, M. J. (1987). Accountability in the public sector: Lessons from the Challenger tragedy. *Public Administration Review, 47*(3), 227–238.

Rounds, J. (1979). Social theory, public policy and social order. Unpublished Ph.D. dissertation, University of California, Los Angeles.

Rounds, J. (1981). Information and ambiguity in organizational change. Paper presented at the Carnegie–Mellon Symposium on Information Processing in Organizations. Pittsburgh, PA: Carnegie–Mellon University.

Rowan, B. (1980). Organizational structure and the institutional environment: The case of public schools. Unpublished manuscript, Texas Christian University, Fort Worth.

Rudduck, J. (1977). Dissemination as encounter of cultures. *Research Intelligence, 3,* 3–5.

Rueda, R. (1989). Defining mild disabilities with language-minority students. *Exceptional Children, 56*(2), 121–128.

Sarason, S. B. (1982). *The culture of the school and the problem of change* (rev. ed.). Boston: Allyn & Bacon.

Sarason, S. B., & Doris, J. (1979). *Educational handicap, public policy, and social history.* New York: Free Press.

Schein, E. H. (1972). *Professional education.* New York: McGraw-Hill.

Schempp, P. G., & Graber, K. C. (1992). Teacher socialization from a dialectical perspective: Pretraining through induction. *Journal of Teaching in Physical Education, 11*(4), 329–348.

Schön, D. A. (1983). *The reflective practitioner: How professionals think in action.* New York: Basic Books.

Scott, R. W. (1981). *Organizations: Rational, natural, and open systems.* Englewood Cliffs, NJ: Prentice-Hall.

Segal, M. (1974). Organization and environment: A typology of adaptability and structure. *Public Administration Review, 34*(3), 212–220.

Senge, P. M. (1990). *The fifth discipline: The art and practice of the learning organization.* New York: Doubleday.

Simon, H. (1947). *Administrative behavior.* New York: Macmillan.

Simon, H. A. (1977). *The new science of management decision.* Englewood Cliffs, NJ: Prentice-Hall.

Singer, J. D., & Butler, J. A. (1987). The Education for All Handicapped Children Act: Schools as agents of social reform. *Harvard Educational Review, 57*(2), 125–152.

Sirotnik, K. A., & Oakes, J. (1986). *Critical perspectives on the organization and improvement of schooling*. Boston: Kluwer-Nijhoff Publishing.

Skrtic, T. M. (1985). Doing naturalistic research into educational organizations. In Y. S. Lincoln (Ed.), *Organizational theory and inquiry: The paradigm revolution* (pp. 185–220). Beverly Hills, CA: Sage.

Skrtic, T. M. (1987). An organizational analysis of special education reform. *Counterpoint, 8*(2), 15–19.

Skrtic, T. M. (1988). The organizational context of special education. In E. L. Meyen & T. M. Skrtic (Eds.), *Exceptional children and youth: An introduction* (pp. 479–517). Denver: Love Publishing.

Skrtic, T. M. (1991a). *Behind special education: A critical analysis of professional culture and school organization*. Denver: Love Publishing.

Skrtic, T. M. (1991b). The special education paradox: Equity as the way to excellence. *Harvard Educational Review, 61*(2), 148–206.

Skrtic, T. M. (1995). The organizational context of special education and school reform. In E. L. Meyen & T. M. Skrtic (Eds.), *Special education and student disability: Traditional, emerging, and alternative perspectives* (pp. 729–791). Denver: Love Publishing.

Skrtic, T. M., Guba, E. G., & Knowlton, H. E. (1985). *Interorganizational special education programming in rural areas: Technical report on the multisite naturalistic field study*. Washington, DC: National Institute of Education.

Skrtic, T. M., & Ware, L. P. (1992). Reflective teaching and the problem of school organization. In E. W. Ross, J. W. Cornett, & G. McCutcheon (Eds.), *Teacher personal theorizing: Connecting curriculum practice, theory, and research* (pp. 207–218, 298–303). Albany: State University of New York Press.

Spring, J. (1980). *Educating the worker-citizen: The social, economic, and political foundations of education*. New York: Longman.

Stainback, S., & Stainback, W. (1984). A rationale for the merger of special and regular education. *Exceptional Children, 51*(2), 102–111.

Stainback, S., & Stainback, W. (1987). Integration versus cooperation: A commentary on educating children with learning problems: A shared responsibility. *Exceptional Children, 54*(1), 66–68.

Taylor, F. W. (1947). *Scientific management*. New York: Harper & Row. (Original work published 1911)

Thompson, J. D. (1967). *Organizations in action*. New York: McGraw-Hill.

Toffler, A. (1970). *Future shock*. New York: Bantam Books.

Turnbull, H. R. (1986). *Free appropriate public education: The law and children with disabilities*. Denver: Love Publishing.

Turnbull, H. R. (1993). *Free appropriate public education: The law and children with disabilities*. Denver: Love Publishing.

Turnbull, H. R., & Turnbull, A. P. (1978). *Free appropriate public education: Law and implementation*. Denver: Love Publishing.

Turnbull, H. R., & Turnbull, A. P. (1986). *Free appropriate public education: The law and children with disabilities*. Denver: Love Publishing.

Tyack, D., & Hansot, E. (1982). *Managers of virtue: Public school leadership in America, 1820–1980*. New York: Basic Books.

Tye, K. A., & Tye, B. B. (1984). Teacher isolation and school reform. *Phi Delta Kappan, 65*(5), 319–322.

United States Department of Education, Office of Special Education and Rehabilitative Services. (1988). *Annual report to Congress on the implementation of the Education for All Handicapped Children Act*. Washington, DC: Author.

Walker, L. J. (1987). Procedural rights in the wrong system: Special education is not enough. In A. Gartner & T. Joe (Eds.), *Images of the disabled/disabling images* (pp. 97–115). New York: Praeger.

Wang, M. C., Reynolds, M. C., & Walberg, H. J. (1986). Rethinking special education. *Educational Leadership, 44*(1), 26–31.

Wang, M. C., Reynolds, M. C., & Walberg, H. J. (Eds.). (1987). *Handbook of special education: Research and practice: Vol. 1. Learner characteristics and adaptive education*. Oxford: Pergamon Press.

Weatherley, R. (1979). *Reforming special education: Policy implementation from state level to street level*. Cambridge, MA: MIT Press.

Weber, M. (1946). Bureaucracy. In H. H. Gerth & C. W. Mills (Eds. and Trans.), *From Max Weber: Essays in sociology* (pp. 196–244). New York: Oxford University Press. (Original work published 1922)

Weber, M. (1947). *The theory of social and economic organization* (T. Parsons, Ed.; A. M. Henderson & T. Parsons, Trans.). Glencoe, IL: Free Press. (Original work published 1924)

Weick, K. E. (1976). Educational organizations as loosely coupled systems. *Administrative Science Quarterly, 21*(1), 1–19.

Weick, K. E. (1979a). Cognitive processes in organization. In B. M. Staw (Ed.), *Research in organizational behavior* (Vol. 1, pp. 41–74). Greenwich, CT: JAI Press.

Weick, K. E. (1979b). *The social psychology of organizing* (2nd ed.). Reading, MA: Addison-Wesley.

Weick, K. E. (1982a). Administering education in loosely coupled schools. *Phi Delta Kappan, 63*(10), 673–676.

Weick, K. E. (1982b). Management of organizational change among loosely coupled elements. In P. Goodman (Ed.), *Change in organizations* (pp. 375–408). San Francisco: Jossey-Bass.

Weick, K. E. (1985). Sources of order in underorganized systems. In Y. S. Lincoln (Ed.), *Organizational theory and inquiry: The paradigm revolution* (pp. 106–136). Beverly Hills, CA: Sage.

Wise, A. E. (1979). *Legislated learning: The bureaucratization of the American classroom*. Berkeley: University of California Press.

Woodward, J. (1965). *Industrial organizations: Theory and practice*. Oxford: Oxford University Press.

Worthy, J. C. (1959). *Big business and free men*. New York: Harper & Row.

Wright, A. R., Cooperstein, R. A., Reneker, E. G., & Padilla, C. (1982). *Local implementation of P.L. 94–142: Final report of a longitudinal study*. Menlo Park, CA: SRI International.

Wright, J. S. (1967). *Hobson vs. Hansen: Opinion by Honorable J. Skelly Wright, Judge, United States Court of Appeals for the District of Columbia*. Washington, DC: West Publishing.

Zucker, L. G. (1977). The role of institutionalization in cultural persistence. *American Sociological Review, 42*, 726–743.

Zucker, L. G. (1981). Institutional structure and organizational processes: The role of evaluation units in schools. In A. Bank & R. C. Williams (Eds.), *Evaluation and decision making* (CSE Monograph Series, No. 10). Los Angeles: UCLA Center for the Study of Evaluation.

CHAPTER 10

Deconstructing/Reconstructing Public Education:
Social Reconstruction in the Postmodern Era

Thomas M. Skrtic

To this point in the book we have been concerned with deconstructing and reconstructing special education, both as a professional practice and as an institutional practice of public education. I began the process in Part 1 by deconstructing the modern objectivist view of the professions and professional knowledge relative to the rise of subjectivism and the emergence of postmodernism. We continued the process in Parts 2 and 3, first by exposing the inconsistencies, contradictions, and silences in special education's functionalist knowledge tradition (Chapter 3), and then by presenting optional metatheoretical (Chapters 4 through 6) and theoretical (Chapters 7 through 9) descriptions of special education and student disability as possible knowledges for reconstructing the field and its practices. And, of course, the aim of deconstructing special education is to clear the way for special educators to reconstruct it in a manner that is more consistent with the ideal of serving the best educational and political interests of their consumers.

In this concluding chapter I want to consider three additional problems that must be addressed if the field of special education is to undertake the critical project of deconstructing and reconstructing itself. The first problem stems from special education's role as an institutional practice of public education. Because special education is a structural and cultural artifact of twentieth-century schooling (Skrtic, 1987, 1991a; Chapters 3 and 9), deconstructing and reconstructing it necessarily requires deconstructing and reconstructing public education itself. The second problem is the necessity of adequate methods and conditions for deconstructing and reconstructing social practices, discourses, and institutions. In this regard, of course, I have recommended the epistemological and moral framework of pragmatism as the method of critical discourse (Chapters 2 and 3). What needs to be resolved, however, is the matter of achieving the institutional conditions in which such a discourse can emerge and be sustained. Finally, there is the political problem of justifying the deconstruction and reconstruction of public education to others. In a society such as ours, those who propose such a project must be able to make their case on more than moral arguments; they must have convincing political and economic arguments for change as well.

I address these problems by relating the inclusion debate in special education to the restructuring debate in general education, and then relating the broader discourse on educational reform to the emerging political and economic conditions of the twenty-first century. In the first section, I reconsider the inclusion debate from a critical perspective and show that it deconstructs special education as an institutional practice of public education. Then, by relating the inclusion debate in special education to the restructuring debate in general education, I show that, together, they deconstruct the twentieth-century discourse on school failure and, ultimately, the institution of public education. Moreover, by considering the inclusive education and school restructuring reform proposals from the organizational perspective developed in Chapter 9, I show that, in principle, both reforms require schools to be reconfigured as adhocracies and, furthermore, that restructuring schools in this way creates the institutional conditions for the critical, pragmatic discourse necessary to deconstruct and reconstruct public education. Finally, I reappropriate the social reconstructionist idea of cultural transformation through progressive education and, by relating it to the historical conditions of the emerging postindustrial era, argue that reconstructing public education as an integrative system is a distributive good that serves the best moral, political, and economic interests of all Americans.

CRITICAL IMPLICATIONS OF THE INCLUSION DEBATE

As we know from Chapter 3, the problem with the inclusion debate is that, like the mainstreaming debate, it is a form of naive pragmatism, a method of discourse that reproduces problems of professional practice rather than resolving them because, although it criticizes professional models and practices, it treats their grounding assumptions and theories as unproblematic. Just as the mainstreaming debate reproduced the special education problems of the 1960s in the 1980s, the danger today is that, rather than resolving the special education problems of the late twentieth century, the inclusion debate will reproduce them in the twenty-first century (Skrtic 1991a, 1991b, 1995a, 1995b).

In this section I want to help avoid this possibility by reading the empirical arguments of the inclusion debate critically, in terms of their implications for the functionalist theories and assumptions that guide and justify special education as a profession and an institutional practice. Although I have deconstructed special education as a professional (Chapter 3) and an institutional practice (Chapter 9), deconstructing it from the perspective of the inclusion debate serves two important purposes. First, it permits me to deconstruct special education in the language of the field, in terms of it own standards (see the discussion of this point in Chapter 3). Second, deconstructing special education in this way permits me to compare the inclusion and restructuring debates, thus setting the stage for deconstructing the twentieth-century discourse on school failure.

There are two lines of argument within the inclusion debate: one about the ethics and efficacy of the current special education system, and one about the wisdom and feasibility of the inclusive education reform proposals (see Reynolds, 1988; Skrtic, 1991b). I begin my critical reading by considering both lines of argument in terms of their implications for special education's grounding theories of human pathology and organizational rationality, and the corresponding assumptions that disabilities are pathological, diagnosis is objective and useful, special education is a rational system, and progress in the field is a rational-technical process.[1] Then, I use the metatheory of school organization and change developed in Chapter 9 to conduct a critical reading of the reform proposals and counterproposals of the inclusion proponents and opponents.

The Nature of Disability and Diagnosis

Although the inclusion debate has been quite heated, there is virtually no disagreement on the question of the nature of disability.[2] The inclusion proponents (see Gartner & Lipsky, 1987; Pugach & Lilly, 1984; Stainback & Stainback, 1984; Wang, Reynolds, & Walberg, 1986, 1987b) and opponents (see Braaten, Kauffman, Braaten, Polsgrove, & Nelson, 1988; Bryan, Bay, & Donahue, 1988; Council for Children with Behavioral Disorders, 1989; Kauffman, Gerber, & Semmel, 1988; Keogh, 1988) agree that there are some students for whom the handicapped designation is a pathological distinction, but that, for a variety of technical, social, and political reasons (see below), most students identified as handicapped in school are not disabled in a pathological sense. Moreover, both sides in the debate agree that there are additional students in school who have special educational needs but remain unidentified and unserved (see, e.g., Braaten et al., 1988; Bryan et al., 1988; CCBD, 1989; Keogh, 1988; Stainback & Stainback, 1984; Wang et al., 1986 1987b). Although inclusion proponents recognize that students with spec educational needs can pose problems for classroom teachers, their poir that neither the general education system nor the special education syst sufficiently adaptable to serve those students adequately (e.g., Gartner & Lipsky, 1987; Pugach & Lilly, 1984; Wang et al., 1986), a position with which most inclusion opponents agree, implicitly or explicitly (see Bryan et al., 1988; Kauffman, 1988, Kauffman et al., 1988; Keogh, 1988).[3]

Inclusion proponents argue that differential diagnosis does not result in objective distinctions, either between the disabled and nondisabled designations or among the three high-incidence disability classifications of learning disabilities, emotional disturbance, and mild mental retardation (Gartner & Lipsky, 1987; Stainback & Stainback, 1984; Wang, Reynolds, & Walberg, 1986, 1987a). Inclusion opponents generally agree that the disabled–nondisabled distinction is not objective. Moreover, they also agree that distinctions among the three high-incidence disability classifications are not objective because, in addition to measurement and definitional problems, the process for making these decisions in schools is "embedded in a powerful economic, political, and philosophical network" (Keogh, 1988, p. 20; see also CCBD, 1989; Gerber & Semmel, 1984; Hallahan & Kauffman, 1977; Kauffman, 1988).

On the matter of the utility of differential diagnosis, inclusion proponents argue that there are no instructionally relevant reasons for making the disabled–nondisabled distinction or for distinguishing among the three high-incidence classifications. Their point is that all students have unique learning needs and, moreover, that students in the high-incidence disability classifications, as well as those in the other special needs programs (e.g., Chapter 1, bilingual education, migrant education), can be taught using similar instructional methods (e.g., Gartner & Lipsky, 1987; Lipsky & Gartner, 1989c; Reynolds, Wang, & Walberg, 1987; Stainback & Stainback, 1984, 1989; Wang, 1989a, 1989b; Wang et al., 1986, 1987a). Here, too, most of the inclusion opponents agree, admitting that "effective instructional and management procedures will be substantially the same for nonhandicapped and most mildly handicapped students" (Kauffman, Gerber, & Semmel, 1988, p. 8; Gerber, 1987; Hallahan & Kauffman, 1977).[4] At this point in my critical reading of the inclusion debate, both the proponents and opponents implicitly reject special education's first two guiding assumptions and thus the functionalist theory of human pathology.

The Nature of Special Education and Progress

Inclusion proponents argue that the only rational justification for the special education system is that it confers instructional benefit on students who are designated handicapped (e.g., Gartner & Lipsky, 1987; Lilly, 1986; Reynolds, 1988; Reynolds et al., 1987; Stainback & Stainback, 1984; Wang et al., 1987a), and on this basis reject the idea that special education is a rationally conceived and coordinated system. That is, by pointing to the weak effects of special education instructional practices and the social costs of labeling, inclusion proponents argue that special education is no more justifiable than simply permitting most students to remain unidentified in general education classrooms, and far less justifiable than making such placements in conjunction with appropriate in-class support services (see Gartner & Lipsky, 1987; Lipsky & Gartner, 1989a, 1989b; Pugach & Lilly, 1984; Stainback & Stainback, 1984; Wang et al., 1987a; below). Moreover, they argue that special education is coordinated neither with the general education system nor with the other special needs programs, characterizing the entire special needs enterprise as a collection of operationally separate programs added to schools over time, an extreme case of "disjointed incrementalism" (Reynolds & Birch, 1977; Reynolds & Wang, 1983; Reynolds et al., 1987; Wang, Reynolds, & Walberg, 1985, 1986).

On the question of whether special education can be improved incrementally through rational-technical refinements in conventional diagnostic and instructional practices, inclusion proponents argue that the current system of special education is fundamentally flawed and that neither it nor its associated practices can be improved incrementally. Rather, they believe that the current approach to special education must be replaced by restructuring the special and general education systems into a new adaptable system of public education in which students with special educational needs are taught in general education classrooms (see Gartner & Lipsky, 1987; Lilly, 1986; Lipsky & Gartner, 1989a, 1989b; Pugach & Lilly, 1984; Reynolds et al., 1987; Stainback & Stainback, 1984; Stainback, Stainback, & Forest, 1989; below).

Inclusion opponents agree with the proponents that to be rationally justifiable the special education system must confer benefit on students who are designated handicapped (see Kauffman et al., 1988; Keogh, 1988), as well as that the field's *instructional* practices have not been shown to benefit students (see Hallahan, Keller, McKinney, Lloyd, & Bryan, 1988; Keogh, 1988).[5] Nevertheless, they justify the current system of special education by arguing that it is beneficial to students in a *political* sense. The argument here is that, given the nonrational process by which resources are allocated in schools, the current system of special education targets otherwise unavailable special educational resources to designated students, instructional inadequacies notwithstanding (CCBD, 1989; Kauffman, 1988, 1989; Kauffman et al., 1988). The logic behind this argument turns on the inclusion opponents' position on the nature of progress.

Although inclusion opponents agree with the proponents that there are serious problems with the current system of special education that need to be corrected, they believe that incremental progress is possible through additional research and development aimed at improving conventional diagno<

and instructional practices, while maintaining the current system, including the pull-out approach of mainstreaming (see Braaten et al., 1988; Bryan et al., 1988; CCBD, 1989; Hallahan et al., 1988; Kauffman, 1988; Kauffman et al., 1988; Keogh, 1988; Lloyd, Crowley, Kohler, & Strain, 1988). In effect, then, the inclusion opponents say that, although special education is not an instructionally rational system *at present*, it is a politically rational system that can become instructionally rational *in the future* through incremental improvements in conventional diagnostic and instructional practices (see Bryan et al., 1988; Hallahan et al., 1988). The inclusion opponents' position on the sense in which special education is a rational system cannot be separated from their position on the nature of progress because, although one can justify retaining an instructionally ineffective but politically essential system *if* it will become effective in the future, such a system cannot be justified politically or ethically if incremental progress is not possible. Moreover, although inclusion opponents recognize the obvious lack of coordination among general education, special education, and the other special needs programs, they consider this problem to be an unfortunate but inevitable and unavoidable consequence of the targeting strategy that is required to make special education a politically rational system (Kauffman et al., 1988).

At this point in my critical reading, the proponents of inclusion reject all four of special education's guiding assumptions and thus the functionalist theories of human pathology and organizational rationality. This is why the inclusion debate has been so unsettling for the field; by rejecting the theories upon which the field's practices and discourses are premised, the inclusion proponents reject functionalism, the metatheoretical paradigm that guides and justifies everything that special educators think, do, say, write, and read as professionals (see Chapter 3). Although the opponents reject the first two guiding assumptions and thus the theory of human pathology, by arguing that special education is a politically rational system that can be improved incrementally, they retain the third and fourth assumptions and thus the theory of organizational rationality. This is why the inclusion debate is so contentious. Both sides agree (implicitly) that special education's assumptions about the nature of disability and diagnosis are inadequate, but they are at odds over an appropriate course of ameliorative action because they disagree over the nature of special education and progress. The proponents argue that, given the weak effects of special education *and* the nonadaptability of general education, a completely new system should be formed by restructuring the current special and general education systems into a single adaptable one. The opponents argue that, weak effects notwithstanding, the current system of special education should be retained for political purposes, *given* the nonadaptability of general education and the fact that current special education practices can be improved incrementally. At bottom, then, the inclusion debate turns on the question of the nature of school organization and change, a matter I will consider in more depth after briefly reviewing the reform proposals of four teams of inclusion proponents whose names have become synonymous with the inclusive education concept.

The Inclusion Reform Proposals

All four reform proposals call for eliminating both the student classification system of P.L. 94–142, the Education for All Handicapped Children Act (EHA) (now Individuals with Disabilities Education Act), and the pull-out approach of mainstreaming, and restructuring the separate general and special education systems into a new "unitary" system in which students with special needs are educated in general education classrooms. Although all four teams characterize the restructured system as "flexible, supple and responsive" (Lipsky & Gartner, 1987, p. 72), a "totally adaptive system" (Reynolds & Wang, 1983, p. 199) designed to personalize instruction through "group problem solving . . . shared responsibility, and . . . negotiation" (Pugach & Lilly, 1984, p. 52), they disagree on which students currently classified as handicapped should be integrated into it on a full-time basis.[6] The Lilly/Pugach proposal is the least inclusive. It includes only "the vast majority of students [currently] served as 'mildly handicapped'" (Pugach & Lilly, 1984, p. 53), excluding students with moderate, severe, and profound disabilities, who are to be taught in separate settings within typical school buildings.[7] The Reynolds/Wang proposal is somewhat more inclusive in that it includes "most students with special learning needs" (Wang et al., 1985, p. 13), while reserving the option of separate settings for some students, presumably those with severe and profound disabilities (see Reynolds & Wang, 1983; Wang et al., 1985). The Gartner/Lipsky proposal calls for including all students currently served under each EHA disability classification, except those with the most severely and profoundly disabling conditions (Gartner & Lipsky, 1987; Lipsky & Gartner, 1989b), who are to be taught in separate classrooms located in age-appropriate school buildings (cf. Sailor, 1989). Finally, in what is the most inclusive proposal, Stainback and Stainback (1984, 1987b; Stainback et al., 1989) argue for the integration of all students, including those with the most severely and profoundly disabling conditions.[8]

The strategy for creating the adaptable system in all four proposals is characterized as a merger (to one degree or another) of the general and special education systems. For example, Reynolds and Wang (1983) propose eliminating most categorical special needs pull-out programs by merging the professionals who work in special education's three high-incidence disability programs and the other categorical special needs programs, forming "a 'generic' or noncategorical base" of support staff (p. 206). Supported by paraprofessionals, these generic specialists form a school-based support team that works "mostly in the regular classrooms . . . to supply technical and administrative support to regular classroom teachers" (p. 206). Above the classroom teachers and generic specialists, Reynolds and Wang (1983) propose a merger of district-level consultants who provide the classroom teachers and generic specialists with consultation and training (see also Wang et al., 1985).

Lilly and Pugach merge current special education resource programs that serve "the mildly handicapped, and primarily . . . the learning disabled" (Pugach & Lilly, 1984, p. 54) with the general education support service of remedial education, forming a single, coordinated system of in-class support services based in general education. This approach, they argue, would be less stigmatizing and more efficient than the current array of special pull-out programs (Lilly, 1986; Pugach & Lilly, 1984). Although the Reynolds/Wang and Lilly/Pugach proposals modify the current system of support services, both retain traditional classrooms in which one teacher has primary responsibility for a group of students. The primary difference is that some or most of the students that would have been served in separate settings for all or part of the school day remain in the classroom on a full-time basis, where they and their teacher are provided with in-class support services and consultation.

Stainback and Stainback (1984) call for merging the current "dual system" of general and special education into a "unified system" (p. 102). They propose disbanding special education programs and redeploying some of the residual personnel in the general education system to teach a particular general education (e.g., science, reading) or special education (e.g., alternative communication systems, supported employment) subject. The remaining special education personnel and some of the general education staff are reassigned as consultants who provide in-class, subject-area support services to classroom teachers, each of whom works individually in a separate subject-area classroom (Stainback & Stainback, 1987a; Stainback et al., 1989). As in the case of the other two support services models, this one also retains traditional classrooms and places the subject-area consultants above them (see Stainback & Stainback, 1984, 1987a).

Finally, Gartner and Lipsky call for a merged system in which education is "both one and special for all students" (Lipsky & Gartner, 1987, p. 73). They propose complete abandonment of separate special education programs except for students with the most severely and profoundly disabling conditions. Although initially they also emphasized the support services level (see Gartner & Lipsky, 1987), more recently (Lipsky & Gartner, 1989a) they stressed the classroom level by linking their reform proposal to several of those within the excellence movement in general education (see below), particularly the "effective schools" approach pioneered by Edmonds (1979) and promoted by Lezotte (1989). Through broad adoption of effective schools principles and practices, they argue, "the education of students labeled as handicapped can be made effective" (Lipsky & Gartner, 1989b, p. 281). Toward this end, they call for a new legal mandate to replace the EHA, "an effective schools act for all students" (1989b, p. 282).

Opponents' Reactions to the Inclusion Proposals

The inclusion opponents argue against these and other reform proposals on historical and political grounds, concluding that special educational needs have not and simply cannot be accommodated in general education classrooms. Kauffman (1988, 1989) and others (CCBD, 1989) argue that, historically, the separate special education system emerged to serve students who were forced out of a single system "in which . . . general educators were expected to teach nearly all students regardless of their characteristics" (Kauffman, 1988, p. 493). Arguing that very little has changed in general education classrooms to make them more accommodating, Kauffman predicts that abandoning the special education system will result in the rediscovery of the need for a separate system in the future (see also CCBD, 1989; Keogh, 1988). In their political or microeconomic critique of the inclusion proposals, Kauffman, Gerber, and Semmel (1988; cf. Gerber, 1988; Gerber & Semmel, 1985) argue that "teachers, whether in regular or special class environments, cannot escape the necessary choice between higher means [i.e., maximizing mean performance by concentrating resources on the most able learners] and narrower variances [i.e., minimizing group variance by concentrating resources on the least able learners] as long as resources are scarce and students differ" (Gerber & Semmel, 1985, p. 19, cited in Kauffman et al., 1988, p. 10). This is true, they say, "whenever a teacher instructs a group of students . . . [except] when new resources are made available or more powerful instructional technologies are employed" (Kauffman et al., 1988, p. 10).

Although the historical and microeconomic arguments are important, they are not criticisms of the inclusive education proposals. The historical argument is silent about the fact that the inclusive proponents' proposals call for restructured schools, not a return to traditional classrooms. And the microeconomic argument is silent about the new human resources and more powerful instructional technologies that are to be available in inclusive schools, the exact conditions that can narrow variances without negatively affecting class means, according to the argument itself. Rather than arguments against the inclusive education reform proposals, implicitly the historical and microeconomic arguments are compelling critiques of the traditional notion of a classroom. In fact, by arguing that general education and special education classrooms are nonadaptable in a microeconomic sense, Kauffman and coauthors make a stronger case against the current system of special education than the inclusion proponents. Moreover, by arguing that general education classrooms have not changed historically, and that neither they nor special education classrooms can change politically, the inclusion opponents contradict their position on the possibility of rational-technical change, and thus their argument for the political rationality of the current system of special education.

At this point in my critical reading of the inclusion debate, we have seen that, in their criticism of the current system of special education, the proponents of inclusion reject all four of the field's guiding assumptions and thus the theories of human pathology and organizational rationality. In their defense of the current system the opponents also reject the assumptions about the nature of disability and diagnosis, and thus the theory of human pathology, but retain those about the nature of special education and progress, and thus the theory of organizational rationality. In their criticism of the inclusive education proposals, however, the opponents reverse their position on the third and fourth assumptions and thus, like the inclusion proponents, reject all four guiding assumptions, which means that they also reject the field's grounding theories of human pathology *and* organizational rationality. Moreover, we will see below that, when their reform proposals are considered from an organizational perspective, the inclusion proponents also reverse their position on the third and fourth assumptions (also see Skrtic, 1988, 1991a, 1991b, 1995b). In their criticism of the current system, they argue against the rationality of special education and the possibility of rational-technical change and call for a fundamental restructuring of school organizations. However, considered from an organizational perspective, their reform proposals actually call for a rational-technical approach to change that reproduces and extends the current systems of special and general education and thus the traditional organization of schools. What is so troubling about this confusion over the third and fourth assumptions is that the inclusion debate, and thus the nature of special education as a professional and institutional practice in the 1990s and beyond, hangs on the question of the nature of school organization and change, the very question about which there is so much confusion and uncertainty in the field.

Organizational Analysis of the Inclusion Proposals

Drawing on the metatheory of school organization and change presented in Chapter 9, the problem with the inclusive education reform proposals is that each of them reproduces the structural and cultural contradictions of the EHA and mainstreaming. This is so because, even though the inclusion proponents reject the theory of human pathology, ultimately they retain the theory of organizational rationality, and thus the assumptions that school organizations are rational and that changing them is a rational-technical process. As we will see, although the inclusive education reform proposals require an adhocratic structure for schools, they reproduce the traditional two-structure, machine-professional bureaucratic configuration (see Chapter 9). The result is that, like the EHA and mainstreaming, they retain the professional bureaucracy inner structure of schools and extend their outer machine bureaucracy structure.[9]

The Lilly/Pugach, Reynolds/Wang, and Stainback/Stainback proposals call for collaborative problem solving between a classroom teacher and a support services staff. However, by retaining the traditional role of classroom teacher, each of these proposals retains a specialized division of labor and a professionalized means of coordination, which of course yields a loosely coupled form of interdependence and thus deflects the goal of collaboration. As we know from Chapter 9, as long as the work in schools is divided by specialization and coordinated through professionalization, there is no need for teachers to collaborate. Collaboration emerges when work is distributed on the basis of a collaborative division of labor and coordinated through mutual adjustment, an arrangement that is premised on shared responsibility and a team approach to problem solving and yields a form of interdependence premised on reflective discourse.

Moreover, although these proposals call for collaborative problem solving between a classroom teacher and a support services staff, by retaining the notion of a classroom and placing the support services staff above it, they actually extend the rationalization and formalization of the machine bureaucracy configuration and thus undermine the ideals of problem solving and personalized instruction. This is so because placing a support staff above the classroom teacher maintains the misplaced, machine bureaucratic practice of separating theory from practice, implying that the theory of teaching is at the support level, while the mere practice of teaching takes place in the classroom. Moreover, this politicizes and thus undermines the ideal of collaboration, since placing support personnel above the practice context makes them technocrats rather than support staff (see Mintzberg, 1983). In an actual machine bureaucracy, technocrats are the people with the theory; they control and define the activities of the other workers. This is not collaboration in an organizational sense; it is bureaucratic control and supervision. In professional bureaucracies, the notion of a technocracy within the organization violates the logic of professionalization and thus technocrats are resisted, particularly change agents and other school improvement personnel (see Mintzberg, 1979; Wolcott, 1977).

The same problems are inherent in the Gartner/Lipsky proposal. This reform proposal retains general education classrooms and proposes to make them effective for all students by implementing the principles of effective schools research through school improvement projects (Lipsky & Gartner, 1989b). Here, the assumption is that the theory of effective teaching, which is known by the effective schools specialists apart from and prior to the classroom context, is contained in the principles identified in effective schools research, and that implementing these principles in the practice context is simply a matter of the teacher making a commitment to follow them (see Lezotte, 1989; Lipsky & Gartner, 1989b). In principle, imposing such standards from above, their apparent efficacy in some other context notwithstanding, can only lead to an extension of existing rationalization and formalization, and thus to an increase in professionalization and a corresponding decrease in personalization (see Cuban, 1983, 1989; Slavin, 1989; Stedman, 1987; below). As Cuban (1989) noted in this regard, under the effective schools formula many schools have returned to the nineteenth-century practice of standardizing curriculum and instruction and thus ignore individual differences.

Although the arguments put forth in the inclusion debate reject the assumption of human pathology and thus represent progress relative to the mainstreaming debate, the outcome is the same. Like the EHA and mainstreaming, the adhocratic ends of the inclusion proponents are distorted by the bureaucratic structure and culture of school organizations. Moreover, because the inclusion proponents retain the presupposition of organizational rationality, their adhocratic ends are deflected by the bureaucratic value orientation of their own reform proposals.

PUBLIC EDUCATION AND THE DISCOURSE ON SCHOOL FAILURE

To this point in the book we have been concerned with deconstructing (and reconstructing) special education, both as a professional practice and as an institutional practice of public education. In this section I consider the implications of deconstructing special education for the discourse on school failure and the legitimacy of the institution of public education. This requires expanding the discussion to include the voice of the general education professional community and what it has to say (and not say) about school failure from the perspective of educational excellence. By reading the mainstreaming and inclusion debates as two phases in a *discourse on equity*, and the "effective schools" and "school restructuring" debates in general education as two phases in a *discourse on excellence*, I compare the similarities and differences between the two discourses and show how they converge upon one another to deconstruct the twentieth-century discourse on school failure and, ultimately, the institution of public education itself.

By the effective schools debate I mean the early phase of the excellence movement, which was shaped largely by the thinking in *A Nation at Risk* (National Commission on Excellence in Education, 1983). The effective schools approach seeks excellence through means that are quantitative and top-down. It is quantitative in that it simply calls for more of existing school practices – more difficult courses and homework, additional time in school, higher standards, and more standardized testing. It is top-down because it is characterized by attempts to further bureaucratize (rationalize and formalize) work in schools, an increase in "state control, with its emphasis on producing standardized results through regulated teaching" (Wise, 1988, p. 329). Like the proponents of the EHA and mainstreaming, advocates of the effective schools approach to excellence do not question the traditional bureaucratic structure of schools; "their passion . . . is . . . for making those structures more efficient" (Cuban, 1989, p. 784), which ultimately turns the goal of higher standards into more standardization (see Bacharach, 1990; Cuban, 1983, 1989; Meier, 1984; Resnick & Resnick, 1985).

By the school restructuring debate I mean the more recent phase of the excellence movement, which has been shaped by the thinking in books like *A Place Called School* (Goodlad, 1984), *Horace's Compromise* (Sizer, 1984), and *High School* (Boyer, 1983), and in commission reports like *Children in Need* (Committee for Economic Development, 1987) and *An Imperiled Generation* (Carnegie Foundation for the Advancement of Teaching, 1988). The difference is that the participants in this debate seek excellence through means that are qualitative and bottom-up: qualitative in that they call for fundamental changes in the structure of schools; bottom-up in that they call for an increase in professional discretion and personalized instruction through collaborative problem solving among professionals and consumers at local school sites (see Bacharach, 1990; Clark, Lotto, & Astuto, 1984; Cuban, 1983, 1989; Elmore, 1987; Elmore & McLaughlin, 1988; Lieberman & Miller, 1984; McNeil, 1986; Oakes, 1985; Sergiovanni & Moore, 1989; Sirotnik & Oakes, 1986; Wise, 1979, 1988).

The first similarity between the excellence and equity discourses is that the initial debate in each discourse is an extreme form of naive pragmatism that merely reproduces and extends the problems it sets out to solve (see Chapter 3). As in the case of the EHA and mainstreaming, the new practices that emerged out of the effective schools debate largely reproduced the original problems (see Clark & Astuto, 1988; Cuban, 1983, 1989; Meier, 1984; Resnick & Resnick, 1985; Slavin, 1989; Stedman, 1987; Timar & Kirp, 1988; Wise, 1988). A second similarity is that the failure of the first debate in each discourse gives rise to a second one that, although it is less naive in the sense that it implicitly questions grounding assumptions and theories, is also a form of naive pragmatism that promises to reproduce current problems. Although the restructuring debate is less naive than the effective schools debate, it does not explicitly recognize the connection between general education models and practices and the functionalist theories and assumptions in which they are grounded. [10] As such, like the inclusion debate in special education, the restructuring debate promises to reproduce and extend the general education problems of the 1980s and 1990s into the next century (see Cuban, 1983, 1989; Skrtic, 1991a; Wise, 1988; Chapter 3; below).

Although the restructuring and inclusion debates are similar in this second respect, the effects of this pattern in each debate are mirror images of one another. As we have seen, the inclusion debate is less naive than the mainstreaming debate because it implicates school organization in the problem of school failure. The mirror image of this in the restructuring debate is that, by pointing to the emergence and persistence of homogeneous grouping practices—curricular tracking, in-class ability grouping, and compensatory pull-out programs—as an indication of deep structural flaws in traditional school organization (see Cuban, 1989; Oakes, 1985, 1986a, 1986b; Stedman, 1987; Wise, 1988), the participants in the restructuring debate implicate school failure in the problem of school organization.

The second way the inclusion and restructuring debates mirror each other is that, although both reject two of the four functionalist assumptions and question the other two, in the final analysis they retain the assumptions that they question. We saw this pattern for the inclusion proponents, who reject the assumptions about the objectivity of disability and diagnosis and question but ultimately retain those about the rationality of school organization and change. The mirror image in the restructuring debate is that, although it rejects the assumptions about the rationality of school organization and change, it questions but ultimately retains those about the objectivity of school failure and diagnosis. That is, although restructuring advocates criticize the institutional practices of tracking and compensatory pull-out programs (Goodlad, 1984; Sizer, 1984), and even the overrepresentation of minority students in certain special education programs (Oakes, 1986a, 1986b), they do not criticize special education as an institutional practice (see Skrtic, 1991a, 1991b). Thus, in the end, the participants in the school restructuring debate retain the assumptions that, at least for students identified as handicapped, school failure is pathological and diagnosis is objective and useful.

The restructuring debate fails to recognize special education as a form of tracking because its criticism of homogeneous grouping practices stops at the point of presumed pathology, which is the third and most important way that the two debates mirror one another. Whereas the inclusion debate rejects the theory of human pathology but retains that of organizational rationality, the restructuring debate rejects the theory of organizational rationality but ultimately retains that of human pathology. The significance here is that, in their inclusive education and school restructuring phases, the discourses on excellence and equity converge to deconstruct the twentieth-century discourse on school failure by rejecting both of the functionalist theories that ground and legitimize it. Moreover, the broader significance of the deconstruction of the discourse on school failure is that it provides the grounds for an immanent critique of the institution of public education.

As the institution through which America "sought to hold itself together and prepare its citizens for the greatest of all experiments in democracy" (Greer, 1972, p. 17), public education had to achieve several largely contradictory goals simultaneously, the most basic of which is that, in a democracy, education must be both excellent and equitable. If America was to remain democratic and avoid tyranny, Thomas Jefferson argued, public education must be excellent; it must produce intelligent citizens and thoughtful leaders (Ford, 1904). Moreover, he cautioned that if America was to remain a free society, one in which positions of power are open to all on the basis of merit, public education also must be equitable, that is, it must ensure "that [persons] of talent might rise whatever their social and economic origins" (Greer, 1972, p. 16).[11] The significance of the convergence of the discourses on excellence and equity is that it exposes the immanent contradiction between public education's democratic ideals and bureaucratic practices. In the late twentieth century, public education finally must confront the fact that it is neither excellent nor equitable. Moreover, it must do so without recourse to the distorting and legitimizing effects of the functionalist discourse on school failure. To continue making the claim that it is democratic, the institution of public education must, at a minimum, reconstruct itself to be both excellent and equitable.

EXCELLENCE, EQUITY, AND ADHOCRACY

We can begin the process of reconstructing public education by considering the convergence of interests in the inclusive education and school restructuring reform proposals from the organizational perspective developed in Chapter 9. As we know, the inclusion debate calls for eliminating the bureaucratic means of the EHA and mainstreaming. The corresponding argument in the restructuring debate is for eliminating scientific management, the traditional bureaucratic approach to administration and change (see Boyer, 1983; Cuban, 1983, 1989; Goodlad, 1984; Oakes, 1985, 1986a, 1986b; Sirotnik & Oakes, 1986; Sizer, 1984; Wise, 1988; Chapters 3 and 9). In organizational terms, the first convergence of interests is that inclusion and restructuring both call for eliminating rationalization, formalization, and tight coupling, the misplaced structural contingencies of the outer machine bureaucracy configuration of traditional school organizations.

The second convergence is between the inclusion proponents' arguments for merging the general and special education systems and those of the restructuring proponents' for merging general education curricular and instructional tracks. Here, both sets of reform proposals are calling for the elimination of specialization, professionalization, and loose coupling, the structural contingencies of the inner professional bureaucracy configuration of schools. In practical terms, the proponents of inclusive education (see above) and school restructuring (see Boyer, 1983; Cuban, 1983, 1989; Goodlad, 1984; McNeil, 1986; Oakes, 1985; Sizer, 1984) seek an adaptable system in which teachers personalize instruction for "all" students through collaborative problem solving among themselves and with their clients. Of course, because the restructuring proponents retain the theory of human pathology, there are differences between the two sets of proposals in terms of the definition of "all" students, just as there are within the inclusion debate itself. But these are differences in degree, not in kind. In organizational terms, the proponents of inclusion and restructuring are arguing for the introduction of collaboration, mutual adjustment, and discursive coupling, the structural contingencies of the adhocratic form. In principle, inclusion and restructuring both require an adhocratic school organization and professional culture.

As we know, the inclusion opponents' position on equity and excellence is that, given the nonadaptablity of traditional schools and classrooms, the targeting function of the EHA and the pull-out logic of mainstreaming must be maintained for political purposes, diagnostic and instructional inadequacies notwithstanding. The moment of truth in this position is the argument that, as long as resources are constant and students differ, no teacher, whether in a general or special education classroom, can escape the necessary choice between higher class means (excellence) and narrower class variances (equity). In organizational terms, this is true because the structural contingencies of specialization and professionalization yield a finite repertoire of standard practices relative to a corresponding set of presumed client needs, a situation in which students with atypical needs must be forced into the available standard practices (a problem of excellence) or out of the classroom (a problem of equity). Given the inevitability of human diversity, a professional bureaucracy can do nothing but create students who do not fit the system. In schools, all forms of tracking, including compensatory, bilingual, migrant, gifted, and special education, are organizational artifacts, unintended consequences of using specialization and professionalization to divide and coordinate work, consequences that are compounded by misguided attempts to rationalize and formalize teaching. Students are subjected to—and subjugated by–homogeneous grouping practices because, given their structural and cultural contingencies, traditional schools cannot accommodate diversity and so must screen it out by containing it in decoupled special needs programs.

The problem with the inclusion opponents' argument, however, is that it assumes that nonadaptability is inherent to schooling rather than to bureaucratic school organizations. Student diversity is a problem for schools only when they are premised on standardization and thus configured as bureaucracies, performance organizations that perfect standard practices for known contingencies. As we know from Chapter 9, the adhocratic form is premised on innovation and thus configured as a problem-solving organization that invents new practices for unfamiliar contingencies. Regardless of its cause or extent, student diversity is not a liability in a problem-solving organization; it is an asset, an enduring source of uncertainty and thus the driving force behind innovation, progress, and the growth of knowledge.

The problem with the inclusion and restructuring proposals in this regard is that, although the goal of personalized instruction through collaborative problem solving requires the adhocratic configuration, they reproduce the professional bureaucracy configuration. This is so because, by retaining the notion of a classroom, they retain a specialized division of labor and professionalized means of coordination, and thus a loosely coupled form of interdependence among teachers. Ultimately, both sets of reform proposals eliminate rationalization and formalization, the misplaced machine bureaucracy outer structure of schools, while retaining specialization and professionalization, the professional bureaucracy inner structure. From an organizational perspective, the argument for eliminating rationalization and formalization is an argument for uniting theory and practice in the professional, the essence of the professional bureaucracy form. The problem with this move in the inclusion and restructuring proposals, however, is that by retaining the professional bureaucracy configuration, they unite theory and practice in the *individual* professional specialist rather than in a multidisciplinary *team* of professionals. [12] From a structural perspective, innovation is "the building of new knowledge and skills [which] requires the combination of different bodies of existing ones" (Mintzberg, 1979, p. 434). Innovation in organizations requires collaboration, mutual adjustment, and discursive coupling, and thus the division of labor, means of coordination, and form of interdependence of the adhocratic configuration, structural contingencies that "break through the boundaries of conventional specialization," creating a situation in which "professionals must amalgamate their efforts . . . [by joining] forces in multidisciplinary teams, each formed around a specific project of innovation" (Mintzberg, 1979, pp. 434–435). From a cultural perspective, repertoires or paradigms of practice are social constructions. As in the case of scientific communities (Kuhn, 1970; Chapter 1), innovation occurs when new paradigms emerge through confrontations over uncertainty within social groups (Brown, 1978; Rounds, 1981; Weick, 1979). Innovation is not a solitary act in organizations; when it does occur, it is a social phenomenon that requires a reflective, dialogical discourse, a social process of paradigm construction, deconstruction, and reconstruction (see Skrtic, 1991a; Skrtic & Ware, 1992).

Beyond the problem of innovation, eliminating rationalization and formalization (machine bureaucracy) while retaining specialization and professionalization (professional bureaucracy) creates a purely professional mode of accountability, which places virtually all decisions about the adequacy of practice in the hands of individual professionals. As we know from Chapter 2, this creates a political problem because of the subjectivity of professional knowledge and the inherent power/knowledge implications of professional practice. From an organizational perspective, the source of the political problem is the very professional bureaucracy configuration that the inclusion and restructuring advocates leave in place. Structurally, the convergent thinking and deductive reasoning of professionals tends to create a means–ends inversion in these organizations, a situation in which, working alone, professionals confuse the needs of their clients with the skills they have to offer them (Mintzberg, 1979; Perrow, 1970; Segal, 1974). Moreover, professionals are rarely conscious of this confusion because their commitment to the prevailing paradigm of practice tends to distort negative information about its validity, turning anomalies of practice into client pathologies, thus preserving the legitimacy of the professional culture (see Brown, 1978; Rounds, 1979, 1981; Weick, 1985; Chapter 9).[13]

From a structural perspective, proponents of restructuring and inclusion are right about eliminating scientific management and the bureaucratic means of the EHA. The misplaced rationalization and formalization associated with these practices separates theory from practice. At a minimum, achieving the adhocratic ends of restructuring and inclusion will require returning discretion to teachers by merging theory and practice in schools. However, if merging theory and practice is to result in the innovation that is required to personalize instruction, the structural contingencies of specialization, professionalization, and loose coupling must be eliminated as well. And this requires more than simply eliminating general education tracks and merging the general and special education systems in the manner proposed. Tracking and special needs pull-out programs are not the problem in today's schools; they are symptoms of the means–ends inversions caused by the structural contingencies of the professional bureaucracy configuration. Achieving the adhocratic ends of inclusive education and school restructuring requires merging theory and practice *and* eliminating specialization and professionalization, which means eliminating *classrooms* and uniting theory and practice in multidisciplinary teams of specialists and consumers.

Furthermore, from a cultural perspective, achieving the innovation that is required to personalize instruction will require that an adhocratic professional culture emerge and be sustained in public education. To emerge, such a culture will require the structural contingencies of the adhocratic form. To be sustained, however, an adhocratic culture requires an enduring source of uncertainty because, as the case of NASA illustrates (Chapter 9), without problems to solve adhocracies eventually reconfigure themselves as bureaucracies. Politically, the institution of public education cannot be democratic unless its practices are excellent and equitable, which, in organizational terms, cannot be the case unless schools are organized as adhocracies. And, in structural and cultural terms, school organizations and the professionals who staff them can neither become nor remain adhocratic without the uncertainty of student diversity. In the adhocratic school, educational equity is the way to educational excellence.

PROGRESSIVE EDUCATION AND SOCIAL RECONSTRUCTION

In addition to being excellent and equitable, public education in a democracy also must promote stability and change. When the historical conditions of the late nineteenth century produced a rapidly expanding economy and an increasingly diverse population, leaders in government, business, and education argued that public education had to represent a stabilizing force, a mechanism for America to socialize its citizens (Callahan, 1962; Cremin, 1961; Haber, 1964). At the same time, however, educational pioneers from Horace Mann to William Torrey Harris argued that public education in a rapidly expanding democracy had to be dynamic enough to change with the spiritual mood of the public and the material needs of society (Cremin, 1961, 1965). Moreover, when the historical conditions associated with industrialization produced unprecedented changes in the social and material needs of society, early-twentieth-century political and educational reformers argued for a more proactive role for public education. Not only did public education have to promote excellence and equity, and stability and change; it also had to transform the cultural sensibility of the public when, in the interest of responding to changing historical conditions, it was necessary for America to reconstruct itself and its social institutions (Cremin, 1961; Dworkin, 1959; Kloppenberg, 1986).

Industrialization and Individualism

The first test of the idea that public education should transform society occurred during the progressive era, a period in which the notion of a rational democratic society was shaken by industrialization and its associated problems of urbanization and immigration. America's first response to the problem of industrialization was shaped by the idea of "social efficiency" (Haber, 1964, p. 59), which was promoted by a generation of progressive reformers who were grounded in the prescriptive discourse of scientific management and machine bureaucracy, and thus in the functionalist theories of organizational rationality and human pathology (see Chapter 9). Although the social efficiency phase of the progressive movement was short lived, its intensity and timing were sufficient to instill the idea in government, business, and education that the problem with democracy is that it is inefficient and, more important, that things could be set right if government and education simply adopted industry's bureaucratic form and its emerging "science" of efficiency (see Callahan, 1962; Haber, 1964). Applied to education, the social efficiency approach gave America the segregated special classroom and eventually the profession of special education, which became the principal structural and cultural mechanisms for containing and decoupling students who threaten bureaucratic efficiency (see Lazerson, 1983; Sarason & Doris, 1979; Skrtic, 1991a).

The idea of social transformation through education took on a new significance in the social disarray following World War I and the stock market crash of 1929. During this period, a second generation of progressive reformers grounded in philosophical pragmatism and shaped by the idea of "social reconstruction" argued that the problem with democracy *is* bureaucracy.[14] Drawing on Weber's theories of bureaucracy (1922/1946, 1924/1947) and economy (1922/1978) and Dewey's philosophy of education, they argued that nothing short of a reconstruction of society was necessary to save democracy from the distorting effects of bureaucracy (Kliebard, 1988; Kloppenberg, 1986). According to Weber (1922/1978), democracy and bureaucracy grow coincidentally because the actualization of an egalitarian democratic government requires the development of the bureaucratic administrative form. The problem arises in the contradiction between the substantive rationality of democracy (democratic ends) and the formal rationality of bureaucracy (bureaucratic means) because, although democracy is intended to be dynamic, the bureaucratic form on which it depends resists change. Weber believed that the contradiction between democracy and bureaucracy is the central and irresolvable fact of the modern state. But the social reconstructionists tempered his pessimism with Dewey's (1927/1988) optimistic argument that, although industrialization intensifies the very real problem of bureaucracy, it also provides an opportunity for America to recover democracy by reconstructing the modern state itself.

According to Dewey (1899/1976, 1927/1988), industrialization intensifies the problem of bureaucracy because it places more of life – particularly work and education – under the bureaucratic form, which, by design, virtually eliminates the need to think reflectively and to solve problems collaboratively through discourse. And since these are the essential skills of democratic citizenship, the extension of bureaucracy under industrialization ultimately undercuts the ability of the public to govern itself democratically. Nevertheless, Dewey (1929–30/1988, 1927/1988) argued that industrialization also had created an expanding network of regional, national, and international interdependencies, which in turn had created the need for a new cultural sensibility in America, a shift from the rugged or *possessive* form of individualism that had served it well in the eighteenth and nineteenth centuries, to a *social* form of individualism that was more suited to democratic life under the inherently interdependent conditions of an industrial age. Dewey pointed to the mounting social and political costs of the cultural contradiction between possessive and social individualism, and argued that the new conditions of interdependence made possible and begged a new approach to public education, one premised on developing in the public a new sense of itself as an interdependent community of interests. Dewey and the other social reconstructionists believed that the cultural transformation to social individualism would produce a new American public, one that was capable of carrying out the reconstruction of society needed to save democracy from bureaucracy (Kloppenberg, 1986).

Progressive Education

Before industrialization, Dewey (1899/1976) argued, children's daily experiences at home provided them with a multitude of problems to solve through their encounters with adults and other children. But when industrialization removed work and education from the home, children lost the rich problem-solving context that had provided their parents and grandparents with ample opportunity to develop imagination and intelligence. Although Dewey was an optimist, he was not a romantic. Rather than arguing for a return to the past, he proposed that we should return problems to the lives of children by turning public schools into problem-rich contexts, communities of inquiry in which teachers engage their students' minds with problems rather than simply fill their heads with "facts." The approach Dewey recommended was progressive education, a pedagogy in which teachers engage their students' native capacities and enthusiasm by linking learning to life through concrete problem solving, or what he called the "concrete logic of action" (1899/1976, p. 69).

Understanding what Dewey meant by progressive education is difficult because it "has been so distorted by generations of well-meaning but ill-equipped educational administrators that its original significance has been almost entirely lost" (Kloppenberg, 1986, p. 374). Nevertheless, in the space remaining I can note some of its most distinctive features by referring to my previous discussion of pragmatism, the antifoundational philosophy of knowledge and ethics upon which progressive education is premised. As we know from Chapter 2, pragmatism rejects the subjective–objective and order–conflict dichotomies of the modern framework, thus avoiding the foundational question of which paradigm is the correct one for grounding social practices and institutions. Rather, it proposes a critical and radically democratized form of dialogical social discourse in which all forms of knowledge are accepted or rejected on the basis of their consequences for the realization of social ideals, not on the basis of whether they are true in a foundational sense (Bernstein, 1991; Rorty, 1979, 1989, 1991). Whereas the aim of modern social inquiry is to justify social practices and institutions by showing that they are based on accurate representations of the social world, pragmatism seeks to change social practices and institutions by reconciling them with democratic ideals (Bernstein, 1971, 1991; Rorty, 1982, 1989).

Given its grounding in pragmatism, progressive education is a pedagogy in which students deconstruct and reconstruct knowledge and experiences under conditions of uncertainty. It conceives of thinking as arising from the need to solve concrete problems, "from the need of meeting some difficulty, in reflecting upon the best way of overcoming it, and thus leads to planning, to projecting mentally the result to be reached, and deciding upon the steps necessary and their serial order" (Dewey, 1899/1976, p. 69). Dewey favored problem solving because he saw it as the best means for developing students' capacity to think critically, which is important because, for him, education is a dialogical process of critical reflection leading to "reconstruction . . . of experience which adds to the meaning of experience, and . . . increases the ability to direct the course of subsequent experience" (Dewey, 1899/1976, p. 93). As such, the goal of the progressive educator "is not to train students to perform familiar tasks in time-honored ways, but to help them learn to solve unanticipated problems with imagination, not to impart bodies of knowledge but to develop the capacity to think . . . without the assistance of inherited methods or the reassurance of knowing that a correct answer always exists" (Kloppenberg, 1986, p. 375).

Moreover, because the purpose of reconstructing knowledge and experience is to reconcile them with ideals, progressive education is also grounded in the pragmatist theory of ethics, which conceives of ethical activity as it does all other activity, in terms of problem solving through dialogical discourse within a community of interests (Dewey, 1910/1989). For Dewey, ethics is the concrete task of applying inventiveness and the broadest lessons of experience to the "reconstruction and resolution of conflicts and problems in particular situations . . . not the application of rules that simply sum up past experience" (Edel & Flower, 1989, p. xxv). Dewey considered the ethical dualism between freedom and responsibility, or individual interests (excellence) and the common good (equity), to be a pseudo-problem created by the artificial split between the individual and the social in modern knowledge (Kloppenberg, 1986; Chapter 2). The key to Dewey's analysis of freedom and responsibility is in the pragmatist theory of ethics actualized through progressive education. In this view:

> freedom is essentially the capacity to learn and to make creative and innovative use of learning in guiding conduct. The pragmatic emphasis is on responsibility as prospective rather than retrospective . . . on sensitivity, learning and self-development. (Edel & Flower, 1989, p. xxv)

Drawing on Dewey's philosophy of education, and thus on the pragmatist theories of knowledge and ethics, the social reconstructionists rejected the prevailing idea put forth by advocates of social efficiency that public education should serve as a vehicle for conditioning individuals to follow the rules. Instead, they proposed the progressive theory that people should be freed from external restraints and expected to freely choose to be responsible. As such, progressive education is essential to democracy; it is the principal mechanism by which society cultivates its citizens to want to be socially responsible, which it does by developing in them an awareness and appreciation of interdependence or community, a critical attitude toward received knowledge, and an appreciation of uncertainty (see Bourgeois, 1896/1912; Croly, 1909/1965, 1914; Dewey, 1897, 1928/1959, 1899/1976, 1916/1980).

Dewey framed the social reconstructionists' concern over the decline of democracy as a twofold problem arising from the new form of interdependence that emerged with industrialization (1927/1988). The first problem was a bewildered public, which, because it lacked the social form of individualism required by an inherently interdependent world, could no longer express its interests and thus was unfit for participation in democracy. The second problem was "the essential need . . . [for] improvement of the methods and conditions of debate, discussion and persuasion" (1927/1988, p. 365), which was essential if the public was to develop a sense of itself as a community of interests. Of course, Dewey and the other reconstructionists believed that philosophical pragmatism and a reformed, progressive system of public education would provide the methods and conditions of discourse for achieving cultural transformation and social reconstruction (Kloppenberg, 1986). But it was in the public schools that the social reconstructionists were confronted with the circularity in their argument for transforming society through education. As Kloppenberg (1986) noted in this regard:

> Education inevitably involves institutions as well as the ideas to be communicated, and unshackling students from a false individualism and a false subservi-

ence to [received knowledge] must therefore await the unshackling of their teachers. . . . If the problems facing society can be traced to its individualism, as these thinkers believed, and reform must proceed by means of education, how can reformers get around the awkward fact that the educational system is imbued with precisely the values that they have isolated as the source of the problem? (p. 377)

As in the case of inclusion and restructuring, the circularity in the reconstructionist argument for transforming society through education turns on the contradiction between the adhocratic value orientation of progressive education and the bureaucratic structure and culture of public schools.

No one grasped the circularity problem better than Weber (1922/1978). Whereas the problem of an unreflective public could be traced to the contradiction between democracy and bureaucracy in the modern state, he explained that the circularity of trying to solve the problem through education turns on a double contradiction in the logic of modernity itself: the contradiction between democracy and bureaucracy, on one hand, and between education and professionalization, on the other. The ever-increasing push to further bureaucratize the economy and government creates the need for more and more experts and thus continually increases the importance of specialized knowledge. But the logic of expertise contradicts democracy because it creates "the struggle of the 'specialist' type of [person] against the older type of 'cultivated' [person]" (1922/1978, p. 1090). And since the progressive project is premised on restoring democracy by educating the cultivated citizen, it is stymied because public education itself becomes increasingly bureaucratized in the interest of training experts for a bureaucratized economy. Democracy continues to decline, not only because the bureaucratic form resists change but because the cultivated citizen continues to disappear. Moreover, as more of life comes under the control of the specialization and professionalization of the professional bureaucracy, the need to solve problems and to engage in discourse diminishes even further. This reduces the capacity for critical thought and dialogical discourse in society *and* in the professions, which not only undercuts the ability of the public to govern itself democratically, but reduces even further the capacity of the professions to view themselves and their practices critically.

EDUCATIONAL REFORM, SOCIAL RECONSTRUCTION, AND POSTINDUSTRIALISM

We can assess the significance of the social reconstructionist debate for the contemporary situation in society, education, and special education by comparing the emerging historical conditions of the twenty-first century with those of the early twentieth century, the conditions under which the reconstructionist debate took shape.

> By 1932 . . . industrialism has moved into overdrive and an urban society is clearly in the making. . . . A new physics has replaced the Newtonian outlook and a new logic is shaking philosophy. . . . The social sciences have been staking claims for the study of human life and thrusting different perspectives of method and research into the arena. Ethics is in a particularly precarious position: formerly it had coasted on the comfortable assumption that people agreed about morality but only argued about how it was to be justified. . . . Now it is startled into the perception that there are fundamental conflicts on moral questions. (Edel & Flower, 1989, pp. viii–ix)

In the late twentieth century, we know that the very idea that there can be a "new physics" has deconstructed the modern view of science and, moreover, that this has forced the social disciplines to question their earlier objectivist claims about methods of representing social life. Moreover, we have had over a century to think about antifoundationalism, the new logic of pragmatism that began shaking philosophy in the 1870s and has continued to shake it and social theory ever since. And, as we know, this has produced new and reappropriated old methods for addressing fundamental conflicts on moral questions, particularly questions about power/knowledge relations in the emerging postmodern world. Finally, and most important in terms of determinate possibilities for the future, industrialism has stalled out in the late twentieth century and is being overtaken by postindustrialism.

The significance of the emergence of postindustrialism is that it is premised on an even greater and more pervasive form of interdependence and social responsibility than is industrialism. The difference is that, whereas the new form of social interdependence that Dewey associated with industrialization stopped at the boundaries of industrial organizations themselves, postindustrialization extends interdependence into the very core of organizations and, from there, back out into the community (see Dertouzos, Lester, & Solow, 1989; Drucker, 1989; Kearns & Doyle, 1988; Naisbitt & Aburdene, 1985; Reich, 1983, 1990). As performance organizations premised on standardization, industrial firms are designed to mass produce the same product or service by standardizing work processes and worker behavior. As such, they are configured as machine bureaucracies, organizations that use rationalization and formalization to separate theory from practice, which produces an unreflective, mechanical form of interdependence among workers. However, the emerging postindustrial firm invents personalized products and services by deploying its workers on problem-solving teams. As a problem-solving organization premised on innovation, it is configured as an adhocracy because innovation requires the structural contingencies of collaboration and mutual adjustment to unite theory and practice in teams of workers, which in turn yields a discursive form of interdependence premised on collaborative problem solving through reflective discourse. Moreover, because personalization requires a close and continuous relationship with consumers, postindustrial firms require a professional-political form of accountability, one premised on a community of interests among workers and managers, and, ultimately, among the organization's members, consumers, and host community (Dertouzos et al., 1989; Drucker, 1989; Kearns & Doyle, 1988; Mintzberg, 1979; Reich, 1983).

Reich (1990) characterized the adhocracies of the postindustrial economy as "environments in which people can identify and solve problems for themselves" (p. 201), as contexts in which

> individual skills are integrated into a group. . . . Over time, as group members work through various problems . . . they learn about each others' abilities. They learn how they can help one another perform better, what each can contribute to a particular project, and how they can best take advantage of one another's experience. (p. 201)

The system of education that is needed for the postindustrial economy is one that prepares young people "to take responsibility for their continuing education, and to collaborate with one another so that their combined skills and insights add up to something more than the sum of their individual contributions" (Reich, 1990, p. 202). As such, educational excellence in the postindustrial era is more than basic numeracy and literacy or the mastery of facts; it is a capacity for working collaboratively with others and for taking responsibility for learning (Dertouzos et al., 1989; Drucker, 1989; Kearns & Doyle, 1988; Naisbitt & Aburdene, 1985; Reich, 1983, 1990). Moreover, educational equity is the precondition for excellence because collaboration means learning collaboratively with and from persons with varying interests, abilities, skills, and cultural and linguistic perspectives, and taking responsibility for learning means taking responsibility for one's own learning *and* that of others (Dertouzos et al., 1989; Drucker, 1989; Kearns & Doyle, 1988). Ability grouping and tracking have no place in such a system because they "reduce young people's capacities to learn from and collaborate with one another" (Reich, 1990, p. 208). Homogeneous grouping practices work against promoting social responsibility in students and developing their capacity for negotiation within a community of interests, outcomes that require public schools to be settings in which "unity and cooperation are the norm" (Reich, 1990, p. 208; Dertouzos et al., 1989).[15]

Given the relevancies of an emerging postmodern culture and postindustrial economy, successful schools in the twenty-first century will be those that produce cultivated citizens—liberally educated young people who can live and work responsibly and interdependently under conditions of uncertainty. The curriculum and pedagogy in these schools will promote students' sense of social responsibility, awareness of interdependence, and appreciation of uncertainty by cultivating their capacity for experiential learning through collaborative problem solving and reflective discourse within a democratic community of interests. These schools will achieve excellence and equity simultaneously, recognizing equity as the way to excellence. They will be those that produce cultivated citizens by giving all of their students a progressive education in an adhocratic setting.

Where do we stand in terms of the problems that Dewey identified earlier in the century? One need do little more than consider the state of political and cultural life today to see that the problem of a bewildered public is still with us. Indeed, given a nascent postmodern culture and postindustrial economy, the public is perhaps more bewildered than ever before. The prospects for reflective discourse have improved considerably, however. As we have seen, the postmodern turn and the vindication and reappropriation of pragmatism are providing new methods of critical discourse. Not only are these methods useful in educational inquiry, but the methods themselves are premised on and aimed at education, edification, and self-formation. Moreover, decades of failed attempts to improve schools have resulted in enough uncertainty about public education to create a convergence of interests over the problem of school failure. And, of course, the most significant development is the emergence of postindustrialism, which holds out the possibility of a convergence of interest among government, business, labor, and education over the problems of public education and democracy in America.

The significance of postindustrialism for the special education advocacy community is that it raises the possibility of the type of reform that will be required to actualize the adhocratic values of inclusion. Indeed, these are the very values upon which postmodernism and postindustrialism are premised, and, more important, the precise values that are needed to reconcile the institutional practice of education with its democratic ideals. Given the historical conditions of a postmodern society and postindustrial economy, and the fact that democracy *is* collaborative problem solving through reflective discourse within a community of interests, progressive education and the adhocratic school provide us with the methods and conditions to resume the critical project of cultural transformation and social reconstruction. With adequate methods and conditions of discourse, we may yet be able to transform the American public and save democracy from bureaucracy.

NOTES

1. My use of the qualifiers "explicit" and "implicit" in the sections to follow requires some clarification because I am using three different types or levels of explicitness and implicitness. First, there is the type that refers to the nature of agreement between the inclusion proponents' and opponents' assessments of various aspects of the current system of special education. In these cases, I simply use the terms explicit and implicit in the customary way. Second, there is the type I use when discussing the implications of the inclusion proponents' and opponents' empirical arguments for special education's grounding assumptions, theories, and metatheories. It should be clear by this point that the participants in the inclusion debate are not speaking explicitly to the the field's assumptions, theories, and metatheories. Indeed, that is the problem with the inclusion debate—what I referred to above as the problem of naive pragmatism (see Chapter 3). In these cases I will at times omit the qualifiers explicit and implicit, particularly when including them would be cumbersome. In any event, when I say, for example, that the inclusion proponents or opponents "reject" or "retain" an assumption, theory, or metatheory, it should be understood that they do so implicitly. Finally, at the end of the section I use a third type of explicitness and implicitness in referring to the source of special education's grounding assumptions, theories, and metatheories, that is, with reference to whether they are explicit (derived from the field's disciplinary grounding in psychology and biology) or implicit (derived from a social norm), as explained in Chapter 3.

I should note here as well that, as a pragmatist, I am not concerned with the question of whether special education's four guiding assumptions are right or wrong, but with whether they are *useful* in the (pragmatist's) sense of reducing the gap between the field's claims about itself (that it serves the best educational and political interests of its clients and the democratic needs of society) and its actual practices (see Chapters 1 and 2). In this sense, I am arguing in this section and the ones to follow that special education's conventional assumptions are not useful, and that the field should drop them as a guide to practice. For ease of reference, these assumptions, as noted in Chapter 3 in their full form, are that

1. Student disability is a pathological condition.
2. Differential diagnosis is objective and useful.
3. Special education is a rationally conceived and coordinated system of services that benefits diagnosed students.
4. Progress in special education is a rational-technical process of incremental improvements in conventional diagnostic and instructional practices.

If the field of special education is to reduce the gap between its claims and its practices, I am contending, it should base its models, practices, and discourses on a different set of assumptions. That is, in effect, that: (1) student disabilities are organizational pathologies; (2) differential diagnosis is subjective and harmful to students and to public education as a whole; (3) special education is a nonrational and uncoordinated system that serves the political interests of school organizations; and (4) progress in the field is nonrational, a revolutionary process of replacing the current system rather than an evolutionary process of improving it incrementally. Here again, I am not claiming that the conventional assumptions are wrong and mine are right, only that my alternatives are more useful, in the pragmatist sense noted. Also see notes 2 and 10.

2. There is no argument over the fact that most low-incidence disabilities (those in the severe to profound range of severity) are associated with observable patterns of biological symptoms (or syndromes) and are thus comprehensible under the pathological model (see Mercer, 1973; Chapter 3). Accordingly, the concern with regard to these students is not whether their disabilities are the result of a pathology, but whether they are being served adequately and ethically under the largely segregated approach of the current system, and whether the pathological distinction is of any *use*, in the pragmatist sense (note 1), in designing effective and ethical instructional placements and practices (see Sailor, 1989; Sailor et al., 1986; Stainback & Stainback, 1984; below). The question of whether student disabilities are pathological refers primarily to the high-incidence EHA classifications of learning disabilities, emotional disturbance, and mild mental retardation, which in most cases do not show biological signs of pathology (see Algozzine, 1976, 1977; Apter, 1982; Hobbs, 1975; Mercer, 1973; Rhodes, 1970; Chapter 3). Here too, however, it is helpful to keep the pragmatist's notion of usefulness in mind (note 1).

3. On the related matter of the attribution of student failure, the inclusion opponents and proponents agree that an exclusive "student-deficit" orientation is inappropriate. Although some inclusion opponents argue that the proponents favor an exclusive "teacher-deficit" orientation (Kauffman et al., 1988; Keogh, 1988), the inclusion proponents clearly recognize the responsibility of students in the learning process (see Gartner, 1986; Wang, 1989b; Wang & Peverly, 1987).

4. The only inclusion opponent who makes a case for the potential instructional relevance of differential diagnosis, considers it to be an empirical question that, if answered in the negative, should signal the discontinuance of the practice of differential diagnosis and the categorical approach to special education (Keogh, 1988). Although Bryan et al. (1988) do not make an explicit argument for the instructional relevance of differential diagnosis, by arguing that "one cannot assume that any two learning disabled children would be any more similar than a learning disabled child and a normally achieving child, or a normally achieving child and an underachieving child" (p. 25), they actually make an implicit argument against the instructional utility of differential diagnosis, and thus agree (implicitly) with the inclusion proponents' position that all students have unique learning needs and interests, even those within the traditional high-incidence disability classifications.

5. Although some inclusion opponents argue that the handicapped designation is beneficial, none argue that it has been shown to lead to direct instructional benefit (see Hallahan et al., 1988; Keogh, 1988). The only arguments in favor of instruction in special education settings are based on either the perception that general education teachers are incapable of addressing diverse learning needs in their classrooms (Bryan et al., 1988) or the speculation that more powerful instructional techniques might be easier to implement in separate settings (Hallahan et al., 1988; cf. Hallahan & Keller, 1986).

6. Each of the reform proposals calls for educating all students currently served in compensatory, bilingual, migrant, and remedial education programs in the general education classrooms of the restructured system on a full-time basis. Disagreement over which students classified as handicapped under the EHA should be served in general education classrooms on a full-time basis has split the four teams of inclusion proponents into two camps of "inclusion" (Reynolds/Wang and Lilly/Pugach) and "full inclusion" (Lipsky/Gartner and Stainback/Stainback) advocates (see Chapter 3, note 5). Although I will not use this distinction in the text, the full inclusion teams have distanced themselves from the inclusion teams, noting that their reform proposals ultimately maintain two separate systems and thus are merely "blending at the margin" (Lipsky & Gartner, 1989a, p. 271), or that they are too exclusive because they do not "address the need to include in regular classrooms . . . those students labeled severely and profoundly handicapped" (Stainback & Stainback, 1989, p. 43).

7. This proposal also excludes students who are classified as mildly handicapped but have "developmental" or pathological learning disabilities (cf. Kirk & Chalfant, 1983).

8. Although this is the most inclusive proposal, it includes the proviso that "in some instances" students with severe and profound disabilities will need to be grouped in "specific courses and classes according to their instructional needs" (Stainback & Stainback, 1984, p. 108; Stainback et al., 1989).

9. Virtually all of the citations in this section are references to empirical and interpretive research findings that support my theoretical claims about organization and change (presented in Chapter 9). That is, in virtually all cases the author or authors cited in conjunction with an assertion have not made the assertion. The assertions are mine, based on the discussion of organization and change in Chapter 9, and they are supported by the empirical or interpretive research of the authors cited.

10. The models, practices, and discourses of special education, general education, and educational administration are based on the same set of disciplinary and normative assumptions grounded in the functionalist theories of human pathology and organizational rationality (see note 1 and Chapter 3). Thus, my reference to general education's "functionalist theories and assumptions" refers to the same theories (human pathology and organizational rationality) and virtually the same assumptions considered in the previous section. The only difference is that the guiding assumptions of general education and educational administration are stated in the broader terms of "school failure" and "special programming," rather than the more specific terms of "student disability" and "special education." As noted in Chapter 3, the more broadly stated assumptions are that

1. School failure is a (psychologically or sociologically) pathological condition that students have.
2. Differential diagnosis (i.e., homogeneous classification by ability or need) is an objective and useful practice.
3. Special programming (e.g., in-class ability grouping, curricular tracking, and segregated and pull-out special needs programs) is a rationally conceived and coordinated system of services that benefits diagnosed students.
4. Progress in education (i.e., greater academic achievement and efficiency) is

a rational-technical process of incremental improvements in conventional diagnostic and instructional practices.

In this section and the ones to follow, I am making the same claim about these assumptions as I am about special education's guiding assumptions (see note 1). As a pragmatist, I am concerned not with the question of whether the assumptions are right or wrong, but with whether they are *useful* in the (pragmatist's) sense of reducing the gap between public education's claims about itself (that it serves the best educational and political interests of its clients and the best political and economic interests of a democratic society) and its actual practices (see note 1; Chapters 1 and 2; below). In this sense, I am arguing that the conventional assumptions are not useful, and that the field and institution of education should drop them as a guide to practice. As in the case of special education (see note 1 and Chapter 3, note 7), I am contending that, if public education is to reduce the gap between its claims and its practices, it should base its models, practices, and discourses on a different set of assumptions, in effect, that: (1) school failure is an organizational pathology; (2) differential diagnosis is subjective and harmful to students and to society as a whole; (3) special needs programming is a nonrational and uncoordinated system that serves the political interests of school organizations and public education itself; and (4) progress in public education is nonrational, a revolutionary process of replacing the current system rather than an evolutionary process of improving it incrementally. Here again, I am not claiming that the conventional assumptions are wrong and mine are right, only that my alternatives are more useful, in the pragmatist sense noted.

11. I am treating the idea that public education in a democracy must be both excellent and equitable as a minimum requirement (see Chapter 3, note 4). Drawing on the discussion of the place of values in critical pragmatism in Chapter 2 (also see Chapter 9), I provide an expanded view of the requirements for democratic education in a subsequent section of this chapter. Also see MacPherson (1974) on various forms of liberal democracy, Barber (1984) on "strong" or participatory democracy, Gutmann (1987) on democratic education, and Soltis (1993) on the relationship between forms of democracy and approaches to teaching.

12. The best articulation of this position within the restructuring debate is Schön's (1983, 1987, 1988) argument for developing reflective practitioners by eliminating in schools the "normal bureaucratic emphasis on technical rationality" (Schön, 1983, p. 338), thus permitting teachers to become "builders of repertoire rather than accumulators of procedures and methods" (1988, p. 26). Although Schön clearly recognized that the reflective practitioner requires a reflective organization (see Schön, 1983, 1988), he conceptualizes the reflective practitioner as an individual professional engaged in a monological discourse with a problem situation, rather than a team of professionals engaged reflectively in a dialogical discourse with one another and their consumers, which retains the structural contingencies of specialization and professionalization and thus the professional bureaucracy configuration. For a deconstruction of Schön's notion of the reflective practitioner, see Skrtic (1991a) and Skrtic and Ware (1992).

13. Although I will not pursue the issue of accountability in any great depth here (see Skrtic, 1991a, 1995a; Chapter 9), the mode of accountability that emerges

in the adhocracy represents an alternative to the two extreme positions on account-ability that have shaped the current debate on school restructuring, what Timar and Kirp (1988, p. 130) called the "romantic decentralist" (professional) and the "hyperrationalist" (bureaucratic) modes of accountability (also see Murphy, 1989; Timar & Kirp, 1988, 1989), as well as Conley's (1990, p. 317) middle ground or "constrained decision maker" position. Modes of accountability are shaped by the logic of the division of labor, means of coordination, and form of interdependence in organizations. There is no way out of the professional–bureaucratic accountability dilemma in schools as they are currently organized. And the constrained decision maker position merely tries to strike a balance between the two extremes, while leaving the current configuration of schools intact. The key to accountability in the adhocracy is that it avoids all three positions by assigning responsibility to *groups* of professionals and politicizing discretion within a discourse among professionals and consumer constitutiencies (see note 12 and Chapter 9).

14. The social reconstructionist movement, which generally sought to use pub-lic education as a means to reconstruct society on a more democratic and egalitarian footing, emerged in the 1920s, peaked in the 1930s, and virtually disappeared under the conservative pressures of World War II, the Cold War, and McCarthyism (see Bowers, 1970; Stanley, 1992). Within education, social reconstructionism was pro-moted by a small faction within the Progressive Education Association (Bowers, 1970); more broadly, however, it was the principal reform strategy of progressive liberalism, the American political theory based on the "social gospel" (ethical renewal through religious dissent) and pragmatism (Kloppenberg, 1986). A comprehensive treatment of the various (and changing) positions and camps within the reconstruc-tionist movement is beyond the scope of this chapter (see Kliebard, 1986; Kloppen-berg, 1986; Stanley, 1992), but for present purposes we can think of two basic forms of social reconstructionism, the second of which I follow in the text.

"Radical" reconstructionism was (to varying degrees) Marxist-oriented and sought to restore democracy by committing schools and teachers to the doctrinal position of restructuring the socioeconomic order toward a collectivist society (Hleb-owitsh & Wraga, 1992). "Reformist" or "gradualist" reconstructionism was based on the social theory of Weber (see Chapter 5) and the educational philosophy of Dewey (see below). Although ultimately they too were concerned about *economic* restructur-ing, the reformists (e.g., Bode, 1938; Dewey, 1938) sought to restore democracy by using public education as a vehicle for *ethical* renewal, that is, by restructuring schools as dialogical communities of inquiry that produce cultivated citizens who, armed with democratic values and pragmatist methods, are capable of carrying out the necessary reconstruction of society (see Kloppenberg, 1986; Skrtic, 1991a; below). The prob-lem for the reformists was not the capitalist industrial order *per se*, but the bureaucratic administrative form that accompanied industrialization, which they believed dimin-ished the public's capacity for democratic governance.

15. The positive implications of postindustrialization are more an ideal than a reality at present. Indeed, faced with the dynamism of a globalized economy, the initial response of industry largely has been attempts to increase competitiveness through conventional, bureaucratic approaches to "restructuring" (e.g., "down-sizing," temporary workers, more standardization), which have not solved the com-

petitiveness problem and have had negative social consequences within organizations and in society at large (Aktouf, 1992; Lawler, 1992; Chapter 5). Nevertheless, a substantial body of theoretical (Aktouf, 1992; Argyris, 1957; Brown, 1978; Likert, 1961; McGregor, 1960) and practical (Kanter, 1985; O'Toole, 1985; Ouchi, 1981; Peters & Waterman, 1982) knowledge on participatory organization and management has existed for some time and continues to grow (for a review, see Lawler, 1986, 1992). The major problem has been bringing conventional management practices in line with the democratic, participatory requirements of the adhocratic form (see Aktouf, 1992; Best, 1990; Brown, 1978; Lawler, 1992).

The advantage today is that, having reached the limits of conventional "restructuring" practices, the business community and investors have begun to see the competitive advantage of participatory or democratic forms of organization and management, even if they have not accepted completely "the responsibility of organizations to create meaningful and satisfying work" (Lawler, 1992, p. xiii; Naisbitt & Aburdene, 1985; Reich, 1983). Of course, we should not expect a sharp rise in altruism in the business community; the motivation for change is largely, if not purely, profitability. Japan's economic success, based largely on the principles of total quality management (Deming, 1986; see Chapter 9, note 2), has been important in this regard, not because Japan's management approach is the answer for America, but because it drew attention to the advantages of worker participation and, more important, to the idea that effective organizations require an approach to management that "fits the national cultural values of the country . . . in which they operate" (Lawler, 1992, p. 24). Japanese management emphasizes Japan's core national values, such as uniformity, discipline, group membership, conformity, and loyalty to employer and to country (Ouchi, 1981). In a diverse and democratic society such as ours, however, we need an approach to management that is tied to our historical context and our core national values of justice, liberty, equality, and community. In principle, the participatory or democratic approach to management that is associated with the adhocratic form is completely consistent with these values (Lawler, 1992; Mintzberg, 1979, 1983; Naisbitt & Aburdene, 1985; Reich, 1983). Indeed, in its idealized form, adhocracy, or collaborative problem solving through reflective discourse within a community of interests, is another name for democracy, an organizational configuration in which diversity is an asset and democracy a virtue because it is premised on the principle of innovation through voice, participation, and inclusion.

REFERENCES

Aktouf, O. (1992). Management and theories of organization in the 1990s: Toward a critical radical humanism. *Academy of Management Review, 17*(3), 407–431.

Algozzine, B. (1976). The disturbing child: What you see is what you get? *Alberta Journal of Education Research, 22,* 330–333.

Algozzine, B. (1977). The emotionally disturbed child: Disturbed or disturbing? *Journal of Abnormal Child Psychology, 5*(2), 205–211.

Apter, S. J. (1982). *Troubled children, troubled systems.* New York: Pergamon Press.

Argyris, C. (1957). *Personality and organization*. New York: Harper.

Bacharach, S. B. (Ed.). (1990). *Education reform: Making sense of it all*. Boston: Allyn & Bacon.

Barber, B. R. (1984). *Strong democracy: Participatory politics for a new age*. Berkeley: University of California Press.

Bernstein, R. J. (1971). *Praxis and action: Contemporary philosophies of human activity*. Philadelphia: University of Pennsylvania Press.

Bernstein, R. J. (1991). *The new constellation*. Cambridge: Polity Press.

Best, M. H. (1990). *The new competition: Institutions of industrial restructuring*. Cambridge, MA: Harvard University Press.

Bode, B. H. (1938). *Education at the crossroads*. New York: Newson & Company.

Bourgeois, L. (1912). *Solidarité* (7th ed.). Paris: Colin. (Original work published 1896)

Bowers, C. A. (1970). Social reconstructionism: Views from the left and the right, 1932–1942. *History of Education Quarterly, 10*(1), 22–52.

Boyer, E. L. (1983). *High school*. New York: Harper & Row.

Braaten, S. R., Kauffman, J. M., Braaten, B., Polsgrove, L., & Nelson, C. M. (1988). The regular education initiative: Patent medicine for behavioral disorders. *Exceptional Children, 55*(1), 21–27.

Brown, R. H. (1978). Bureaucracy as praxis: Toward a political phenomenology of formal organizations. *Administrative Science Quarterly, 23*, 365–382.

Bryan, T., Bay, M., & Donahue, M. (1988). Implications of the learning disabilities definition for the regular education initiative. *Journal of Learning Disabilities, 21*(1), 23–28.

Callahan, R. E. (1962). *Education and the cult of efficiency: A study of the social forces that have shaped the administration of public schools*. Chicago: University of Chicago Press.

Carnegie Foundation for the Advancement of Teaching. (1988). *An imperiled generation: Saving urban schools*. Princeton, NJ: Author.

Clark, D. L., & Astuto, T. A. (1988). *Education policy after Reagan—What next?* (Occasional Paper No. 6). Charlottesville: University of Virginia, Policy Studies Center of the University Council for Educational Administration.

Clark, D. L., Lotto, L. S., & Astuto, T. A. (1984). Effective schools and school improvement: A comparative analysis of two lines of inquiry. *Educational Administration Quarterly, 20*(3), 41–68.

Committee for Economic Development. (1987). *Children in need: Investment strategies for the educationally disadvantaged*. New York: Author.

Conley, S. C. (1990). Reforming paper pushers and avoiding free agents: The teacher as a constrained decision maker. In S. B. Bacharach (Ed.), *Education reform: Making sense of it all* (pp. 313–324). Boston: Allyn & Bacon.

Council for Children with Behavioral Disorders. (1989). Position statement on the regular education initiative. *Behavioral Disorders, 14*, 201–208.

Cremin, L. A. (1961). *The transformation of the school*. New York: Knopf.

Cremin, L. A. (1965). *The genius of American education*. New York: Vintage Books.

Croly, H. (1914). *Progressive democracy*. New York: Macmillan.

Croly, H. (1965). The promise of American life. In J. W. Ward (Ed.), *The American heritage series*. Indianapolis: Bobbs-Merrill. (Original work published 1909)

Cuban, L. (1983). Effective schools: A friendly but cautionary note. *Phi Delta Kappan, 64*(10), 695–696.

Cuban, L. (1989). The "at-risk" label and the problem of urban school reform. *Phi Delta Kappan, 70*(10), 780–784, 799–801.

Deming, W. E. (1986). *Out of the crisis*. Cambridge, MA: MIT Press.

Dertouzos, M. L., Lester, R. K., & Solow, R. M. (1989). *Made in America: Regaining the productive edge*. Cambridge, MA: MIT Press.

Dewey, J. (1897). My pedagogic creed. *The School Journal, 54*(3), 77–80.

Dewey, J. (1938). Education, democracy and socialized economy. *The Social Frontier, 5*(40), 71–73.

Dewey, J. (1959). Progressive education and the new science of education. In M. S. Dworkin (Ed.), *Dewey on education* (pp. 113–126). New York: Teachers College Press. (Original work published 1928)

Dewey, J. (1976). The school and society. In J. A. Boydston (Ed.), *John Dewey: The middle works, 1899–1924* (Vol. 1, pp. 1–109). Carbondale: Southern Illinois University Press. (Original work published 1899)

Dewey, J. (1980). Democracy and education. In J. A. Boydston (Ed.), *John Dewey: The middle works, 1899–1924* (Vol. 9, pp. 1–370). Carbondale: Southern Illinois University Press. (Original work published 1916)

Dewey, J. (1988). Individualism, old and new. In J. A. Boydston (Ed.), *John Dewey: The later works, 1925–1953* (Vol. 5, pp. 41–123). Carbondale: Southern Illinois University Press. (Original work published 1929–30)

Dewey, J. (1988). The public and its problems. In J. A. Boydston (Ed.), *John Dewey: The later works, 1925–1953* (Vol. 2, pp. 235–372). Carbondale: Southern Illinois University Press. (Original work published 1927)

Dewey, J. (1989). How we think: A restatement of the relation of reflective thinking to the educative process. In J. A. Boydston (Ed.), *John Dewey: The later works, 1925–1953* (Vol. 8, pp. 105–352). Carbondale: Southern Illinois University Press. (Original work published 1910)

Drucker, P. F. (1989). *The new realities*. New York: Harper & Row.

Dworkin, M. S. (Ed.). (1959). John Dewey: A centennial review. In M. S. Dworkin (Ed.), *Dewey on education* (pp. 1–18). New York: Teachers College Press.

Edel, A., & Flower, E. (1989). Introduction. In J. A. Boydston (Ed.), *John Dewey: The later works, 1925–1953* (Vol. 7, pp. vii–xxxv). Carbondale: Southern Illinois University Press.

Edmonds, R. (1979). Some schools work and more can. *Social Policy, 9*(5), 26–31.

Elmore, R. F. (1987). *Early experiences in restructuring schools: Voices from the field*. Washington, DC: National Governors Association.

Elmore, R. F., & McLaughlin, M. W. (1988). *Steady work: Policy, practice, and the reform of American education*. Santa Monica, CA: Rand Corporation.

Ford, P. L. (Ed.). (1904). *Thomas Jefferson, works*. New York: Knickerbocker Press.

Gartner, A. (1986). Disabling help: Special education at the crossroads. *Exceptional Children, 53*(1), 72–79.

Gartner, A., & Lipsky, D. K. (1987). Beyond special education: Toward a quality system for all students. *Harvard Educational Review, 57*(4), 367–390.

Gerber, M. M. (1987). Application of cognitive-behavioral training methods to teach basic skills to mildly handicapped elementary school students. In M. C. Wang, M. C. Reynolds, & H. J. Walberg (Eds.), *Handbook of special education: Research and practice* (pp. 167–186). Oxford: Pergamon Press.

Gerber, M. M. (1988). Tolerance and technology of instruction: Implications for special education reform. *Exceptional Children, 54*(4), 309–314.

Gerber, M. M., & Semmel, M. I. (1984). Teacher as imperfect test: Reconceptualizing the referral process. *Educational Psychologist, 19*, 137–148.

Gerber, M. M., & Semmel, M. I. (1985). The microeconomics of referral and reintegration: A paradigm for evaluation of special education. *Studies in Educational Evaluation, 11*, 13–29.

Goodlad, J. I. (1984). *A place called school: Prospects for the future.* New York: McGraw-Hill.

Greer, C. (1972). *The great school legend: A revisionist interpretation of American public education.* New York: Basic Books.

Gutmann, A. (1987). *Democratic education.* Princeton, NJ: Princeton University Press.

Haber, S. (1964). *Efficiency and uplift: Scientific management in the progressive era, 1890–1920.* Chicago: University of Chicago Press.

Hallahan, D. P., & Kauffman, J. M. (1977). Categories, labels, behavioral characteristics: ED, LD, and EMR reconsidered. *Journal of Special Education, 11*, 139–149.

Hallahan, D. P., & Keller, C. E. (1986). *Study of studies for learning disabilities: A research review and synthesis.* Charleston: West Virginia Department of Education.

Hallahan, D. P., Keller, C. E., McKinney, J. D., Lloyd, J. W., & Bryan, T. (1988). Examining the research base of the regular education initiative: Efficacy studies and the adaptive learning environments model. *Journal of Learning Disabilities, 21*(1), 29–35, 55.

Hlebowitsh, P. S., & Wraga, W. G. (1992, April). Social class analysis in the early progressive tradition. Paper presented at the annual meeting of the American Educational Research Association, San Francisco.

Hobbs, N. (1975). *The futures of children: Categories, labels, and their consequences.* San Francisco: Jossey-Bass.

Kanter, R. M. (1985). *Change masters: Innovation for productivity in the American workplace.* New York: Simon & Schuster.

Kauffman, J. M. (1988). Revolution can also mean returning to the starting point: Will school psychology help special education complete the circuit? *School Psychology Review, 17*, 490–494.

Kauffman, J. M. (1989). The regular education initiative as Reagan–Bush education policy: A trickle-down theory of education of the hard-to-teach. *Journal of Special Education, 23*(3), 256–278.

Kauffman, J. M., Gerber, M. M., & Semmel, M. I. (1988). Arguable assumptions underlying the regular education initiative. *Journal of Learning Disabilities, 21*(1), 6–11.

Kearns, D. T., & Doyle, D. P. (1988). *Winning the brain race: A bold plan to make our schools competitive.* San Francisco: Institute for Contemporary Studies.

Keogh, B. K. (1988). Improving services for problem learners: Rethinking and restructuring. *Journal of Learning Disabilities, 21*(1), 19–22.

Kirk, S. A., & Chalfant, J. D. (1983). *Academic and developmental learning disabilities.* Denver: Love Publishing.

Kliebard, H. M. (1986). *The struggle for the American curriculum, 1893–1958.* Boston: Routledge & Kegan Paul.

Kliebard, H. M. (1988). The effort to reconstruct the modern American curriculum. In L. E. Beyer & M. W. Apple (Eds.), *The curriculum: Problems, politics, and possibilities* (pp. 19–31). Albany: State University of New York Press.

Kloppenberg, J. T. (1986). *Uncertain victory: Social Democracy and Progressivism in European and American thought, 1870–1920.* New York: Oxford University Press.

Kuhn, T. (1970). *The structure of scientific revolutions* (2nd ed.). Chicago: University of Chicago Press.

Lawler, E. E. (1986). *High-involvement management: Participative strategies for improving organizational performance.* San Francisco: Jossey-Bass.

Lawler, E. E. (1992). *The ultimate advantage: Creating the high-involvement organization.* San Francisco: Jossey-Bass.

Lazerson, M. (1983). The origins of special education. In J. G. Chambers & W. T. Hartman (Eds.), *Special education policies: Their history, implementation, and finance* (pp. 15–47). Philadelphia: Temple University Press.

Lezotte, L. W. (1989). School improvement based on the effective schools research. In D. K. Lipsky & A. Gartner (Eds.), *Beyond separate education: Quality education for all* (pp. 25–37). Baltimore: Paul H. Brookes.

Lieberman, A., & Miller, L. (1984). *Teachers, their world and their work: Implications for school improvement.* Alexandria, VA: Association for Supervision and Curriculum Development.

Likert, R. (1961). *New patterns of management.* New York: McGraw-Hill.

Lilly, M. S. (1986). The relationship between general and special education: A new face on an old issue. *Counterpoint, 6*(1), 10.

Lipsky, D. K., & Gartner, A. (1987). Capable of achievement and worthy of respect: Education for handicapped students as if they were full-fledged human beings. *Exceptional Children, 54*(1), 69–74.

Lipsky, D. K., & Gartner, A. (Eds.). (1989a). *Beyond separate education: Quality education for all.* Baltimore: Paul H. Brookes.

Lipsky, D. K., & Gartner, A. (1989b). Building the future. In D. K. Lipsky & A. Gartner, *Beyond separate education: Quality education for all* (pp. 255–290). Baltimore: Paul H. Brookes.

Lipsky, D. K., & Gartner, A. (1989c). The current situation. In D. K. Lipsky & A. Gartner, *Beyond separate education: Quality education for all* (pp. 3–24). Baltimore: Paul H. Brookes.

Lloyd, J. W., Crowley, E. P., Kohler, F. W., & Strain, P. S. (1988). Redefining the applied research agenda: Cooperative learning, prereferral, teacher consultation, and peer-mediated interventions. *Journal of Learning Disabilities, 21*(1), 43–52.

MacPherson, C. B. (1974). *The life and times of liberal democracy*. Oxford: Oxford University Press.

McGregor, D. (1960). *The human side of enterprise*. New York: McGraw-Hill.

McNeil, L. M. (1986). *Contradictions of control: School structure and school knowledge*. New York: Methuen/Routledge & Kegan Paul.

Meier, D. (1984). "Getting tough" in the schools. *Dissent, 31*(1), 61–70.

Mercer, J. (1973). *Labeling the mentally retarded: Clinical and social system perspectives on mental retardation*. Berkeley: University of California Press.

Mintzberg, H. (1979). *The structuring of organizations*. Englewood Cliffs, NJ: Prentice-Hall.

Mintzberg, H. (1983). *Structure in fives: Designing effective organizations*. Englewood Cliffs, NJ: Prentice-Hall.

Murphy, J. T. (1989). The paradox of decentralizing schools: Lessons from business, government, and the Catholic Church. *Phi Delta Kappan, 70*(10), 808–812.

Naisbitt, J., & Aburdene, P. (1985). *Re-inventing the corporation*. New York: Warner Books.

National Commission on Excellence in Education. (1983). *A nation at risk: The imperative for educational reform*. Washington, DC: U. S. Government Printing Office.

Oakes, J. (1985). *Keeping track: How schools structure inequality*. New Haven, CT: Yale University Press.

Oakes, J. (1986a). Keeping track, part 1: The policy and practice of curriculum inequality. *Phi Delta Kappan, 68*(1), 12–17.

Oakes, J. (1986b). Keeping track, part 2: Curriculum inequality and school reform. *Phi Delta Kappan, 68*(2), 148–154.

O'Toole, J. (1985). *Vanguard management*. New York: Doubleday.

Ouchi, W. (1981). *Theory Z*. Reading, MA: Addison-Wesley.

Perrow, C. (1970). *Organizational analysis: A sociological review*. Belmont, CA: Wadsworth.

Peters, T. J., & Waterman, R. H. (1982). *In search of excellence*. New York: Harper-Collins.

Pugach, M., & Lilly, M. S. (1984). Reconceptualizing support services for classroom teachers: Implications for teacher education. *Journal of Teacher Education, 35*(5), 48–55.

Reich, R. B. (1983). *The next American frontier*. New York: Penguin Books.

Reich, R. B. (1990). Education and the next economy. In S. B. Bacharach (Ed.), *Education reform: Making sense of it all* (pp. 194–212). Boston: Allyn & Bacon.

Resnick, D., & Resnick, L. (1985). Standards, curriculum, and performance: Historical and comparative perspectives. *Educational Researcher, 14*(4), 5–20.

Reynolds, M. C. (1988). A reaction to the JLD special series on the regular education initiative. *Journal of Learning Disabilities, 21*(6), 352–356.

Reynolds, M. C., & Birch, J. W. (1977). *Teaching exceptional children in all America's schools*. Reston, VA: Council for Exceptional Children.

Reynolds, M. C., & Wang, M. C. (1983). Restructuring "special" school programs: A position paper. *Policy Studies Review, 2*(1), 189–212.

Reynolds, M. C., Wang, M. C., & Walberg, H. J. (1987). The necessary restructuring of special and general education. *Exceptional Children, 53*(5), 391–398.

Rhodes, W. C. (1970). A community participation analysis of emotional disturbance. *Exceptional Children, 36*(5), 309–314.

Rorty, R. (1979). *Philosophy and the mirror of nature.* Princeton, NJ: Princeton University Press.

Rorty, R. (1982). *Consequences of pragmatism.* Minneapolis: University of Minnesota Press.

Rorty, R. (1989). *Contingency, irony, and solidarity.* New York: Cambridge University Press.

Rorty, R. (1991). *Objectivity, relativism, and truth: Philosophical papers* (Vol. 1). Cambridge: Cambridge University Press.

Rounds, J. (1979). *Social theory, public policy and social order.* Unpublished doctoral dissertation. University of California, Los Angeles.

Rounds, J. (1981, May). Information and ambiguity in organizational change. Paper presented at the Carnegie–Mellon Symposium on Information Processing in Organizations, Pittsburgh.

Sailor, W. (1989). The educational, social, and vocational integration of students with the most severe disabilities. In D. K. Lipsky & A. Gartner (Eds.), *Beyond separate education: Quality education for all* (pp. 53–74). Baltimore: Paul H. Brookes.

Sailor, W., Halvorsen, A., Anderson, J., Goetz, L., Gee, K., Doering, K., & Hunt, P. (1986). Community intensive instruction. In R. Horner, L. Meyer, & H. D. Fredericks (Eds.), *Education of learners with severe handicaps: Exemplary service strategies* (pp. 251–288). Baltimore: Paul H. Brookes.

Sarason, S. B., & Doris, J. (1979). *Educational handicap, public policy, and social history.* New York: Free Press.

Schön, D. A. (1983). *The reflective practitioner: How professionals think in action.* New York: Basic Books.

Schön, D. A. (1987). *Educating the reflective practitioner: Toward a design for teaching and learning in the professions.* San Francisco: Jossey Bass.

Schön, D. A. (1988). Coaching reflective thinking. In P. Grimmett & G. Erickson (Eds.), *Reflection in teacher education.* New York: Teachers College Press.

Segal, M. (1974). Organization and environment: A typology of adaptability and structure. *Public Administration Review, 34*(3), 212–220.

Sergiovanni, T. J., & Moore, J. H. (1989). *Schooling for tomorrow.* Boston: Allyn & Bacon.

Sirotnik, K. A., & Oakes, J. (1986). Critical inquiry for school renewal: Liberating theory and practice. In K. A. Sirotnik & J. Oakes (Eds.), *Critical perspectives on the organization and improvement of schooling* (pp. 3–93). Boston: Kluwer-Nijhoff Publishing.

Sizer, T. R. (1984). *Horace's compromise: The dilemma of the American high school.* Boston: Houghton Mifflin.

Skrtic, T. M. (1987). An organizational analysis of special education reform. *Counterpoint, 8*(2), 15–19.

Skrtic, T. M. (1988). The organizational context of special education. In E. L. Meyen & T. M. Skrtic (Eds.), *Exceptional children and youth: An introduction* (pp. 479–517). Denver: Love Publishing.

Skrtic, T. M. (1991a). *Behind special education: A critical analysis of professional culture and school organization.* Denver: Love Publishing.

Skrtic, T. M. (1991b). The special education paradox: Equity as the way to excellence. *Harvard Educational Review, 61*(2), 148–206.

Skrtic, T. M. (1995a). The organizational context of special education and school reform. In E. L. Meyen & T. M. Skrtic (Eds.), *Special education and student disability: Traditional, emerging, and alternative perspectives* (pp. 729–791). Denver: Love Publishing.

Skrtic, T. M. (1995b). The special education knowledge tradition: Crisis and opportunity. In E. L. Meyen & T. M. Skrtic (Eds.), *Special education and student disability: Traditional, emerging, and alternative perspectives* (pp. 609–672). Denver: Love Publishing.

Skrtic, T. M., & Ware, L. P. (1992). Reflective teaching and the problem of school organization. In E. W. Ross, J. W. Cornett, & G. McCutcheon (Eds.), *Teacher personal theorizing: Connecting curriculum practice, theory, and research* (pp. 207–218, 298–303). Albany: State University of New York Press.

Slavin, R. E. (1989). PET and the pendulum: Faddism in education and how to stop it. *Phi Delta Kappan, 70*(10), 752–758.

Soltis, J. F. (1993). Democracy and teaching. *Journal of Philosophy of Education, 27*(2), 149–158.

Stainback, S., & Stainback, W. (1984). A rationale for the merger of special and regular education. *Exceptional Children, 51*(2), 102–111.

Stainback, S., & Stainback, W. (1987a). Facilitating merger through personnel preparation. *Teacher Education and Special Education, 10*(4), 185–190.

Stainback, S., & Stainback, W. (1987b). Integration versus cooperation: A commentary on educating children with learning problems: A shared responsibility. *Exceptional Children, 54*(1), 66–68.

Stainback, S., & Stainback, W. (1989). Integration of students with mild and moderate handicaps. In D. K. Lipsky & A. Gartner (Eds.), *Beyond separate education: Quality education for all* (pp. 41–52). Baltimore: Paul H. Brookes.

Stainback, S., Stainback, W., & Forest, M. (Eds.). (1989). *Educating all students in the mainstream of regular education.* Baltimore: Paul H. Brookes.

Stanley, W. B. (1992). *Curriculum for utopia: Social reconstructionism and critical pedagogy in the postmodern era.* Albany: State University of New York Press.

Stedman, L. C. (1987). It's time we changed the effective schools formula. *Phi Delta Kappan, 69*(3), 215–224.

Timar, T. B., & Kirp, D. L. (1988). *Managing educational excellence.* New York: Falmer Press.

Timar, T. B., & Kirp, D. L. (1989). Education reforms in the 1980's: Lessons from the states. *Phi Delta Kappan, 70*(7), 504–511.

Wang, M. C. (1989a). Accommodating student diversity through adaptive instruction. In S. Stainback, W. Stainback, & M. Forest (Eds.), *Educating all students in the mainstream of regular education* (pp. 183–197). Baltimore: Paul H. Brookes.

Wang, M. C. (1989b). Adaptive instruction: An alternative for accommodating student diversity through the curriculum. In D. K. Lipsky & A. Gartner (Eds.), *Beyond separate education: Quality education for all* (pp. 99–119) Baltimore: Paul H. Brookes.

Wang, M. C., & Peverly, S. T. (1987). The role of the learner: An individual difference variable in school learning and functioning. In M. C. Wang, M. C. Reynolds, & H. J. Walberg (Eds.), *Handbook of special education: Research and practice: Vol. 1. Learner characteristics and adaptive education* (pp. 59–92). Oxford: Pergamon Press.

Wang, M. C., Reynolds, M. C., & Walberg, H. J. (1985, December). Rethinking special education. Paper presented at the Wingspread Conference on the Education of Students with Special Needs: Research Findings and Implications for Policy and Practice, Racine, WI.

Wang, M. C., Reynolds, M. C., & Walberg, H. J. (1986). Rethinking special education. *Educational Leadership, 44*(1), 26–31.

Wang, M. C., Reynolds, M. C., & Walberg, H. J. (Eds.). (1987a). *Handbook of special education: Research and practice: Vol. 1. Learner characteristics and adaptive education*. Oxford: Pergamon Press.

Wang, M. C., Reynolds, M. C., & Walberg, H. J. (1987b, October). Repairing the second system for students with special needs. Paper presented at the Wingspread Conference on the Education of Children with Special Needs: Gearing Up to Meet the Challenges of the 1990s, Racine, WI.

Weber, M. (1946). Bureaucracy. In H. H. Gerth & C. W. Mills (Eds. and Trans.), *From Max Weber: Essays in sociology* (pp. 196–244). New York: Oxford University Press. (Original work published 1922)

Weber, M. (1947). *The theory of social and economic organization* (T. Parsons, Ed. & A. M. Henderson & T. Parsons, Trans.). Glencoe, IL: Free Press. (Original work published 1924)

Weber, M. (1978). *Economy and society* (G. Roth & C. Wittich, Eds.; E. Fischoff, H. Gerth, A. M. Henderson, F. Kolegar, C. W. Mills, T. Parsons, M. Rheinstein, G. Roth, E. Shils, C. Wittich, Trans.) (Vols. 1–2). Berkeley: University of California Press. (Original work published 1922)

Weick, K. E. (1979). Cognitive processes in organization. In B. M. Staw (Ed.), *Research in organizational behavior* (Vol. 1, pp. 41–74). Greenwich, CT: JAI Press.

Weick, K. E. (1985). Sources of order in underorganized systems. In Y. S. Lincoln (Ed.), *Organizational theory and inquiry: The paradigm revolution* (pp. 106–136). Beverly Hills, CA: Sage.

Wise, A. E. (1979). *Legislated learning: The bureaucratization of the American classroom.* Berkeley: University of California Press.

Wise, W. E. (1988). The two conflicting trends in school reform: Legislated learning revisited. *Phi Delta Kappan, 69*(5), 328–333.

Wolcott, H. F. (1977). *Teachers versus technocrats: An educational innovation in anthropological perspective.* Eugene, OR: Center for Educational Policy and Management.

Author Index

Subject Index

About the Contributors

DIANNE L. FERGUSON is an Associate Professor of Special Education and Rehabilitation at the University of Oregon. She directs a series of personnel preparation and research and development projects related to improving the schooling experiences of students with severe disabilities. Over the past several years she has published research in the areas of curriculum and curriculum theory, personnel preparation, schooling reform in both regular and special education, and the experiences of families with severely disabled adults. She is coeditor of *Interpreting Disability: A Qualitative Reader* (with P. M. Ferguson and S. J. Taylor, 1992).

PHILIP M. FERGUSON is an Associate Professor of Special Education and Rehabilitation at the University of Oregon. He coordinates research and demonstration projects that support families of children and adults with severe disabilities. He also coordinates an interdisciplinary doctoral program that focuses on disability policy. He has a background in policy research and qualitative methods, and has done extensive research on the history of mental retardation in the twentieth century. He is coeditor of *Interpreting Disability: A Qualitative Reader* (with D. L. Ferguson and S. J. Taylor, 1992).

LOUS HESHUSIUS is a Professor of Education at York University, Toronto. Her present research focuses on the relationships between different world views and modes of consciousness, and education and special education theories and practices, and on the epistemological underpinnings of various conceptions of research. She wrote *Meaning in Life as Experienced by Persons Labeled Retarded* and *Portraits*, a translation of portraits of marginalized persons by the Dutch award-winning author Lize Stilma. She has published in, among others, *Exceptional Children, Journal of Learning Disabilities, Educational Researcher*, and *Journal of Education*.

DWIGHT C. KIEL is an Associate Professor of Political Science at the University of Central Florida. He teaches courses and directs research in public policy and political theory. He has published articles on eighteenth- and nineteenth-century American and European political thought and is the coauthor of *Great Ideas, Grand Schemes* (with P. Schumaker and T. Hielke), a forthcoming text on political ideologies.

THOMAS M. SKRTIC is a Professor of Special Education at the University of Kansas. In addition to his primary work in special education policy and administration, he teaches and directs research in the areas of curriculum and instruction and educational inquiry. His research interests include organization analysis, policy implementation, and American pragmatism. He is author of *Behind Special Education: A Critical Analysis of Professional Culture and School Organization* (1991) and coeditor of *Special Education and Student Disability: Traditional, Emerging and Alternative Perspectives* (with E. L. Meyen, 1995).

CHRISTINE E. SLEETER is a Professor of Teacher Education at the California State University at Monterey Bay. She teaches and consults nationally in the area of multicultural education and has published on this and related topics in journals such as the *Harvard Educational Review, Journal of Education*, and *Teachers College Record*. Her most recent books include: *Empowerment Through Multicultural Education* (1991); *Keepers of the American Dream* (1992); *Turning on Learning* (with C. Grant, 1989); and *Making Choices for Multicultural Education* (with C. Grant, 1993). She also edits a book series entitled "The Social Context of Education."

SALLY TOMLINSON is Dean of Education and Professor of Educational Policy and Management at Goldsmiths College, University of London. She teaches and does research in the areas of educational policy, special education, and minority education. Her publications include: *Educational Subnormality: A Study in Decision Making* (1981); *A Sociology of Special Education* (1982); *The School Effect: A Study of Multiracial Comprehensives* (with D. Smith, 1989); and *The Assessment of Special Educational Needs: Whose Problem?* (with D. Galloway and P. Armstrong, 1994).